The Historical Ecology of Some Unimproved Alluvial Grassland in the Upper Thames Valley

Alison McDonald

BAR British Series 441
2007

This title published by

Archaeopress
Publishers of British Archaeological Reports
Gordon House
276 Banbury Road
Oxford OX2 7ED
England
bar@archaeopress.com
www.archaeopress.com

Archaeopress
10 years

BAR 441

The Historical Ecology of some Unimproved Alluvial Grassland in the Upper Thames Valley

© A McDonald 2007

ISBN 978 1 4073 0122 8

Printed in England by Chalvington Digital

All BAR titles are available from:

Hadrian Books Ltd
122 Banbury Road
Oxford
OX2 7BP
England
bar@hadrianbooks.co.uk

The current BAR catalogue with details of all titles in print, prices and means of payment is available free from Hadrian Books or may be downloaded from www.archaeopress.com

To my family, without whose help...

Plus ca change, plus c'est la meme chose.
Karr (1849) Les Guepes, vii.

Frontispiece: Oxford mead flowers. (Rosemary Wise 1983)

TABLE OF CONTENTS

ACKNOWLEDGEMENTS   vii

PREFACE   ix

INTRODUCTION   1

PART I – DESCRIPTION

CHAPTER 1 – DESCRIPTION OF METHODS

1.1	Historical methods	5
1.2	Scientific methods	5
1.2.A	Introduction	5
1.2.B	Choice of sample method	5
1.2.C	Location of sample Stands and size of grid	6
	i. Port Meadow with Wolvercote Common	6
	ii. Picksey Mead	6
1.2.D	Choice of sample number	6
1.2.E	Method of laying out sample Stands	8
1.2.F	Method of recording	8
1.2.G	Nomenclature	8
1.2.H	Collection and analysis of soil samples	9
	i. Measurement of pH	9
	ii. Measurement of conductivity	9
1.2.I	Seasonality	9
1.2.J	Analysis of data	10
1.2.K	Species diversity	10
1.2.L	Limitations of methods	10
1.3	Multivariate analyses of data	10
1.3.A	Introduction	10
1.3.B	Association analysis	11
1.3.C	Principal component analysis (PCA)	11
1.3.D	Correspondence analysis (Twinspan)	13

CHAPTER 2 – EDAPHIC FACTORS

2.1	Gravel	19
2.2	Soil including alluvium	19
2.3	Water	20
2.3.A	Introduction	20
2.3.B	Ground water	20
2.3.C	Surface water	22
	i. Port Meadow with Wolvercote Common	22
	ii. Picksey Mead	24
2.4	Nutrient status	25
2.4.A	Introduction	25
2.4.B	pH	25
2.4.C	Conductivity	25

CHAPTER 3 – CLASSIFICATION OF PLANT COMMUNITIES IN THE OXFORD GRASSLAND

3.1	Introduction	27
3.2	Description of grassland types	27

3.3	The Oxford Grassland – Class: *Molinio-Arrhenatheretea*	30
3.3.A	Introduction	30
3.3.B	Group I – Port Meadow Marsh	30
3.3.C	Group II – Port Meadow Moist Pasture	34
	i. Section 1 – River bank and ditch	35
	ii. Section 2 – Raised area and dredgings	35
	iii. Section 3 – Wet pasture	37
3.3.D	Group III – Port Meadow Dry Pasture	38
	i. Section 1 – Disturbed pasture	40
	ii. Section 2 – Less disturbed pasture	43
3.3.E	Group IV – Picksey Mead	46
	i. Section 1 – Fen	46
	ii. Section 2 – Meadow	49
	iii. Section 3 – River banks	51

PART II – HISTORY

CHAPTER 4 – RIVER CONTROL

4.1	Prehistoric period	53
4.2	Historic period	54
4.2.A	Weirs	54
	i. King's Weir	55
	ii. Godstow Weir	55
	iii. Medley Weir	55
4.2.B	Water mills	55
4.3	Navigation	55
4.3.A	Introduction	55
4.3.B	Up to the Sixteenth Century	55
4.3.C	Post Sixteenth Century	56
4.3.D	Ecological appraisal	58
	i. Water-table	58
	ii. Flora	59
	iii. Fauna	59

CHAPTER 5 – CONTINUITY OF THE OXFORD GRASSLAND

5.1	Climax vegetation and its replacement	60
5.1.A	Introduction	60
5.1.B	Woodland destruction and grassland establishment	60
5.1.C	Summary	61
5.2	Grassland management	61
5.2.A	Introduction	61
5.2.B	Iron Age and Roman settlement (700 B.C. – A.D. 400)	62
5.2.C	Effect of increased settlement	64
5.2.D	Summary of pre-Saxon land-use	64
5.2.E	Legal evidence of transition to the Anglo-Saxon period	65
5.2.F	The Anglo-Saxon period	65
5.2.G	The political background	66
5.2.H	A conglomerate estate?	67
5.2.I	The sub-division of estates	68
5.2.J	Summary of Anglo-Saxon land-use	69
5.2.K	Medieval period – Port Meadow with Wolvercote Common	69
5.2.L	Impact of common rights of grazing	70
5.2.M	Regulating the grazing	71
5.2.N	Enclosure/encroachment	72
5.2.O	Medieval period - Picksey Mead	73
5.2.P	Water meadows	76

5.2.Q	Sixteenth Century Lammas land	77
5.2.R	Seventeenth Century management	78
5.2.S	Eighteenth Century management.	79
5.2.T	Nineteenth Century changes	80
5.2.U	Twentieth Century management	81

PART III – COMPARISONS

CHAPTER 6 – THE OXFORD GRASSLAND IN THE LIGHT OF MANAGEMENT

6.1	Fluxes in grassland systems	83
6.1.A	Introduction	83
6.1.B	Effect of defoliation	83
6.1.C	Impact of fertilizer	84
6.1.D	Effect of grazing animals	84
	i. Impact of dung on grassland	84
	ii. Feeding preferences	85
	iii. Impact of treading and poaching	87
	iv. Overgrazing	87
	v. Undergrazing	87
6.2	Disturbance to the Oxford grassland	87
6.2.A	Access points	89
6.2.B	Animal refuge/rubbish tip	89
6.2.C	Dump road	89
6.2.D	Allotment gardens	89
	i. Port Meadow	89
	ii. Wolvercote Common	90
6.2.E	Oxford Model Aircraft Club	90
6.2.F	Port Meadow Airfield (1917–1922)	90
6.3	Management problems on the Oxford grassland	90
6.3.A	Introduction	90
6.3.B	Weed control	93
6.4	Changing community patterns in the Twentieth Century	97
6.4.A	Introduction	97
6.4.B	Change in water-table and flooding levels	98
6.4.C	The Oxford grassland in the 1920s	100
	i. Area A – Now Port Meadow Marsh	100
	ii. Area B – Now Moist Pasture	100
	iii. Area C – Now Dry Pasture	103
	iv. Summary of change on Port Meadow	103
	v. Picksey Mead	103
6.4.D	Port Meadow in the 1950s	104
	i. Moisture tolerances of some *Ranunculus* species	104
	ii. *Agrostis* hybrids	105
	iii. *Festulolium loliacium*	105
6.4.E	The Oxford grassland in the 1970s	106
	i. Introduction	106
	ii. Lower-level grassland	106
	iii. Mid-level grassland	107
	iv. Higher-level grassland	107
	v. Area of dense thistles	107
	vi. Consequences of changing community patterns	107
6.4.F	Other recent changes on the Oxford grassland	109
6.5	Comparisons with other grasslands	110
6.5.A	Introduction	110
6.5.B	Lowland England	110
6.5.C	The upper Thames valley	112
6.6	Conclusions	112

6.7	Considerations for future management	113
6.7.A	Port Meadow with Wolvercote Common	113
	i. Overgrazing in winter	113
	ii. Port Meadow Marsh	114
6.7.B	Picksey Mead	114
6.8	Future research and development	114
6.8.A	Availability of mineral salts in the soil and soil water	114
6.8.B	Variation of pH in the Oxford grassland	114
6.8.C	Comparison between pasture and meadow seed banks	114
6.8.D	Seral movement	115
6.8.E	Pollination and seed set	115
6.8.F	Are there significant associations between past management of unimproved grassland and individual plant species?	115
6.8.G	Autecology	115

GLOSSARY 117

APPENDICES

A	Grid references of Stands and date of sampling	119
B	All species recorded in this monograph	120
C	Principal Component Analysis graphs	123
	i. Boundaries of communities indicated by Twinspan	123
	ii. pH at each Stand	124
	iii. Conductivity at each Stand	125
	iv. Altitude (+50m) at each Stand	126
	v. Twinspan Grassland Types at each Stand	127
D	Make-up of river gravels on the Oxford grassland (Institute of Hydrology)	128
E	Minerals in Port Meadow soil water (Institute of Hydrology)	129
F	Memories of Port Meadow (Henry Minn)	133
G	Iron Age species list (Dr M.A. Robinson)	135
H	Ownership of Yarnton and Begbroke lot balls	
	Mowing the meads: the lot ceremony (F. Charlett)	136
I	Horse and cow feeding preferences	139
J	*Poaceae* species of grassland interest	140
K	Access points to the the Meadow and Picksey Mead	142
L	Plant species found on Port Meadow (1923–1973)	145
M	Survey of the hedge species on the eastern boundary of Port Meadow (McDonald 1980)	148

HISTORICAL SOURCES NOT INCLUDED UNDER AUTHOR'S NAME 149

SOURCES CITED UNDER AUTHOR'S NAME 151

MAPS

1	The Oxford grassland and its neighbourhood	x
2	The Oxford grassland: Port Meadow with Wolvercote Common, and Picksey Mead, in the upper Thames valley, near Oxford.	4
3	Stand numbers and distribution of grassland Types on Port Meadow	7
	Inset: Stand numbers and distribution of grassland Types on Picksey Mead	
4	Inundation zones on Port Meadow and Wolvercote Common	17
5	Position of bore holes on Port Meadow and Wolvercote Common additional to map 7 (Institute of Hydrology)	18
6	The upper Thames valley gravels and archaeological sites	20
7	Ground water flow beneath the Oxford grassland (Institute of Hydrology, unpublished report)	21

8	The south end of Port Meadow (Ordnance Survey 1st Edition 1877).	24
9	Distribution of archaeological sites on Port Meadow. Sites A, B and C investigated by the Oxford Archaeological Unit. Botanical transect recorded across Site C	54
10a	Redistribution of the hay lots on Picksey Mead – 1845	77
10b	Redistribution of the hay lots on Picksey Mead – 1958	78
11	Water courses and potential areas of disturbance in the Oxford grassland	86
12	2,4–D amine solution was sprayed over Port Meadow on several occasions	94
13	Distribution of weed species on Port Meadow with Wolvercote Common	96
14	The position of Areas A, B and C on Port Meadow according to Baker (1937)	99
15	Distribution of *Ranunculus* species on Port Meadow 1981	105
16	Nature Conservancy Council's Vegetation Map of Port Meadow with Wolvercote Common	106
17	Nature Conservancy Council's recording sites on Port Meadow with Wolvercote Common	107

FIGURES

la	Sampling density was increased by sampling the centre of each 200m x 200m square. The new grid was laid out upon the diagonal of the old grid	8
lb	The quadrats in each Stand were numbered consecutively	8
2	Classification of the Oxford grassland (Association Analysis)	12
3	Illustration of the square-root scale used as "cut off" points for Twinspan's "pseudospecies"	13
4	The number of days per annum when the river was above typical low flood level at Godstow lock tail water. Medley weir removed in 1931	22
5	Cross section of the Thames valley at Binsey adjacent to Port Meadow with Wolvercote Common (Institute of Hydrology)	53
6	The reduction in pasture as a result of the river flooding	88
7	Fluctuations in the number of animals counted at the annual drive (Oxford City Solicitor *pers. comm.*)	88
8	A comparison of the species recorded in 1981 (this study) and 1973 (Nature Conservancy Council) typifies the problems faced in the interpretation of species lists	109

TABLES

1	The Oxford grassland association table (Twinspan)	14-15
2	Environmental variables at Stands on Port Meadow with Wolvercote Common and Picksey Mead	26
3	Summary of the Oxford grassland classification	29
4	*Poa trivialis* (Type A) grassland	32
5	*Myosotis scorpioides* (Type B) grassland	33
6	*Gallium palustre* (Type C) grassland	33-34
7	*Potentilla anserina* (Type D) grassland	35
8	*Achillea millefolium* (Type E) grassland	36
9	*Plantago major* (Type F) grassland	36-37
10	*Alopecurus geniculatus* (Type G) grassland	37
11	*Deschampsia cespitosa* (Type H) grassland	38
12	*Agrostis capillaris* (Type I) grassland	40
13	*Poa annua* (Type J) grassland	42
14	*Cirsium arvense* (Type K) grassland	42-43
15	*Cirsium vulgare* (Type L) grassland	43-44
16	*Galium verum* (Type M) grassland	44-45
17	*Carex panicea* (Type N) grassland	45
18	*Phragmites australis* (Type 0) grassland	46-47
19	*Succisa pratensis* (Type Q) grassland	48
20	*Cardamine pratensis* (Type R) grassland	49-50
21	*Arrhenatherum elatius* (Type S) grassland	50-51
22	*Bromus commutatus* (Type P) grassland	52
23	The Sixteenth Century Freemen of Oxford regulated the number of animals grazing on Port Meadow	71

24   Fluctuations in the number of Freemen of Oxford may reflect the grazing pressures on the Meadow   71

25   Ragwort control experiment showed that neither forage harvesting, nor hand pulling, reduced
        species-richness, and herbicide produced a species-poor sward   96

26   Comparison of *Ranunculus* species growing on Port Meadow (Baker 1937)   104

PHOTOGRAPHS

Frontispiece: Oxford mead flowers (Rosemary Wise)

1   The grid laid out on Stand 32. The recorder was examined by horses and cattle on most days.
        (Mr J. Steane)   9

2   Aerial photographs show up Bronze and Iron Age ditches as well as underground stream beds.
        (Royal Commission for Historic Monuments 1976)   23

3   Port Meadow with Wolvercote Common. Meadow Buttercups (*Ranunculus acris*) are avoided by
        grazing animals. Compare this photograph with Photograph 25   28

4   Picksey Mead. *Succisa pratensis* (Type Q) grassland in the foreground   28

5   The tall form of Hardhead (*Centaurea nigra*) flowering on Picksey Mead   41

6   The stunted form of Hardhead (*Centaurea nigra*) flowering on Port Meadow after the forage
        harvester had been through   41

7   The whole of Port Meadow was frequently flooded in winter before Medley Weir was removed
        in 1931. The floods attracted a large population of winter migrants. (H. Minn)   57

8   Zones between mead and willow swamp show up on the south side of the Spinney on Picksey Mead   58

9   Dr M.A. Robinson excavating dark bluish-brown gleyed soil containing biotic material from an
        Iron Age ditch   62

10   Mr E. Harris, First Meadsman, holding the cherry-wood balls used for allocating the hay on Picksey
        Mead by lot   75

11   The merestone, which separated the Begbroke Tydalls from those of Yarnton on Picksey Mead,
        rescued by Mr E. Harris after a contractor had cast the others into the Thames   76

12   A branding iron and hot tar were used to mark Yarnton animals put into Picksey Mead to graze the
        aftermath. "E" stands for Eardington, the old name for Yarnton   79

13   The Meadsman and his team allocating hay on Yarnton Mead. (Taunt 1911)   82

14   Horses making use of the "refuge" during the floods of January 1982   89

15   *Plantago major* (Type F) grassland has developed on the levelled allotment gardens since 1968   90

16   The Oxford Model Aircraft Club mow their "flying area" and so provide a short turf in which
        daisies (*Bellis perennis*) are abundant   91

17   Shooting target on Port Meadow Airfield in 1918. (H.Minn)   91

18   Bombing target and rifle butts on Port Meadow Airfield in 1918. Godstow Weir in the background.
        (H.Minn)   92

19   Rotting hay and wheel ruts indicate poor management on Picksey Mead. January 1983   92

20   Inundation Zones E and F on Port Meadow are overgrazed in winter by ponies belonging to the
        Wolvercote Commoners   95

21   Port Meadow after the Thistles had been cut. The height of the vegetation in the background
        suggests that the Meadow is not overgrazed in summer. August 1983   97

22   A mud bank community growing on Port Meadow opposite Binsey before Medley Weir was removed.
        (Church 1922)   101

23   *Poa trivialis* (Type A) grassland has developed in the mud bank area since the river was confined
        to a deeper channel. August 1983   101

24   Sheep were grazing on Port Meadow in 1911 and the willows along the Line Ditch were pollarded.
        (H.Minn)   102

25   Contrary to all reports, sheep were also grazing on Port Meadow in 1917. The view is the same as
        Photo 3. The trees in the hedge between Hook Meadow and Wolvercote Common have gone and
        the Long Ditch has a rich aquatic community   102

26   The different moisture tolerances of Meadow, Bulbous and Creeping Buttercup are illustrated on a
        Bronze Age barrow   104

27   The horses mark the edge of Port Meadow Marsh which has spread into the Mid-level Grassland
        (NCC) since 1972   108

28   Most of the grass in the High-level Grassland dies down in summer and can be seen as a
        light-coloured line behind the animals   108

ACKNOWLEDGEMENTS

First of all I should like to acknowledge the debt I owe to Prof. Joan Thirsk and Dr Tim King, the examiners of my thesis, who gave me very helpful suggestions for the improvement of the text in several places. I am indebted to Dr Roger Hall for his support after the retirement of Prof. Thirsk. I am also grateful to the late Dr Stan Woodell, Dr John Sheail and John Steane for their helpful discussions; to Miss Jasmine Howse for the help she gave me with proof-reading this volume and to Dr David Davison and Dr Wendy Logue of Archaeopress for technical help in bringing the work into a state fit for publication.

PREFACE

This volume is the result of 25 years work starting with "The historical ecology of Port Meadow and Wolvercote Common, Oxford" an undergraduate dissertation submitted to Oxford Polytechnic in May 1980 (McDonald 1980). It was a desk study which generated sufficient interest for me to work (during the following two years) on a base line botanical survey of Port Meadow with Wolvercote Common, ancient pasture and to contrast it with a similar survey of Picksey Mead, ancient hay-meadow, under Dr S.R.J. Woodell, the Botany School, Oxford University and Dr John Sheail of the Institute of Terrestrial Ecology, Monks Wood, Huntingdon. The historical research was extended to look at the history of the management of both these flood-plain areas in order to understand something of the differences in their species-composition and to enable me to relate them to their past management. The thesis I produced in 1984 resulted in the award of a D.Phil from the University of Oxford.

The pioneering environmental archaeology by Prof. Mark Robinson mentioned in this volume is now an authoritative discipline and the ground-breaking use of a multi-disciplinary approach to grassland studies is at last being recognised by Natural England and others as an essential element in management plans for Sites of Special Scientific Interest. Since the early 1980s grants have been available for increasingly in-depth studies of a single topic. The publication of this volume represents a change of view in which multi-disciplinary studies, especially those relating to the history of man and the landscape he has influenced are recognized for the breadth of vision which is their strength.

The description of the vegetation I made in 1984 has proved invaluable when working with English Nature (now Natural England) over the intervening years as it provided a base-line from which natural and man-made changes in the vegetation could be measured. In particular, the description of Port Meadow Marsh was vital in connection with the study of *Apium repens* carried out by the Rare Plants Group of the Ashmolean Natural History Society of Oxfordshire for English Nature from 1996–2006 (McDonald and Lambrick 2006). I have brought the descriptions of the various communities into line with the relevant volumes of John Rodwell's British Plant Communities (1991–2002). The historical sections of the work have also stood the test of time and have been brought up to date where necessary and incorporated into this new volume.

With the current interest in flood-alleviation plans for West Oxford, which include the possibility of constructing new channels associated with overflow areas within the river Thames flood-plain above Oxford, which could affect the hydrology and therefore the vegetation of these ancient pastures and meads, publication of this work is timely.

Alison W. McDonald
24 January 2007.

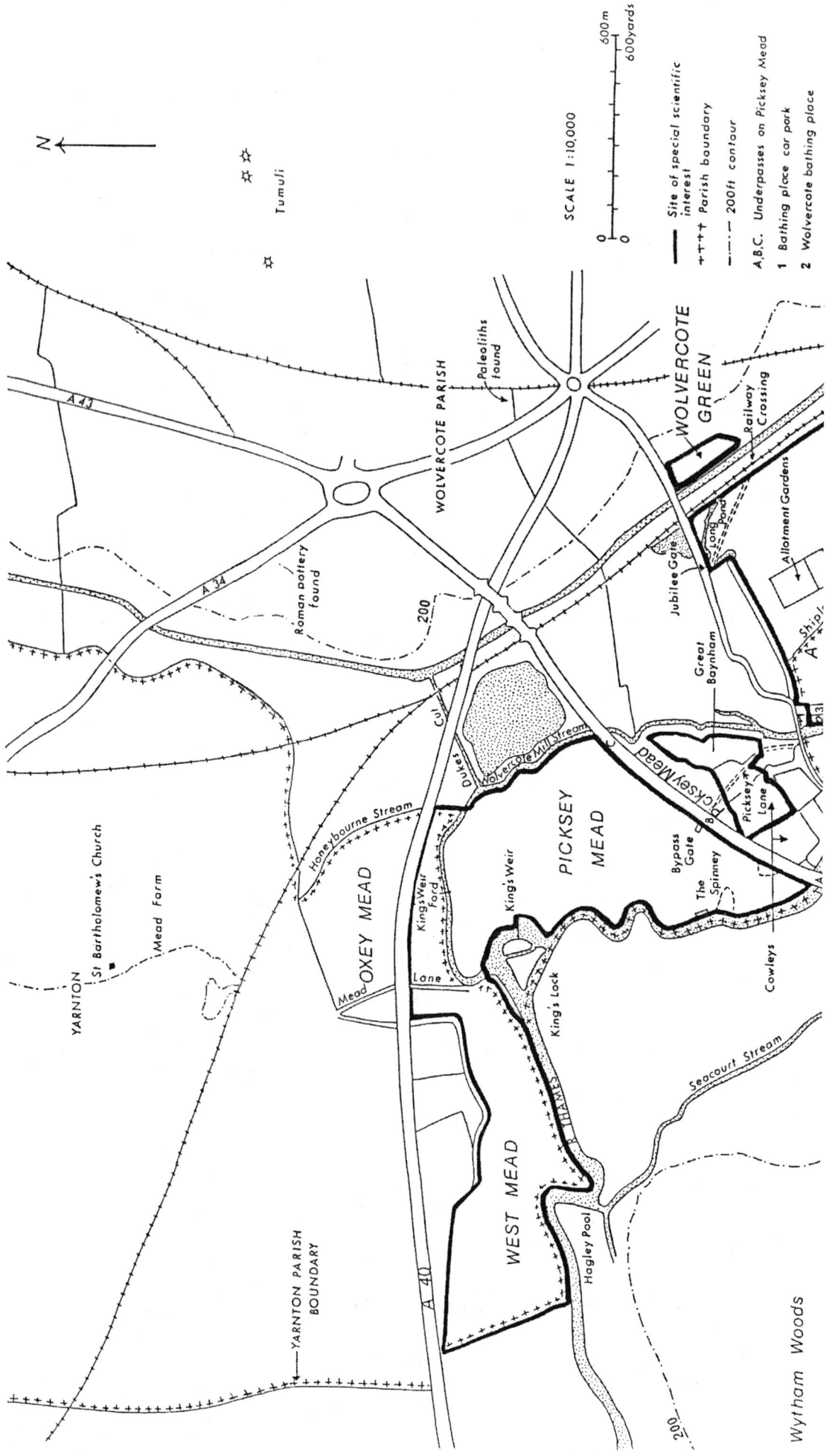

N

Tumuli

☆ ☆
☆

SCALE 1:10,000

0 ——— 500m
0 ——— 600yards

━━━ Site of special scientific interest
+++++ Parish boundary
—·—·— 200ft contour

A,B,C. Underpasses on Picksey Mead
1 Bathing place car park
2 Wolvercote bathing place

WOLVERCOTE PARISH

Paleoliths found

Roman pottery found

A 44

A 34

200

Dukes Cut

Wolvercote Mill Stream

WOLVERCOTE GREEN

Railway Crossing

Long Pond

Jubilee Gate

Great Baynham

Allotment Gardens

A Shipl

PICKSEY MEAD

Picksey Mead

Picksey Lane

Bypass Gate

The Spinney

Cowleys

Honeybourne Stream

OXEY MEAD

King's Weir Ford

King's Weir

Mead Lane

YARNTON

St Bartholomew's Church

Mead Farm

King's Lock

THAMES

WEST MEAD

Seacourt Stream

A 40

YARNTON PARISH BOUNDARY

Hagley Pool

200

Wytham Woods

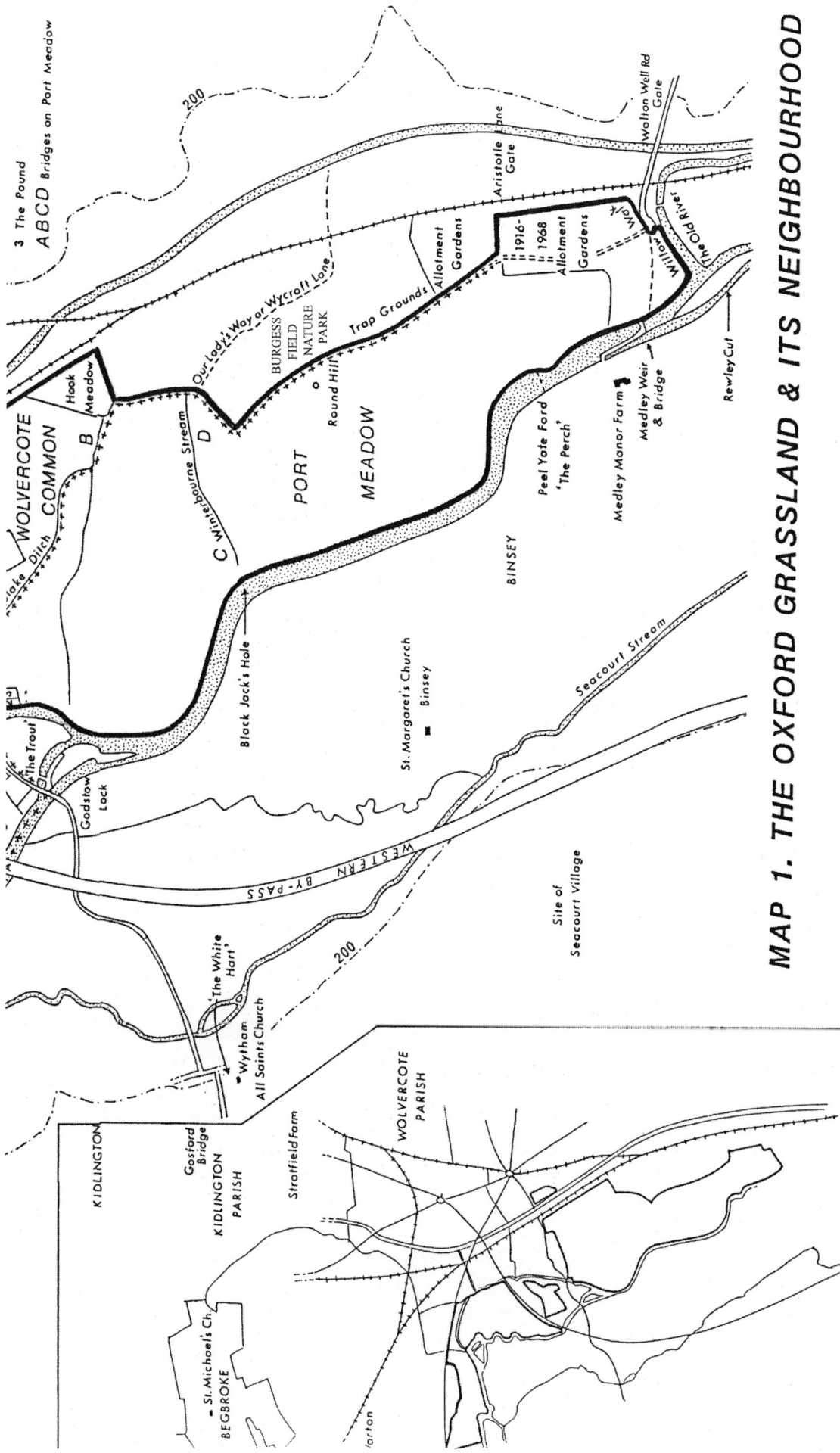

MAP 1. THE OXFORD GRASSLAND & ITS NEIGHBOURHOOD

3 The Pound
ABCD Bridges on Port Meadow

200

Walton Well Rd Gate

Aristotle Lane Gate

Allotment Gardens

1916–1968 Allotment Gardens

Willow

The Old River

Trap Grounds

Our Lady's Way or Wycroft Lane

BURGESS FIELD NATURE PARK

Round Hill

Medley Weir & Bridge

Rewley Cut

HOOK Meadow

WOLVERCOTE COMMON

B

C Winterbourne Stream

D

PORT MEADOW

Peel Yate Ford 'The Perch'

Medley Manor Farm

Godstow Lock

The Trout

Black Jack's Hole

BINSEY

St. Margaret's Church Binsey

Seacourt Stream

WESTERN BY-PASS

200

Site of Seacourt Village

The White Hart

Wytham All Saints Church

Gosford Bridge

KIDLINGTON

KIDLINGTON PARISH

Stratfield Farm

WOLVERCOTE PARISH

St. Michael's Ch.

BEGBROKE

Yarton

INTRODUCTION

Historical ecology is a relatively new subject brought to the notice of the general public in studies such as that of Hayley Wood, Cambridgeshire (Rackham 1974). Using botanical and topographical surveys, supplemented by printed and manuscript records, pollen analysis and dendrochronology, the history of the use and management of woodland, its constituent communities and species, can in some measure be traced (Rackham 1980; Peterken 1981). The historical ecology of grassland poses different problems and has received very little attention, possibly because grassland in lowland Britain is either a temporary seral stage or a man-made vegetation type, much of which is recent, or is poorly documented historically.

This work focuses on some common land within three miles of Oxford City centre known as Port Meadow (325 acres/132 ha.) with Wolvercote Common (75 acres/30.4 ha.), widely believed to have been pasture since Domesday, and Picksey Mead (115 acres/46.6 ha.), a hay meadow of similar antiquity (Tansley 1939: 568) (Map 1). For the sake of convenience they have been called, collectively, the Oxford grassland. The principal features of these unimproved grasslands, and their neighbourhood, are shown in Map 1. Port Meadow measures about a mile and a half from north to south and is bordered by the river Thames on the west and south. Shiplake Ditch, which was for centuries part of the northern boundary of Oxford City, separates Port Meadow from Wolvercote Common to the north. The eastern boundary is more varied. In the north Wolvercote Common has been divided into two parts by the Oxford canal and the railway line. Hook Meadow (a species-rich meadow similar to Picksey Mead) is tucked into a corner between the railway, the common land and the Trap Grounds to the south. The Trap Grounds have been the depository for Oxford City rubbish. The tip is now closed and the area landscaped and seeded with a grassland mixture, and planted with trees and shrubs and designated by Oxford City Council "Burgess Field Nature Park". South of the tip or dump are some allotment gardens. The boundary then turns east until it meets the railway line ditch which it follows southwards until it joins the old navigation channel of the river Thames.

Port Meadow gives the appearance of being flat but in reality there is a fall in the ground-level from 58.1m above O.D. in the north to 56.9m in the south near Aristotle Lane. Here the land rises abruptly onto an area raised approximately 1m by the dumping of Oxford City rubbish between 1888 and the early 1920s. Picksey Mead appears to be flat, too, but has a fall of 0.5m from north to south. It is bordered on the west, north and east by the Thames and on the south by meadowland, part of which is a Site of Special Scientific Interest (Nature Conservancy Council Southern Region). Unlike Port Meadow, which is owned by Oxford City Council, and Wolvercote Common, which is held in trust by Oxford City Council and Oxfordshire County Council, Picksey Mead has several owners. The Duke of Marlborough owns 51 acres (20.7 ha.) in the north, about 3 acres (1.2 ha.) on the west side and the grazing of the aftermath of the whole mead in alternate years. In the south-west, 18 acres (7.3 ha.) are divided from the rest by a silted up stream bed. They and the grazing in alternate years belong to Mrs Wise of Wytham. In the central-southern area are 3 acres (1.2 ha.) called the Tythals or Tidals, once church property in lieu of tithe, and now belonging to Mr R.D.A. de la Mare, who also owns a strip of land opposite King's Weir and is a major owner of the final 43 acres (17.4 ha.). These are held in movable fee simple by the "Yarnton Farmers" but the ownership of each of the 13 unfenced divisions can change by the annual drawing of named balls. In the Thirteenth Century rights to the hay lots and grazing in Picksey Mead were attached to 13 farms in Yarnton and Begbroke. By 1980 only Mr W.A. Bayliss of Stonehouse Farm retained some of these rights. The rest were sold to Mr R.D.A. de la Mare of Cumnor and the Nature Conservancy Council. The Oxford bypass extends over 8 acres of Picksey Mead (Nature Conservancy Council Southern Region).

In the course of completing an undergraduate project on "The Historical Ecology of Port Meadow with Wolvercote Common" (McDonald 1980) it became clear that the vegetation of this tract of unimproved pasture had undergone significant change since the last major botanical survey was made by Baker (1937) and that this might be due, among other factors, to its management or to the removal of Medley Weir in 1931.

In this book the wealth of ecological, historical and archaeological information, now available for the Oxford grassland and elsewhere, has been described as fully as possible in an attempt to relate the different grassland types to historical factors and present day conditions. Despite the grassland's proximity to Oxford and its designation as a Grade 1 Site of Special Scientific Interest more than 50 years ago (Nature Conservancy Council Southern Region), its ecology has not been recently studied in any detail. The ecology of individual species such as *Ranunculus spp.* (Harper & Sagar 1953) and *Agrostis spp.* (Bradshaw 1958, 1959a, 1959b, 1960) has, however, been studied and others have been sampled as part of a genecological study of lawn weeds (Warwick 1980; Warwick & Briggs 1978a, 1978b, 1979, 1980a, 1980b). References to Port Meadow in the Victoria County History (Crossley 1979) gave information relating to changes in the management of Port Meadow. Baker's (1937) study, made in 1922/23, has provided valuable material for certain comparisons which showed changes in the vegetation in relation to the management of the grassland and of the adjacent river.

The base lines provided by Baker's survey of the 1920s and that made about 60 years later underline the value of such records in discovering where and when changes have occurred in the incidence of plant species and communities. How and why such events have come about becomes clear when assessing the significance of such trends in the management of that environment. By contrast data from herbarium specimens and published floristic records have been of little value because they were insufficiently precise. In completing this work I consulted an extremely diverse literature. I have attempted to check all references and to present them in a standardised form, but in view of the magnitude of the task absolute accuracy cannot be guaranteed.

Of necessity not all aspects of grassland ecology could be covered in this study. Effort was concentrated on the features of the main grassland types in relation to flooding and past management, particularly grazing and mowing regimes. Many management activities, such as planting Willow Walk, the polo field or horse racing are not very relevant to the present study and so have been set aside. It would, however, have been desirable to have more information on the nutrients in particular grassland species in order to test the nutritional value, rather than palatability, of grazing preferences of both horses and cattle.

The ecological importance of the study area has increased over the last forty years due to the rapid advance of agricultural techniques. Less than 5% of the unimproved flood-land present in 1945, for example, remains in the Thames valley and elsewhere in lowland England (Nature Conservancy Council Southern Region).

The Oxford grassland occurs on variable thicknesses of riverine alluvium and gravel of pH 5.2 to 7.6 on the floodplain of the River Thames, although there are a few areas not reached by flood-water. Because of their physiographic position, annual flooding has been a natural feature in the lower areas since their origin from woodland thousands of years ago, though at different times the details of the flooding regime have been greatly altered by human intervention.

This study extends Baker's work by recording, as far as possible, the plant communities growing on Port Meadow with Wolvercote Common and Picksey Mead between May and August 1981–83 and relating them to current environmental factors. Since the aim of the botanical survey was to obtain an objective description of the vegetation of the Oxford grassland, it was thought that association, ordination and classification techniques would be valuable and that their interpretation could be facilitated by soil analyses (pH and conductivity) and by information relating to river levels, the height of the water-table and to land-use history.

The name Port Meadow with Wolvercote Common sounds rather clumsy if used too often. I have therefore used the local name "the Meadow" in general statements about what is more properly "the pasture". Hay fields or hay meadows beside the Thames near Oxford are known locally as "meads". I have used this term, which describes alluvial grassland cut for hay and then grazed, when referring to Picksey Mead and similar grassland.

This book has been arranged in three sections. Part I includes a description of the methods (p.5) used in researching the Oxford grassland as it is today. Botanical data were subjected to association (p.11), principal component (p.11) and correspondence (p.13) analyses and the results compared. Correspondence analysis (derived from the program Twinspan) proved to be the most useful, since it divided the grassland into manageable groups. A description of the edaphic factors which underlie the Oxford grassland (p.17) is followed by a description of the Oxford grassland itself. Group I, Port Meadow Marsh (p.28), was isolated at the first division of the data and Group IV, Picksey Mead (p.44) at the second division. The third division separated Group II, Port Meadow Moist Pasture (p.32) from Group III, Port Meadow Dry Pasture (p.36). These terms have been used for convenience only. The communities they describe are obviously different from each other. They are only relatively "moist" or "dry" and the "fen" on Picksey Mead is based on alluvium not on the peat which the name implies. The broad categories in the classification suggested by the Twinspan program (see Fig. 4) were useful, but there is an element of arbitrariness in the method which caused a few borderline Stands to be misplaced. For example, two similar grassland Types, *Deschampsia cespitosa* (Type H) and *Agrostis capillaris* (Type I) grassland have been placed in Groups II and III, respectively, when an inspection of the community itself would have placed them in the same Group.

Part II of this study is devoted to the history of the control or management of the upper reaches of the River Thames (p.55) and of the adjacent Oxford grassland (p.62). It is presented in historical periods from the prehistoric to the present day. Where direct evidence of the Oxford grassland is lacking, its history has been suggested by analogy, particularly in relation to the prehistoric and historic periods up to and including the Anglo-Saxon period.

Finally, Part III is devoted to comparisons. The Oxford grassland is seen in the light of present and recent management. This section begins with a description of the changes which occur in a grassland community as it is subjected to various forms of management (p.85). Some of these changes are related to the Oxford grassland (p.99) which is then compared with other grassland systems in lowland England (p.112) and in the upper Thames valley (p.114). This is followed by a section called "Conclusions" (p.114), which summarises the changes in the plant communities on Port Meadow with Wolvercote Common and on Picksey Mead, as a result of variations in the management of the land and the adjacent river over a period of some 4,000 years. Considerations for the future management of the Oxford grassland and topics which require further research and development conclude the monograph.

Nomenclature follows Stace (1997) for higher plants and Smith (1980) for bryophytes (see Nomenclature p.8). A complete species list is to be found in Appendix A.

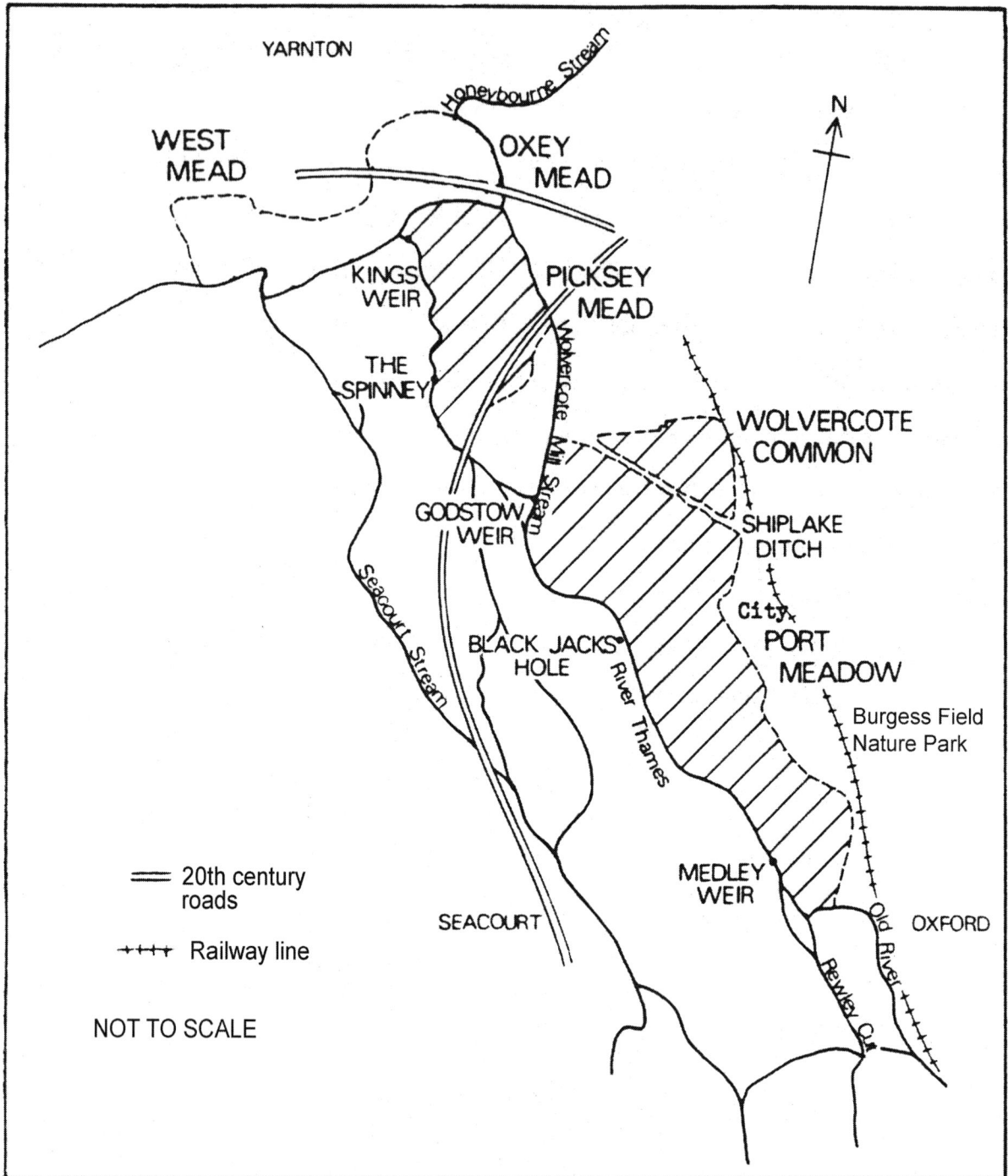

Map 2. The Oxford grassland: Port Meadow with Wolvercote Common, and Picksey Mead, in the upper Thames valley, near Oxford

PART I – DESCRIPTION

CHAPTER 1

DESCRIPTION OF METHODS

1.1 HISTORICAL METHODS

In 1969 John Sheail and Terry Wells organised a Symposium "Old Grassland: its archaeological and ecological importance". Their unpublished report advocates a closer contact between ecologists, archaeologists, historians and geographers in order to obtain a better understanding of the character of ancient grassland. They commented on the paucity of detailed descriptions of alluvial grassland in particular and expressed the need for more information on features of grassland ecology associated with land-use history, as a basis for sound nature conservation management.

The multidisciplinary approach thus described has been used in this study of unimproved grassland near Oxford. Living in Wolvercote overlooking part of the Oxford grassland (see Map 2), I was in a good position to have useful discussions with local people throughout the study period. It was known that archaeological sites on Port Meadow were scheduled as Ancient Monuments and that there was a documented history of pasture management going back into the early medieval period, together with a botanical survey carried out in the 1920s which had been compared with the haymead flora of Picksey Mead (Baker 1937). It seemed to be an ideal area upon which to base a study of the historical ecology of ancient grassland.

As a result of searching a wealth of published and unpublished sources, a draft history of the Oxford grassland was constructed using both direct evidence and inferences of likely management practises based on analogy of broadly comparable sites where historical or ecological evidence was available. This draft was discussed with several specialists including an archaeologist, a historian, a historical geographer and an ecologist (acknowledged at the beginning of this volume) and was afterwards amended in the light of their comments.

1.2 SCIENTIFIC METHODS

1.2.A INTRODUCTION

Subjective assessments of trends in plant communities, which are inherent in the Zurich-Montpellier methods of plant community classifications (Poore 1955), have been much used and accepted in the past (Braun-Blanquet 1932; Kershaw 1964: 71; Shimwell 1971: 185), but on this occasion have been avoided wherever possible. It was considered particularly important to do this in order to provide base line data for comparison at a later date.

Plant communities are recognisable units of vegetation made up of species living together in both an interdependent and dependent fashion in a common habitat (Tansley 1939: 213). Such communities are sometimes detected by sight, by random or by systematic sampling methods. Dawkins and Field (1978), in their computer-drawn models, showed that a random survey can be less efficient at detecting plant communities than a systematic method. A regular sampling pattern, in the form of a grid, defines a limit to the size of a community which may be unsampled. This is not possible with a random sampling method in which samples can be clumped as well as scattered and in which the size of an undetected community is always potentially larger than that with a grid sample. Systematic sampling is therefore more likely to produce a comprehensive description of the vegetation and can provide a base line from which to record future changes. It was therefore decided to sample in a grid of squares based on the National Grid and to subject the data to statistical analysis in order to make an objective framework within which to describe the Oxford grassland.

It is intended that, as with extensive and general studies, the analysis of the data should generate hypotheses and provide the groundwork for later more specific and intensive work (Poore 1956, 1962; Cain & Castro 1959: 104; Foin & Jain 1977; Gauch 1982: 13). The success of this study rests with the extent to which these aims and the interlocking of the ecological and historical elements have been achieved.

1.2.B. CHOICE OF SAMPLE METHOD

A quadrat one metre square was chosen as a convenient minimal area sampling unit (Mueller-Dombois & Ellenberg 1974: 48–9) which was applied in the field to both hay-meadow and pasture grasslands. This unit had already been used successfully on chalk grassland, Thames-side and Wendlebury hay-meadows and pasture (Wells *et al.* 1976; Allen 1979; Scruby 1979). Having decided that sampling would not be random, it was considered that it would be more economical, in terms of maximum information obtained in minimum time spent, if the quadrats themselves were arranged in square Stands, rather than transects or strips, and the Stands sampled in a grid pattern. This arrangement would have additional benefits for four reasons:

i. A square is more efficient in the detection of local irregularities. Strips tend to require the sampling of a larger area than squares, unless they are extremely narrow.
ii. A square encloses the minimal sample area that must be recorded for a given sampling error which depends on the number of units sampled (Dawkins and Field 1978).
iii. Regular clustering frequently occurs due to natural causes (e.g. limestone pavement) or human activity (e.g. ridge-and-furrow farming methods). Such phenomena may coincide with a regular sampling pattern but they are detectable by eye and were not present in the Oxford grassland.
iv. By adopting similar techniques it may be possible at a later date to compare the Oxford grassland with other species-rich meadows in, for example, the north of England, bearing in mind that the method is not suitable for studies on limestone pavement (Ratcliffe 1977, II: 129).

1.2.C   LOCATION OF SAMPLE STANDS AND SIZE OF GRID

i. Port Meadow with Wolvercote Common

The Thames Water Authority's photogrammetric map of the Thames valley (scale 1:1250, 1978) is based on a mosaic of aerial photographs upon which both contour lines at quarter metre intervals, and the National Grid have been drawn. This combination proved to be invaluable for the location of sample areas shown on Map 3. The intersections of the grid on the map were at 200m intervals and were chosen for the position of sampling Stands. This is represented by the letters A, B, C and D on Fig. 1a. To locate the intersections on the ground, compass bearings (adjusted 9 degrees west for magnetic north) were used. The land is very flat and lacks landmarks. Sightings on Oxford spires or chimneys had to be used in a few instances, as well as bridges across the adjacent river. These included Wolvercote Mill chimney which was taken down in 2006. On Port Meadow the intersections of paths made by horses were also used, because they showed up well on the photogrammetric map (Thames Water 1978). Sampling began at the north end of

Wolvercote Common in the last week of May 1981 and finished at the south end of Port Meadow in the first week of August 1981. This was followed by a transect across an Iron Age hut complex (Stand 44). The National Grid reference for each Stand and the date it was sampled are presented in Appendix B. After collecting the data from the Stands on Port Meadow with Wolvercote Common, the method was assessed and the possibility that it might be inadequate on such a heterogeneous area was accepted, but not tested, in view of the time limitation.

ii. Picksey Mead

In the light of the experience gained on the Meadow, the sampling density on Picksey Mead was doubled by placing an extra Stand in each of the grid squares. The sampling grid was, therefore, placed on the diagonal of the National Grid, represented by the line AD in Fig. la. and the new grid is represented on Fig. la by the letters a, b, c and d.

> If the line AD is the hypotenuse of the triangles ABD and ACD then, by Pythagoras, $AD^2 = AB^2 + BD^2$ and $(1/2AD)^2 = 1/2\ (AB^2)$

Therefore the Stands were thus placed at 141.4 metre intervals in a grid pattern and the area of each grid square sampled was reduced from 40,000 square metres to 20,000 square metres. If this density of sampling on Picksey Mead proved to be inadequate, one could reduce the area sampled to 10,000 square metres by sampling on a grid at 100m intervals on the National Grid. This is represented by the numerals i, ii, iii and iv on Fig. 1a. The latter was not, however, found to be necessary.

In order to include the south, detached portion of Picksey Mead (see Map 3), Stand 45 was placed 10m towards the centre of the meadow instead of in the ditch at the intersection of the grid, and Stands 46 and 47 were placed 25m towards the centre of the mead. They would otherwise have been located on the bypass (see Map 3). Sampling began at Stand 45 in the first week of May 1982 and finished at Stand 67 in the first week in July 1982. The Grid reference and date of sampling each Stand is to be found in Appendix A.

A total of 67 Stands and 1675 quadrats were sampled in the Oxford grassland.

1.2.D   CHOICE OF SAMPLE NUMBER

Statistical analyses of the data to be collected were considered in choosing 25 x 1m quadrats arranged in a square 5m x 5m per Stand. 25 quadrats per Stand were likely to be more convenient than, for example, 16 or

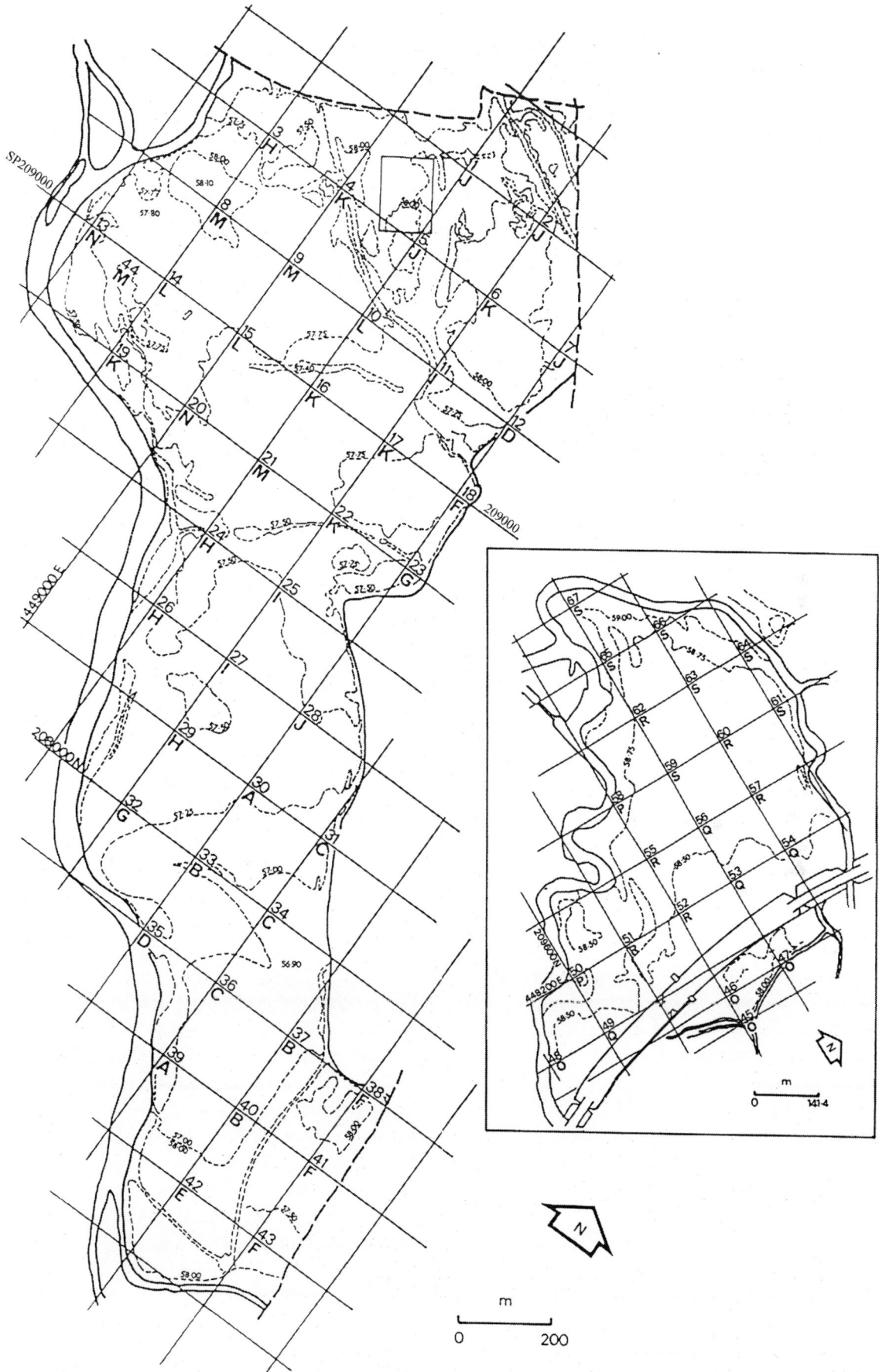

Map 3. Stand Numbers and Distribution of grassland Types on Port Meadow
Insert: Stand Numbers and Distribution of grassland Types on Picksey Mead

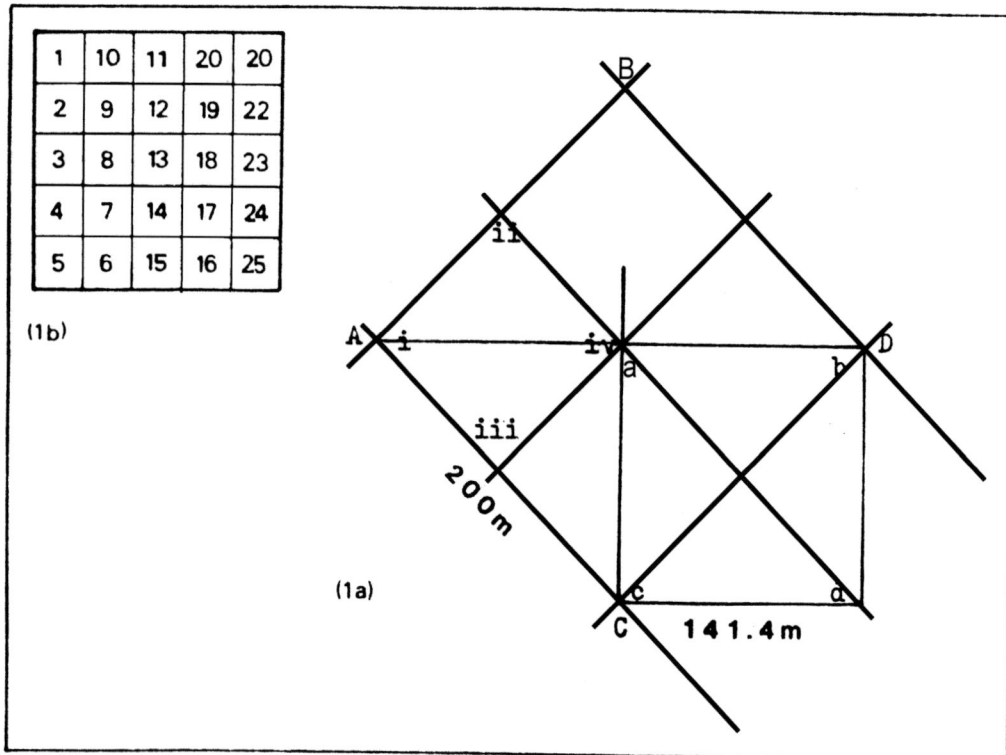

Fig. 1a. Sampling density was increased by sampling the centre of each 200m x 200m square. The new grid was laid out upon the diagonal of the old grid.

Fig. 1b. The quadrats in each Stand were numbered consecutively.

36 in terms of maximum information obtained within the constraints of the time available for the collection, and money available for the computer processing of the data. In recording the flora, estimates of percent cover by, for example, Braun-Blanquet's or the Domin cover-abundance scales, were rejected as being too subjective and non-comparable between different plant forms. Instead, the presence of each species in a quadrat was recorded and these frequency scores amalgamated to give scores for each Stand (up to 25 per species per Stand). These were accepted as a more objective approximation of cover abundance for analysis purposes. The scores were subjected to Correspondence Analysis and were expressed in terms of presence/absence data for Associaton Analysis and Principal Component Analysis in an attempt to overcome the problems of abundance and cover estimations (see Chapter 1.3). By combining the scores of the 1m minimum area sampling units at each Stand, the units became sub-units for the statistical analyses.

1.2.E METHOD OF LAYING OUT SAMPLE STANDS

A surveyor's pole was placed on each of the sites identified by compass bearings, and a second pole was set up 5m due east. A 5m x 5m square was then laid out south of these poles and pegs placed round it at 1m intervals. Pegs were then used to lay out a grid of fine rope representing 25 x 1m squares on the ground (see Photo 1).

1.2.F METHOD OF RECORDING

The quadrats in the Stand are numbered consecutively 1–25 i.e. the first row is oriented north-south, the second south-north, the third north-south (see Fig. 1b). Sampling begins in the northwest corner of the Stand in quadrat no. 1.

The presence of every plant species occurring in the quadrat is recorded on a Nature Conservancy Council meadow recording card (Wells 1981). A new card is used for each quadrat and includes notes on altitude, pH, conductivity, approximate soil depth, unusual features and problems of identification of plant species. A few species, gathered for identification purposes, have been pressed and placed in the Fielding-Druce Herbarium, Oxford University. A list of all species' names, both Latin and English, appears in Appendix B.

1.2.G NOMENCLATURE

Nomenclature follows Stace (1997) for higher plants and Smith (1980) for bryophytes. For the sake of clarity, botanical names have only been italicised when they occur as species in the text.

Photograph 1. The grid laid out on Stand 32. The recorder was examined by both horses and cattle on most days.
(Mr J. Steane)

1.2.H COLLECTION AND ANALYSIS OF SOIL SAMPLES

A sample from the top 10cm of soil at the north-west and south-east corners of each Stand was collected for analysis in the laboratory in July and August 1981.The analysis of soil and water samples for pH and conductivity was carried out according to the methods described in Allen (1974) and set out below.

i . Measurement of pH

30 ml of fresh (i.e. still damp) soil was placed in a 100 ml tripour beaker and covered with distilled water to a depth of 10 mm (this approximates to a soil to water weight ratio of 1:1). The mixture was well stirred and allowed to stand for 15 minutes before taking a reading with a Pye pH meter. A sample of water from the river Thames at Wolvercote Bathing Place was also measured with a Pye pH meter.

ii. Measurement of conductivity

The mixture was then further diluted to a soil to water weight ratio of 1:3, well stirred and allowed to settle for a further 15 minutes. Conductivity was then measured by a 5-range "Dionic" conductivity tester on the supernatant liquid and expressed as units, each one equivalent to one micromho/cm at 2°C. The results of both conductivity and pH are set out in Table 2.

1.2.I SEASONALITY

The chances of species being seen and, therefore, recorded will vary according to their natural seasonal cycles. Ephemeral species, such as mudwort (*Limosella aguatica*) were not recorded. Their presence is rare in the Oxford grassland and I do not consider their absence from the data to be significant. They have, however, been mentioned in the description of some grassland Types. For example those seen on Stand 12. However, strawberry clover (*Trifolium fragiferum*) is a perennial which shows leaf and flower parts only in the summer months. It is abundant in Port Meadow Marsh but was not recognised when this area was sampled. This omission is regretted but is not considered to be significant since it was included in the description of the *Mentha aquatica* community (see Chapter 3.4.B). Wild onion (*Allium vineale*) is an annual which germinates and sets seed during one season. The presence of this and other annuals on Picksey Mead is thought to be more significant and related to some disturbance which offered a germination site. Their distribution on the Oxford grassland is sparse and varies from year to year, reflecting the activity of moles, destruction of the sward by hay making machinery, or poaching by grazing animals. In an attempt to overcome the problem of detecting out-of-season species, frequent walks were taken over the Oxford grassland and additional species noted at different seasons between September 1981 and August 1983. These species are mentioned in the description of the appropriate grassland Type. Their presence showed small variations within the four communities described and were interesting but not significant.

1.2.J ANALYSIS OF DATA

The bryophytes had not been identified by the time the data were analysed so they have been omitted from the numerical analysis. Their presence, however, has been indicated in the description of the appropriate grassland Types.

The scores for each Stand were added up and arranged in a matrix of Stands and species in which every species had a score of up to 25 for each Stand. These data were first stored on floppy discs using the RML 3802 computer, then transmitted to the Oxford University VAX and ICL 2988 computers. After checking, the matrix was submitted to a selection of the Department of Forestry's classification and ordination programs (Dawkins 1968a; 1968b) and to Cornell University's Twinspan (Hill 1976) (see Chapter 1.3).

1.2.K SPECIES DIVERSITY

Species diversity has been defined by Legendre and Legendre (1983) as:

"a measure of the species composition of an ecosystem, in terms of the number and relative abundance of these species."

There are a number of ways of measuring diversity depending upon the way the data are collected. The Shannon-Weiner measure should, for example, be used when all the species in a large community are known and the data have been collected from random samples. When non-random methods are used and the samples are not known to be representative, as in this case, Brillouin's (1956) formula is preferable (Krebs 1978: 456; Pielou 1966; Margalef 1958; Williams 1964; Peet 1974).

The Oxford grassland species data were fed into a computer and Brillouin's diversity index for each Stand (see Table 2) obtained using an unpublished program belonging to the Forestry Department, Oxford University.

1.2.L LIMITATIONS OF METHODS

Irrespective of whether random or systematic methods are used, there is always a chance that a community, such as the willow swamp south of Stand 50, may remain unsampled. This is less likely to occur with systematic sampling if the area between the sampling points is less than the area of the community, depending upon its shape. Sampling at 200m intervals on Port Meadow could have resulted in the omission of some communities. For example, there are several areas on the Meadow from which gravel has been extracted (see Map 5) but only one of these (Stand 19) was sampled. The inspection of these areas detected no differences in the vegetation. Communities such as the Spinney on Picksey Mead were missed but species in them were also noted at the nearest Stand.

The possibility that there was a significant omission of bryophytes from the data has not been tested due to lack of time.

The value of carrying out a further season's sampling was considered, particularly in view of the possibility that some communities or species might remain undetected, especially on Port Meadow. Three methods of overcoming this problem were assessed:

i.   The completed sample grid could have been treated as a skeleton framework and an index of diversity used to indicate where further samples should be interpolated (Lambert 1972; Smartt 1978).
ii. An extension of the survey by placing a Stand in the centre of each grid square on Port Meadow as had been done on Picksey Mead.
iii. A series of random samples.

These three methods are equally objective and each could just as easily have sampled a community for the second time as detect a "new" community. They are also time-consuming in terms of the collection and the analysis of the data. I decided that further sampling would not be cost effective, in terms of time spent for additional data obtained, because the aim of the survey was to provide a description of the Oxford grassland and analyses of the data already provided a basis for this.

1.3 MULTIVARIATE ANALYSES OF DATA

1.3.A INTRODUCTION

Classification, association and ordination techniques were used as tools to interpret the structural complexities of the floral communities. The efficiency of these methods must be judged by evaluating the time spent in organizing the data and the amount of understanding of the structure of the data acquired from the product of a particular program.

Numerical methods are important for objective sampling. Complex multivariate methods of analysis which compare each Stand with all the others, using a variety of statistical tests, are only feasible because of recent advances in the ability of computers to deal with large data sets. The function of multivariate analysis is to show structure in the data by a progression of small steps and to make an easily read and objective summary which will facilitate an understanding of the results (Clymo 1980; Poore 1962; Gauch 1982: 12). The final hierarchy is not an end in itself but is treated as a pattern from which hypotheses can be generated (Williams & Gillard 1971: 245–60). The testing of such hypotheses comes at a later stage when general relationships of species, communities and environmental factors are refined, perhaps to those of single species showing restricted tolerance in their habitat requirements.

The data were, initially, put through association and ordination (principal component analysis) programs. Although each generated broad hypotheses, neither proved as useful as the more robust combination of ordination and classification methods as represented in the program Twinspan (Hill 1978) – a so-called two-way indicator species analysis (Simon 1962; Crovello 1970; Shimwell 1971; Moore, Fitzsimons, Lambe & White, 1970; Blashfield & Aldenderfer 1978).

Twinspan produced a hierarchical table, in which similar Stands and species were grouped together. Dissimilar Stands and species were placed far apart. This table (Table 1) illustrating the hierarchical classification of the Stands, was used as a "skeleton" and was "clothed" with an ecological description of the area.

A description and evaluation of these methods are given separately in the following sections of this chapter.

1.3.B ASSOCIATION ANALYSIS

A divisive monothetic classification technique based on earlier work by Goodall (1953), was adapted for primary vegetation surveys by Williams and Lambert (1959) and called association analysis. The modifications subsequently introduced to this program are described by Gauch (1982: 196–7). In this analytical technique, the Stands are clustered together and then divided hierarchically into progressively smaller clusters, according to whether a particular species is present or absent. Each division is made on the species with the maximum sum of chi-squared values, when compared with all the other species at each level of the hierarchy. (Goodall 1953; Williams & Lambert 1959, 1960, 1961; Lambert & Williams 1962, 1966; Ivimey-Cook & Proctor 1966; Dale & Anderson 1973).

Unfortunately, this method produces a high misclassification rate (Coetzee & Werger 1975; Hill,

Bunce & Shaw 1975; Ladd 1979). Where there is only a relatively small range of variation in the community, as in the Oxford grassland, problems arise when the quantitive differences in the abundance of species are analysed (Hill 1977).

When an Association Analysis program (Dawkins 1968a) was applied to the Oxford grassland data (Fig. 2), the first division was made on the damp hayfield species, *Lathyrus pratensis* (meadow vetchling) and *Filipendula ulmaria* (meadow sweet). Port Meadow with Wolvercote Common was separated from Picksey Mead. At the second level *Leontodon autumnalis* (autumn hawkbit) and *Phragmites communis* (reed) on Picksey Mead and *Myosotis scorpioides* (water forget-me-not) and *Oenanthe fistulosa* (water dropwort) on Port Meadow, isolated the two wet areas from the rest. As the analysis proceeded through the divisions, one Stand was picked out at each level on the basis of the presence or absence of a single species until the remaining Stands were clustered into groups of two or three. The final hierarchy identified 19 communities and placed the Picksey Mead river bank Stands 50 and 58 with the Port Meadow Stands (see Fig. 2). The classification was broadly similar to that of Twinspan but it failed because too many single Stands were unclassified.

1.3.C PRINCIPAL COMPONENT ANALYSIS (PCA)

PCA is an ordination technique which was invented by Pearson (1901) and developed by Hotelling (1933), but was not applied to ecological data until the advent of the computer allowed Goodall (1954) to use it on Australian scrub vegetation. The advantage of this form of analysis is that the scores are taken from the data matrix without any subjective introduction of weights or endpoint selections. An individual Stand or species may be singled out as the principal component of each axis. The first axis lies on the line of greatest variance, while the second lies perpendicular to the first in order to account for the maximum remaining variance (Gauch 1982: 137).

PCA programs (Dawkins 1968b) using variance-covariance and equalized means, in which the values of all the species recorded in the Stands are compared for the ordering of the Stands, produced similar results. In the variance-covariance matrix (Appendix C) the first (hydrological) axis has a variance of 1422.4 and the second (anthropogenic) axis a variance of 822.29, with a total variance from the diagonal of 4910.6. The Stands are arranged in three dispersed clusters representing a continuum from dry to moisture-loving species on Port Meadow with Wolvercote Common and the community

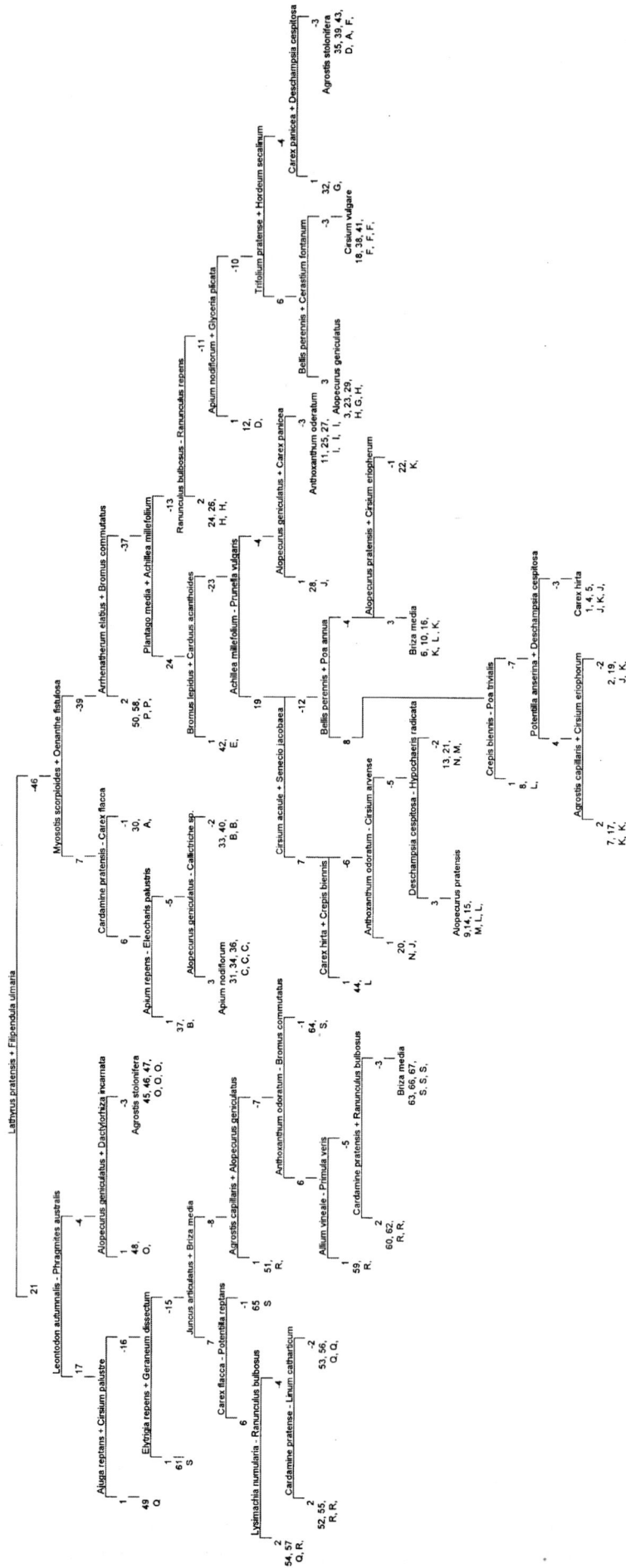

Fig. 2. Classification of the Oxford Grassland (Association Analysis)

on Picksey Mead is in an open cluster in a central position (see Appendix Ci where PCA is compared with the Twinspan results). This technique confirms the simple structure in the data suggested by the Association Analysis. It separates the hay meadow Stands from those of the pasture, but, apart from a continuum of Stands on the Meadow, does not provide a more detailed classification. PCA's correspondence between Stands and the plotting of pH conductivity and altitude on the PCA graph (Appendix Cii, Ciii, Civ) revealed no clear pattern either so this line of analysis was abandoned in favour of correspondence analysis as represented by Twinspan. The Twinspan grassland types and their relationship to the PCA classification are shown in Appendix Cv.

1.3.D CORRESPONDENCE ANALYSIS (TWINSPAN)

Correspondence analysis as represented by Twinspan (Hill 1978) is a combination of classification and ordination techniques which was recommended to me by Dr John Rodwell of Lancaster University in order to compare the Oxford grassland with the National Vegetation Classification now called British Plant Communities. Twinspan is a divisive, hierarchical, polythetic method of making what is called a two-way indicator species analysis of samples and species (Hill 1979; Gauch & Whittaker 1981). It is based on an earlier one-way system that only classified samples (Hill, Bunce & Shaw 1975). However, contrary to the impression given by its name, Twinspan divides ordinations rather than selects indicator species (Hill 1979). The significant, new feature of Twinspan is that it primarily classifies the Stands and uses this classification to construct a secondary classification of the species. These two classifications are expressed as an ordered two-way table in which similar Stands and species appear close together, and dissimilar Stands and species, far apart. The odd species or Stands are placed in an anomalous position. Twinspan also identifies differential species; these reflect discontinuities in the vegetation due to environmental or historical conditions.

In making the classification, reciprocal averaging of chi-squared scores is first used to ordinate the data. Then one or several species that characterise the extremes of the first axis are emphasised to polarise the Stands. The axis is broken near the middle to divide the Stands into two clusters which are identified as (+) or (−). Stands near the middle of the axis are identified as "borderline" or "misclassified" positive and negative to draw attention to the possibility that such Stands may be misclassified. Next, species that are preferential to one end or the other of the axis are identified and used as a basis for a "refined"

ordination and the axis is divided at an appropriate point to make the desired dichotomy. Finally an "indicator" ordination is constructed with the most preferential species and compared with the refined ordination.

Quantitative data are expressed as preferential species, using "pseudospecies" to give the qualitative element (Hill, Bunch & Shaw 1975; Hill 1977, 1979). The idea follows that of Braun-Blanquet's scale of cover abundance (Mueller-Dombois & Ellenberg 1974: 82; Westhoff & Maarel 1973: 639) but the levels used to define the scale are "pseudospecies cut levels".

Because a computer has a binary system, numerical data are supplemented by "pseudospecies" which were invented for the Twinspan program to weight species, especially those which occur more than once in a Stand. The program is so designed that the weighting can be varied according to the type of data or method of collection. In this case the data were collected from a series of 25 quadrats in square Stands placed on a grid. A square root scale (see Fig. 3) has, therefore, been used to provide "cut off" points for the pseudospecies (see below).

The first pseudospecies cut level, 0, was chosen so as to place more emphasis on presence/absence than on quantity. Class 1 contains those hypothetical species occurring in

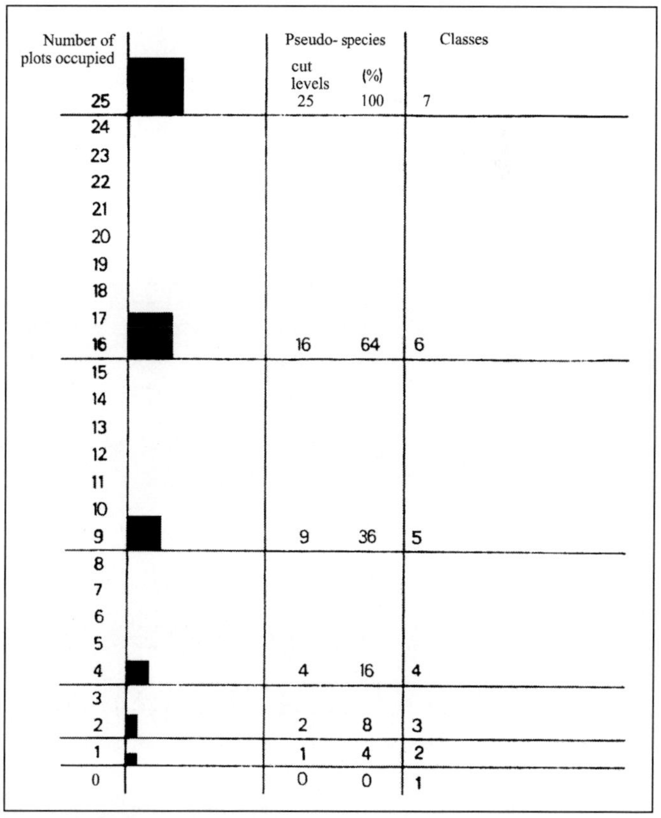

Fig. 3. Illustration of the square root scale used as "cut off" points for Twinspan's "pseudospecies".

13

MEAD   FEN

TWINSPAN output: cut levels 0, 1, 2, 4, 9, 16, only real species as indicators.

Grassland type: B C A D F G H I J K L M N Q R S P O

Species (Plot no. / Species):

- 50 Equi pal
- 6 Alli ven
- 21 Anis ste
- 10 Anth odo
- 11 Anth syl
- 15 Arrh ela
- 18 Brom com
- 19 Brom hor
- 33 Cent nig
- 43 Dact fuc
- 2 Elyt rep
- 55 Fili ulm
- 60 Gera dis
- 65 Hera sph
- 77 Lath pal
- 78 Lath pra
- 82 Leuc vul
- 83 Linu cat
- 84 List ova
- 89 Lysi num
- 96 Ophi vul
- 112 Prim ver
- 113 Prun vul
- 119 Rhin min
- 123 Sang off
- 126 Sila sil
- 128 Stel gra
- 142 Urti dio
- 147 Vici cra
- 148 Vici sat
- 45 Dact inc
- 88 Lych flo
- 124 Sene aqu
- 131 Succ pra
- 136 Trif cam
- 143 Vale dio
- 9 Ajug rep
- 23 Ange syl
- 26 Calt pal
- 26 Care acu
- 27 Care dis
- 30 Care nig
- 32 Care rip
- 48 Eleo uni
- 49 Epil hir
- 51 Fest aru
- 58 Gali uli
- 63 Glyc max
- 70 Hype tet
- 75 Junc con
- 90 Medi lup
- 93 Myos lax
- 97 Pedi pal
- 98 Phal aru
- 100 Phra aus
- 109 Poly hyd
- 117 Ranu fic
- 132 Symp off
- 134 Thal fla
- 28 Care fla
- 38 Cirs pal
- 79 Leon aut
- 20 Brom lep
- 53 Fest pra
- 120 Rume ace
- 17 Briz med
- 80 Leon his
- 86 Lotu cor
- 115 Ranu bul
- 141 Tris fla
- 8 Alop pra
- 34 Cera fon

TABLE 1. THE OXFORD GRASSLAND ASSOCIATION TABLE (TWINSPAN) SHOWS THE HIERARCHY OF BOTH STANDS AND SPECIES. PORT MEADOW MARSH IS SEPARATED FROM THE REST AT THE FIRST DIVISION OF STANDS AND SPECIES.

14

Column group labels (top to bottom along divisions): **2nd division** — **PASTURE** — **1st division** — **2nd division** — **MARSH**

Species (row labels):

42 Cyno cri
44 Dact glo
46 Desc ces
54 Fest rub
68 Holc lan
69 Hord sec
101 Plan lan
114 Ranu acr
121 Rume con
135 Trag pra
138 Trif pra
40 Crep bie
85 Loli per
99 Phle pra
133 Tara off
35 Cirs aca
59 Gali ver
66 Pilos off
71 Hypo gla
76 Koel mac
81 Leon tar
87 Luzu cam
105 Poa com
125 Sene jac
137 Trif dub
146 Vero ser
1 Achi mil
16 Bell per
37 Cirs eri
39 Cirs vul
41 Crep cap
52 Fest hyb
56 Gali mol
103 Plan med
111 Pote rep
36 Cirs arv
72 Hypo rad
25 Card aca
61 Gera mol
64 Glyc pli
74 Junc buf
108 Poly avi
127 Sonc pal
129 Stel med
144 Vero ana
106 Poa pra
107 Poa tri
67 Hier spp
102 Plan maj
104 Poa ann
3 Agro cap
139 Trif rep
110 Pote ans
122 Rume cri
4 Agro sto
7 Alop gen
29 Care hir
118 Ranu rep
31 Care pan
73 Junc art
62 Glyc flu
91 Ment aqu
95 Oena fis
140 Trig pal
12 Apiu inu
14 Apiu rep
22 Call spp
57 Gali pal
92 Myos dis
94 Myos sco
116 Ranu fla
130 Stel pal
145 Vero scu
13 Api nod
47 Eleo pal
24 Card pra

TABLE 1 CONTINUED

less than one quadrat and so emphasises the absence of a species. This leads to an anomaly. Because there are no scores between 0 and 1, no species are recorded in Class 1 on the final table (see Table 1). Fig. 3 shows that if a species is recorded in one quadrat or plot, it is counted as a pseudospecies and placed in Class 2. If it occurs in more than 16 quadrats in a Stand it is counted as six pseudospecies and placed in Class 6. This study involves a detailed insight into one type of vegetation, neutral grassland, so the species which occur in more than 16 Stands are common and relatively unimportant. There is no significant difference between species occurring in 24 and those occurring in 25 quadrats per Stand. Class 7 is not, therefore, required.

When the ordination is being constructed each Stand accumulates a value from three different sources:

1. Each species in the Stand scores 1.
2. Each differential species in the Stand scores 1.
3. Each pseudospecies in the Stand scores 1.

The values on the final table represent Classes with the following values:

Class 1 – Species scoring <1
Class 2 – Species scoring 1
Class 3 – Species scoring 2–3
Class 4 – Species scoring 4–8
Class 5 – Species scoring 9–15
Class 6 – Species scoring 16–25

In the data from the Oxford grassland, which involve scores between 1 and 25, 6 cut levels provide adequate classes and express the structure of the data without any additional weighting.

Table 1 not only presents the data in the style of traditional continental phytosociology, but it indicates the hierarchy of both the Stands and the species. The hierarchy of the Stands is shown at the foot of Table 1 and of the species to the right, together they show the classification of the Oxford grassland. It shows the Oxford grassland divided into four groups each evolved in response to particular or a combination of edaphic and management factors. Group I, Port Meadow Marsh, appears to be controlled by variations in water availability, in this case flooding and drainage. Group II, Port Meadow Moist Pasture is subject to less flooding but more disturbance due to man's management of the grazing animals. Port Meadow Dry Pasture is not a homogenous area either, but is distinguished by the rare occurrence of floods, heavy grazing, particularly in winter, and lack of alluvium. It is immediately apparent that Group IV, Picksey Mead, has been separated from the rest because of its characteristics as a hay meadow rather than permanent pasture.

At the bottom of the hierarchy the clusters of Stands have been described as grassland types A to S. They are shown on Map 4 as they occur at each Stand and in Appendix Cv where they are substituted for the Stand numbers shown in Appendix Ci. No attempt has been made to delineate boundaries between grassland types because the vegetation between Stands was not recorded. The contour lines shown on Map 4 are, however, useful in interpreting the vegetation in terms of the topography and height of the water-table.

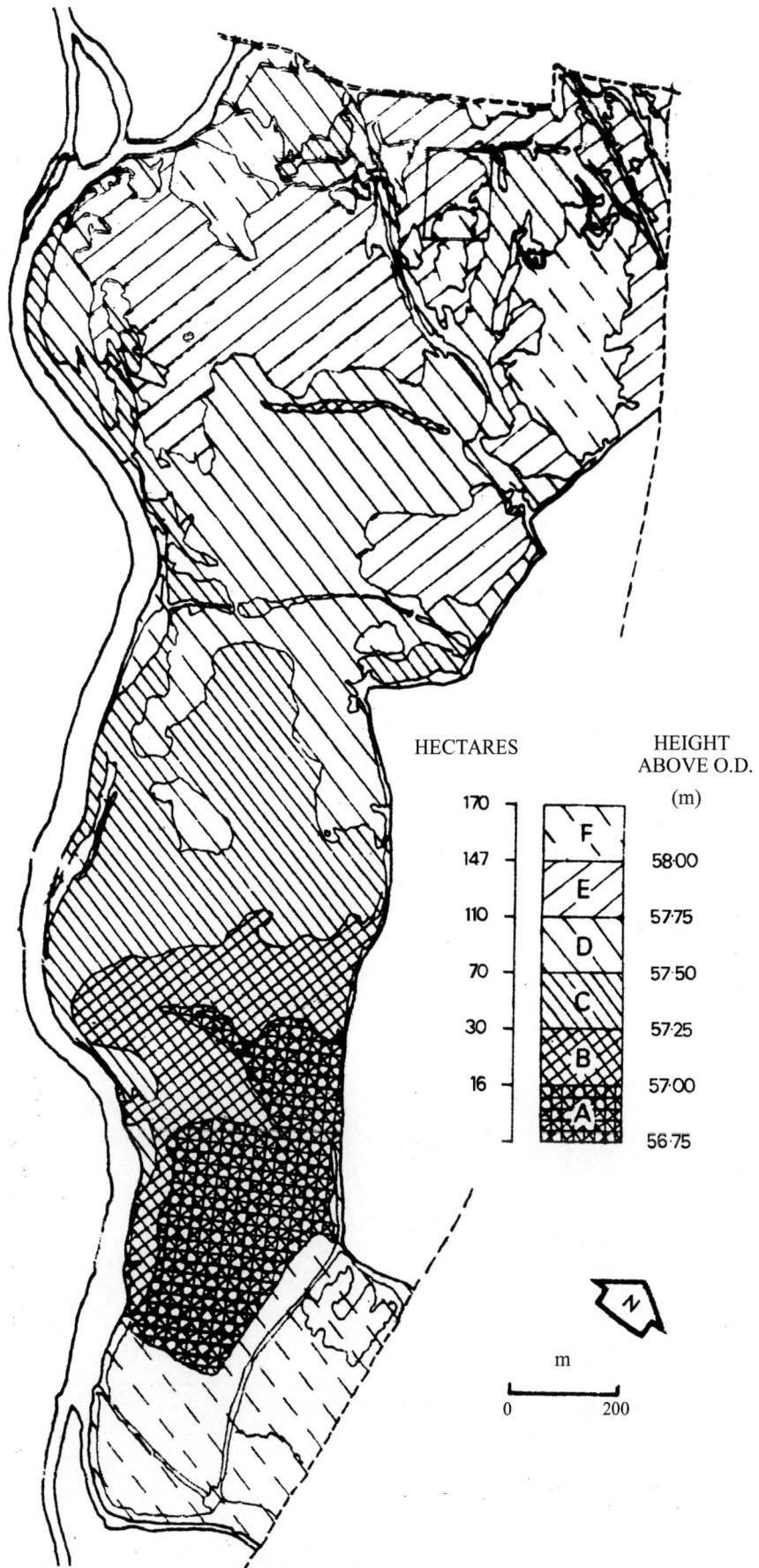

HECTARES		HEIGHT ABOVE O.D. (m)
170	F	
147	E	58·00
110	D	57·75
70	C	57·50
30	B	57·25
16	A	57·00
		56·75

m
0   200

Map 4. Inundation zones on Port Meadow and Wolvercote Common

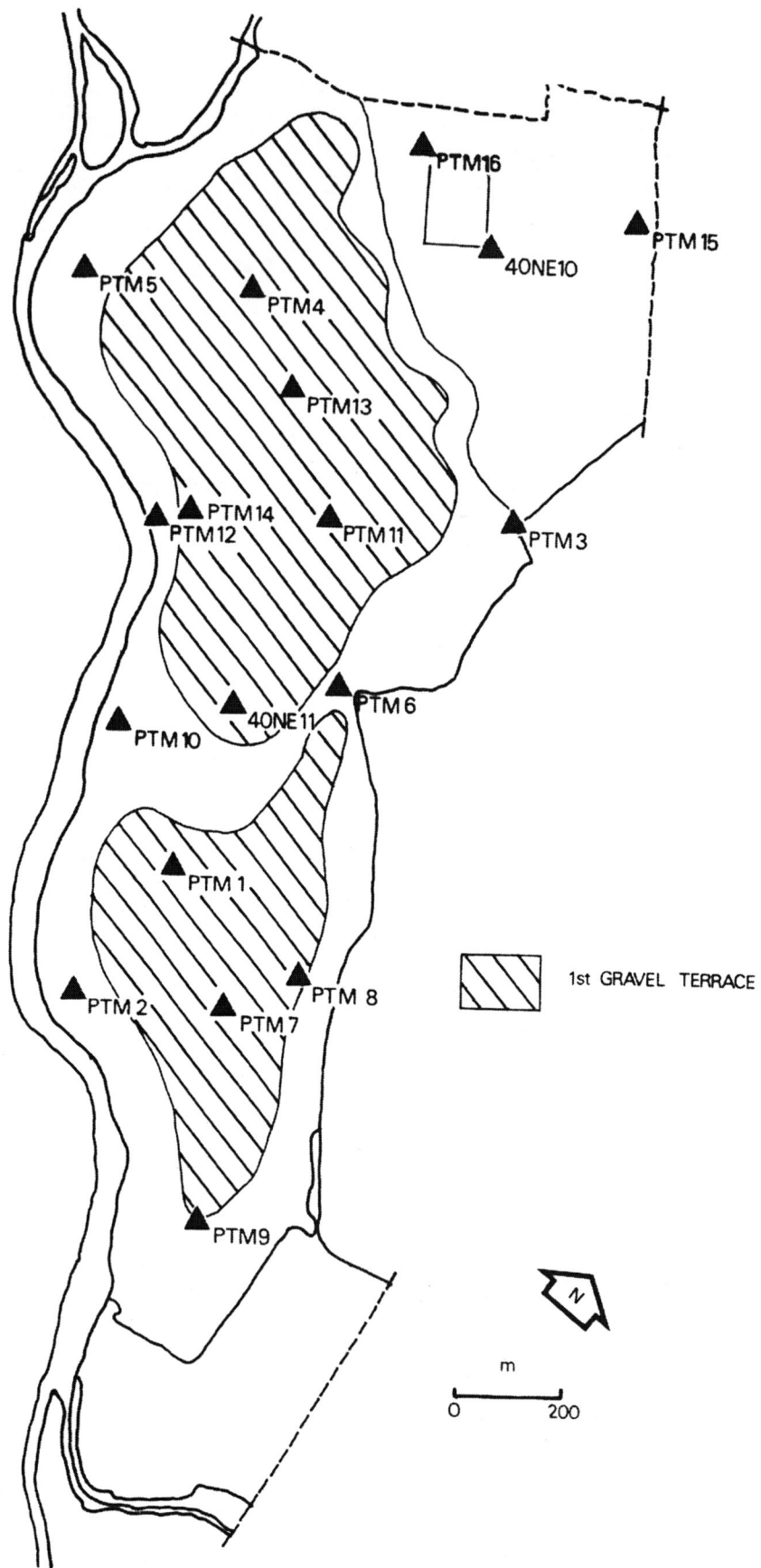

Map 5. Position of bore holes on Port Meadow additional to Map 7 (Institute of Hydrology).

CHAPTER 2

EDAPHIC FACTORS

2.1 GRAVEL

The Oxford grassland developed on gravel, and alluvium over gravel, on the floodplain or first Thames terrace, which is the youngest of the Thames terraces (Sandford 1954: 22). These calcareous gravels, together with loess and weathering products, were laid over Oxford Clay during the late Pleistocene. The Thames became more restricted to its bed, and eroded a complex pattern of ephemeral channels which generally became stabilised into a few major channels before the end of the Devensian period.

The composition of the gravel varies on Port Meadow with Wolvercote Common and Picksey Mead (see Appendix D) from five different layers of gravel with sand and/or alluvial mixtures at PTM (Port Meadow) 1 (see Map 5) to a mixture of sand and gravel at PTM 3 and PTM 5, and apparently solid gravel at 40NE8 at the south end of Picksey Mead. Over this gravel a layer of alluvium of varying thickness on the Oxford grassland was deposited (Institute of Hydrology 1979), mostly during the Iron Age (Robinson & Lambrick 1984).

2.2 SOIL INCLUDING ALLUVIUM

Gradually, a thin soil, not necessarily of alluvial origin, developed over the gravel. Old stream beds subsequently became silted up as the volume of water was reduced during the afforestation of the catchment area. Where these soils have been observed by archaeologists, they show no sign of water-logging, nor the marked alkalinity which one might expect from a soil closely associated with calcareous gravels beside a flooding river derived from an oolitic limestone catchment area. Any limestone pebbles surviving in the soil tend to be severely decayed and molluscan shells are generally absent. Some molluscs were preserved beneath a Bronze Age barrow at King's Weir. They were protected from leaching by the calcareous material of the barrow. Aquatic species indicative of flooding were absent. The absence of waterlogged organic remains or much gleying in Neolithic and Bronze Age ditches also suggests a lack of flooding, or at least a seasonally low water table, on the Thames floodplain in the Neolithic and Bronze Ages.

(Lambrick & Robinson 1979: 141–2; Briggs & Gilbertson 1980; Robson 1976; Bowler & Robinson 1980).

Robinson & Lambrick's (1984) lucid exposition of Holocene flooding and deposition of alluvium in the upper Thames valley distinguishes periods when the uplands were ploughed, soil surfaces eroded and alluvium deposited along the Thames valley floor, from periods when pasturalism was dominant and flooding without the deposition of silt occurred. The process of the gradual accretion of alluvium over the Thames floodplain has been described as "alluviation" (Robinson & Lambrick 1984: 810). The correlation of archaeological evidence with hydrological conditions such as the laying down of alluvium indicates changes in land-use and farming practice. In the Iron Age the water-table rose and flooding occured, but this was associated with little or no deposition of alluvium. This probably reflects increased clearance of woodland for pasturalism in the catchment area. In the late Iron Age and Roman periods, the grassland gave way to more extensive arable and both flooding and deposition of alluvium were recorded. In the Saxon period arable farming was reduced and did not become important again until the earlier Middle Ages when flooding was again accompanied by the movement of silt into the valley bottom. In the later middle ages it was the turn of pasturalism to dominate the landscape in both the upland and lowland areas in the Thames basin. When corn prices were raised in the Nineteenth Century, ploughing began once more in upland areas (Robinson & Lambrick 1984).

Environmental evidence for this hypothesis has been found on Port Meadow, as well as at six other sites in the upper Thames valley (see Map 6), where alluvial clay and aquatic molluscs seal prehistoric deposits. Robinson & Lambrick (1984) consider that this layer was laid down no earlier than the mid Iron Age and that deposition of alluvium was common-place on these areas in the Roman period. They suggest that the depth of organic preservation in Iron Age features on Port Meadow indicates that the water table remained high to the present day. The accuracy of this hypothesis is crucial to the understanding of early land-use in the upper Thames valley but this argument must remain

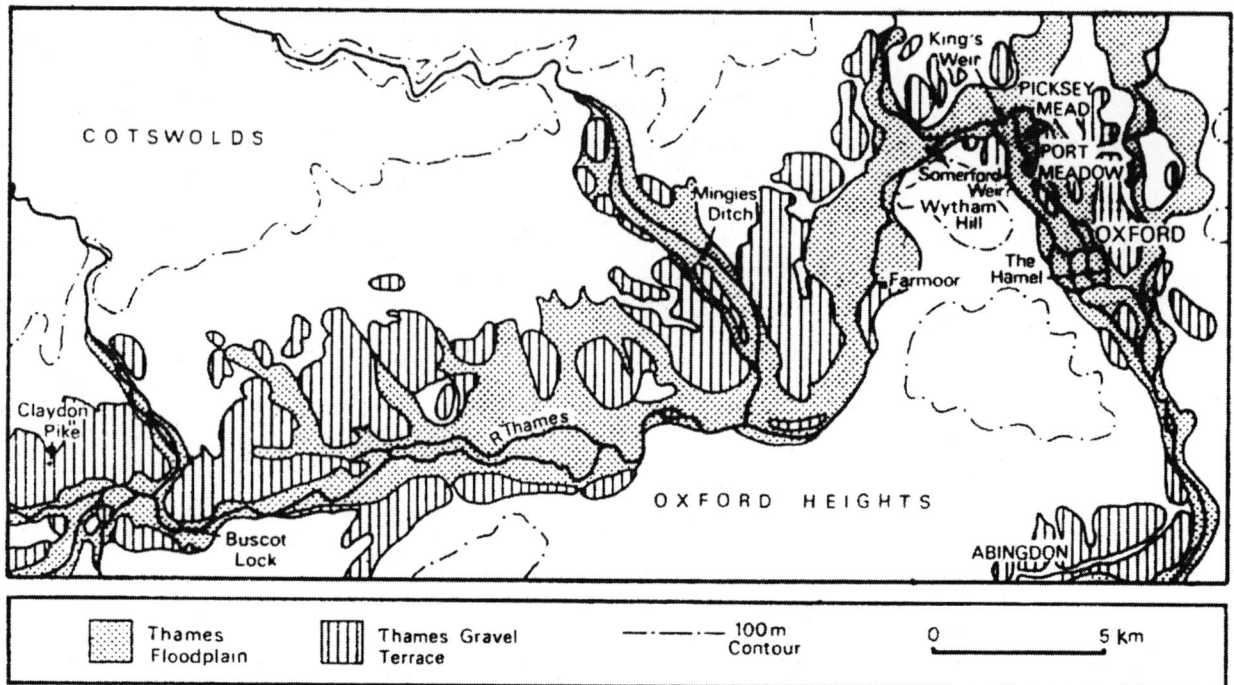

Map 6. The upper Thames valley river gravels and archaeological sites.

tentative until soil scientists have reported on the evidence put forward by the archaeologists. Its effect on the land use of the Oxford grassland is discussed in Chapter 5.2.B.

In Port Meadow Marsh, there is about one metre of very clayey gravel topped with alluvium (PTM9 see Map 5 and Appendix D). The soil is well structured and is similar to true meadow soils; it is not acid nor deficient in oxygen due to the constant movement of water to and from the Thames (Tansley 1939: 88; Nature Conservancy Council Southern Region). In the Twentieth Century the structure of the soil has, however, been affected by the presence of cattle and horses during periods when the water-table was high. Apart from compaction near gateways, the excessive treading of these animals has caused some poaching of the pasture, but not enough to impede drainage, even in Port Meadow Marsh (Nature Conservancy Council 1983). Picksey Mead has a floodplain soil with a fluctuating water-table in which sufficient organic material has accumulated to form a "floating" meadow. Clarke (1954: 55) suggested that this soil "rolls and reverberates when jumped upon" but I felt no such activity.

2.3. WATER

2.3.A INTRODUCTION

The movement of water, both above and below ground, is an important aspect of the ecology of the grassland. It helps to explain why there are no waterlogged conditions, particularly on Port Meadow Marsh where one might

expect to find them. The significance of ground and surface water regimes is considered in the two following sections.

2.3.B GROUND WATER

The bi-weekly ponding up of the water as a result of the flash lock system in the Nineteenth and early Twentieth centuries, may have affected the vegetation on Port Meadow where the height of the water table reflects, to some extent, that of the river (see Chapter 4.3.C). Thacker (1911: 176) suggested that the extra time needed for the water to flow from Godstow to Medley, a mere mile and a half, was because of the width of the river as it passed Port Meadow. It may also have reflected the fall of the river along that reach which is very slight.

Recent work of the Institute of Hydrology (see Fig. 5 and below) suggested, however, that water may have appeared to be lost by flowing into the adjacent Port Meadow gravel until it was saturated. The gravel allows ground water to pass freely from and to the river so that the water table of the Meadow rises and falls with the height of the river. Today, Port Meadow Marsh is wet for much of the year yet cannot be described as waterlogged with standing, stagnant water. On the contrary, the constant flow of the ground water aerates the soil and prevents a reduction in pH normally associated with waterlogging.

This ground water system is currently being investigated by the Institute of Hydrology, as part of a larger study in the Oxford area, by monitoring and analysing the water from observation wells situated at intervals across the Thames valley floor (see Map 7 and Appendix E). The Institute has found that when the river rises (particularly in winter) the gravel on Port Meadow adjacent to Burgess Field Nature Park (see Maps 2 & 3) and in the area of Stands 30, 33 and 34 becomes saturated and the ground water flows in a

north-westerly direction. In summer when the river level is generally lower, the gravel can take in water from the east. A westerly flow then occurs (Institute of Hydrology 1979).

On Picksey Mead the general direction of the ground water is south south-westerly (see Map 7). It flows from the area

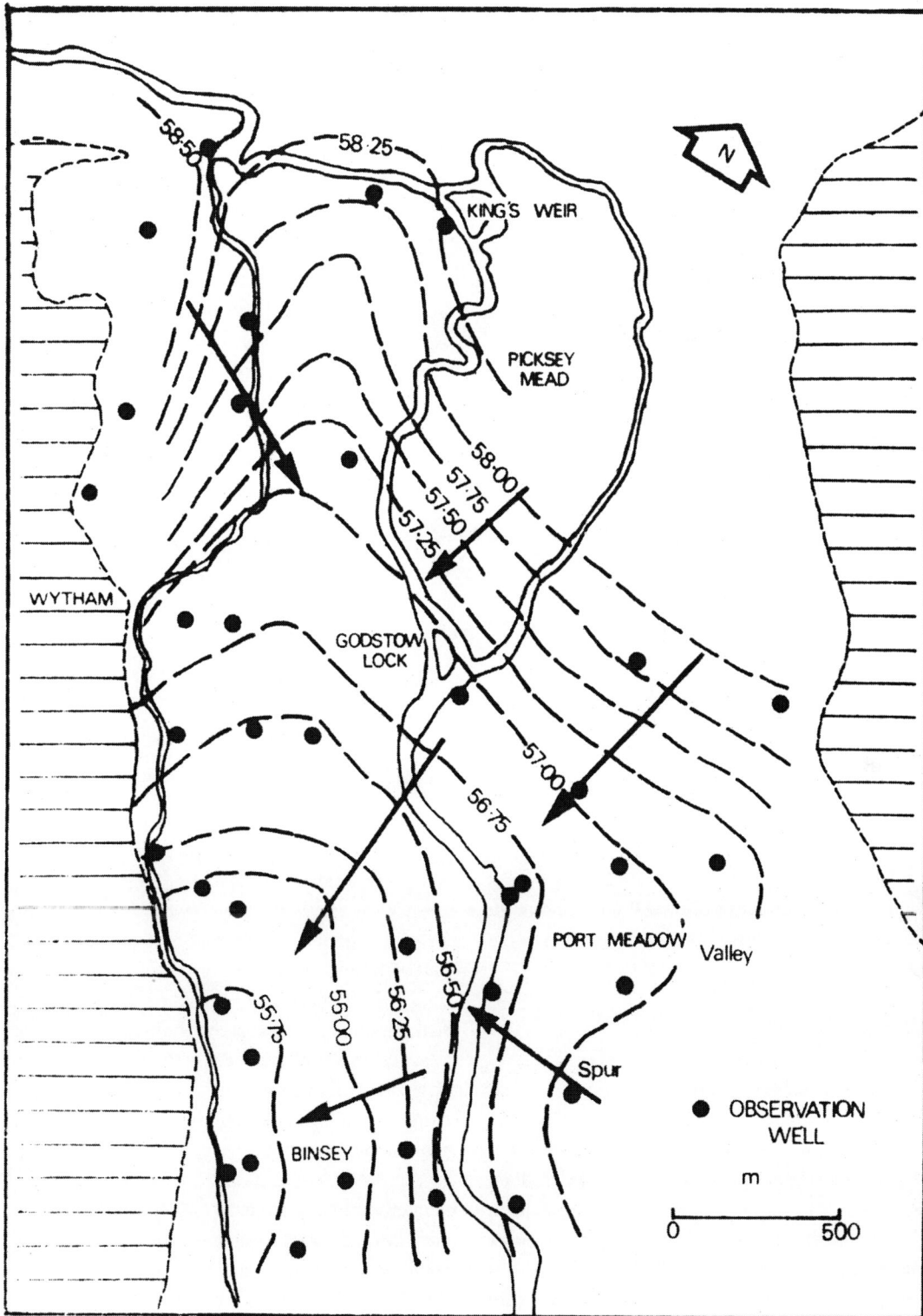

Map 7. Ground water flow beneath the Oxford grassland, contours show height of water-table in metres O.D. (Institute of Hydrology, unpublished report).

21

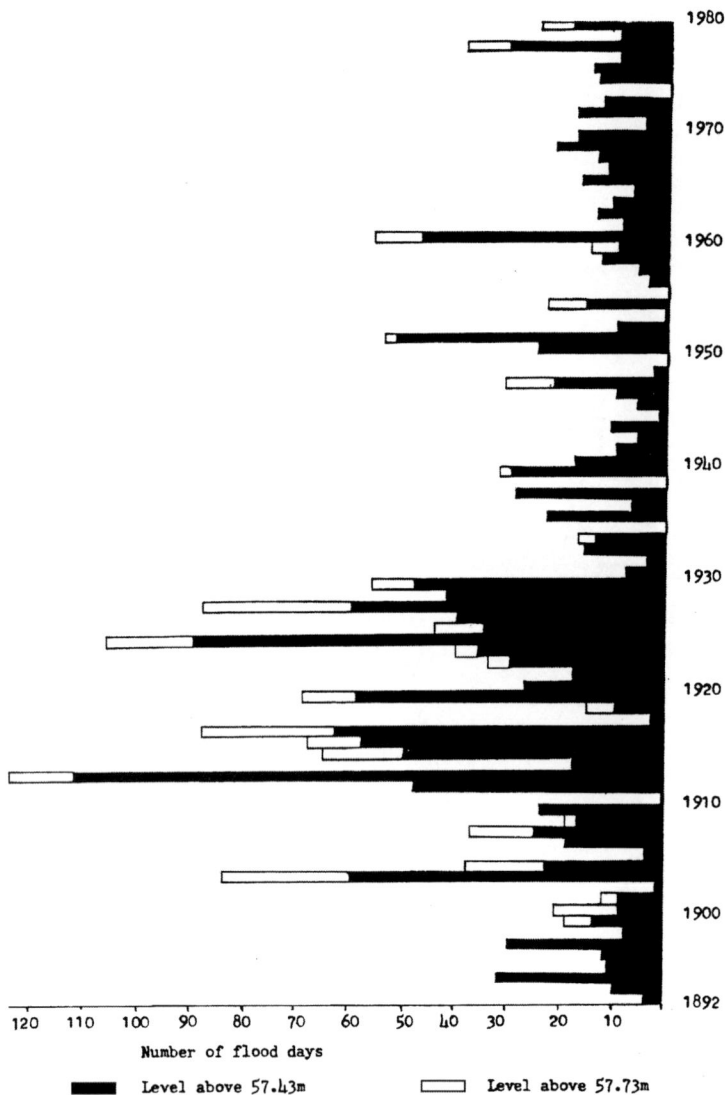

Fig. 4. *The number of days per annum when the river was above typical low flood level at Godstow Lock tail water. Medley weir was removed in 1931.*

water level but does not receive floodwater because of the levée. At this time the water table is raised to the height of the river and gives the appearance of flooding but with no deposition of alluvium. New farming methods such as piped drainage interrupting overland flow and, to a lesser extent, direct drilling to "improve" pasture too wet to plough, may also be factors on other sites.

The improvements to the Thames near Oxford in the late Nineteenth and early Twentieth Centuries were very effective in improving navigation and reducing flood periods. The number of days each year when the river was at flood level between 1898 and 1978 are recorded in Figure 4. Map 4 shows contours on Port Meadow with Wolvercote Common (from the Thames Water photogrammetric map (1978) but not checked for accuracy) expressed as inundation zones to give a visual aid for the description of the grassland. Figure 6 (p.88) shows how much of the Meadow is flooded when the river reaches low and high flood levels and, therefore, the amount of grassland not affected by flood water and available for grazing.

2.3.C.i. Port Meadow with Wolvercote Common

The aerial photograph (Photo 2) taken in the dry summer of 1976 (Royal Commission for Historic Monuments) shows the silted-up remains of ditches draining across Port Meadow towards the river (see Map 1). They are as follows:

Shiplake Ditch is the largest of the ditches and has formed part of the boundary of Oxford since at least the 15th century until 1927 (Crossley 1979). In the early Saxon period it was striking enough to be given the name "Shiplake" – slow flowing stream of the sheep – (Gelling 1953). Perhaps the sheep were dipped in it prior to shearing. Shiplake Ditch continues to be the boundary between Port Meadow and Wolvercote Common.

Winterbourne Stream used to flow from Upper Wolvercote and through Port Meadow, but was cut off by the construction of the canal in 1781. The streambed forms the boundary between Wolvercote Common and Hook Meadow, but its direction is otherwise unclear. The name "Winterbourne" suggests that it was once more active but that water flowed in it only during the winter months.

of high water in the river above King's Weir in the north and east, to the lower river level below King's Weir, in the south-west (Map 7).

2.3.C SURFACE WATER

At the end of the Eighteenth Century and in the Nineteenth there is evidence that, within the area of the Oxford grassland, Wolvercote paper mill required a greater head of water (Carter 1957). King's Weir was raised and silt laden flood water backed up over the meads and into Yarnton (Stapleton 1893: 315). The probable low level of alluvial deposition over Picksey Mead during the last fifty years, despite its being a period of extensive arable expansion, may be related to the formation of levées along the river bank, by the dumping of material dredged from the river, which acts as a barrier. When the Thames is high much of Picksey Mead is below the river-

Photograph 2. Aerial photographs show up Bronze and Iron Age ditches as well as underground stream beds.
(Royal Commission for Historic Monuments 3 August 1976).

Water may still flow along its course underground across Port Meadow just south of Stands 22 and 24 and into the river at Black Jack's Hole.

A third ditch runs across the Meadow in between Shiplake Ditch and Winterbourne Stream and drains into the river near the south end of Picksey island. This ditch holds water when Zones A, B and C are flooded (see Maps 1 and 4). The ditches round Wolvercote Common were last cleaned in the autumn of 1963. The direction of the flow was changed and the water now flows from west to east, into the Line Ditch. The excavated earth was spread and harrowed the following spring (Wolvercote Commoners' Committee Minutes 10.9.63, 31.12.63).

This flow of water relates to the surface drainage which may be different from that of the ground water. Under the raised area (see Maps 1 and 8) there was at one time a deep ditch draining this part of Port Meadow which flowed into the Old River (see Map 8; Minn 1939; Appendix F). The silted-up remains of the northern part of the ditch

may underlie Stands 33 and 34. Rubbish, which is said to have included builders' rubble, may have blocked the outflow. In 1925 the City Council built a road northwards from Walton Well gate across the Meadow. A culvert was built to take water under the road, from whence it passed into a ditch that flowed into the Line Ditch (so called because it follows the railway line). The water eventually flowed into the Old River above the railway line bridge.

The nature of the plant communities growing on this part of Port Meadow (Stands 34, 36, 37 & 40), compared with those in the 1920s (see Chapter 6) suggests that the Old River and, therefore, the water-table is now kept at a higher level than before. This would lead to a cessation of any movement of surface water off the Meadow. The land is very flat, (56.9m above sea level) and water cannot flow into the river on those parts where the surface water is held back by the raised path which runs parallel to the river bank, and the bank itself which has been built up to 57.2m. The situation is exacerbated by the silting up of the following ditches:

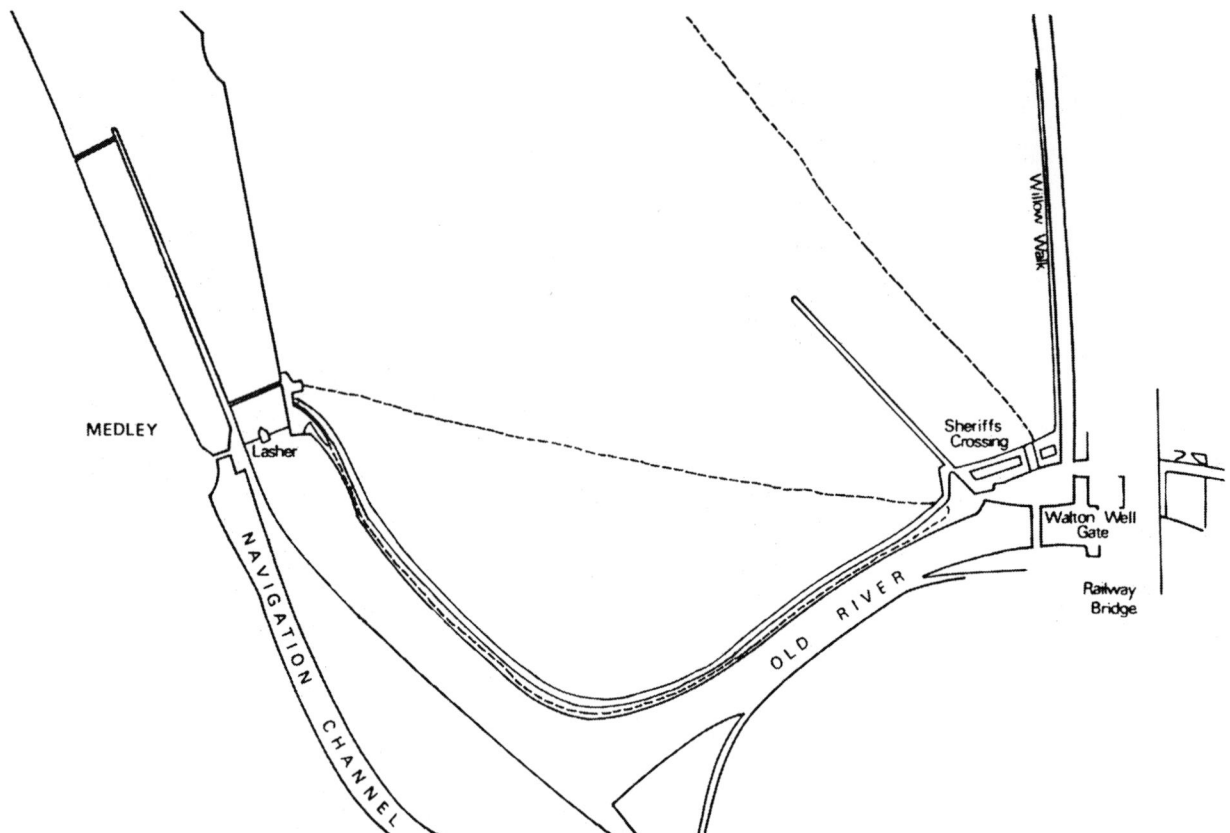

Map 8. The south end of Port Meadow (Ordnance Survey 1st Edition 1877).

1 The drainage channel running north-west from Walton Well Gate has been filled in with City refuse.

2 The culvert and drainage ditches running along the eastern boundary of the Meadow are in an unkempt state. These ditches were designed to drain into the Old River just before it passes under the railway line to the east.

3 The ditch to the south-west (at the north end of Medley Boat Station) now acts more for the access of flood water than for the egress of surface water.

4 On the east, the culvert built under the road to the tip in 1935 has been allowed to silt up and the road itself acts as a further barrier to the flow of surface water.

5 In the south west, the ditch adjacent to Medley Boat Station, designed to take water from the Meadow to a discharge point below Medley Weir, has been filled in. This ditch is less important now than it was prior to the removal of the weir in 1931. Nevertheless, since it has been filled in it is more difficult for water to flow off Port Meadow Marsh, particularly in times of flood.

2.3.C.ii. Picksey Mead

There is a slight fall in the land from north to south-east which takes the surface drainage away from the river towards the old weir on the Wolvercote Mill Stream shown

on Map 2 (Nature Conservacy Council 1958). A ditch running along the southern border of the Mead and one between the Wytham Piece and the Yarnton and Begbroke Piece (See Map 10a), once helped to dry out the southern end as soon as the floods abated. They were part of a system of ditches which could either be used to take flood water from the Mead or for watering stock. Water would have entered from the river above King's Weir and the Mill Weir, and left just above Godstow Bridge (Nature Conservancy Council 1958). This system was changed when the A34, Oxford Bypass was built across the south end of Picksey Mead. The dual carriageway took six acres from Yarnton and Begbroke Piece and two acres from Wytham Piece, leaving an 8 acre remnant of Picksey Mead on the south-east of the road (Nature Conservancy Council 1958).

New ditches along both sides of the Bypass embankment were dug and connected to the Mill Stream, in addition to the Honeybourne Stream (sometimes called Yarnton Ditch or King's Bridge Brook, Nature Conservancy Council 1958). The Thames Water Authority brought Honeybourne Stream under the Mill Stream and along a new channel at the edge of Picksey Mead and then by way of a siphon under the Bypass embankment and so into the Mill Stream. It is regularly dredged, the last occasions being 1961 and 1975. The dredged material is spread over an area of Picksey Mead, 10–15m wide. Unfortunately it is impossible to get modern machinery onto the opposite bank in order to dump the dredged material on the island between the Mill Stream and the new bed of Honeybourne Stream.

The new drainage system is not effective. The area west of Picksey Lane has become a reedswamp dominated by (*Phragmites australis* and *Epilobium hirsutum*) since the road was built.

On the main part of Picksey Mead river dredging, including gravel, has been deposited and spread over the alluvium within 15m of the river bank. A raised bank has been formed and examples of the vegetation cover were recorded at Stands 50 and 58 (see Map 3). Although the bank has reduced the amount of flooding in winter, the water table rises above the ground level, particularly in the neighbourhood of Stand 60, whenever the head water at King's Weir is high. The raised bank impedes the flow of water off the Mead into the river below King's Weir. The altitude of each Stand is shown in Table 2 and Appendix Civ where these values have been substituted for the Stand numbers shown in Appendix Ci.

2.4 NUTRIENT STATUS

2. 4. A INTRODUCTION

One set of soil samples taken from each Stand was analysed (see above p.9) for pH and conductivity and the results are shown on Table 2. They show a more intricate situation on both the Meadow and Picksey Mead than had been indicated by Baker (1937). Port Meadow appears to be affected by minerals emanating from the City Dump and the nutrient poor situation on part of Picksey Mead may be the result of a reduction in flooding and hence deposition of alluvium and, perhaps, the filtering of ground water as it passed from the river under Picksey Mead. Analysis of soil samples taken at regular intervals throughout the year will be required in order to test the annual range of fluctuation in nutrient status.

2.4.B pH

Bearing in mind the difference in measuring pH by a colorometer and by a Pye pH meter, the range in pH values on both Port Meadow and Picksey Mead appears to be much greater now than when it was last recorded in 1923/4. Baker (1937) found that the pH varied between 6.5 and 8.0. Table 2 shows that in 1982 there was a variation from 5.2 to 7.6; most Stands were between pH 6.0 and 7.3. They are also shown in Appendix Cii where they have been substituted for the Stand numbers shown in Appendix Ci. On the Meadow the cause of this apparent decline in alkalinity may be due to increased leaching of

the soil since the removal of Medley Weir in 1931. At that time the flooding of the river was reduced both in extent and in the number of flood days (see Fig. 4). The pH of the river water, stated by Baker (1937) to be 8.0 (compared with 7.8 today) may also be compared with a pH of 5.6 for rain water. This may have contributed to the high pH level recorded in the soil. Although acid rain may affect the leaves of the vegetation it may have no direct influence on the soil where the alkaline influences of limestone gravel, and river water are so great. In the north-west part of Port Meadow, however, which may not have been flooded even in 1947 and 1981, leaching by relatively acidic rain may have reduced the pH of the soil.

A look at each grassland type (See Tables 3–21 (in Chapter 3) and 2) shows that although the height of the water-table and flooding have a significant effect on grassland composition, there is very little correlation with pH values. In particular, *Deschampsia cespitosa* (Type H) grassland grows mostly on Stands with pH 7.3 but also on Stand 3 with a pH of 6.9. On Picksey Mead, *Cardamine pratense* (Type R) grassland grows on Stands 51, 52, 57 and 60 at pH 6.0, 6.1 or 6.3 and Stand 62 with a pH of 7.4, Stand 55 with a pH of 5.2. This complex situation needs further elucidation with samples being tested at, say, monthly intervals throughout the year.

2.4.C CONDUCTIVITY

The pattern of conductivity readings (p.9) from the top 10cm of soil (see Table 2) suggests that most of the Stands had a conductivity level below 100. These values are shown in Appendix Ciii where they replace the Stand numbers shown in Appendix Ci. The difference between these and the 15 Stands with a level between 120 and 500 may reflect the influence of calcium carbonate in the gravel under Port Meadow with Wolvercote Common, the nutrient status of ground water or simply the increase in the free ions present in the soil as a result of dunging. The tests were made in August 1982 when animals tended to graze mostly in the low-lying area of Port Meadow. The majority of the high readings occurred in this area.

When the readings are compared with those of the survey carried out by the Institute of Hydrology (Appendix E), the position becomes clearer. An analysis was made of the water from between 3 and 5 levels in boreholes numbers PTM 1, 2, 3 and 5. Calcium, magnesium, sodium, potassium, bicarbonate, sulphate, chlorine, nitrate and silicon were isolated, using methods described by Allen (1974). The Institute found that the fluctuations in the amount of these mineral salts at different levels may be related to the differences in the composition of the gravel

Stand number	1	2	3	4	5	6	7	8	9	10	11	12
pH	7.2	6.4	6.9	5.9	6.1	5.6	5.9	7.2	6.7	5.5	6.8	7.3
Conductivity	89	82	105	59	67	35	64	92	68	39	93	205
Altitude (50m)	8.7	7.6	7.6	8.2	7.8	8.1	7.9	8.1	7.8	7.8	7.6	7.2
No of species	26	30	22	27	24	33	30	27	36	31	32	22
Diversity Index	1.27	1 .30	1.20	1.32	1.25	1.36	1.29	1.29	1.37	1.33	1.41	1.13
Mean (quad)	16.04	16.48	13.64	17.76	14.96	16.69	15.44	17.80	19.04	19.04	22.48	8.04

13	14	15	16	17	18	19	20	21	22	23	24	25	26
6.2	6.2	6.2	6.0	5.9	6.5	7.2	6.0	6.2	6.0	7.2	7.4	5.9	7.3
48	56	66	52	48	79	253	49	51	46.5	200	98	48	105
7.7	7.8	7.8	7.7	7.7	7.6	7.4	7.8	7.7	7.8	7.6	7.3	7.6	7.4
32	36	32	28	32	21	29	30	31	29	29	27	33	27
1.34	1.42	1.34	1.31	1.33	1.12	1.34	1.30	1.34	1.32	1.29	1.25	1.36	1.28
17.52	21.28	17.08	17.28	18.40	11.16	16.80	16.88	17.92	18.24	15.52	14.72	18.32	16.04

27	28	29	30	31	32	33	34	35	36	37	38	39	40
7.3	6.8	7.3	6.8	7.4	6.9	7.2	6.6	7.3	7.3	7.0	7.5	7.3	6.5
120	50	94	333	131	135	495	550	295	158	190	82	140	290
7.4	7.6	7.4	7.2	7.1	7.3	7.2	6.9	7.4	6.8	6.9	7.8	7.2	6.90
32	29	23	21	22	21	17	20	14	15	16	19	16	15
1.34	1.30	1.20	1.11	1.11	1.19	1.08	1.14	1.03	1.02	1.02	1.10	1.05	1.03
18.76	16.84	13.12	11.24	9.48	14.92	9.88	11.80	8.48	9.08	9.20	9.92	10.68	9.24

41	42	43	44	45	46	47	48	49	50	51	52	53	54
7.2	7.4	7.1	–	6.4	5.5	6.0	7.2	6.9	7.6	6.1	6.0	6.1	6.8
225	103	89	–	60	33	71	100	54	56	43	39	26	47
7.8	7.6	7.5	7.8	8.3	8.3	8.2	8.6	8.3	8.6	6.6	8.4	8.4.	8.6
14	33	10	41	40	51	54	63	49	30	44	45	49	45
0.97	1.24	0.87	1.42	1.41	1.52	1.58	1.52	1.56	1.31	1.52	1.51	1.54	1.54
7.80	10.72	6.84	19.88	18.08	27.40	30.32	19.80	32.40	18.12	20.48	27.72	30.60	32.36

55	56	57	58	59	60	61	62	63	64	65	66	67	
5.2	7. 1	6.3	7.0	6.0	6.0	7.3	7.4	6.2	7.4	7.4	7.1	6.1	
19	60	36	51	24	25	76	70	38	62	59	50	31	
8.6	8.6	8.6	8.8	8.6	8.6	8.6	8.6	8.6	8.8	9.1	8.8	9.1	
4	48	41	25	40	38	41	39	41	40	47	40	34	
1.49	1.55	1.52	1.21	1.42	1.45	1.43	1.44	1.45	1.45	1.54	1.45	1.42	
24.60	32.28	30.36	14.76	21.32	25.32	18.44	24.40	24.28	23.60	31.36	23.68	24.08	

TABLE 2. ENVIRONMENTAL VARIABLES AT STANDS ON PORT MEADOW WITH WOLVERCOTE COMMON AND PICKSEY MEAD.

and that the mineral salts may be more concentrated in an underground valley (see Map 7, p.21). More work would be required to confirm this.

The direction of flow of the ground water (see above) gives strength to the hypothesis that the high conductivity levels at Stands 30, 31 and 33 may be due to mineral salts brought in from the adjacent Burgess Field Nature Park. Phenol and trace element tests have not been made to establish the extent of any pollution from industrial waste materials dumped here.

CHAPTER 3

CLASSIFICATION OF PLANT COMMUNITIES IN THE OXFORD GRASSLAND

3.1 INTRODUCTION

There is little point in setting down a description of a community unless it is put into context. The reader needs to know its constituent parts as well as its relative size and how and where it differs from similar communities. This is the case with grassland. The British Plant Communities (NVC) (Rodwell, 1992) and the phytosociological associations of the Zurich-Montpellier school (Braun-Blanquet 1932; Moore 1962; Kershaw 1964; Shimwell 1978; O'Sullivan 1968a, 1968b, 1968c), have been referred to in the process of classifying unimproved alluvial grassland in the upper Thames valley into the Molinio-Arrhenatheretea Tüxen 1937; emend. Tüxen 1970. The continental phytosociologists have built up a description of European grasslands within which British grasslands are included, although they differ owing to their geographical position. Other differences such as those between hay mead and pasture are the result of management and have been described in Britain by, for example, Baker (1937) and Tansley (1939). Changes in the composition of a sward as a result of human and animal pressures are discussed in Chapter 6.

Single, easily distinguished plant species have been used for many years to indicate various plant communities and associations. It is perhaps significant that, to differentiate forest Stands, the descriptions *Pinus*, *Fagus* or *Quercus* forest are apparently satisfactory for scientific purposes (Mueller-Dombois & Ellenberg 1974: 171). To describe grassland, however, soil types such as chalk or limestone, or terms descriptive of alkalinity such as neutral or acid, are accepted as being more informative. This is due, perhaps, to the greater ecological amplitude of a core of grassland species. The concept derives from Tansley's (1911) original description of, for example, mesotrophic grassland as "*Graminetum neutra*" which, in accordance with good scientific practice, has been successively refined by ecologists (Tansley 1939; Page 1980) and by agriculturalists (Stapledon 1925, 1936; Fenton 1927, 1931a, 1931b; Williams & Davis 1946) whose interest was centred on the abundance and distribution of particularly nutritious species such as *Lolium perenne*, *Dactylis glomerata* and *Trifolium repens*.

The NVC is used by Natural England as one of the tools in assessing the nature conservation value of particular habitats. Since the Oxford grassland is a Grade 1 Site of Special Scientific Interest and, under European legislation, a Special Area of Conservation, it is important to fit its description into this framework. The following chapter is, therefore, an attempt to show where the Oxford grassland is placed in a more comprehensive phytosociological hierarchical classification of European and British mesotrophic grasslands. At the top of the hierarchy the fit is loose because, at the Class level the Molinio-Arrhenatheretea includes grasslands from different geographical areas and under different management. Even the Association level includes species absent from the Oxford grassland for various reasons which have been discussed in the relevant sections. The Sub-Association called a "Community" has been invented in order to describe the vegetation found in the four categories of grassland, isolated by Twinspan, and growing on Port Meadow with Wolvercote Common and Picksey Mead in 1981–2.

3.2 DESCRIPTION OF GRASSLAND TYPES

In contrast to Association Analysis (see Chapter 1.3.B), in which the hierarchy is set up by the presence or absence of one species, Twinspan (see Chapter 1.3.D), includes all the species in each section as a means of deciding the dichotomy at each division. The indicator species for each group are not necessarily constant species for the group. In the present study the name for each of the communities and grassland types has been given either because a particular species was a Twinspan indicator species AND constant species in the group (T), or because it was a constant species with a high score in most of a particular group of Stands (S).

Since this is a hierarchical classification in which constant species at a high level are understood to be included at the lower levels, the names of these constant species have not been repeated. The Stand numbers in each group are given in brackets (Table 3). The grassland type letters are shown on the Oxford Grassland Map 3 as well as on the graph in Appendix Cv.

Photograph 3. Port Meadow with Wolvercote Common. Meadow Buttercups (Ranunculus acris) *are avoided by grazing animals. Compare this photograph with Photograph 25.*

Photograph 4. Picksey Mead. Succisa pratensis *(Type Q) grassland in the foreground.*

The Tables (nos 4–21) for each grassland type show the scores for each species. Stands and species are arranged in the same order as the Twinspan table in which similar species and Stands are placed together and dissimilar Stands and species, far apart.

The grassland is classified in the Class Molinio-Arrhenatheratea Tüxen 1937; emend. Tüxen 1970, and is divided into 4 groups and 19 grassland types according to the hierarchy produced by the program Twinspan. It will be shown that the communities comprising each Group are controlled by different major factors. Group I, Port Meadow Marsh, by annual flooding; Group II, Port Meadow Moist Pasture, by anthropogenic disturbance; Group III, Port Meadow Dry Pasture, by lack of floods and heavy grazing; and Group IV, Picksey Mead, by annual hay cutting followed by grazing. The major differences are expressed in Photograph 3 (Groups I to III) and Photograph 4 (Group IV).

It is acknowledged that species lists in alphabetical order are easy to consult, but it is considered that the position of species and Stands placed in the hierarchy by Twinspan is more important in a base line study of this nature. It is hoped that in future additional samples may be taken in Port Meadow with Wolvercote Common and that Oxey and West Meads, Yarnton (the remaining meads in this Site of Special Scientific Interest) will also be sampled and the data combined with that in this study. This added information should confirm the four communities (Groups I to IV) described in this work and clarify the grassland types at the lowest level of the hierarchy. The hierarchy is set out in Table 1. The grassland communities and types are summarised in Table 3 and are presented in the order in which they were distinguished, and are shown on Map 3. In the text, however, Types O and Q grassland are treated in succession, as they are both forms of mire vegetation as opposed to mesotrophic grassland. The main mead community, MG4, is then described and the river bank community, MG1, comes last.

TABLE 3. SUMMARY OF THE OXFORD GRASSLAND CLASSIFICATION

CLASS: MOLINIO-ARRHENATHERETEA

GROUP 1
PORT MEADOW MARSH
ORDER: Trifolio-Agrostietalia
ALLIANCE: Elyto-Rumicion crispi
ASSOCIATION: Rumici-Alopecuretum geniculati
BRITISH PLANT COMMUNITY
MG11 Festuca rubra-Agrostis stolonifera-Potentilla anserina inundation grassland, Lolium perenne sub-community

GRASSLAND TYPE	STAND NO.
A – *Poa trivialis*	30, 39

BRITISH PLANT COMMUNITY
MG13 Agrostis stolonifera-Alopecurus geniculatus grassland (Rodwell, 1992)
Mentha aquatica community
GRASSLAND TYPE

B – *Myosotis scorpioides*	33, 37, 40
C – *Galium palustre*	31, 34, 36

GROUP II
PORT MEADOW MOIST PASTURE
ORDER: Trifolio-Agrostietalia
ALLIANCE: Elyto-Rumion crispi
ASSOCIATION: Lolio-Agrostetum stoloniferae
BRITISH PLANT COMMUNITY
MG12 Festuca arundinacea grassland
Agrostis stolonifera Community

SECTION 1
Riverbank and ditch
GRASSLAND TYPE

D – *Potentilla anserina*	12, 35

SECTION 2
Raised area and dredgings
GRASSLAND TYPE
BRITISH PLANT COMMUNITY
MG7 Lolium perenne leys and related grasslands

E – *Achillea millefolium*	42
F – *Lolium perenne*	18, 38, 41, 43

SECTION 3
Wet pasture
BRITISH PLANT COMMUNITY
MG9 Holcus lanatus-Deschampsia cespitosa grassland
GRASSLAND TYPE

G – *Alopecurus geniculatus*	23, 32
H – *Deschampsia cespitosa*	3, 24, 26, 29

GROUP III
PORT MEADOW DRY PASTURE
ORDER: Arrhenatheratalia
ALLIANCE: Cynosurion cristati

SECTION 1
Disturbed pasture
BRITISH PLANT COMMUNITY
MG11 Festuca rubra-Agrostis stolonifera-Potentilla anserina grassland
Lolium perenne sub-community
GRASSLAND TYPE

I – *Agrostis capillaris*	11, 25, 27
J – *Poa annua*	1, 2, 5, 7, 28

BRITISH PLANT COMMUNITY
MG6 Lolium perenne-Cynosurus cristatus grassland
GRASSLAND TYPE

K – *Cirsium arvense*   4, 6, 16, 17, 19, 22

SECTION 2
Less disturbed pasture
BRITISH PLANT COMMUNITY
MG5 Centaurea nigra-Cynosurus cristatus grassland
GRASSLAND TYPE

L – *Cirsium vulgare*   10, 14, 15
M – *Galium verum*   8, 9, 21, 44
N – *Carex panicea*   13, 20

GROUP IV
PICKSEY MEAD
ORDER: Molinetalia
ALLIANCE: Calthion palustris

SECTION 1
Fen
BRITISH PLANT COMMUNITY
M24 Cirsio-Molinietum fen-meadow
GRASSLAND TYPE

O – *Phragmites australis*   45, 46, 47, 48

SECTION 2
River banks
BRITISH PLANT COMMUNITY
MG1 Arrhenatherum elatius grassland
GRASSLAND TYPE

P – *Bromus commutatus*   50, 58

SECTION 3
Meadow
BRITISH PLANT COMMUNITY
M22 Juncus sub-nodulosus-Cirsium palustre fen, Briza
media-Trifolium spp sub-community
GRASSLAND TYPE

Q – *Succisa pratensis*   49, 53, 54, 56
BRITISH PLANT COMMUNITY
MG4 Alopecurus pratensis-Sanguisorba officinalis
grassland
GRASSLAND TYPE

R – *Cardamine pratense*   51, 52, 55, 57, 60, 62
S – *Arrhenatherum elatius*   59, 61, 63, 64, 65, 66, 67

3.3. THE OXFORD GRASSLAND – CLASS: MOLINIO-ARRHENATHERETEA

3.3.A. INTRODUCTION

The Class Molinio-Arrhenatheretea includes lowland
and upland pastures and hay meadows, roadside verges,
footpaths and neglected grassland in continental Europe
and the British Isles. O'Sullivan (1965) and Shimwell
(1968) identified the character species as:

Alopecurus pratensis	*Ophioglossum vulgatum*
Helictotrichon pubescens	*Poa pratensis*
Cardamine pratensis	*Poa trivialis*
Cerastium fontanum	*Ranunculus acris*
Festuca pratensis	*Rhinanthus minor*
Festuca rubra	*Rumex acetosa*
Holcus lanatus	*Vicia cracca*
Lathyrus pratensis	

Later possible additions were included by Ellenberg (1978):

Agrostis gigantea	*Dactylorhisa incarnata*
Colchicum autumnale	*Euphrasia rostkoviana*
Dactylis glomerata	*Prunella vulgaris*

Some of these species have not been found in the
Oxford grassland. There are several reasons for this. For
example, *Agrostis gigantea* is a grass of rough grassland,
Euphrasia rostkoviana is a European species not native
in Britain. *Colchicum autumnale* is a poisonous herb
often handweeded from pastures (Clapham *et al.* 1962).
It has not been seen in Picksey Mead for about forty
years.

3.3.B GROUP I - PORT MEADOW MARSH

CLASS: Molinio-Arrhenatheretea Tüxen 1937 emend. Tx.
1970
ORDER: Trifolio-Agrostietalia Tx. 1970
ALLIANCE: Elyto-Rumicion crispi Nordh. 1940; emend.
Tx. 1950
ASSOCIATION: Rumici-Alopecuretum geniculati Tx.
1937 emend. Tx. 1950
BRITISH PLANT COMMUNITY
MG13 Agrostis stolonifera-Alopecurus geniculatus
grassland. Rodwell 1992.
COMMUNITY: *Mentha aquatica* (T)

ORDER: TRIFOLIO-AGROSTIETALIA
This Order occurs in grassland subject to periodic flooding
(Tüxen 1970). Its character species are:

Alopecurus geniculatus	*Mimulus guttatus*
Carex hirta	*Myosurus minimus*
Elymus pycnanthus	*Pulicaria dysenterica*
Inula britannica	*Rorippa sylvestris*
Juncus compressus	*Spergularia rubra*
Juncus inflexus	*Trifolium fragiferum*
Mentha longifolia	*Trifolium hybridum*
Mentha pulegium	*Trifolium resupinatum*

It is notable that there are several species included in this list which are not found in the Oxford grassland. These include:

i. an element reflecting salt marsh or dune vegetation subject to tidal inundation, for example *Elymus pycnanathus*.
ii. a European element: these species are now extinct or introduced into Britain, for example, *Inula britannica, Mentha longifolia, Mimulus guttatus, Trifolium hybridum, T. resupinatum*.
iii. species of wet places now rare in both continental Europe and Britain, for example, *Mentha pulegium, Myosurus minimus*. The former has not been seen on Port Meadow for more than 30 years.
iv. calcifuge species, for example, *Spergularia rubra*.
v. species common in Britain but normally not part of the Oxford grassland community, for example, *Pulicaria dysenterica, Rorippa sylvestris*.

ALLIANCE: ELYTO-RUMION CRISPI

The character species for the Elyto-Rumion crispi, normally a river bank community, but also found in extensive areas of seasonally flooded alluvium in Eastern England (Rodwell 1992), are all found in Port Meadow Marsh. They are:

Agrostis stolonifera	*Ranunculus repens*
Potentilla anserina	*Rumex crispus*
Potentilla reptans	

ASSOCIATION: RUMICI-ALOPECURETUM GENICULATI

The *Mentha aquatica* Community on Port Meadow Marsh is not a typical example of the Rumici-Alopecuretum geniculati Association since, of the character species *Alopecurus geniculatus, Inula britannica, Rorippa sylvestris* and *Lysimachia nummularia*, only the first was found there. However, Braun-Blanquet and Tüxen (1952) suggest that the character species in Eire are *Agrostis stolonifera, Alopecurus geniculatus* and *Potentilla reptans* and that the constant species are *Alopecurus geniculatus* and *Glyceria fluitans* – all Port Meadow Marsh species. Wells (1974) and Ratcliffe (1977) include this community in the "Wet Alluvial Meadows" group. Rodwell (1992) refers to it as MG 13 *Agrostis stolonifera–Alopecurus geniculatus* inundation grassland and Page (1981) may be right in suggesting that it is a transition between the Class Phragmitea and the Holco-Juncetum (effusi) in the Order Molinetalia, as well as belonging to the Alliance Calthion palustris.

COMMUNITY: *Mentha aquatica* (T)
CONSTANT SPECIES:

Mentha aquatica	*Glyceria fluitans*

The *Mentha aquatica* Community falls into the MG 13 *Agrostis stolonifera–Alopecurus geniculatus* inundation grassland described in the British Plant Community (Rodwell 1992). It is probably related to the Lolio-Potentillion anserinae (Tüxen 1947) known to be common on inundated, well-grazed, European pastures (Sýkora 1982: 65). The community is characterized by creeping hemicryptophytes and rhizome geophytes which spread rapidly over temporary gaps caused by poaching, and over areas which are free from water, and so available for colonization, only during the summer months. The community is subjected to frequent flooding during the winter and spring and sometimes in the summer too.

In general, flooding leads to the depletion of oxygen in the soil and the formation of manganese and ferrous ions; sulphate becomes sulphide, ferric ions are replaced by ferrous ions and the decomposition of the organic material in the soil produces carbon dioxide, methane and organic acids (Brummer 1974). Many of these substances are toxic to plants, which are further stressed by low oxygen tension limiting respiration (Odum *et al.* 1979). This problem was well-studied in the 1960s (Henshaw *et al.* 1962; Crawford 1966; Crawford and McMannon 1968; Crawford 1969; Crawford and Tyler 1969). It has been found that there are several strategies for survival. For example, of the species growing in the Oxford grassland, *Alopecurus geniculatus, Agrostis stolonifera, Deschampsia cespitosa* and *Potentilla anserina* are able to avoid oxygen stress by the diffusion of oxygen through the aerenchymous tissue from the stems to the roots (Coult and Vallance 1958; Rahman 1976). McMannon and Crawford (1971) found that some flood-tolerant species, such as *Glyceria maxima*, produce non-toxic malic acid instead of the ethanol which normally results from an increased rate of glycolysis induced by anaerobic conditions. Jones and Etherington (1971) also studied the effect of waterlogging on four species which represented different habitats in a dune slack system. These species, *Festuca rubra, Carex flacca, C. nigra* and *Agrostis stolonifera* grow in the Oxford grassland where they are also subjected to varying degrees of flooding. Jones and Etherington found that waterlogging caused both tillering and root production to be reduced in the grasses, but only the roots of *Carex nigra* increased during the treatment and *Agrostis stolonifera* was unaffected. These results paralleled the ecological responses of the species and were found to be due in part to varying tolerance of increasing manganese concentrations. High concentrations of manganese (200 p.p.m.) were toxic to *Festuca rubra* and to some plants of *Carex nigra*. The growth of *Agrostis stolonifera* was unaffected but the growth of *Carex flacca* was actually promoted by high concentrations of manganese (Jones 1972). Barclay and Crawford (1982) have now tested the hypothesis that some species have a way of overcoming a lack of oxygen by growing a range of species under experimental conditions which ensured a total exclusion of oxygen. *Glyceria maxima* and *Juncus effusus* died within a week, but *Schoenoplectus lacustris* continued to grow for two weeks. These species are absent from even the wettest parts of the Oxford grassland (excluding boundary ditches). Is this because there is too little waterlogging for them to gain a competitive advantage? It would be interesting to know whether *Glyceria fluitans* and *G. maxima* have similar strategies.

On Port Meadow Marsh the top-soil is well-structured and freely draining (Nature Conservancy Council 1983) so that the water-table rises and falls with the height of the river. This allows the top-soil to dry out completely during the summer months. It suggests that in the Oxford grassland waterlogged conditions and the lack of oxygen normally associated with it is mainly a problem during the winter. This, and the dominance of *Mentha aquatica*, plus the absence of *Polygonum hydropiper* again suggest that Port Meadow Marsh does not support the Typical Association of the Rumici-Alopecuretum geniculati.

The *Mentha aquatica* Community in Port Meadow Marsh is very different from the Picksey Mead Fen which is also based on alluvium (See *Phragmites australis* (Type 0) grassland). Its character species, *Mentha aquatica*, would make an interesting study. It has two forms, one with exserted stamens and the second with inserted stamens. Both forms have a creeping habit and relatively small leaves.

The community on Port Meadow Marsh is divided into two communities and three grassland types. The first community has been misclassified. It is better placed with Types I and J grassland.

TYPE A (30, 39) *Poa trivialis* (S)
BRITISH PLANT COMMUNITY
MG11 Festuca rubra-Agrostis stolonifera-Alopecurus geniculatus inundation grassland, Lolium perenne sub-community (Rodwell 1992).
CONSTANT SPECIES:

Agrostis capillaris	*Poa trivialis*
Alopecurus geniculatus	*Potentilla anserina*
Cirsium arvense	*Ranunculus repens*
Eleocharis palustris	*Trifolium repens*
Lolium perenne	

STANDS		30	39
PH.		6.8	7.3
COND.		333	140
Carex	fla	1	
Leont	aut	1	
Plant	lan		1
Loliu	per	1	24
Phleu	pra	3	2
Tarax	off	2	
Poa	tri	25	25
Hiera	pil	1	
Plant	maj		25
Poa	ann		15
Agros	cap	22	25
Trifo	rep	25	25
Poten	ans	25	25
Rumex	cri		1
Agros	sto	25	
Alope	gen	16	23
Carex	hir		17
Ranun	rep	25	25
Carex	pan	15	
Juncu	art	22	
Glyce	flu	18	25
Menth	aqu	1	2
Oenan	fis	9	
Trigl	pal	2	
Eleoc	pal	25	7
TOTAL	SPP.	20	16

TABLE 4. GRASSLAND TYPE A – POA TRIVIALIS (S)

The constant species in Type A are the same as a *Lolium perenne* Sub-community of the MG11 *Festuca rubra-Agrostis stolonifera-Potentilla anserina* inundation grassland (Rodwell 1992). Type A represents an intermediate zone between the Elyto-Rumician crispi Alliance (*Achillea millefolium* (Type E) and *Plantago major* (Type F) grasslands) to the south and east and the Cynosurion cristati (*Deschampsia cespitosa* (Type H) grassland and *Agrostis capillaris* (Type I) grassland) to the north. *Eleocharis palustris* (in Stand 30) is not a normal constituent of the *Lolium perenne* Sub-community because its rhizomes need an open sward to spread into. Perhaps its intolerance of shade (Walters 1949) reflects the absence of tall-growing species in its neighbourhood due to the heavy grazing on Port Meadow Marsh as soon as the floodwater recedes. *Triglochin palustris* and *Oenanthe fistulosa* suggest a transition to true fen.

Stand 39 is at the other end of the transition. Here the constant species are accompanied by abundant *Poa annua* and *Plantago major*. Both these species are colonizers of disturbed ground and reflect the heavy use of the adjacent path by animals and people.

TYPE B (33, 37, 40) *Myosotis scorpioides* (S)
BRITISH PLANT COMMUNITY
MG13 Agrostis stolonifera-Alopecurus geniculatus grassland. Rodwell 1992.

Mentha aquatica community
CONSTANT SPECIES:

Agrostis stolonifera	*Myosotis scorpioides*
Cardamine pratensis	*Oenanthe fistulosa*
Galium palustre	*Ranunculus flamula*
Juncus articulatus	*Veronica scutellata*

STANDS		33	37	40
PH		7.2	7.0	6.5
COND.		495	190	290
Agros	cap			2
Poten	ans	11		24
Agros	sto	24	25	21
Alope	gen		22	
Ranun	rep	4		1
Carex	pan		2	
Juncu	art	7	22	19
Glyce	flu	25	25	24
Menth	aqu	24	25	25
Oenan	fis	24	25	25
Apium	inu	3		
Apium	rep		1	
Calli	spp	19		3
Galiu	pal	19	17	11
Myoso	dis		2	
Myoso	sco	25	23	25
Ranun	fla	4	12	12
Stell	pal		4	
Veron	scu	7	19	7
Apium	nod	11		
Eleoc	pal	25		24
Carda	pra	14	4	8
TOTAL	SPP.	16	15	15

TABLE 5. GRASSLAND TYPE B – MYOSOTIS SCORPIOIDES (S)

Myosotis scorpioides grassland is the wettest in Port Meadow and is characterised by perennials rather than the annuals and ruderal species normally associated with poached Rumici-Alopecuretum geniculati (R. Tüxon (1937) 1950). *Myosotis discolor*, an annual and *Cirsium palustre*, a biennial, were, however, recorded. It is classified as MG13 Agrostis stolonifera-Alopecurus geniculatus grassland (Rodwell 1992).

Page (1980) took a sample from between Stands 37 and 40 to describe the Rumici-Alopecuretum geniculati. He seems to have taken it a little to the east of the Grid reference given, near the foot of the bank of the raised area. This bank shows distinct zones as it changes from *Plantago major* (Type F) grassland to *Myosotis scorpioides* (Type B) grassland. The zones include a *Rumex conglomeratus* rather than a *Rumex crispus* sub-community along the

edge of the flood line near the foot of the raised area (see Map 4).

It was the red pigment in the leaves and stems of *Mentha aquatica* that drew attention to the aquatic nature of the *Myosotis scorpioides* (Type B) grassland and its similarities to that of the long pond on Wolvercote Common which contained the following species on the 2nd July 1983:

Agrostis stolonifera	*Limosella aquatica* (1982 only)
Alisma plantago-aquatica	*Mentha aquatica*
Alopecurus geniculatus	*Myosotis scorpioides*
Apium nodiflorum	*Oenanthe fistulosa*
Callitriche spp.	*Plantago major*
Cardamine flexuosa	*Potentilla anserina*
Carex hirta	*Ranunculus repens*
Eleocharis palustris	*Rumex crispus*
Glyceria maxima	*Trifolium repens*
Glyceria plicata	

Bryophytes do not normally form a part of the Rumici-Alopecuretum geniculati, however, in the *Myosotis scorpioides* (Type B) grassland the calcicolous bryophyte *Brachythecium rutabulum* becomes conspicuous and Stand 40 was distinguished by *Amblystegium riparium, B. rutabulum* and a filamentous algae which grew on the soft, silty soil.

TYPE C (31, 34, 36) *Galium palustre* (S)
CONSTANT SPECIES:

Agrostis stolonifera	*Juncus articulatus*
Alopecurus geniculatus	*Myosotis scorpioides*
Cardamine pratense	*Oenanthe fistulosa*
Carex panicea	*Potentilla anserina*
Eleocharis palustris	*Ranunculus repens*
Galium palustre	*Trifolium repens*

STANDS		31	34	36
PH		7.4	6.6	7.3
COND.		131	550	158
Crepi	bie	1		
Poa	pra	4		
Agros	cap	3	1	
Trifo	rep	21	7	4
Poten	ans	18	23	24
Rumex	cri	1		
Agros	sto	23	24	24
Alope	gen	2	8	1
Carex	hir	5	5	
Ranun	rep	24	23	24
Carex	pan	1	9	6
Juncu	art	21	25	20
Glyce	flu	23	24	24
Menth	aqu	8	25	24

Oenan	fis	20	24	24
Trigl	pal	1		
Galiu	pal	1	20	19
Myoso	dis			2
Myoso	sco	16	25	8
Ranun	fla		4	
Stell	pal		11	
Veron	scu		3	
Apium	nod	6		
Eleoc	pal	20	25	20
Carda	pra	6	6	3
TOTAL	SPP.	21	19	15

TABLE 6. GRASSLAND TYPE C - GALIUM PALUSTRE (S)

This grassland type is intermediate between *Poa trivialis* grassland (Type A) and *Myosotis scorpioides* grassland (Type B). It is characterized by *Potentilla anserina* and *Oenanthe fistulosa* which, together with the constant species, make up a dense, springy sward in which strawberry clover (*Trifolium fragiferum*) is abundant. This clover was not recorded in the survey but was seen flowering on the 1st August 1983 and in subsequent years, sometimes accompanied by *Trifolium repens*. *Galium palustre* grassland (Type C), as well as *Poa trivialis* (Type A) and *Myositis scorpioides* (Type B) are heavily grazed as soon as the water table falls to below ground level. *Mentha aquatica* seems to be the least palatable of these species and yet it rarely reaches more than 20cm in height in common with the rest of *Galium palustre* (Type C) grassland.

3.3.C GROUP II – PORT MEADOW MOIST PASTURE

CLASS: Molinio-Arrhenatheretea Tüxen 1937 emend. 1970
ORDER: Trifolio-Agrostietelia Tx. 1970
ALLIANCE: Elyto-Rumion crispi Nordh. 1940; emend. Tx. 1950
ASSOCIATION: Lolio-Agrostetum stoloniferae Page 1980
BRITISH PLANT COMMUNITY
MG12 Festuca arundinacea grassland Rodwell 1992
COMMUNITY: *Agrostis stolonifera* (S)

For a description of the Trifolio-Agrostietalia and the Elyto-Rumion crispi see Chapter 3.3.B. Port Meadow Marsh.

ASSOCIATION: LOLIO-AGROSTETUM STOLONIFERAE

Page (1980) described the character species of the inundation grassland, Lolio-Agrostetum stoloniferae (MG12 Festuca arundinacea grassland), as follows:

Agrostis stolonifera	*Lolium perenne*
Festuca arundinacea	*Potentilla anserina*

With the exception of *Festuca arundinacea*, which is an element of the *Phragmites australis* (Type 0) grassland, these species are a significant part of the *Agrostis stolonifera* Community. This Association is widely distributed, usually on clay loams which dry out completely in summer but are wet or inundated in winter. It appears to be maintained by grazing. On Port Meadow Moist Pasture the constants *Agrostis stolonifera*, *Holcus lanatus* and *Lolium perenne* are present together with *Phleum pratense* and *Poa trivialis*, and the herbs *Cirsium arvense*, *Hypochaeris radicata*, *Plantago lanceolata*, *P. major*, *Ranunculus acris*, *Trifolium pratense* and *T. repens*.

COMMUNITY: *Agrostis stolonifera* (S)
CONSTANT SPECIES:

Agrostis stolonifera	*Ranunculus repens*
Cirsium arvense	*Trifolium repens*
Lolium perenne	

The *Agrostis stolonifera* Community is characterised by species adapted to spreading rapidly over bare soil. Its constituents in the Oxford grassland include the three grassland Types which do not fall into the *Mentha aquatica* or the *Plantago media* communities, placed at either end of the hydroscale. The majority of the grassland Types are to be found in Inundation Zones B, C and D (see Map 4). The exceptions are *Achillea millefolium* (Type E) and *Plantago major* (Type F) grasslands, which are to be found well above high flood-level on the raised area at the south end of Port Meadow (see Map 3). They may be better classified in the *Poo-Lolietum* (see *Plantago major* (Type F) grassland below).

The *Agrostis stolonifera* Community is one which reflects considerable disturbance by the hooves of grazing animals, particularly in winter. For this reason it was first classified in the Order Plantaginetalia majoris (Tüxen 1970). On reflection such a classification put too great an emphasis on the reseeded *Plantago major* (Type F) grassland and nullified the self-perpetuating aspects of this ancient pasture. Reclassification into a separate Order, Trifolio-Agrostietalia, underlines the long history of periodic flooding which, with periodic heavy grazing, is the major influence in the formation of the *Agrostis stolonifera* Community. This Community is synonymous with the MG11 *Festuca rubra-Agrostis stolonifera-Potentilla anserina* inundation grassland described by Rodwell (1992) and with the *Potentilla anserina* nodum described by Adam (1976).

In the Oxford grassland there is a high water-table for much of the year, but where there is movement of water through the underlying gravel, as it flows to and from the river, the soil is kept well aerated (Tansley 1939, 560). Soil heterogeneity is also an important factor in the variation of the *Agrostis stolonifera* community. Fitter (1982) has shown that soil variation influences the co-existence of some grass species such as *Holcus lanatus*, *Lolium perenne*, *Festuca rubra*, *Poa trivialis* and the herb *Plantago lanceolata*. The distribution of their roots in this and the *Plantago media* Community, where the ground is also crossed by many filled-in ditches of various ages, reflects the importance of the distribution of environmental factors in space. This phenomenon has, similarly, been identified in chalk heath (Grubb, Green and Merrifield 1969) and in limestone heath (Etherington 1981).

Except for *Cirsium arvense*, the constant species are those which Stapledon (1925) considered to represent a well-managed grassland component of a dairy farm. But the presence of *Senecio jacobaea* on Stand 26 and *Cirsium arvense* in abundance on all four Stands show that this is not the case on Port Meadow (p.95). These Stands are overgrazed and trampled, particularly in winter and spring, with the result that there is a short sward in which *Bellis perennis*, a light-demanding rosette species is able to flower.

TYPE D (12, 35) *Potentilla anserina* (S)
CONSTANT SPECIES:

Poa annua	*Agrostis capillaris*
Potentilla anserina	*Alopecurus geniculatus*
Cardamine pratensis	

STANDS		12	35
PH		7.3	7.3
COND.		205	295
Alope	pra	10	
Ceras	fon	2	
Cynos	cri	3	
Dacty	glo	1	
Desch	ces	4	
Rumex	con	19	
Trifo	pra	2	
Loliu	per	9	251
Phleu	pra	18	
Belli	per	4	
Cirsi	arv	2	18
Glyce	pli	22	
Poa	pra		3
Poa	tri		4
Plant	maj		12
Poa	ann	5	12
Agros	cap	11	22
Trifo	rep	10	25
Poten	ans	18	25
Rumex	cri		4
Agros	sto	22	16
Alope	gen	9	9
Ranun	rep	18	21
Juncu	art	8	
Apium	nod	1	
Carda	pra	3	16
TOTAL	SPP.	22	14

TABLE 7. GRASSLAND TYPE D – POTENTILLA ANSERINA (S)

3.3.C.i. SECTION 1 – RIVER BANK AND DITCH

This grassland has affinities with *Poa trivialis* grassland (Type A) in the Rumici-Alopecuretum geniculati of Group I. It does not represent the botanically interesting community (Nature Conservancy Council 1972; Appendix K) which grows only on the side of the river bank down to the edge of the water where the ground is well-trodden by cattle and horses moving across it to take a drink. The Type occurs on the river bank and in a ditch, two apparently dissimilar Stands. Nevertheless, they have a similar community characterized by species such as *Lolium perenne*, *Trifolium repens* and *Potentilla anserina* which are generally found on moist, well-trampled soils.

Stand 12 is botanically interesting because it is more species-rich. Perennial herbs and the grasses *Glyceria plicata* and *Agrostis stolonifera*, comprise the characteristic species of winter and early spring. By late summer (29th August 1981) the community was augmented by the following species, which are becoming increasingly rare in lowland England. In the dry summers of the early 21st century they were also common in Port Meadow Marsh (McDonald and Lambric 2006).

Apium nodiflorum	*Polygonum arenastrum*
Atriplex prostrata	*P. aviculare sensu strictu*
Chenopodium vulvaria	*P. minus*
Juncus bufonius	*P. mite*
J. articulatus	*Trifolium medium*
Veronica beccabunga	

The rarity of these annuals is the result of an increase in land drainage as farmers take advantage of the European Economic Community agricultural grants, and to eutrophication of ditches affected by chemical nitrogenous fertilisers carried in "run off" from adjacent land.

3.3.C.ii. SECTION 2 – RAISED AREA AND DREDGINGS

This area supports calcareous grassland Types on soil with a pH level of 7.1–7.5. The relatively high conductivity readings (p.53) (between 82 and 225) may reflect the movement of mineral salts, from the old City rubbish underneath or calcium carbonate from the gravel dredgings.

TYPE E (42) *Achillea millefolium* (T)
CONSTANT SPECIES:

Achillea millefolium	*Plantago major*
Bellis perennis	*P. media*
Bromus lepidus	*Poa pratensis*
Carduus acanthoides	*P. trivialis*
Carex hirta	*Potentilla anserina*
Cerastium fontanum	*Ranunculus acris*
Cirsium vulgare	*Rumex crispus*
Dactylis glamerata	*Senecio jacobaea*
Festuca rubra	*Sonchus arvensis*
Geranium molle	*Taraxacum officinale*
Hordeum secalinum	*Trifolium pratense*
Leontodon autumnalis	*Trisetum flavescens*
Phleum pratense	*Veronica anagallis-aquatica*

STANDS		42
PH		7.4
COND.		102
Prune	vul	2
Leont	aut	1
Bromu	lep	1
Trise	fla	1
Ceras	fon	6
Dacty	glo	10
Festu	rub	4
Horde	sec	2
Plant	lan	10
Ranun	acr	16
Trifo	pra	20
Loliu	per	25
Phleu	pra	14
Tarax	off	9
Senec	jac	9
Achil	mil	2
Belli	per	3
Cirsi	vul	1
Plant	med	1
Cirsi	arv	16
Cardu	aca	1
Geran	mol	2
Sonch	arv	3
Veron	ana	2
Poa	pra	23
Poa	tri	6
Plant	maj	16
Trifo	rep	21
Poten	ans	1
Rumex	cri	6
Agros	sto	25
Carex	hir	4
Ranun	rep	5
TOTAL	SPP.	33

TABLE 8. GRASSLAND TYPE E – ACHILLEA MILLEFOLIUM (T)

This was the only Stand to occur on the 1920s tip which forms the raised area at the south-west end of Port Meadow. It is representative of the area but is not homogeneous insofar as it contains the bottom of a hollow as well as the side of a hump. It is the only species-rich area with a domestic rubbish substrate and has been distinguished by TWINSPAN from other heterogeneous Stands on natural gravel and alluvium which carry the *Poa annua* (Type J) grassland. Heavy grazing and trampling occurs, particularly in winter when floods reduce the amount of grassland otherwise available and separate the south from the north end of the Meadow. Dense patches of *Urtica dioica*, adjacent to Stand 42, indicate a high level of phosphate (Pigott and Taylor 1964), while *Senecio jacobaea*, also growing in large clumps in the area, suggests poor soil and inadequate pasture management. These two species protect other more palatable plants from hungry cattle and horses.

TYPE F (18, 38, 41, 43) *Lolium perenne* (S)
CONSTANT SPECIES:

| *Plantago major* | | *Poa pratensis* | |

STANDS		18	38	41	43
PH		6.5	7.5	7.2	7.1
COND.		79	82	225	89
PRUNE	VUL			1	
FESTU	PRA	3			
ALOPE	PRA	3			
DACTY	GLO	5	1		
HOLCU	LAN	1		6	
HORDE	SEC	13	23	4	
PLANT	LAN	1	12	3	
RANUN	ACR	21	2	25	
TRIFO	PRA	6	9	9	
LOLIU	PER	25	25	25	25
PHLEU	PRA	25			3
TARAX	OFF		6		
SENEC	JAC		1		
CIRSI	VUL	1		5	
CIRSI	ARV	25	21	25	23
POLYG	AVI		2		
STELL	MED		2		
POA	PRA	11	24	25	25
POA	TRI	21	10		14
PLANT	MAJ	6	25	13	9
POA	ANN	1	19		
TRIFO	REP	25	25	25	21
POTEN	ANS	23			
RUMEX	CRI		8		1
AGROS	STO	25	17	25	25
CAREX	HIR	13			

RANUN	REP		25	16	4	25	
TOTAL			21	19	14	10	

TABLE 9. GRASSLAND TYPE F – LOLIUM PERENNE

Although this grassland Type has been classified by the TWINSPAN program with the Moist Pasture, Lolio-Agrostetum stoloniferae, it has a resemblance to the leys and related grasslands of the Poo-Lolietum (De Vries & Westhoff apud Bakker 1965) (MG7 Lolium perenne leys (Rodwell 1992)), probably as a result of sowing a grassland mixture over the old allotment gardens (Stands 38, 41 and 43) when they were discontinued in 1968 (p.90). The Plantaginetalia majoris, into which the Poo-Lolietum is placed, is composed of disturbed grasslands generally found on recreation areas and near poached gateways and footpaths. These communities are often part of leys and pastures. At one time this Order was in a Class on its own, but in 1970 Tüxen (reference unseen) suggested that it should be placed in the Molinio-Arrhenatheretea (Page 1970). This is in keeping with the evidence from the Oxford grassland which shows a continuum of vegetation in which change is generally related to management of the grassland and adjacent river, including periodic flooding. This community is distinguished from the Lolio-Cynosuretum (Lolium perenne-Cynosurus cristatus grassland (Rodwell 1992)) by the absence of *Cynosurus cristatus*.

Plantago major, a component of Type F grassland, is a trampling-resistant perennial, characterizing a community which gets churned up by animals or man and his machines, especially in winter time. The dominance of *Trifolium repens* and *Agrostis stolonifera* indicates the moist condition of *Lolium perenne* (Type F) grassland; *Cirsium arvense* may reflect its poor management. This grassland is found where flooding is rare and where shelter from the wind is provided by trees and embankments, which encourages cattle and horses to gather in bad weather.

3.3.C.iii. SECTION 3 – WET PASTURE
CONSTANT SPECIES:

Agrostis stolonifera	*Lolium perenne*
Carex hirta	*Phleum pratense*
Cirsium arvense	*Poa trivialis*
Deschampsia cespitosa	*Ranunculus acris*
Holcus lanatus	*Trifoiolilum repens*

TYPE G (23, 32) *Alopecurus geniculatus* (T) (Table 7)
CONSTANT SPECIES:

Alopecurus geniculatus	*Poa pratense*
Juncus articulatus	*Potentilla anserina*
Plantago major	

STANDS		23	32
PH		7.2	6.9
COND.		200	135
Leont	aut	7	
Rumex	ace		1
Ceras	fon	2	
Cynos	cri	18	
Dacty	glo	4	
Desch	ces	17	23
Festu	rub		23
Holcu	lan	9	1
Horde	sec	1	
Plant	lan	4	
Ranun	acr	24	18
Trifo	pra	1	
Loliu	per	23	24
Phleu	pra	25	24
Tarax	off	11	
Belli	per	9	
Cirsi	arv	23	25
Hypoc	rad	3	
Juncu	buf	8	
Poa	pra	8	14
Poa	tri	25	23
Plant	maj	9	23
Poa	ann	2	
Agros	cap		25
Trifo	rep	24	25
Poten	ans	23	25
Rumex	cri		2
Agros	sto	25	25
Alope	gen	18	22
Carex	hir	3	20
Ranun	rep	24	25
Carex	pan		2
Juncu	art	23	3
Eleoc	pal	15	
TOTAL		29	21

TABLE 10. GRASSLAND TYPE G – ALOPECURUS CENICULATUS (T)

Although both Stands have the same vegetation type, Stand 23 is in a silted-up stream which used to flow across Port Meadow to the river and Stand 32 is on the edge of Port Meadow Marsh (Maps 3 and 4). *Plantago major*, and the annuals *Poa annua* and *Juncus bufonius*, indicate a disturbed soil in a situation similar to that which resulted in *Lolium perenne* (Type F) grassland. *Alopecurus geniculatus* (Type G) grassland is, however, a more species-rich variant of *Potentilla anserina* (Type D) grassland, kept short by grazing geese and other animals all the year round because this grassland receives less flooding than Port Meadow Marsh (see Map 4).

TYPE H (3, 24, 26, 29) *Deschampsia cespitosa* (S)
CONSTANT SPECIES:

Bellis perennis	*Plantago lanceolata*
Cerastium fontanum	*Trifolium pratense*
Festuca rubra	

STANDS		3	24	26	29
PH		6.9	7.4	7.3	7.3
COND.		103	98	105	94
Filip	ulm		3		
Festu	pra		3	1	
Lotus	cor			4	
Ranun	bul		25	23	
Trise	fla			1	3
Alope	pra		3		
Ceras	fon	2	6	8	1
Cynos	cri	2	4	3	
Dacty	glo		2	4	
Desch	ces	20	17	11	11
Festu	rub	23	25	24	22
Holcu	lan	11	25	23	11
Horde	sec	9	8	25	
Plant	lan	3	3	13	20
Ranun	acr	25	22	18	25
Trifo	pra	21	15	21	21
Loliu	per	25	23	25	23
Phleu	pra	25	25	24	25
Tarax	off				3
Senec	jac			4	
Cirsi	vul		2	3	
Cirsi	arv	23	23	21	8
Poa	pra		6	16	3
Poa	tri	25	24	22	25
Plant	maj	25			13
Poa	ann	9			
Agros	cap			22	
Trifo	rep	23	23	24	25
Poten	ans		24	22	17
Agros	sto	25	24	23	25
Carex	hir	15	12	23	12
Ranun	rep	13			20
Carex	pan	8			
TOTAL		20	24	26	20

TABLE 11. GRASSLAND TYPE H – DESCHAMPSIA CESPITOSA (S)

This grassland Type can be equated with Deschampsietum cespitosae Horv. 1935 or the MG9 Holcus lanatus-Deschampsia cespitosa grassland (Rodwell 1992), but the

grazing pressure and water movement on Port Meadow restrict the abundance of *Deschampsia cespitosa* in wet areas where its capacity for aerating waterlogged soil round its roots might otherwise give it the competitive advantage (Rahman 1976; Davy 1980). *Deschampsia cespitosa* does, however, reflect the amount of winter flooding received by Zone C (See Map 4).

The boundary between *Alopecurus geniculatus* (Type G) and *Deschampsia cespitosa* (Type H) is not clear. It may be on the boundary between Inundation Zones C and D (See Map 4). Stand 3 appears at first sight to have been misclassified, but its presence in Inundation Zone D may account for its presence in *Deschapsia cespitosa* (Type H) grassland. Although it is classified as Wet Pasture, Stands 24 and 26 are sufficiently dry to allow the moisture-intolerant *Ranunculus bulbosus*, as well as the more tolerant *R. acris*, to grow in abundance (Harper & Sagar 1953). Deschampsia cespitosa (Type H) grassland is, therefore, a link with the Disturbed Pasture group.

3.3.D GROUP III – PORT MEADOW DRY PASTURE

CLASS: Molinio-Arrhenatheretea Tüxen 1937 emend Tx. 1970
ORDER: Arrhenatheretalia Pawlowski 1928
ALLIANCE: Cynosurion cristati Tx. 1947
ASSOCIATION: Centaureo-Cynosuretum Br.-Bl. & Tx. 1952
BRITISH PLANT COMMUNITY
MG5 Cynosurus cristatus-Centaurea nigra grassland. Rodwell 1992.
COMMUNITY: *Plantago media* (T)

ORDER: ARRHENATHERETALIA

This Order contains grasslands growing on nutrient-rich, neutral and slightly acid soils where the ground is well-drained. They can be managed as pastures or hay meadows and include the related communities of neglected land and roadside verges (Page 1980: 83). The Order was described by O'Sullivan (1965) who gave the following character species:

Bellis perennis	*Leucanthemum vulgare*
Bromus hordeaceus	*Taraxacum Sect. Vulgaria*
Dactylis glomerata	*Trifolium dubium*
Daucus carota	*Trisetum flavescens*
Knautia arvensis	*Veronica chamaedrys*

With the exception of *Daucus carota* and *Knautia arvensis* all these species were recorded on Port Meadow Dry Pasture in 1981. The two exceptions are herbs with tall growth forms which are probably excluded from the pasture by the heavy grazing.

Subsequently, Ellenberg (1978) made the following additions for central Europe and the Alps:

Achillea millefolium	*Ornithogalum umbellatum*
Anthriscus sylvestris	*Saxifraga granulata*
Carum carvi	*Stellaria graminea*
Crepis capillaris	*Tragopogon orientalis*
Heracleum sphondylium	*Tragopogon pratensis*

Of these species only *Achillea millefolium* and *Crepis capillaris* grow in Port Meadow Dry Pasture. *Anthriscus sylvestris, Heracleum sphondylium, Stellaria graminea* and *Tragopogon pratensis* grow on Picksey Mead and, except for the latter rare in August 1984 and subsequently, may be barred from Port Meadow by the heavy grazing. The remaining four species are continental species occurring rarely in Britain, generally in East Anglia, and so would not be expected in the Oxford grassland. The grouping of these species in the Arrhenatheretalia suggests a link with the Molinetalia in which the Picksey Mead communities have been placed.

ALLIANCE: CYNOSURION CRISTATI

The Arrhenatheretalia is divided into four Alliances. The Arrhenatherion elatioris Br.–Bl. 1925 (Koch 1926) includes communities of roadside verges and ungraded hay meadows, the Polygono-Trisetion Br.–Bl. 1948 includes upland hay meadows, the Poion alpinae Oberdorfer 1950 (reference unseen) includes subalpine grasslands and the Cynosurion cristati communities of grazed lowland and submontane areas (Page 1980: 83-4). The character species for the latter are:

Cynosurus cristatus	*Phleum bertolonii*
Hordeum secalinum	*Phleum pratense*
Leontodon autumnalis	*Trifolium repens*
Lolium perenne	*Veronica filiformis*
Odontites verna	*Veronica serpyllifolia*

These are all common species in the upper Thames valley near Oxford but *Odontites verna*, *Phleum bertolonii* and *Veronica filiformis* were not recorded on Port Meadow in 1981. The latter is an unexpected character species for the Cynosurion cristati in Britain where it is classed as a garden escape.

ASSOCIATION: CENTAUREO-CYNOSURETUM

This used to be confined to hay meadows but now includes other old unimproved grassland. Its constant species, *Centaurea nigra, Lotus corniculatus* and *Briza media*, are also found in the Alopecurus-Sanguisorbetum (MG4 Alopecurus pratensis-Sanguisorba officinalis grassland (Rodwell 1992)), but the Centaurea-Cynosuretum (MG5

Centaurea nigra-Cynosurus cristatus grassland (Rodwell 1992)) is less species-rich and is distinguishable from other Associations by its lack of their differential and preferential species. For example, *Sanguisorba officinalis* is rare in Port Meadow Dry Pasture and flowers at only 10cm high, whereas it is abundant in Picksey Mead. The Cynosurion cristati Alliance of British calcicolous grassland is closely related to the European Mesobromion erecti (Rodwell 1992).

COMMUNITY: *Plantago media* (T)
CONSTANT SPECIES:

Cynosurus cristatus	*Plantago media*
Lolium perenne	*Trifolium pratense*
Phleum pratense	*Trifolium repens*

The *Plantago media* Community covers the driest part of the Meadow. Here the limestone gravel is covered by a layer of alluvium only about 10cm thick and it is doubtful, despite the evidence of Minn (Appendix L) and the local people, whether the part colonised by *Galium verum* (Type M) grassland has ever been subjected to flooding in the modern period. This hypothesis was evoked by a comparison of the height of the grassland, (Fig. 7) the amount of flooding since 1894 (Fig. 5) and the height of the water at Godstow Lock tail water. Minn himself mentions finding *Gentiana amarella* (*Gentianella amarella* (Stace 1997: 523)) in the north-west corner of the Meadow in 1907 when records show that the Meadow was flooded extensively for long periods (see Fig. 5). There is no modern record of this biennial species on Port Meadow. It is normally found in dry calcareous pastures and dunes and one concludes that there is a lack of summer-flooding at least, in its habitat. Despite a trend towards acidity due to leaching, felwort (*Gentianella amarella*) may have been a part of the *Galium verum* (Type M) grassland in 1907 indicating its calcicolous nature then as the presence of *Cirsium acaule* does today. Whether or not this situation will continue in the future depends as much on the management of the Thames and, therefore, the water-table, as on the management of the grazing animals.

Group III grassland is broadly classified as MG5 Cynosurus cristatus-Centaureo nigra grassland. It is distinguished by the base-demanding *Plantago media*, a species generally found only in old and relatively undisturbed pastures. This is a hemicryptophyte which can reproduce by lateral tillers. It is well adapted to shallow soils where there is shorter turf and, therefore, greater light-intensity (Harper & Sagar 1964). On Port Meadow this is reflected by its greatest abundance on Stands 8 and 19, *Poa annua* (Type J) and *Cirsium arvense* (Type K) grasslands respectively. The *Plantago media* community has wet and dry facies. The wet facies tends to be transitional to the *Cirsium arvense* (Type K) grassland while in the dry facies *Cirsium vulgare* (Type L) and *Carex panicea* (Type N) grasslands are transitional to the driest grassland on the highest part of the Meadow, *Galium verum* (Type M). The presence of *Cirsium acaule* and *C. eriphorum* in the latter grassland type suggests an affinity with both chalk and limestone pasture rather than with alluvial meadows.

3.3.D.i. SECTION 1 - DISTURBED PASTURE
TYPE I (11, 25, 27) *Agrostis capillaris* (T)
CONSTANT SPECIES:

Agrostis capillaris	*Potentilla anserina*
Cirsium arvense	*P. reptans*
Deschampsia cespitosa	*Poa trivialis*
Festuca rubra	*Prunella vulgaris*
Pilosella officinarum	*Ranunculus acris*
Holcus lanatus	*R. repens*
Plantago major	*Taraxacum officinale*

STANDS		11	25	27
PH		6.8	5.9	7.3
COND.		93	48	120
Antho	odo			2
Centa	nig	22	1	
Ophio	vul	2		
Prune	vul	15	7	1
Carex	fla	23		1
Leont	aut		15	11
Rumex	ace		18	14
Leont	his	16		1
Lotus	cor		21	22
Trise	fla		1	
Ceras	fon	8	12	
Cynos	cri	25	25	25
Desch	ces	12	5	6
Festu	rub	25	25	25
Holcu	lan	21	25	23
Horde	sec		6	
Plant	lan	22	25	23
Ranun	acr	25	23	13
Trifo	pra	13	23	24
Loliu	per	20	23	25
Phleu	pra	25	25	25
Tarax	off	25	18	16
Luzul	cam		3	
Senec	jac			6
Belli	per	21	7	
Cirsi	vul		6	1
Festu	hyb			7
Plant	med	17	13	19
Poten	rep	24	13	24
Cirsi	arv	23	21	25
Poa	pra			17
Poa	tri	12	7	12
Hiera	pil	4	1	2
Plant	maj	19	9	10
Poa	ann	4		
Agros	cap	20	25	24
Trifo	rep	24	25	25
Poten	ans	25	9	11
Agros	sto	15		25
Carex	hir	17	9	
Ranun	rep	20	11	4
Juncu	art	8		
Carda	pra	10	1	
TOTAL	SPP.	32	33	32

TABLE 12. GRASSLAND TYPE I – AGROSTIS CAPILLARIS (T)

This relatively species-rich community is totally "unimproved" in contrast to the remaining Stands to the north on Port Meadow which have received herbicide treatment (see Chapter 6.3.B). In addition to many plants associated with the Cynosurion, *Agrostis capillaris* (Type I) grassland contains *Centaurea nigra* and *Prunella vulgaris*. These species are constant constituents of the hay meadow grassland in Picksey Mead where the tall form of *Centaurea nigra* contrasts strongly with the stunted form on Port Meadow (see photographs 5 and 6). *Agrostis capillaris* (Type I) grassland is easily distinguished on the ground, particularly in summer when the turf is springy with the accumulation of litter and *Trifolium fragiferum* is in flower. *T. fragiferum* spends the winter in a vegetative state underground and so avoids problems of anoxia due to floods (Harper & Clatworthy 1963). *Agrostis capillaris* (Type I) grassland is similar to the *Lolium* sub-community of the MG11 *Festuca rubra-Agrostis stolonifera-Potentilla anserina* grassland (Rodwell 1992). To the east of Stand 25 *Juncus compressus* was recorded in August 1983.

Trifolium fragiferum was recorded on Stand 11 in August 1982 and 1983. This Stand covers a shallow dip 5m away from Shiplake Ditch upon which the bryophytes *Eurynchium swartzii* and *Amblystegium riparium* were recorded in association with two plants of *Ophioglossum vulgatum*. Although the latter was not found elsewhere on the Meadow it is often associated with ancient grassland and is frequent on Picksey Mead. The presence of the constant species, *Deschampsia cespitosa*, links *Agrostis capillaris* (Type I) grassland with *Deschampsia cespitosa* (Type H).

Photograph 5. The tall form of Hardhead (Centaurea nigra) *flowering on Picksey Mead.*

Photograph 6. The stunted form of Hardhead (Centaurea nigra) *flowering on Port Meadow after the forage harvester had been through.*

TYPE J (1, 2, 5, 7, 28) *Poa annua* (T)
CONSTANT SPECIES:

Bellis perennis	*Ranunculus acris*
Plantago major	*R. bulbosus*
Poa annua	*Taraxacum officinale*
Poa trivialis	

STANDS		1	2	5	7	28
PH		7.2	6.4	6.1	5.9	6.8
COND.		39	82	67	64	50
Prune	vul					2
Leont	aut			7	2	8
Rumex	ace					4
Lotus	cor	16	1			
Ranun	bul	17	1	3	24	17
Alope	pra				15	
Ceras	fon		9		4	10
Cynos	cri	22	25	17	25	25
Dacty	glo	21	5	25	23	
Desch	ces		1		2	2
Festu	rub	23	11	24	3	
Holcu	lan	1	2		8	1
Horde	sec	1	21		23	9
Plant	lan	3	16	21	17	25
Ranun	acr	19	17	8	15	25
Trifo	pra	14	15	25	8	22
Loliu	per	25	25	25	25	25
Phleu	pra	25	24	23	21	23
Tarax	off	24	15	13	8	24
Galiu	ver			3		
Poa	com	6				
Achil	mil	19	3	23	1	
Belli	per	23	17	20	6	24
Cirsi	eri				4	
Cirsi	vul		2			
Crepi	cap			1		
Plant	med	21	9	9	7	6
Poten	rep	17	16	15	5	
Cirsi	arv		2	19		
Poa	pra	2		1	4	22
Poa	tri	2	24	9	23	20
Plant	maj	17	24	22	25	23
Poa	ann	1	17	13	22	4
Agros	cap	25		23	24	25
Trifo	rep	25	25	25	25	24
Poten	ans		20		13	
Rumex	cri					12
Agros	sto		25		3	22
Alope	gen					3
Carex	hir	17	18			9
Ranun	rep		21		1	
Carex	pan	15				2
Juncu	art		1			3
TOTAL	SPP.	26	30	24	30	29

TABLE 13. GRASSLAND TYPE J – POA ANNUA (T)

The main factors which distinguish *Poa annua* (Type J) grassland from the rest are anthropogenic rather than environmental. The inundation map shows that they are rarely flooded and Table 13 shows no strong relationship between the pH and conductivity values of the Stands. The varied topography of these Stands, and consequent differences in drainage, have resulted in a mixture of species with differing tolerances to soil moisture. *Poa annua* (Type J) grassland therefore includes light-demanding species such, as *Plantago media*, *Trifolium repens* and *Bellis perennis* (Burden 1983) as well the adventive species, *Poa annua* and *Plantago major*, and those adapted to moist conditions such as *Deschampsia cespitosa*.

TYPE K (4, 6, 16, 17, 19, 22) *Cirsium arvense* (T)
CONSTANT SPECIES:

Achillea millefolium	*Holcus lanatus*
Cerastium fontanum	*Plantago major*
Cirsium arvense	*Potentilla reptans*
Festuca rubra	*Poa trivialis*

STANDS		4	6	16	17	19	22
PH		5.9	5.6	6.0	5.9	7.2	6.0
COND.		59	35	52	48	253	46
Centa	nig		1		1		2
Festu	pra			3	7		1
Rumex	ace			8	3		16
Briza	med		4				
Leont	his					17	
Lotus	cor		7		9	12	15
Ranun	bul	25	24	8	7	3	
Trise	fla			5			
Alope	pra		11	9			
Ceras	fon	16	12	12	24	7	11
Cynos	cri	25	7	25	25	8	24
Dacty	glo	25	25	1	21	7	
Desch	ces					7	22
Festu	rub	24	24	25	24	21	25
Holcu	lan	13	24	22	23	18	24
Horde	sec	15	8	22	22		23
Plant	lan	23	20	25	25	20	23
Ranun	acr		24	24	24	16	24
Trago	pra						4
Trifo	pra	18	12	24	25	21	22
Loliu	per	22	22	25	23	25	25

42

Phleu	pra	23	13	24	24	24	25
Tarax	off	10	4		1	22	1
Galiu	ver	9		7			18
Luzul	cam		7				
Senec	jac					3	
Achil	mil	23	16	15	21	6	5
Belli	per	16			2	17	
Cirsi	eri			6	4	1	
Cirsi	vul	7		8	18	18	
Crepi	cap		1				
Festu	hyb	4				2	
Galiu	mol		8				
Plant	med	5	12	4	3	20	6
Poten	rep	16	10	20	23	20	17
Cirsi	arv	25	24	25	8	22	23
Hypoc	rad		1				
Sonch	arv				1		
Poa	pra	7	8	11	2	7	
Poa	tri	24	17	24	13	14	23
Plant	maj	11	8	3	3	7	10
Poa	ann	3					
Agros	cap	24	23	25	24		3
Trifo	rep	23	24	24	23	25	25
Poten	ans				9	7	11
Agros	sto	8	10		21	24	24
Ranun	rep		7				4
TOTAL	SPP.	27	33	28	32	29	29

TABLE 14. GRASSLAND TYPE K – CIRSIUM ARVENSE (T)

This grassland MG6 Lolium perenne-Cynosurus cirstatus grassland (Rodwell 1992) is a species-rich variant of the Lolio-Cynosuretum which contains most of its constant differential species. The exception is *Hordeum secalinum* which was not recorded on Stand 19, an area of gravel extraction in grassland dominated by *Cirsium arvense, C. acaule, C. vulgare* and *Senecio jacobaea.* These species shield others susceptible to grazing such as *Centaurea nigra* and *Trisetum flavescens*, and allow them to flower and set seed. The areas in between the clumps or individual plants (which may be more than one metre high in wet summers) are closely grazed all the year round. Stand 19 is located in one of a series of hollows, facing north-west. The following additional community, reminiscent of *Galium verum* (Type M) grassland, was found near the top of a neighbouring east-facing slope:

Anthoxanthum odoratum	*Linum catharticum*
Briza media	*Pilosella officinarum*
Festuca pratensis	*Potentilla reptans*
Cirsium acaule	*Prunella vulgaris*
Centaurea nigra	*Trifolium pratense*
Galium verum	*Trifolium dubium*

Stand 19 is interesting because the number of conductivity units (253) (p.26) in the soil sample is five times as high as on the other Stands in this group. The pH is also higher by a factor of 10 (6.0–7.2, see Table 3). The reason for this is not clear, but may be associated either with a high level of calcium carbonate in the gravel, or with the fact that, by chance, this area had recently received urine (dung was not sampled).

Between the 17th and 21st May 1984, nine plants thought to be *Orchis morio* were seen by Mrs. Peter Dewar in a hollow to the north of Stand 19. I confirmed their identification in 1985.

3.3.D.ii. SECTION 2 – LESS DISTURBED PASTURE

This grassland occurs in a band across the highest part of Port Meadow (see Map 4) which may not have been flooded since records began in 1894 (see Figs. 5 and 7). It is kept short by grazing all the year round and resembles the Nature Conservation Review's (Ratcliffe 1977: 187, 194) Calcareous Loam Pasture found on basic free draining soils and MG5 Centaurea nigra-Cynosaurus cristatus grassland (Rodwell 1992).

TYPE L (10, 14, 15) *Cirsium vulgare* (S)
CONSTANT SPECIES

Achillea millefolium	*Galium verum*
Agrostis capillaris	*Holcus lanatus*
Cerastium fontanum	*Poa trivialis*
Cirsium arvense	*Potentilla reptans*
C. vulgare	*Ranunculus acris*
Dactylis glomerata	*R. bulbosus*
Festuca rubra	*Trisetum flavescens*

STANDS		10	14	15
PH		5.5	6.2	6.2
COND.		39	56	66
Centa	nig	1	5	
Carex	fla		7	
Rumex	ACE		8	
Briza	med			5
Leont	his			3
Lotus	cor	9	22	
Ranun	bul	20	23	22
Trise	fla	3	4	1
Alope	pra	14	11	
Ceras	fon	17	21	19
Cynos	cri	25	24	25
Dacty	glo	24	24	11
Desch	ces		7	7
Festu	rub	25	23	25
Holcu	lan	21	23	21
Horde	sec	19		

Plant	lan	22	22	23
Ranun	acr	7	9	11
Trifo	pra	24	23	25
Loliu	per	24	25	25
Phleu	pra	25	24	25
Tarax	off		14	12
Cirsi	aca		5	3
Galiu	ver	2	2	11
Pilos	off	3		2
Koele	mac		3	
Luzul	cam	1	3	
Poa	com	20		
Senec	jac		10	13
Veron	ser			1
Achil	mil	25	25	10
Belli	per		8	24
Cirsi	eri	8	5	
Cirsi	vul	13	18	15
Festu	hyb		8	3
Plant	med	1	5	6
Poten	rep	25	21	16
Cirsi	arv	24	21	8
Poa	pra		20	
Poa	tri	23	11	1
Plant	maj	2		8
Agros	cap	23	24	25
Trifo	rep	25	24	21
Agros	sto	1		
TOTAL	SPP.	31	36	32

TABLE 15. GRASSLAND TYPE L – CIRSIUM VULGARE (S)

The indicator species, *Cirsium vulgare*, for Type L grassland, is a biennial weed with a long tap root able to reach down to the water-table in drought periods (Clapham *et al.* 1962: 868). The shallow soil, less than 15cm deep in places, supports a calcicolous sub-community found in all the relatively high and dry areas which comprise islands of first gravel terrace in the alluvium, and suggests a connection between grassland Types L and M. *Heracium pilosella, Centauraea nigra* and *Alopecurus pratensis* characterize the *Cirsium vulgare* (Type L) grassland and show its relationship to the Centaureo-Cynosuretum (MG5 Centaurea nigra - Cynosurus cristatus grassland (Rodwell 1992). As in other grassland Types this one grows on a variable substrate made up of the many holes and ditches dug by man and subsequently silted up.

TYPE M (8, 9, 21, 44) *Galium verum* (S)
CONSTANT SPECIES:

Achillea millefolium	*Galium verum*
Cerastium fontanum	*Lotus corniculatus*
Cirsium arvense	*Plantago major*
C. eriophorum	*Potentilla reptans*
Dactylis glomerata	*Taraxacum officinale*
Festuca rubra	*Trisetum flavescens*

STANDS		8	9	21	44
PH		7.2	6.7	6.2	
COND.		92	68	51	
Antho	odo				7
Prune	vul				2
Leont	aut			3	4
Rumex	ace				2
Briza	med		5		
Leont	his		4	2	4
Lotus	cor	23	23	19	24
Ranun	bul	20	22	5	
Trise	fla	22	21	4	11
Ceras	fon	8	19	11	22
Cynos	cri	25	25	25	24
Dacty	glo	12	24	8	15
Desch	ces	2	2		3
Festu	rub	25	25	25	25
Holcu	lan	1		6	9
Plant	lan	24	24	25	25
Ranun	acr		1	21	5
Trifo	pra	22	25	23	25
Crepi	bie	1			2
Loliu	per	25	25	25	25
Phleu	pra	17	23	23	24
Tarax	off	24	12	12	9
Cirsi	aca		2	3	2
Galiu	ver	6	7	15	7
Hypoc	gla				2
Koele	mac		1		
Leont	tar				1
Luzul	cam		1		1
Poa	com	23			
Senec	jac		8	7	17
Trifo	dub	24	12		11
Achil	mil	25	24	22	22
Belli	per	25	21	18	24
Cirsi	eri		3		
Cirsi	vul		3	8	8
Crepi	cap				14
Festu	hyb		4		
Plant	med	23	9	14	15
Poten	rep	22	20	23	12
Cirsi	arv	1	19	25	15
Hypoc	rad				2
Poa	pra		3		3
Poa	tri		5	9	6
Plant	maj	2	8	15	2
Poa	ann	5		1	
Agros	cap		19		25

Trifo	rep	24	25	25	25
Agros	sto		2	24	7
Carex	hir	14			11
TOTAL	SPP.	27	36	31	41

TABLE 16. GRASSLAND TYPE M – GALIUM VERUM (S)

Galium verum grassland (Type M) is the driest facie of MG5 Centaurea nigra-Cynosaurus cristatus grassland on Port Meadow. It is found in two areas separated by *Cirsium vulgare* grassland (Type L). It is characteristic of areas with shallow base-rich soil in which there may be man-made ditches now silted up almost to ground level. The species which comprise *Galium verum* grassland (Type M) are capable of withstanding drought. For example, *Achillea millefolium*, an abundant species in the area, has a deep rooting system which can reach down to the water-table (Tansley 1939: 566). Stand 8 is an extreme example, located in an area covered by concrete during the First World War and upon which 10cm of top soil and fine gravel (which appeared to have been worm-sorted) have formed. The disintegration of the concrete over the intervening years has allowed invasion by both long (*A. millefolium*) and shallow rooted (*Galium verum*) species. The other Stands in the group were less alkaline and based on gravel.

Stand 44 does not form part of the grid sampling pattern. It was recorded in collaboration with George Lambrick of the Oxford Archaeological Unit. A transect was laid across the centre of an Iron Age house site and its animal enclosure on a north-south orientation (see Site C on Map 9). The frequency of species was recorded in quarter metre rather than 1m quadrats beginning at the south end and omitting the centre of the animal enclosure. The data show a variation in species composition across the site. For example, species less tolerant of wet conditions, such as *Cynosurus cristatus*, *Plantago media* and *Trisetum flavescens*, did not grow over the ditches where *Agrostis stolonifera* and *Poa trivialis* were well represented. *Anthoxanthum oderatum*, a species tolerant of nutrient poor soils (Burdon 1983), grew only in the hut circle from which the turf had been removed in the Iron Age.

TYPE N (13, 20) *Carex panicea* (T)
CONSTANT SPECIES:

Achillea millefolium	Lotus corniculatus
Agrostis stolonifera	Luzula campestris
Bellis perennis	Ranunculus bulbosus
Carex panicea	Senecio jacobaea
Cerastium fontanum	Taraxacum offinale
Cirsium acaule	Trifolium dubium
C. vulgare	Trisetum flavescens

STANDS		13	20
PH		6.2	6.0
COND.		48	49
Antho	odo		24
Carex	fla	17	
Leont	aut	7	
Festu	pra		10
Briza	med		3
Leont	his	1	
Lotus	cor	22	23
Ranun	bul	6	14
Trise	fla	9	7
Ceras	fon	3	24
Cynos	cri	25	25
Dacty	glo	5	
Festu	rub	25	
Plant	lan	23	23
Ranun	acr		1
Trifo	pra	25	25
Loliu	per	25	25
Phleu	pra	21	25
Tarax	off	13	6
Cirsi	aca	6	7
Galiu	ver		6
Luzul	cam	3	3
Senec	jac	18	23
Trifo	dub	13	3
Achil	mil	24	23
Belli	per	25	22
Cirsi	eri		1
Cirsi	vul	19	13
Festu	hyb	1	
Plant	med	3	20
Poten	rep		4
Cirsi	arv	9	
Hypoc	rad	22	
Poa	pra		1
Poa	tri	2	
Hiera	spp	11	
Plant	maj		2
Agros	cap	22	
Trifo	rep	23	25
Agros	sto	3	25
Carex	pan	2	9
TOTAL	SPP.	32	30

TABLE 17. GRASSLAND TYPE N – CAREX PANICEA (T)

Carex panicea (Type N) grassland is the wettest facie of the MG5 Centaurea nigra-Cynosaurus cristatus grassland (Rodwell 1992). It is characterized by the limited presence of *Carex panicea* and *Luzula campestris*. Their preference for moist conditions is met by a ditch running north-west to south-east, 3m from the south-west corner of Stand 20 and an isolated depression on Stand 13. The similarity of *Carex panicea* (Type N) to *Cirsium vulgare* (Type L) grassland is shown by the strong growth of *Senecio jacobaea* and *Cirsium vulgare*, protecting other species from grazing animals and the very short *Cynosurus cristatus* turf. The presence of *Anthoxanthum odoratum* and the low conductivity readings suggest that the soil is nutrient-poor despite the calcareous nature of the gravel substrate. *Carex panicea* (Type N) grassland is the least calcicolous of the Less Disturbed Pasture and provides a link with the Disturbed Pasture.

3.3.E GROUP IV – PICKSEY MEAD

CLASS: Molinio Arrhenatheretea Tx. 1937 emend Tx. 1970
ORDER: Molinetalia Koch 1926
ALLIANCE: Calthion palustris Tx. 1937 emend Tx. 1951

ORDER: MOLINETALIA
This Order includes plant communities of all kinds of wet meadow. Williams (1968) and Ellenberg (1978) give the following character species for it:

Achillea ptarmica	*Lotus uliginosus*
Angelica sylvestris	*Lychnis flos-cuculi*
Carex panicea	*Lysimachia vulgaris*
Cirsium palustre	*Platanthera chlorantha*
Dactylorhiza incarnata	*Sanguisorba officinalis*
Deschampsia cespitosa	*Selinum carvifolia*
Equisetum palustre	*Silaum silaus*
Filipendula ulmaria	*Taraxacum sect. Palustria*
Galium uliginosum	*Thalictrum flavum*
Juncus conglomeratus	*Trollius europaeus*
Juncus effusus	*Valeriana dioica*
Lathyrus palustris	

One would not expect to find that all these species were recorded in Picksey Mead in 1982. For example, Britain is on the northern limit of the range of *Selinum carvifolia* which has only been recorded from three Vice-Counties, Cambridge, North Lincolnshire and Nottingham (Clapham *et al.* 1962) and now only occurs on three Cambridge sites (Stace 1997). *Trollius europaeus* is an upland species not recorded in southern England, *Lysimachia vulgaris* tends to be found in wetter areas such as fens and on the banks of rivers and ponds, and the absence of *Platanthera chlorantha* may be related to the time of hay cutting.

Stachys officinalis was not recorded in Picksey Mead but was seen in West Mead, Yarnton, in June 1984. *Colchicum autumnale* has not been seen in Picksey Mead for about forty years.

ALLIANCE: CALTHION PALUSTRIS
Mire communities of this Order are found in poorly drained permanent pastures and hay meadows where *Caltha palustris*, *Filipendula ulmaria*, *Deschampsia cespitosa*, *Juncus effusus* and *J. inflexus* frequently occur with *Holcus lanatus*, *Poa trivialis*, *Agrostis stolonifera*, *Potentilla anserina*, *Ranunculus repens* and *Rumex crispus*. On Picksey Mead, however, these two *Juncus* species have been replaced by *Juncus articulatus*. The reason for this is not clear but may be related to greater or less movement in the water-table.

3.3.E.i. SECTION 1 – FEN

TYPE O (45, 46, 47, 48) *Phragmites australis* (T)
BRITISH PLANT COMMUNITY
M24 Cirsio-Molinietum (Rodwell 1991b).
CONSTANT SPECIES:

Agrostis capillaris	*Phragmites australis*
Anthoxanthum odoratum	*Poa trivialis*
Carex nigra	*Prunella vulgaris*
Centaurea nigra	*Ranunculus repens*
Cerastium fontanum	*Rhinanthus minor*
Filipendula ulmaria	*Rumex acetosa*
Juncus articulatus	*Taraxacum officinale*
Lathyrus pratensis	*Trisetum flavescens*
Phleum pratense	*Vicia sativa*

STANDS		45	46	47	48
PH		6.4	5.5	6.0	7.2
COND.		60	33	71	100
Equis	pal		1	15	10
Antho	odo	4	23	25	5
Bromu	com		1		
Centa	nig	3	15	21	7
Filip	ulm	25	25	25	6
Herac	sph	1			
Lathy	pra	10	23	23	22
Leuca	vul			3	
Linum	cat		1		
Lysim	num	2		15	
Prune	vul	10	19	18	2
Rhina	min	1	3	2	9
Sangu	off	15	25	24	
Silau	sil	2	20	20	
Vicia	sat	2	21	23	4
Dacty	inc				1

Genus	sp.				
Lychn	flo			21	5
Senec	aqu			22	
Succi	pra		2	15	
Trifo	cam				11
Valer	dio			15	
Ajuga	rep	1		11	5
Angel	syl	23			1
Calth	pal			6	2
Carex	acu	10	7		
Carex	dis		13	17	4
Carex	nig	11	20	9	18
Carex	rip		1		14
Eleoc	uni				1
Epilo	hir	6	7	1	
Festu	aru		1		
Galiu	uli			15	2
Glyce	max	11			15
Hyper	tet		13		
Juncu	con				1
Medic	lup		1		
Myoso	lax				2
Pedic	pal				1
Phala	aru	8			1
Phrag	aus	11	6	17	1
Polyg	hyd				1
Ranun	fic	21			
Symph	off	9			
Thali	fla			4	1
Carex	fla		17	22	
Bromu	lep		1		
Festu	pra		3		4
Rumex	ace	23	24	17	5
Briza	med			9	1
Leont	his			1	1
Lotus	cor		1	2	2
Trise	fla	11	22	8	25
Alope	pra	13	18		17
Ceras	fon	18	5	16	10
Cynos	cri	4	20	16	16
Dacty	glo	10	20	3	3
Desch	ces	2	15	5	12
Festu	rub		25	25	12
Holcu	lan	22	24	25	18
Plant	lan		25	25	1
Ranun	acr	24	25	25	15
Rumex	con				1
Trifo	pra		20	24	23
Crepi	bie		1	1	
Loliu	per	25	24	17	20
Phleu	pra	21	25	25	23
Tarax	off	5	25	20	12
Belli	per			4	1
Poa	pra	3			3
Poa	tri	10	5	5	23

Genus	sp.				
Agros	cap	22	22	8	5
Trifo	rep		3	8	14
Rumex	cri				16
Agros	sto		3	2	11
Alope	gen				5
Carex	hir	21	3		4
Ranun	rep	4	15	10	25
Carex	pan		17	25	1
Juncu	art	22	23	25	2
Glyce	flu				2
Galiu	pal			7	1
Myoso	sco			6	2
Carda	pra	6	6	5	7
TOTAL	SPP.	40	51	54	63

TABLE 18. GRASSLAND TYPE O – PHRAGMITES AUSTRALIS (T)

Phragmites australis (Type O) grassland is characterised by sedges, (particularly *Carex nigra*), and by early flowering, moisture-loving, plants, such as *Caltha palustris* (the named species for the fen-meadow Alliance (Shimwell 1971)). This is a rich fen-meadow community with between 40 and 63 species per Stand, which has affinities with M24 Cirsio-Molinietum fen-meadow (Rodwall 1991b). Since the river Thames was dredged in the 1920s and the material dumped onto the river bank, this area floods less often. The perception of flooding is, however, maintained as the river rises by the appearance of the water-table above ground-level. Only when the river water is very high does it spill over the bank onto the mead. *Phragmites australis* (Type O) grassland would become a *Phragmites australis* swamp if no management took place. West of Picksey Lane just such a community has evolved since the Western Bypass was built in 1958 (the late Mr E. Harris *pers. comm.*). *Calliergon cuspidatum*, a bryophyte of moist, basic soils, was noticed on this alluvial soil where the pH is on the acid side of neutral (except on Stand 48 where the ground is affected by the river water (pH 7.8) and on the calcareous material dredged from the river).

In the very wet area just to the south of Stand 47 and "outlined" by the 58.0m contour, the additional species, *Glyceria plicata* was found. It also occurred in the Long Pond on Wolvercote Common and in Winterbourne Stream (Stand 12).

TYPE Q (49, 53, 54, 56) *Succisa pratensis* (T)
BRITISH PLANT COMMUNITY
M22 Juncus subnodulosus-Cirsium palustre fen meadow, Briza media-Trifolium spp. sub-community (Rodwell 1991b)
CONSTANT SPECIES:
  Anthoxanthum odoratum   Leucanthemum vulgaris

Briza media *Ophioglossum vulgatum*
Carex flacca *Phleum pratense*
Cerastium fontanum *Succisa pratensis*
Deschampsia cespitosa *Taraxacum officinale*
Equisetum palustris *Trifolium pratense*
Juncus articulatus *Vicia sativa*
Leontodon hispidus

STANDS		49	53	54	56
PH		6.9	6.1	6.3	7.1
COND.		54	26	47	60
Equis	pal	24	6	4	4
Antho	odo	24	25	25	25
Arrhe	ela		14	2	25
Bromu	hor		24	22	7
Centa	nig	21	23	25	24
Dacty	fuc	7			
Filip	ulm	24	11	21	3
Herac	sph		3		
Lathy	pra	22	19	19	23
Leuca	vul	25	12	19	23
Linum	cat		1	2	18
Liste	ova	1			
Lysim	num			16	
Ophio	vul	22	22	22	23
Primu	ver	1		1	4
Prune	vul	11	20	25	24
Rhina	min	17	24	10	23
Sangu	off	25	25	25	24
Silau	sil	23	22	25	21
Urtic	dio	1			
Vicia	sat	8	13	25	24
Dacty	inc	4			
Lychn	flo	1	1		2
Senec	aqu			6	
Succi	pra	24	5	13	5
Trifo	cam	20			
Valer	dio	22			
Ajuga	rep	17			
Carex	acu				7
Carex	nig				3
Carex	rip		2		
Myoso	lax		2		
Carex	fla	25	20	25	25
Cirsi	pal	22			
Leont	aut	13	25	24	25
Festu	pra	16	22	24	17
Rumex	ace		14	4	
Briza	med	25	25	25	25
Leont	his	24	19	21	25

		49	53	54	56
Lotus	cor		8	19	19
Ranun	bul		23		17
Trise	fla	3	1		6
Alope	pra		1		2
Ceras	fon	12	9	12	3
Cynos	cri	24	25	25	25
Dacty	glo	12	19	12	21
Desch	ces	15	20	20	23
Festu	rub	25	25	25	25
Holcu	lan	24	25	25	22
Horde	sec		19	23	13
Plant	lan	25		25	25
Ranun	acr	25	25	24	24
Trifo	pra	25	22	22	17
Crepi	bie	6			
Loliu	per	1	9	18	3
Phleu	pra	17	25	25	25
Tarax	off	19	23	21	25
Pilos	off		3		3
Luzul	cam		1		
Trifo	dub				2
Belli	per	23			
Poa	pra	1			
Poa	tri		24	12	10
Trifo	rep	22		17	20
Agros	sto	22	18	19	8
Alope	gen	7			
Ranun	rep	9		9	
Carex	pan		17	1	19
Juncu	art	24	25	25	24
Trigl	pal		1		
Myoso	sco		1		
TOTAL	SPP.	49	49	45	48

TABLE 19. GRASSLAND TYPE Q – SUCCISA PRATENSIS (T)

The drier zone of this damp meadow grassland is characterised by *Carex acutiformis*, *C. nigra* and *Trifolium dubium*, as well as by *Succisa pratensis*. It is a form of M22 fen meadow where *Juncus subnodulosus* has been replaced by *J. articulatus*. Stand 49 is in the wettest and most species-rich zone of the *Succisa pratensis* (Type Q) grassland in which *Cirsium palustre* was flowering in July 1983 (Photo No.3), in association with such species as *Valeriana dioica* and *Ajuga reptans*. The presence of the latter species suggests a link between the *Phragmites australis* (Types 0) and *Succisa pratensis* (Type Q) grasslands, associated, perhaps, with some disturbance of the drainage system by the Bypass embankment. The polymorphic colour variation in *Dactylorhiza incarnata* (from flesh pink to deep magenta) was very noticeable. North-west of Stand 49, in the corner near the Spinney, a similar rich fen community, including *Achillea ptarmica*,

Dactylorhiza fuchsii and *Thalictrum flavum*, was noted in July 1983. *Calliergon cuspidatum* and a second bryophyte, *Climacium dendroides*, were found and form part of the *Succisa pratensis* (Type Q) grassland

3.3.E.ii SECTION 2 – MEADOW
ASSOCIATION: ALOPECURUS-SANGUISORBETUM

This type of MG4 Alopecurus pratensis-Sanguisorba officinalis (Rodwell 1992) grassland, which Page (1980) named the Fritillario-Sanguisorbetum officinalis, is found on calcareous alluvium in lowland Britain (see Chapter 6). It is distinguished from the sub-montane and the northern hay-meadow MG3 *Anthoxanthum odoratum-Geranium sylvaticum* by the absence of *Geranium sylvaticum, Conopodium majus, Alchemilla glabra* and *A. xanthochlora* (Rodwell 1992). In Europe its counterpart is classified in the Molinion caeruleae Koch 1926.

CONSTANT SPECIES:

Cynosurus cristatus	*Lolium perenne*
Dactylis glomerata	*Ranunculus acris*
Holcus lanatus	*Rhinanthus minor*
Lathyrus pratensis	

The *Rhinanthus minor* and *Lathyrus pratensis* community is distinguished from the rest by the nature of its past management rather than by environmental factors including pH and conductivity (p.26) (Table 2) or the influences of soil (p.19) or moisture (p.20). Very long-term management for hay, followed by grazing, has encouraged the growth of specialist communities which are more species-rich in the *Alopecurus-sanguisorbetum* than in the *Centaurea-cynosuretum*.

Intermediate levels of fertility may play an important part in the diversity of herbaceous plant species owing to the failure of many species in extremely poor acidic soils, and the dominance of a few, such as *Lolium perenne*, in much richer soils (Rorison 1971; Grime 1963). The distribution of high and low fertility levels on the Oxford grassland may be indicated by the contrasting distributions of *Lotus corniculatus* and *Leontodon hispidus*, respectively. Nevertheless both *Trisetum flavescens* (in northern hay meadows) and Arrhenatherium elatius Associations are known to be indicative of nutrient rich soils (Passarge 1969) and analysis of soil from Picksey Mead (Grid Ref: SP485104; Page 1980: 259) and from North Meadow, Cricklade (Wells 1974: 57) respectively, are as follows:

	% loss on ignition	pH	K(%)	Ca	Mg	PO₄
				mg/100gm		
Picksey Mead	25.9	7.4	22.1	1773	22.3	10.4
North Meadow	29.7	6.5	19.0	1620	23.0	—

Despite the fact that these are single samples, they suggest that high fertility of the soil has not reduced the species richness of the *Rhinanthus minor* and *Lathyrus pratensis* community on Picksey Mead. That such a community has been built up in undisturbed grassland over hundreds of years was shown by Richards (1972) who established that there are nine species of *Taraxacum agg.* endemic to this community of which *T. fulgidum, T. tamesense* and *T. litorale* have been found only on Picksey Mead. Specimens collected in April 1983 were identified as *T. fulgidum* Hegl. (Stands 45, 46 & 55), *T. sublaeticolor* Dt. (Stand 47), *T. haematinum* Hagle. (Stand 54) and *T. subundulatum* Dt. (Stand 55), four of which are considered to be rare in MG4 grassland (Rodwell 1992, 56). Subsequently McDonald (2000), reported seven microspecies from Picksey Mead including the endemic *T. richardsianum*, then a new record for Oxfordshire.

TYPE R (51, 52, 55, 57, 60, 62) *Cardamine pratensis* (T)
BRITISH PLANT COMMUNITY
MG4 Alopecurus pratensis-Sanguisorba officinalis grassland (Rodwell 1992).
CONSTANT SPECIES:

Cardamine pratense	*Rumex acetosa*
Hordeum secalinum	*Taraxacum officinale*
Lotus corniculatus	*Trifolium pratense*
Ophioglossum vulgatum	*Vicia sativa*
Poa trivialis	

STANDS		51	52	55	57	60	62
PH		6.1	6.0	5.2	6.3	6.0	7.4
COND.		43	39	19	36	25	70
Equis	pal	8	6	8			1
Alliu	ven		2				
Antho	odo	25	25		24	25	2
Arrhe	ela	4	5	13	4		1
Bromu	hor		25	23	25	25	25
Centa	nig	25	22	11	21	25	20
Filip	ulm	21	25	16	18	14	9
Lathy	pal						12
Lathy	pra	22	10	10	24	10	23
Leuca	vul	19	5		9		3
Lysim	num				14	2	8
Ophio	vul	17	9	4	20	20	22
Prune	vul	25	23	16	24	10	15
Rhina	min	25	11	21	19	6	1
Sangu	off	25	25	24	23	18	2
Silau	sil	24	22	5	16	25	13
Vicia	sat	24	22	23	24	24	23
Lychn	flo	1	1				
Senec	aqu		2				
Succi	pra			4			

49

Carex	rip		1				
Thali	fla						7
Carex	fla	23	25	1	16		
Leont	aut	25	24	13	23	25	23
Bromu	lep	12					
Festu	pra	11	24	3	23	24	24
Rumex	ace	21	19	17	16	12	3
Briza	med		2	7	14		
Leont	his	14		4	7	9	
Lotus	cor	1	5	4	6	24	18
Ranun	bul	25	16	16		13	25
Trise	fla	5	2	2			
Alope	pra	5	19	7	6	1	
Ceras	fon	18	15	16	15	4	
Cynos	cri	25	25	25	24	25	23
Dacty	glo	14	12	23	20	6	19
Desch	ces	21		23	25	14	7
Festu	rub	25	25	25	24	25	25
Holcu	lan	25	24	25	25	25	24
Horde	sec	19	7	21	24	25	25
Plant	lan	25	17	21		7	25
Ranun	acr	25	25	25	25	25	21
Trifo	pra	25	24	19	21	25	7
Loliu	per	15	11	24	21	25	25
Phleu	pra	25	25	25	25	25	25
Tarax	off	23	24	17	22	24	23
Belli	per	12					
Poten	rep	1				6	2
Poa	pra		1		1		
Poa	tri	13	21	5	24	23	24
Agros	cap	4	1				
Trifo	rep				21	11	25
Agros	sto	3	15	25	19	24	25
Alope	gen	10		1			
Carex	hir		11				
Ranun	rep				21		
Carex	pan		22	14		1	
Juncu	art		15	15	25		
Carda	pra	2	9	1	1	1	5
TOTAL	SPP.	44	45	44	41	38	39

TABLE 20. GRASSLAND TYPE R – CARDAMINE PRATENSIS (T)

This, the major grassland Type on Picksey Mead and is distinguished by *Sanguisorba officinalis* and the constant species *Cardamine pratensis* and *Lotus corniculatus*. The latter species is becoming increasingly rare because of its sensitivity to the addition of nitrogenous fertilizers to grassland (Lawes *et al.* 1882), a farming practice which has become increasingly common over the last 40 years. Its presence on the Oxford grassland is limited to those areas which escape flooding. *Cardamine pratensis* (Type R) grassland is characterized by the abundant flowering of *Taraxacum officinale agg.* early in the year, followed by *Leucanthemum vulgare* and *Sanguisorba officinalis*. The distribution and abundance of the grasses are sparse and may be related, perhaps, to the diminished flooding, and the consequent loss of additional nutrients in flood water. The presence of *Bromus lepidus* on Stand 51 is noteworthy since this is not a common meadow plant, being more generally found in waste places and leys (Stace 1997).

TYPE S (59, 61, 63, 64, 65, 66, 67) *Arrhenatherum elatius* (S)

CONSTANT SPECIES:

Arrhenatherum elatius	*Plantago lanceolata*
Deschampsia cespitosa	*Poa trivialis*
Hordeum secalinum	*Rumex acetosa*
Leontodon hispidus	

STANDS		59	61	63	64	65	66	67
PH		6.0	7.3	7.2	7.4	7.4	7.1	6.1
COND.		24	76	33	62	59	50	31
Equis	pal	2		1		17		2
Elymu	rep		11					
Alliu	ven	3	2			1		
Antho	odo	22	1	20		5	14	25
Arrhe	ela	24	16	5	25	23	25	24
Bromu	com				25			
Bromu	hor	25	25	25		25	22	25
Centa	nig	9	14	22	8	24	13	14
Filip	ulm	3	16	24	23	25	16	23
Geran	dis		2					
Herac	sph					2		
Lathy	pal			4				
Lathy	pra	10	15	6	7	24	23	25
Leuca	vul		1	2	15	24	7	11
Linum	cat				2	20		
Lysim	num						1	
Ophio	vul	1	2	1	2	24	1	
Primu	ver	1						
Prune	vul	9	7	9	17	23	17	16
Rhina	min	11		1	25	25	25	25
Sangu	off	25	17	12	25	17	25	23
Silau	sil	8	9	18	5	23	4	5
Stell	gra	6						
Vicia	cra		2	22	11	17		5
Vicia	sat	3	16	16	12			
Lychn	flo					3		
Succi	pra					3		
Leont	aut	3	12	20	17	1	18	12
Festu	pra	9	5	25	17	2	3	11

Rumex	ace	17	9	2	6	1	15	19
Briza	med					23	11	
Leont	his	4	1	10	7	23	3	2
Lotus	cor				8	10	19	17
Ranun	bul	20	9					
Trise	fla	3	1		25	25	11	6
Alope	pra	4	2	4	1		4	
Ceras	fon	5		1	10	17	12	15
Cynos	cri	21	23	25	25	25	23	24
Dacty	glo	25	20	13	25	23	24	25
Desch	ces	22	4	16	5	13	4	4
Festu	rub	25	13	25	25	25	25	25
Holcu	lan	25	25	25	24	24	25	25
Horde	sec	25	11	25	10	12	22	23
Plant	lan	21	3	7	25	18	25	24
Ranun	acr	24	15	21	25	22	24	23
Rumex	con		17					
Trago	pra	1	9					
Trifo	pra	20		17	24	24	3	20
Loliu	per	24	24	25	24	18	16	24
Phleu	pra	23	16	25		18	8	9
Tarax	off	7	25	23	22		25	24
Galiu	ver		11					
Poten	rep				8	7	2	
Cirsi	arv		14		2			
POA	pra					1		
Poa	tri	21	19	23	17	10	25	23
Trifo	rep		11	18	4	24	15	
Agros	sto	17	2	25	2	5	14	25
Carex	hir	5			3	12	1	
Ranun	rep		15	24	15	25	24	16
Carex	pan			1		24		
Juncu	art					13		
TOTAL	SPP.	40	41	41	40	47	40	34

TABLE 21. GRASSLAND TYPE S – ARRHENATHERUM ELATIUS (S)

The major constitutents of Type S grassland clearly place it with the MG4 Alopecurus pratensis-Sanguisorba officinalis grasslands (Rodwell 1992). Here, however, *Arrhenatherum elatius* has become dominant in places. On the Continent *Arrhenatherum elatius* is a common meadow species (Duffy *et al.* 1974: 189). It persists well when cut and produces abundant but poor quality hay (Tansley 1939: 564; Hubbard 1954 2nd ed.: 235). In Britain where there are few old meadows left undisturbed, this tall grass has become well known as a disturbed grassland species, particularly common on roadside verges. Wells *et al.* (1976) noticed that on the ungrazed part of Porton Down, *A. elatius* invaded disturbed sites created during the previous 60 or 70

years. They suggested that this species could not withstand heavy grazing or trampling. It is apparent that on the drier ground in the northern part of Picksey Mead, cutting in early July followed by autumn grazing is insufficient to prohibit the growth of *A. elatius*. In the southern, detached, portion of the mead, however, its absence is probably due to the high water-table which persists throughout the year.

Vicia cracca is a noticeable constituent of *Arrhenatherum elatius* (Type S) grassland and, in contrast to *Sanguisorba officinalis*, was not recorded in the other grassland Types on Picksey Mead. The bryophytes *Amblystegium serpens* (Stands 61 and 66) and *Calliergon cuspidatum* (Stands 62 and 67) were identified. The former prefers shade (Smith 1980), here cast by unpollarded *Salix fragilis* which grow along the river bank at the north end of Picksey Mead. The grassland on the eastern edge of the Mead is influenced by the spreading and seeding of dredgings from the relatively new channel for the Honeybourne Stream (See Chapter 2.3.C.). The standard grass-seed mixture used by Thames Water was as follows:

10	lb.	New Zealand Certified Mother Seed Hawkes Bay Strain Perennial Ryegrass
9	lb.	Aberystwyth S23 British Certified Seed Perennial Ryegrass
1	lb.	Rough Stalked Meadow Grass
3	lb.	Canadian Timothy Grass
3	lb.	Ornia Timothy Grass
1	lb.	New Zealand Certified Mother Seed White Clover
Total	28 lb.	per acre

(Nature Conservancy Council Southern Region 1982)

3.3.E.iii. SECTION 3 – RIVER BANKS

TYPE P (50, 58) *Bromus commutatus* (S) (Table 16)
BRITISH PLANT COMMUNITY
MG 1 Arrhenatherum elatius (Rodwell 1992)
CONSTANT SPECIES:

Agrostis stolonifera	*Festuca rubra*
Alopecurus pratensis	*Poa trivialis*
Anthoxanthum odoratum	*Ranunculus bulbosus*
Arrhenatherum elatius	*Rhinanthus minor*
Bromus commutatus	*Trifolium pratense*
Cerastium fontanum	*Trisetum flavescens*

The importance of soil conditions in influencing succession (Lloyd & Pigott 1967) may be illustrated in the difference between, for example, *Arrhenatherum elatius* (Type S) grassland and the adjacent *Bromus commutatus* (Type P) grassland which is mown less frequently.

STANDS		50	58
PH		7.6	7.0
COND.		56	51
Equis	pal	4	
Alliu	ven		1
Antho	odo	2	2
Anthr	syl	21	
Arrhe	ela	25	23
Bromu	com	14	25
Bromu	hor	25	
Anisa	ste	24	
Centa	nig		3
Geran	dis	22	
Herac	sph	24	
Primu	ver		2
Prune	vul		2
Rhina	min	24	3
Sangu	off		2
Urtic	dio	10	
Vicia	sat	25	
Festu	pra	2	
Rumex	ace		11
Ranun	bul	17	25
Trise	fla	18	23
Alope	pra	1	6
Ceras	fon	9	3
Cynos	cri	24	25
Dacty	glo	25	25
Festu	rub	5	23
Holcu	lan	24	25
Horde	sec		24
Ranun	acr	13	25
Trifo	pra	6	14
Crepi	bie	1	
Loliu	per	25	25
Phleu	pra		25
Trifo	dub	25	
Cirsi	arv	13	
Poa	tri	23	25
Agros	sto	1	2
Carex	pan	1	
TOTAL	SPP.	30	25

TABLE 22. GRASSLAND TYPE P – BROMUS COMMUTATUS (S)

Bromus commutatus (Type P) grassland is classified with MG1 Arrhenatherum elatius (Rodwell 1992) grassland notable on roadside verges in the United Kingdom. It is characteristically lush and thick, except where bare earth thrown up by moles or other agencies, provides a micro-habitat filled by annuals (*Allium vineale*) or perennials

(*Sanguisorba officinalis*) which spread from the *Cardamine pratense* (Type R) grassland on the adjacent land. The inclusion of *Ranunculus bulbosus* and *Primula veris* (intolerant of wet conditions) emphasises that *Bromus commutatus* (Type P) grassland, which grows on a levée beside the river, is usually well above flood level in spring. Parts are shaded by trees which include, *Salix fragilis, Crataegus monogyna* and *Sambucus nigra*, growing along the river bank out of reach of the mower, (Stand 58) and by the Spinney (south of Stand 50). It is, perhaps, worth drawing attention to the abundance of the arable weed *Anisanthus sterilis* on Stand 50. In the early 1980s this grass became prominent in Associations with winter sown wheat (R.J. Chancellor *pers. comm.*). It may have invaded an area disturbed by moles.

The following species were noted in the Spinney[1] on the 10th June 1982:

Agrostis stolonifera	*Poa annua*
Alopecurus pratensis	*Ranunculus acris*
Angelica sylvestris	*R. ficaria*
Anthriscus sylvestris	*R. repens*
Calystegia sepium	*Rhinanthus minor*
Caltha palustris	*Ribes rubrum*
Cardamine pratensis	*R. uva-crispa*
Cirsium arvense	*Rorippa microphylla*
Crataegus monogyna	*Rosa canina*
Dactylis glomerata	*Rubus idaeus*
Epilobium hirsutum	*Rumex conglomeratus*
Filipendula ulmaria	*Salix cinerea*
Fraxinus excelsior	*S. fragilis*
Galium aparine	*S. viminalis*
Glechoma hederacea	*Scutellaria galericulata*
Glyceria maxima	*Stellaria media*
Heracleum sphondylium	*Symphytum officinale*
Iris pseudacorus	*Taraxacum officinale*
Lathyrus pratensis	*Thalictrum flavum*
Lolium perenne	*Trifolium repens*
Lychnis flos-cuculi	*Urtica dioica*
Phalaris arundinacea	*Veronica beccabunga*
Phragmites australis	*Viburnum opulus*
Plantago major	

The Spinney vegetation resembles W6 Alnus glutinosus-Urtica dioica woodland, Salix viminalis sub-community (Rodwell 1991a).

---

[1] Called West Moor point on the 1st edition O.S. map. "In 1540 I note a fishery in the Thames at Wylhan called Westmans Wynde." Thacker (1968) II: 103.

PART II – HISTORY

CHAPTER 4

RIVER CONTROL

4.1 PREHISTORIC PERIOD

The River Thames flows between the oolitic limestone of the Cotswold Hills and the Corallian sand and limestone of the Oxford Heights (see Map 6). In the Oxford area the river meanders over a wide alluvial plain through which islands of the first gravel terrace divide the flow into a series of streams which finally come together at the Sandford Gap below Oxford (Gilbert 1954: 166). Evidence of its early history is sketchy but work undertaken by the Institute of Hydrology can be interpreted to show that in early post glacial times the main stream of the Thames skirted Wytham Hill and followed the course of the present-day Seacourt or Wytham Stream (see Fig. 5). The extent of the silted-up river bed beneath the Seacourt Stream compared with that

of the present River Thames adjacent to Port Meadow is remarkable (Institute of Hydrology 1979). However, large scale dredging in the 1890s and 1930s may have destroyed any early post glacial evidence (if it existed) of the size of the Thames between Hagley Pool and Medley Weir in the Holocene.

On Port Meadow (see Map 9) an excavation through Bronze Age (Site A) and Iron Age (Site B) ditches, carried out by the Oxford Archaeological Unit in the summers of 1982 and 1983 showed that the gravel at the bottom of the Bronze Age ditch is a clear yellow ochre with no alluvium or biotic material in it. This suggests that the water-table was low during the Bronze Age and that there was no flooding. Gravel at the bottom of an Iron Age ditch, on

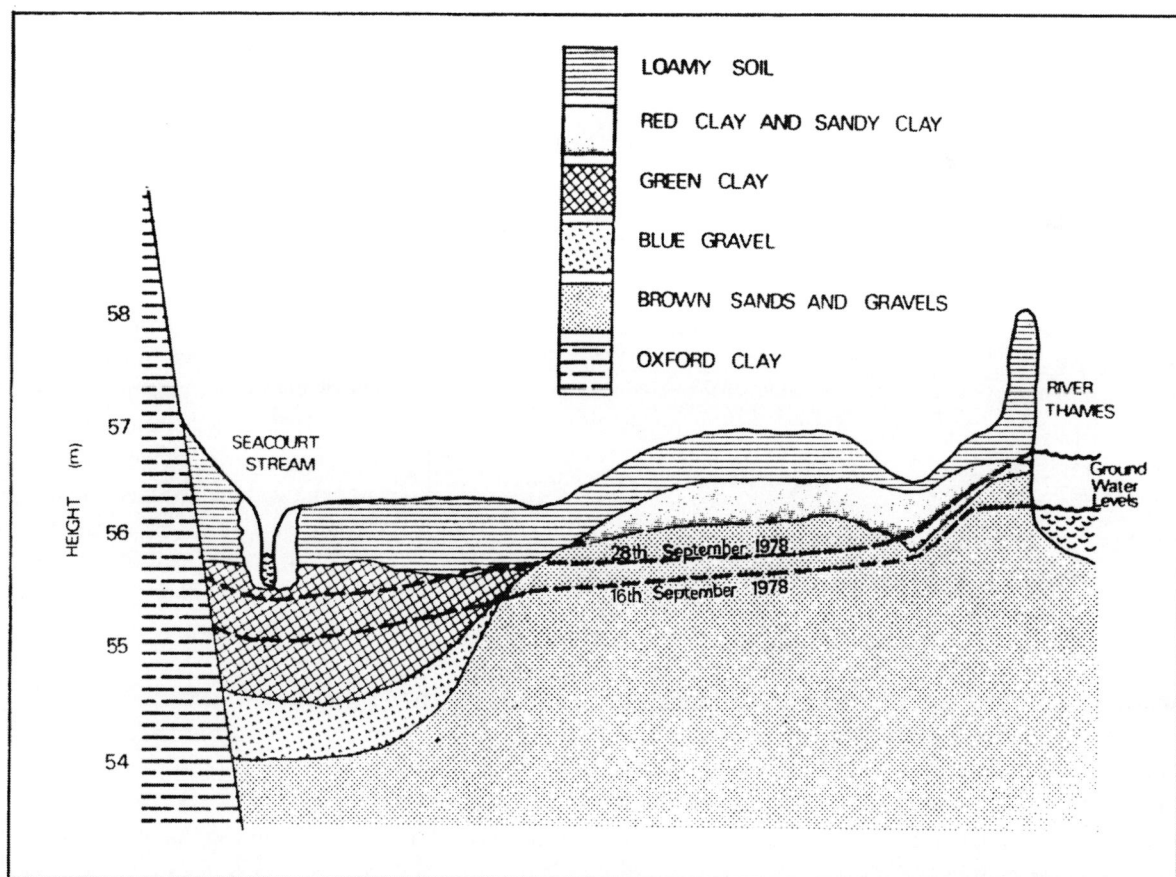

Fig. 5. Cross section across the Thames valley at Binsey adjacent to Port Meadow with Wolvercote Common (Institute of Hydrology).

53

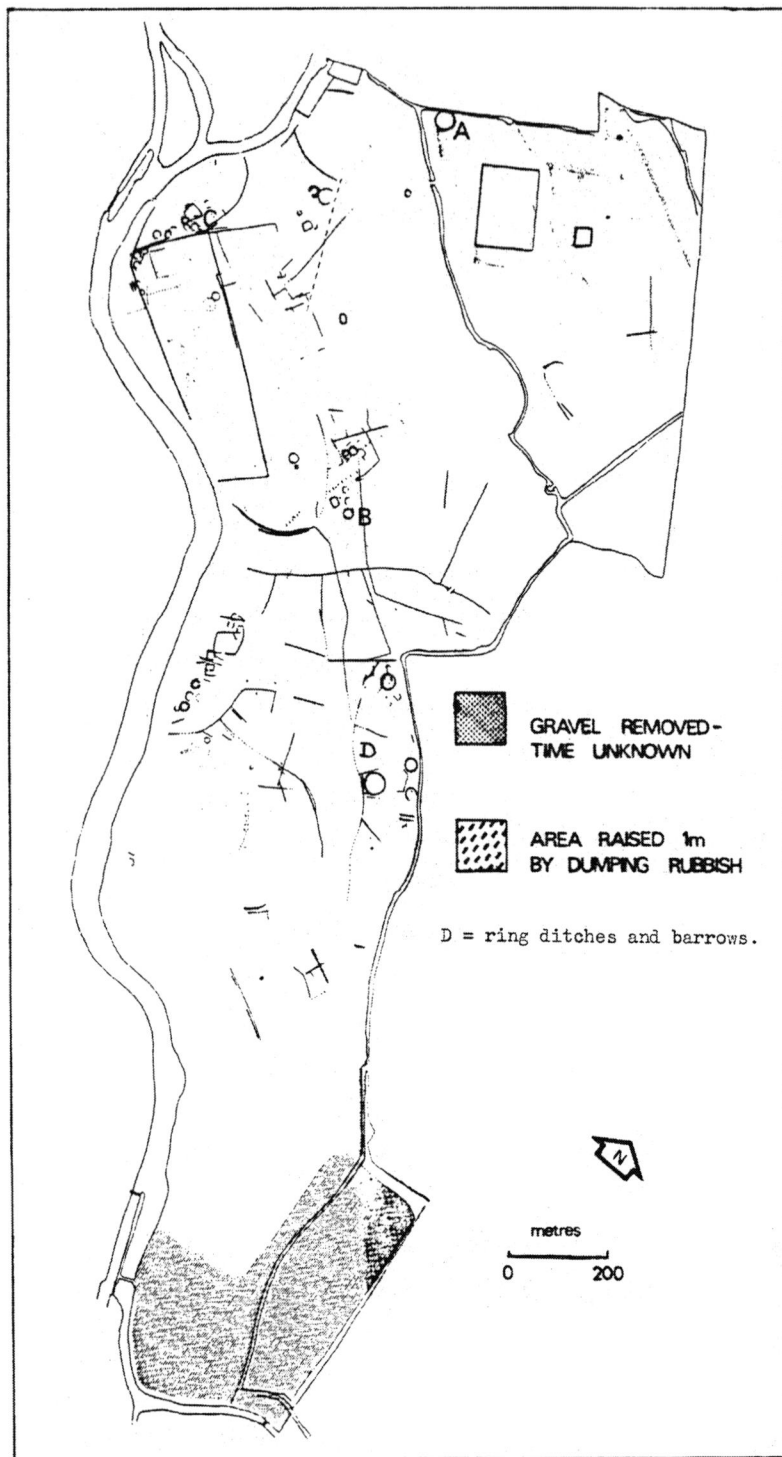

GRAVEL REMOVED -
TIME UNKNOWN

AREA RAISED 1m
BY DUMPING RUBBISH

D = ring ditches and barrows.

N

metres

0   200

Map 9. Distribution of archaeological sites on Port Meadow. Sites A, B and C . investigated by the Oxford Archaeological Unit. Botanical transect recorded across Site C.

by the Oxfordshire Archaeological Unit in August 1983 in Inundation Zone C (see Map 4).

It is known that alluvial and hydrological regimes are influenced by man and that surface run-off, stream flow and ground water levels rise when woodland is replaced by grassland (Limbrey 1978). Although the river flow alongside Port Meadow and Picksey Mead would have been increased by the clearance of woodland in the Neolithic period, there may have been no significant change until the Iron Age when an expanding population began to clear more extensive areas of the uplands. Increased run off from treeless pastures may well have produced the flooding in the river valley evident at the Middle Iron Age floodplain settlement at Farmoor (Lambrick & Robinson 1979). Late Iron Age and Roman arable farming in the upland probably caused the deposition of alluvium which seals Iron Age settlements on the floodplain and which probably gradually increased as the Romans intensified the deforestation and wheat production on their Cotswold estates. The resultant silt-laden water flowing into the valley may account for some of the deposition of alluvium on the Oxford grassland (Robinson 1981; Robinson & Lambrick 1984). By the end of the Fourth Century A.D., the gradual increase of flooding and heavy loads of alluvium had filled in some old river channels and stream beds such as that at Farmoor (Lambrick & Robinson 1979), and so levelled the valley floor. It is not known how fast this occurred but, at a rate of 3.78 grains of solid matter per gallon, even a small flood can carry *c.* 1,125 tons of alluvium in 24 hours (Griffiths 1926: 28).

4.2 HISTORIC PERIOD

4.2.A. WEIRS

Fishweirs, similar to those found in the Trent valley (Salisbury 1980) (but for which there is no evidence so far in the Thames valley), may have been used where the Thames passed Picksey Mead and Port Meadow. It is not

the other hand, is a dark greyish-brown colour mixed with a black humic material, containing biotic remains such as seeds and the exoskeletons of beetles. These are only preserved in soils in a waterlogged, anaerobic, condition (Robinson & Lambrick 1984). The modern water-table is well above the bottom of the Iron Age ditches on Port Meadow, so the movement of water through the gravel was demonstrated particularly well in the trenches dug known when the first fishery was established at King's Weir, nor the first Mill at Wolvercote. Documentary evidence suggests, however, that from the Eleventh Century the river was well-used. For example, there was a mill at Eynsham, recorded in Domesday Book, which must have had an associated fishery because its value included 450 eels. A mill and fishery (175 eels) were being worked at Cassington and a fishery, with meadow attached to it, was recorded at Yarnton (Morris 1978). In 1143 there was a fishery at King's Weir (Carter 1957: 4).

In the Severn valley, there were remnants of possibly-medieval fisheries in the form of small islands which would have allowed navigation on one side and fishing nets or creels to be set on the other (Pannett 1981: 144). They resemble the islands at King's Weir, Wolvercote Mill and, less closely, islands by Black Jack's Hole and at Medley. The fishermen may have planted Osiers (*Salix viminalis*) – an essential component of their craft – on these islands (O.S. Map 1877; Prior 1982: 70; Minn Appendix F). They grow there still, with the exception of those by Black Jack's Hole which disappeared within living memory.

By the Thirteenth Century Godstow Abbey had acquired two mills at Wolvercote and free fishing in the Thames, which seems to have extended from the north of Godstow and Toll Bridges, along both sides of Picksey Mead (which is an island) upstream to Somerford weir (Rot. Hund. Ed. I: 854, 857). The Freemen of Oxford owned the fishery south of these bridges as the waters, including Port Meadow Stream, came within the Franchise of Oxford (Prior 1982: 349).

4.2.A.i. King's Weir

During the medieval period the weirs became more solid and sophisticated. King's Weir, like Eynsham, was described as a strong barrier across the river in 1541. Its construction is described below:

> "A triangular shaped solid projection was built out from the bank on each side of the river in order to reduce the width of the water-way to some 35ft, and in the opening the weir was erected. It consisted of vertical timbers supported at the bottom by a baulk laid horizontally across the river bed, and above water by a beam spanning the gap. At a later date (*c.*1870) a swing beam with moveable tackle was substituted in order to permit of the passage of barges"
>
> (Thames Conservancy 1928: 12)

By 1143, King's Weir, controlled by the Abbess of Godstow, was important, not so much for supplying water to Wolvercote Mill or for trapping fish and eels, but

because it controlled the flow of water to Oxford town and a number of Oxford mills (Carter 1957: 4). In doing so it also influenced the water-table of Picksey Mead, Port Meadow and Wolvercote Common.

4.2.A.ii. Godstow Weir

A weir was probably built onto Godstow bridge for the Abbey about 1138. Such structures generally had wooden rimers (posts) about 18 to 24 inches apart, set into the river bed or into a log set upon the river bed. Paddles up to 3ft 6in high on the end of poles were placed on the upstream side and overlapped the rimers. They were kept in position by the pressure of the river. A second row of paddles could hold back the water up to 6ft deep (Country Life 17 June 1939: 653).

4.2.A.iii. Medley Weir

Medley Weir was built *c.* 1281 in association with a new cut from Medley to Osney (see Map 2) which served Rewley Abbey and its mill. It seems to have been smaller than King's Weir. There is no evidence of the weir causing excessive flooding on Port Meadow until the Eighteenth Century.

4.2.B. WATER MILLS

Mills, too, were important. Water was ponded back above their associated weirs, and cuts were excavated in order to divert the flow of the river. Water mills were used by the Romans at Court Farm, Abingdon, where a Roman mill stone was discovered to have been re-used in the lining of a well (Mr D. Miles *pers. comm.*) but documentary evidence of water mills in the Thames valley does not occur until between *c.* 762 and *c.* 838 (Davis 1973: 260).

4.3 NAVIGATION

4.3.A. INTRODUCTION

River transport was important because of the difficulty of carrying heavy goods by road. Fish weirs and mills were often sited in the shallow stretches of the river where rapid descent provided the fall of water to work the mill (Clark 1889: 431 n.l). Their proliferation made it much more difficult for the bargemen, already confronted by the natural hazards of the river, to trade above and below Oxford.

4.3.B. UP TO THE SIXTEENTH CENTURY

From the time of the Norman Conquest to the Seventeenth Century, each King attempted to limit the number of weirs and mills on the Thames in order to improve both navigation and trade (Thames Conservancy 1928: 1–4). A limited number of weirs was, of course, essential to raise the level of the Thames water sufficiently to allow boats to pass over rapids. King's Weir may have been one of these. It is known that the Thames was navigable as far as Eynsham before Domesday (Salter 1907). Its function in the Middle Ages may have been to maximize the flow of water down Wytham Stream to the pilgrim centre at Seacourt (Biddle 1961/2), and thence to Oxford. There is no evidence at present to show whether or not it served the same purpose in the early Saxon period when an early form of its name suggests that Seacourt was an administrative centre (Gelling 1953). After the medieval village of Seacourt was deserted in the Fifteenth Century, there may have been no one to raise objections when the main stream of the Thames was redirected in order to serve Wolvercote Mill and Oxford.

4.3.C. POST SIXTEENTH CENTURY

In the preamble to the 1623 Act to make the Thames navigable as far as Lechlade, it is recorded that the river was navigable west of Oxford (Thacker 1911: 66). This may have only been relatively true when compared with its state between Oxford and Burcot. Certainly navigation remained difficult; it was necessary for the bargemen to carry portable winches to pull their barges over the shallows and some of the weirs (Thames Conservancy 1928: 4; Prior 1982: 113). Perhaps for political and financial reasons, little is heard of the state of the river above Oxford until 1751. During this period the Oxford-Burcot Commission held the limelight. The natural silting up of the river may have been dealt with on an *ad hoc* basis by the owners of the river banks but I have found no evidence for this.

The passing of the 1751 Act "For the Better Carrying On and Regulating the Navigation of the Rivers Thames and Isis etc." (124 Geo.II c.6.) was a recognition of, but did not at once solve, the problems encountered by millers and bargemen. It was not until 1787, that considerable discussion took place on ways of implementing the 1751 Act. In particular, the Thames and Severn Canal Company would have been anxious to ensure that navigation was not interrupted by flash locks and shoals. One requirement of the Act was to find the best site for a lock to raise the level of water over the shoals in the Port Meadow reach of the river. The possibilities of Black Jack's Hole were considered but the present site at Godstow was finally agreed upon. One might expect that the Freemen of Oxford, anxious to preserve their common pasture intact, had some influence in this decision.

Although there was plenty of water power for Oxford and Wolvercote Mills in wet weather, as well as an improved passage for bargemen, the situation was very different in dry seasons. For example, when water flowed over King's Weir and so to Oxford, the Oxford millers and bargemen might benefit while Wolvercote Mill might be without water (Carter 1957). This remained a bone of contention between river users until the building of the Oxford Canal in 1781, and railways in 1845 and 1850, reduced the pressure of trade on the Thames.

In the Eighteenth and early Nineteenth Centuries, and probably earlier too, there were continual quarrels between bargemen, millers and fishermen over the use of the water. Not only did the pound locks, or flash weirs as they were called, waste considerable amounts of water but they were also time-consuming to operate. A bargeman had to take the weir to pieces, wait until the water-level was right, warp his boat through, rebuild the weir and finally wait until the water had built up to a sufficient depth for onward movement (Thacker 1911: 251). A weir keeper generally collected fees from the bargemen for the use of the water, directed the water to the mill or adjusted the height of the weir to prevent adjoining land from being flooded.

Sometimes the weir keeper caused major problems. At King's Weir in 1813, for example, the tenant of Wolvercote Mill raised the lasher overnight. This simple action flooded Yarnton village, stopped fishing at Godstow Weir, reduced movement of barges at Wolvercote and submerged the adjacent hay meadows and pasture. It was the final straw in a quarrel that had been simmering since the river had been "improved" twenty years earlier. Mr Swann of Wolvercote Mill was building up his paper mill business with the Clarendon Press at this time. Williams, a Wolvercote waterman, took the case to Court and Swann had to pay a fine of £10 (Stapleton 1893: 278, 315; Thacker 1911: 97; Carter 1974: 62).

The problem of allocating water between millers and boatmen remained acute until, in 1826 near Oxford, Tuesdays and Fridays were allocated as "flash" days. On these days the lasher on Godstow Bridge was raised to let more water into the Wolvercote Mill leat to turn the machinery. It was then lowered during the 3-hour flash periods to allow boats with a deeper draft than a punt to go over the weir on a flush or flash of water (Carter 1974: 4; Thacker 1911: 195). A timetable of flashes on and after 10th November 1826 shows that one flash took 70 hours (*c*. 3 days) to travel the 75 to 80 miles downstream from Lechlade to Sonning. It must have been travelling at an average speed of one mile an hour, if delays at each weir are included. A flash reaching

Eynsham on a Monday at 5 p.m. would arrive at King's Weir, two miles dowstream, at 7 p.m. and Godstow at 8 p.m. From there 8 hours were allowed for the water to reach and build up at Medley lock, only one and a half miles downstream, where the tackle of paddles and rimers was not removed until 4 a.m. on Tuesday (Thacker 1911: 175–6).

After 1790, when Rewley Cut became the main stream for navigation, the old river began to silt up. When the railway line was built along the eastern edge of Port Meadow and over the old river Thames it became almost impossible to take any craft down to the Castle Mill Stream because the bridge over the old river was at ground level. At the same time, the stretch of the Thames between King's Weir and Medley lock had gradually silted up and flooding became commonplace (see Photograph 7). River traffic left the Thames above King's Weir, passed along Duke's Cut to the Canal and returned to the river above Osney. Such problems were examined for the Thames Conservancy in the Flood Relief Report (Beardmore & Leach 1869) which made many detailed suggestions for improvements.

These included:

a. Dredging the river between King's Weir and Medley to a depth of nine feet below "flood line".

b. Making a cut 150 yards long bypassing King's Weir (in which there is now a modern pound lock).

c. Building a 100 yard long cut to straighten the river about a third of a mile below King's Weir (leaving an island beside Picksey Mead which has become the Spinney). The succession from meadow to willow swamp can be seen in Photograph 8 (see Chapter 3.3.E.ii for species list).

d. Increasing the weir's height to supply water to Duke's Cut (built 1790 by the Duke of Marlborough to join the river to the canal), to give Wolvercote Mill a good head of water and to relieve flooding in Oxford (Ibid.3).

e. The weir on Godstow Bridge was said to have been divided into eight openings closed by draw-doors, two of which were partially blocked by the bridge pier. This weir and bridge were considered to be wholly inadequate to cope with the flood waters, even if the fishing bucks (traps) were removed, so a navigation channel and pound lock were recommended to take their place.

Photograph 7. The whole of Port Meadow was frequently flooded in winter before Medley Weir was removed in 1931. The floods attracted a large population of winter migrant birds (H. Minn).

Photograph 8. Zones between mead and willow swamp show up on the south side of the Spinney on Picksey Mead.

f. After 80 years in operation Godstow flash lock had become impassable and the Flood Relief Report recommended that this, too, should be repaired and deepened and a second weir built above the new lock.

g. The shoals in the reach above Medley Weir should be removed as well as the weir itself. This weir was in two parts, one on either side of the tip of the island adjacent to Port Meadow that divided the river into two channels.

h. The choked state of the old river was noted and it was suggested that it be filled in as it had been superseded by the channel to the west, Rewley Cut (Beardmare & Leach 1869).

Few of the recommendations of the Thames Commissioners were carried out until 1924 when Godstow Lock was enlarged and

> "the depth of water over the lower sill increased from 3ft 10in. to 6ft 6in. to compensate for the lowering of the tail water upon the abolition of Medley Weir"
>
> (Thames Conservancy 1928)

Between 1924 and 1932 the river between King's Weir and Medley Weir was straightened and confined to a deeper, narrower channel. King's Lock and Godstow Lock, each with an associated weir, were constructed and Medley Weir removed (Stock 1951). The significant reduction in the flooding brought about by this work is illustrated in Fig. 4.

4.3.D ECOLOGICAL APPRAISAL

4.3.D.i. Water-table

The level of the water-table of the Oxford grassland may have changed again when the Thames and Severn Canal was opened in 1790, at the same time as Godstow pound lock and the water pen at King's Weir were constructed. Godstow and Medley pound locks in the 1790s were not modern pound locks. An apparatus was attached to the weir to pen the water upstream until it was required by the millers or bargemen. The water pens drowned Peel Yate Ford between Port Meadow and Binsey Green (Thacker 1911) as well as the ford between Picksey and Yarnton Meads (Vernon-Harcourt 1883: 6; Thacker 1911). This must have raised the water-table in Port Meadow and the Meads and thereby changed the vegetation from that which was adapted to floods in winter and dry summers, to one adapted to floods and a frequently high water-table all the year round. When the navigation channel below Medley, was redirected from the "old river" to the Rewley cut, further changes to the drainage of the south end of Port Meadow may have taken place.

4.3.D.ii. Flora

In the Eighteenth and Nineteenth Centuries, the locks and weirs beside the Oxford grassland changed their drainage. During periods of heavy rain the grassland adjacent to lock headwater was flooded for variable periods. If this happened in late June, for example, the hay crop was ruined, and there were many complaints of this happening after navigation on the Thames was improved above Oxford (Stapleton 1893: 315; Young 1813). The raising of the level at King's Weir meant that water flowed into all the surrounding ditches and raised the water-table to surface level. This had the effect of changing the vegetation from high to low quality hay or pasture (Thames Conservancy 1928: 6; Stapleton 1893: 315). The Spinney was recorded as an island, Westmore Wind Point in the Wytham Enclosure Award 1814 (County Record Office) and as West Point on the Ordnance Survey, 1877, when osiers (*Salix viminalis*) were growing on it. Since the Spinney was joined to Picksey Mead in the 1920s (see Flood Relief Report, item c. above) it provides an example of succession to willow swamp (see Photograph 8).

4.3.D.iii. Fauna

The dredging of the river in the Nineteenth Century changed the riverine habitats. Until the 1890s many parts of the river were wide and shallow with a fine gravel bottom (suitable for punting) very suitable as a habitat for white-clawed crayfish. These were abundant and often caught in creels left in the river overnight by the local boatmen. Other fish, including lampreys, were also abundant. A fine gravel bottom remains in much of the Thames beside Port Meadow, but heavy river traffic and, possibly pollution, may inhibit fish from spawning there. Barbel are, however, known to spawn in Wolvercote Mill Stream which retains its gravel shoals in some places (Minn (see Appendix F)).

CHAPTER 5

CONTINUITY OF THE OXFORD GRASSLAND

5.1 CLIMAX VEGETATION AND ITS REPLACEMENT

5.1.A. INTRODUCTION

It is now widely agreed that the climax community in most parts of lowland England in post-glacial times was deciduous forest, apart from natural glades in the forest where the substrate was unsuitable for the establishment of trees. In regions such as the upper Thames floodplain, the vegetation may have been a dynamic mosaic of marshy woodland, willow swamp and alder carr. Stream courses may have been characterised by a rank vegetation of aquatic plants full of wild fowl and animals (Tansley 1911: 164; Church 1922). Natural vegetation of this type has disappeared from the British Isles except for small, isolated pockets such as the Georgh in Co. Cork. There the plant associations include the Blechno-Quercetum, the Corylo-Fraxinetum and the Osmundo-Saliceteum atrocinerea (Braun-Blanquet & Tüxen 1952). Fitzgerald (1984) comments upon the closed canopy of *Quercus robur* and the attenuation of understorey species as well as on the importance of stream beds as "paths through the maze of braided streams".

5.1.B. WOODLAND DESTRUCTION AND GRASSLAND ESTABLISHMENT

Archaeological evidence of the early Neolithic environment of the floodplain has not yet been found in the Thames valley but later evidence suggests that it may have been alder carr. A detailed archaeological study of material from a silted river channel at Buscot Lock, Lechlade (SU230980) for example (see Map 6), provided biotic evidence, in the form of wood, seeds and beetle exoskeletons, to suggest that there the woodland flora was dominated by alder (*Alnus glutinosa*) at least in the late Neolithic *c.* 2,100 b.c. (Lower case b.c. refers to an uncalibrated radiocarbon date.) Similar evidence for alder carr from the Windrush valley (Robinson 1981a) possibly extended onto the first gravel terrace where open, calcareous, mixed oak woodland probably included the following species:

Lime	*Tilia sp.*
Ash	*Fraxinus excelsior*
Hazel	*Corylus avellana*
Purging Buckthorn	*Rhamnus catharticus*
Willow	*Salix spp.*
Elderbury	*Sambucus nigra*
Blackthorn	*Prunus spinosa*
Blackberry	*Rubus spp.*
Dogwood	*Cornus sanguinea*

The following field-layer species found at Buscot are also those which suggest woodland, or wood pasture.

Nettle	*Urtica dioica*
Hemp Agrimony	*Eupatorium cannabinum*
Dog's Mercury	*Mercurialis perennis*
Red Campion	*Silene dioica*

(Robinson 1981a: 120, 123)

The beginning of the transition from alder wood of the Buscot type to grassland may have begun in the Mesolithic and Neolithic periods for which there is evidence of settlement in the valleys of the upper Thames and its tributaries (Robinson 1981a). Once woodland was cleared grassland was maintained and extended largely as a result of domestic animals eating and trampling the tree seedlings and forest ground-vegetation. At the same time, the seeds of plants from more open country could have been brought in attached to their wool or coat, or in their droppings. The woodland species were thus prevented from regenerating by the grazing animals. Invading plants began to form a continuous turf so that the forest was gradually replaced by grassland. (Tansley 1939: 165; Godwin 1956; Adams 1975).

Near watering places on the river Thames, the grazing and browsing of cattle, red deer, pigs and, by the Bronze Age, horses, would themselves have played a major role in providing clearings colonised initially by disturbed rough-grassland species. Seeds of shade-intolerant plants, including ribwort (*Plantago lanceolata*) and great plantain (*Plantago major*) found at the Buscot site (see Map 6) (Robinson 1981a: 82, 124), support this hypothesis.

In the later Neolithic period farmers entering the upper Thames valley would have found a wooded landscape with clearings into which they settled. Further trampling and browsing of cattle and red deer may have been enough to extend natural or artificial clearings, already made to facilitate hunting or the growing of crops in small areas. Neolithic artefacts have been found on the floodplain at Buscot and at King's Weir, but it is unlikely that the floodplain was extensively cleared at this time. Biological evidence from Buscot and from the Windrush floodplain at Mingies Ditch indicates alder carr. At Drayton the existence of a *Cursus* crossing the floodplain suggests limited clearance. The presence of Bronze Age barrows at, for example, King's Weir and on Port Meadow and Wolvercote Common, may indicate more extensive clearance, and at the Hamel, Oxford (Map 6), possible Bronze Age plough marks were found (Robinson 1981: 85).

Neolithic farmers almost certainly deliberately cleared the forest by felling trees and perhaps by ring-barking and therefore provided pasture as a means of attracting those wild animals suitable for hunting to a convenient area close to their settlement (Coles & Orme 1980: 36; Rackham 1980: 107; Smith 1970: 89). Such a hypothesis is impossible to prove, but it could have happened at Buscot or on what became the Oxford grassland, where the willow swamp may have been cleared by people living at King's Weir (see Map 6) in the Neolithic period. The hazel may have been coppiced, too, and grows today in the hedge which separates Port Meadow from the Burgess Field Nature Park (Robinson 1981: 120–122; McDonald 1980; Appendix M). Evidence from the Somerset Levels suggests that woodland management, including coppicing and pollarding, was practiced in the Neolithic period from *c.* 4,000 B.C. onwards (Cole & Orme 1980: 21).

Evidence of burning associated with early clearance has not been found in the upper Thames valley, but later evidence of this method of clearing timber has been discovered. In the floodplain of the Windrush valley, a tributary of the upper Thames, archaeologists have found burned alder roots at Mingies Ditch (SU391059) in a position which suggested that alder carr may have been cleared by burning in the late Bronze Age *c.* 850+90 b.c. (M.A. Robinson *pers. comm.*). Keeping a fire going over tree stumps for a few days is a very effective method of destroying them. When man destroyed the forest by felling or burning and removed the timber, the process of degeneration was speeded up.

5.1.C. SUMMARY

Robinson (1981) and Robinson & Lambrick (1984) show that in the late Neolithic and Bronze Ages, on the floor of the Thames valley in the Oxford area woodland clearance had been reasonably extensive. Soil profiles, plough marks and biotic remains such as snail shells, have been found at the Hamel (SP507061) in Oxford and in a field west of King's Weir (SP476102) across the river from Picksey Mead (Robinson 1981: 180). These show that, free from floods, the "terrestrial" soil had a high silt content suitable for settlement and arable farming. Aerial photography showing barrows and ring ditches (Photograph 2) which in fact survive as slight earthworks, makes clear that the Meadow was in use in the Bronze Age and during the Iron Age (Atkinson 1942) but the alluvium, which began to be laid down by floods in the Roman period, has concealed any evidence there might be of Bronze Age activity on Picksey Mead. On the Meadow, however, the water-table was lower than it is today and the plants are likely to have been those tolerant of shallow soil and drought conditions. Unfortunately these conditions are not conducive to the preservation of seeds or other plant material which could otherwise have given direct evidence of the Bronze Age environment. At that time the difference between pasture and hay communities could have been less marked. The 2,000 years of management since the Bronze Age have tended to favour geocryptophytes and hemicryptophytes which reproduce vegetatively, on the Meadow, in contrast to early flowering species with cauline leaves and erect shoots now found on Picksey Mead. Although such plants as great burnet (*Sanguisorba officinalis*), tufted vetch (*Vicia cracca*), moon daisy (*Leucanthemum vulgaris*) and knapweed (*Centaurea nigra*) can be found in a stunted form on Port Meadow today. They can be found in less intensively grazed grassland, such as that beside the river Cherwell near Oxford, together with ragged robin (*Lychnis flos-cuculi*) and devil's bit scabious (*Succisa pratensis*) protected from grazing animals by clumps of rushes and tussocky grasses.

5.2 GRASSLAND MANAGEMENT

5.2.A. INTRODUCTION

It is likely that the Bronze Age barrows and ring ditches enclosing burial platforms on the Meadow (Atkinson 1942, 1946; Rhodes 1949; see Photograph 2 and Map 9) indicate that the land had been cleared by then. It was dry enough to form the site of a cemetery for possibly nomadic farmers grazing their animals on the Oxford grassland while their crops were probably growing on the first gravel terrace. Experiments at the Butser Ancient Farm Research Project support the hypothesis that pasture and hay making was as important to Iron Age, Bronze Age and even Neolithic man as it was to Medieval and later farmers (the late Dr P.J. Reynolds, *pers. comm.*). Hay making is important in farming practice because it allows more animals to be kept over the winter when grass does not grow and grazing is not generally available.

In Wessex and Warwickshire some barrows and ring ditches have been found situated on field boundaries, particularly in areas where light, well-drained soils would be easy to till (Ford 1973: 108–114). Similarly, the proximity of the light soil of the first gravel terrace in Burgess Field Nature Park suggests that the eastern group of ring ditches and barrows (marked D on Map 9) may have been placed between an arable field in Burgess Field Nature Park and the pasture on Port Meadow. Evidence for this, if it existed would have been destroyed when the City Dump was made.

5.2.B. IRON AGE AND ROMAN SETTLEMENT (700 B.C.–A.D. 400)

By the Iron Age the Thames valley had become, biologically, an even more diverse landscape. Elements of woodland, cleared areas for arable and grassland, provided the essentials for a more settled Celtic farming community with its tribal units and complicated systems of communal land tenure (see below) (Vinogradoff 1892: 162; Taylor 1981: 20). Silt deposited on riverside land by winter floods enriched the earth. The flood-water protected the surface from frost and therefore brought forward the grass-growing season. Regular grazing would prevent the regeneration of shrubs and trees and form large areas of grassland which gradually developed its own identity. This may have been an important factor in enabling some Celtic farmers to specialise in the production of cattle and horses in the river valleys, while others kept sheep on the hillsides. Large settlements have been identified from air photographs in the Parks, Oxford, in Cassington, and, further away, in Stanton Harcourt, as well as smaller ones at Binsey and Port Meadow. These early Iron Age people are well known for their corn growing, and post holes possibly indicating frames for drying corn, and perhaps hay, have been found at Little Woodbury, Wiltshire (Bersu 1940). See also Jones (1981).

Archaeologists use assemblages of carbonised seeds and those preserved in waterlogged deposits to build up a picture of the local environment and farming practices (Jones 1981; Robinson 1981). This is, however, very difficult because adequate allowance must be made for what was growing in the deposit itself and what was brought into the deposit by wind, water or animal, including worm, activity. The seeds of grassland species, together with the exoskeletons of dung beetles, preserved at the bottom of an Iron Age enclosure ditch on Port Meadow (Photograph 9 and marked C on Map 9), do, however, suggest the presence of a wet grassland landscape with stagnant water in the ditches and trampled, or possibly cultivated, ground in their vicinity (see Appendix G for species list). Near the round houses were long rectangular ditches (see Map 9) which may have been hedged or fenced enclosures used to herd cattle (Robinson 1982; Lambrick & McDonald 1985).

Archaeological sites similar to those on Port Meadow have been described at Farmoor and Claydon Pike, Lechlade (see Map 6) (Lambrick & Robinson 1979; Miles 1979), where the evidence points to a pastoral community grazing animals and, by the Roman period, setting aside some grassland to be cut for hay. Pottery evidence suggests that

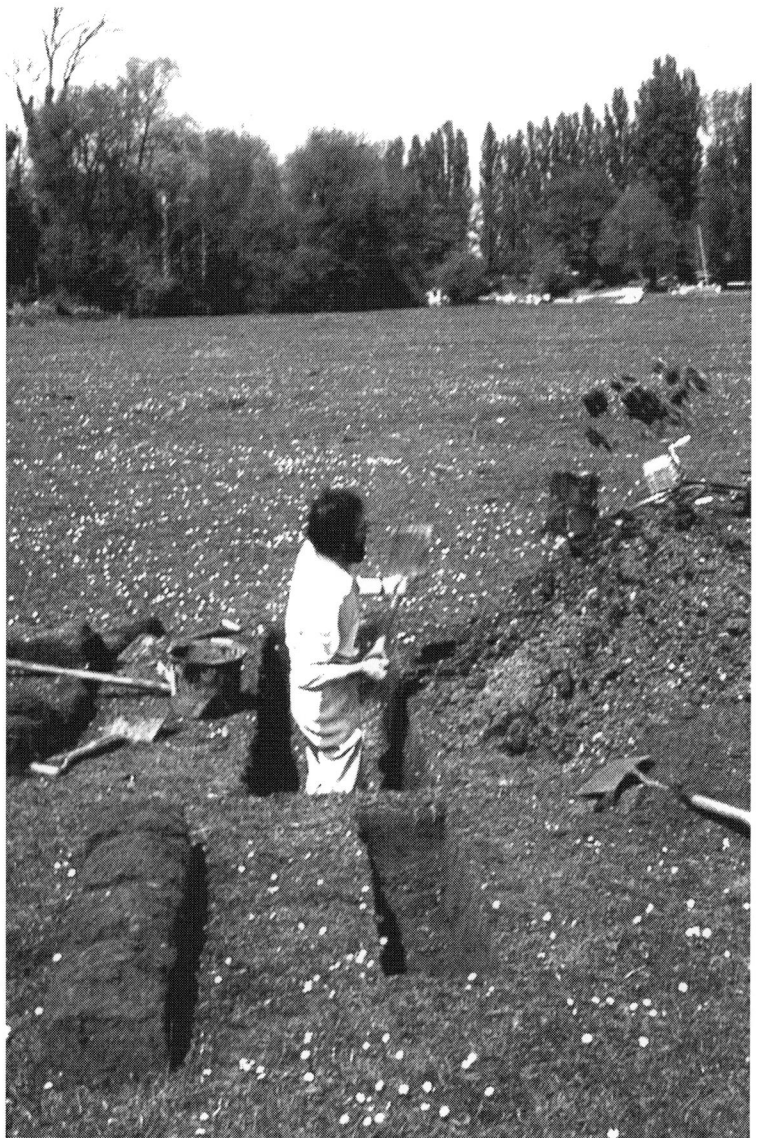

Photograph 9. Dr M.A. Robinson excavating dark bluish-brown gleyed soil containing biotic material from an Iron Age ditch on Port Meadow. 1981

Port Meadow, like Farmoor, was inhabited in the mid-to-late Iron Age (200B.C.–43A.D.) (Atkinson 1942).

Despite their similarities, Lambrick & McDonald (1985) suggest that there may be three types of settlement on the Thames floodplain and lower levels of the first gravel terrace. At Farmoor, for example, where the floodplain was indeed subject to flooding, small single house enclosure groups were inhabited seasonally for a few years and some of the grassland put up for hay. At Claydon Pike, like Port Meadow, the settlement was possibly longer lived and in use all the year round, depending upon whether or not the flooding was serious. There seem to be generally more permanent multiple house enclosure groups placed on drier first-gravel-terrace islands with probable paddocks and other linear boundaries in the vicinity. Whether or not the evidence of several houses indicates several contemporary families or several building phases is not clear. Nor is it clear, although it is possible, that cultivation took place on the floodplain in the middle Iron Age. Examples of the third type of settlement occur at Mingies Ditch and Northmoor which appear to have been longer-lived with at least one house replaced four or five times. Small associated enclosures seem to have functioned as paddocks and larger, probably hedged enclosures may also have been used, at least in part, for animal husbandry and possibly small-scale cultivation.

Such specialization is not confined to the upper Thames valley in the Iron Age. Robinson (1984) describes a division of the Wessex downland into arable and pasture areas, grassland on the Chilterns and Berkshire Downs and an intensification of arable on the higher gravel terraces in the Thames basin. Specialization implies co-operation between settlements which would be in keeping with a tribal organization. The upper Thames valley appears to have been the boundary between the historic tribes of the Catuvellauni (who were derived from the Belgae) to the northeast, the Atrebates to the south and the Dobunni, whose territories may have been encroached upon by the Catuvellauni by the First Century A.D. (Case 1954; Cunliffe 1974: 76–105; Sellwood 1984).

Iron Age Celtic farming was technically advanced and probably organized into land-units based on a complicated tenurial system (Taylor 1981: 20). Celtic farmers grew a variety of crops including spelt (*Triticum spelta*) (a hardy type of wheat which can be sown early in winter or spring), bread wheat (*T. aestivum/compactum*), rye (*Secale cereale*) and Celtic beans (*Vicia faba*). Not only did this extend the growing period and so allow a larger crop to be gathered but each of these species is suited, one way or another, to adverse conditions (Jones 1981, 1984). There is no evidence that the Celtic bean was intentionally

used as a "break-crop" because it, in common with other legumes, can replenish the nitrogen available in the soil. On the contrary, Jones (1984: 123) argues that an increase in leguminous weeds suggests declining fertility through the Iron Age.

Just as in the Neolithic and Bronze Ages, trackways aided the movement of people between settlements (Coles & Orme 1980; Tinsey 1981: 215) so the Iron Age economy probably consisted of networks of settlements, joined to others by communication routes or tracks of the type which crossed Port Meadow from what is now called Aristotle Lane to Binsey Ford (Atkinson 1940). The evidence for this seems tenuous as it is based upon the finding of a set of Bronze Age smith's tools near Aristotle Lane, similar to a set found in Cowley to the east of Oxford. The track may have formed part of a route which ran from the east, through Headington, crossed the Cherwell, and followed the line of the Green Ditch which lies under St. Margaret's Road. From Binsey the track goes over Wytham hill to Eynsham and the west. A second, north-south route, which is more plausible, followed the ridgeway between the Thames and Cherwell valleys along the line of the Banbury Road (Harden 1956: 236; Biddle 1961/2: 70–201).

Each settlement was about two kilometres apart specialising to a greater or lesser extent in the production of particular goods. The kind of product would have been influenced by the geology of the area as well as by economic and other factors. The best evidence for specialist agriculture is the floodplain farmsteads at Farmoor. There is also a clear bias towards pasturalism or arable farming in other settlements which roughly corresponds to geophysical features. There is, for example, more pasturalism than arable on the floodplain and first terrace and more arable than pasture on the second terrace. Differences in the proportions of cows to sheep and horses have also been found including more sheep on the second gravel terrace (Lambrick & Robinson 1979).

The people living on the gravel terrace islands on Port Meadow may have reserved Picksey Mead for hay during the spring and summer, and grazed it only in the months after the hay was cut. Parts of Port Meadow may have been subject to waterlogging in the Iron Age (Lambrick & McDonald 1985) and the pastoralists at that time would have taken their animals to higher ground during the winter months. They would still have been able to use the Oxford grassland from the late spring to early winter.

In addition to the trade links between dependent, specialist townships and the administrative centre of a tribal unit there were agricultural links between the townships themselves. In some places this might have taken the form of "intercommoning", a practice in which two or more settlements shared the products of the land not under cultivation. Ford (1976: 274–294) demonstrated the pattern of linked settlements which suggested units of territory within which meadow, pasture and woodland were shared in the Warwickshire Avon region. He went on to show that the names of many of these settlements were of Saxon origin and that in many cases they were sited beside permeable soils showing evidence of Romano-British settlement. He suggested a continuity of well-ordered estate management over a considerable period, possibly, on some sites, into the Bronze Age.

These tribal units, which maintained their legal, social and agrarian traditions during the period of Roman military government, may have provided the foundation upon which the openfield agricultural system of the Anglo-Saxons was built (Postan 1972; Ford 1976: 294; Laing 1979: 37; Robinson 1981: 71).

Archaeological evidence from Shakenoak, Oxon. shows Romano-British and Saxon people living side by side and suggests that Saxon conglomerate estates were based upon earlier Roman and pre-Roman estates (Brodribb, Hands & Walker 1972). Closer to the Oxford grassland, evidence from Yarnton shows extensive settlement from the Neolithic to the present day. It gradually moves from the flood-plain eastwards and then north-east to the Norman Church. By the Seventeenth Century the village was centred to the north of the Church and in the Twentieth Century the arable fields to the north of the village were developed for housing (Hey 2004). The nearby alluvial meadows, West Mead, Oxey Mead and Picksey Mead, would have been in an ideal position to provide these people with a crop of hay and pasture in the aftermath despite, or perhaps because of, the variations in water-table levels and the deposition of alluvium.

At what time those townships specialising in corn production opened their fields to neighbouring flocks or herds is not known. But it can be argued that it would not be difficult for farmers, living as close to the soil as the Celts, to realise that to use first cattle then sheep to eat down the stubble after harvest would make ploughing easier and solve the problem of too much straw in the soil.

The possibility that the Iron Age people recognised the value of manure in increasing crop production, or, at least, keeping the land in good heart, should not be overlooked. Folding sheep in a different place every night, for example, is a simple way of spreading manure evenly over a field, of any size or shape. To do this in spring and autumn would benefit both the crops and the animals. In spring it is wise to ration the amount of rich young pasture consumed by

cattle, sheep and horses by allowing them to graze the pasture for a few hours and then to move onto the arable. There, their droppings manure the soil and their hooves break the leading shoot of the newly emerged corn and force it to produce several tillers and, therefore, several heads of corn. In autumn the stubble and arable weeds provided good fodder to build up fat in the cattle for the winter. Iron Age cattle kept under cover during the winter gave an accumulation of manure which was spread over the fields after the animals were let out in spring.

5.2.C. EFFECT OF INCREASED SETTLEMENT

Roman civil and military influence allowed the opening up of trade along new and better roads. In the enforced peace, the population expanded and yet more arable land was required to increase the production of corn on the Cotswold estates (Postan 1972). Wet marginal land was, therefore, brought into cultivation. Marginal land is not ideal for cropping as it is generally either too dry and stony, or too wet and heavy, for easy ploughing. It is only brought into use when pressure from an increase in population, or the high price of corn makes the effort involved worthwhile. This changing pattern of cultivation has been described in the modern period in relation to Porton Down, Wiltshire, where chalk downland was grazed by sheep or ploughed for corn, whichever brought the higher economic return (Wells et al. 1976).

The heavy Belgic plough allowed more land to be cultivated in the upland areas, where rainwater washed the newly turned soil into the valleys, and so contributed to the alluvium which was deposited on the floodplain. Romans may have taken advantage of this plough when they established their estates in the Cotswolds and in what later became Wychwood Forest. It would not have been necessary for the many agricultural settlements that occurred on the light soils of the Thames gravel in the Roman period (Frere 1967: 268–9; Limbrey & Evans 1978). Spike rush (Eleocharis palustris) normally grows in wet grassland such as Port Meadow Marsh, so it is significant when its seeds are found amongst grain on several Iron Age sites in the upper Thames valley (Jones 1981). The Romans introduced ditches to drain their arable land with the result that "run off" from the fields increased flooding and the deposition of alluvium in the Thames valley (Robinson & Lambrick 1984).

5.2.D. SUMMARY OF PRE-SAXON LAND-USE

It may be inferred that Bronze Age people maintained at least rough grassland and Iron Age pastoralists utilized the land more extensively for themselves and their herds. The grazing of Port Meadow was first established in the

Bronze Age and fully exploited in the middle Iron Age. It may well have continued in use in the Roman period when there was extensive settlement in the area of north Oxford. There is at present no direct evidence to show that the contrasting land-use of pasture and hay meadow on the Oxford grassland was established as early as the Iron Age.

5.2.E. LEGAL EVIDENCE OF TRANSITION TO THE ANGLO-SAXON PERIOD

Vinogradoff (1882: 162) used the history of land law and jurisprudence to suggest that in England in the "earliest times" the soil was owned by tribal groups rather than by individuals. Laing (1979: 19) paints a similar picture from classical sources. He reminds us that Caesar described the Celtic organisation of *druides*, *equites* and *plebes* and recorded a king Divitiacus in the First Century B.C. who held land in what later became France and in England. In the First Century A.D. Tacitus remarked on the slave market and modern archaeologists have discovered a slave-gang chain of the same period in Anglesey.

Postan (1972) also looked at land law in the Roman Empire. He found that the outlying provinces, including Britain, did not have their own laws reconstructed, but had Roman laws imposed upon them. He suggests that Britain remained in essence a Celtic land ruled by the native aristocrats who followed their traditional laws in legal, social and agrarian matters. This is possible since we find customary and Roman law existing side by side in our Courts today.

Bearing in mind that such early documentary evidence may not be accurate, Jones (1973: 439) cites a Fourth Century case in the Emperor's Court in which there were conflicting claims of ownership of an estate by, presumably important, freemen. One party claimed inheritance according to Roman Law, while the other party claimed under traditional or customary law. The latter was later codified by the Welsh King Hywel Dda *c.* 950 A.D. and suggests that the act of settling entitled the settler to rights in the land for at least thirteen generations. These comprised the four generations needed to acquire proprietorship and the nine generations required before the rights were extinguished. Jones suggests that there is a connection between the Tenth Century law in Wales and the Fourth Century customary law and that it may stem from the Iron Age. If this is the case, then such a law would be important to the Bronze Age and Iron Age pasturalists with a transhumant way of life. They could leave the floodplain in the autumn, for example, secure in the knowledge that they could return the following year or many years later, without let or hindrance. Of course this system would break down when the population increased

and needed more land for settlement and agriculture, as it did in the Iron Age and again in the Fourth Century A.D. The traditional nomadic paturalists would be brought into conflict with their own, more settled, people wishing to increase their corn-growing area. Further problems would arise with invading Romans and Anglo-Saxon settlers.

In the Roman and the early Anglo-Saxon periods, much of Britain was held by great lords and the land worked by slaves. The slaves were either imported, as part of the spoils of war, or were the lowly elements of the indigenous population. By the time that the Anglo-Saxons had settled down, it would make good economic sense to ensure that the slaves were self-supporting and self-replenishing. The model for this type of agricultural system could be in the Celtic tribal laws of the indigenous population. That Celts continued to live in England is suggested in evidence from early Anglo-Saxon charters which refer to Kent villages inhabited by Wealhs. They were probably descended from Welsh or Romano-British people, perhaps farming their land in the traditional way (Postan 1972; Kerridge 1973: 43).

One can argue that people living in a tribal boundary zone, such as the upper Thames valley, would be more likely to continue to live in the customary manner than those living in the tribal centre, or close to a Roman town where the influence of new ideas would be more quickly felt. Pastoral products such as hides, wool and cheese are essential to most economies so their marketability would be maintained. In such circumstances there is no need for a rural community to change its way of life. The ownership of the estates, however, may have changed from the multiple ownership of a tribe to the single ownership of a "great lord". How soon this change was reflected in the day-to-day management of the land-units at village level is not known.

5.2.F. THE ANGLO-SAXON PERIOD

This period has long been described as the Dark Ages because so little was known about it. However, a multidisciplinary approach may enlighten the problem of changing agricultural and settlement patterns and continuing land-use at that time.

The comparative peace of the Roman occupation came to an end in the late Fourth and early Fifth Centuries when the Anglo-Saxons came to Britain. It is thought that they arrived at first as mercenaries in the Roman army and that some of them mutinied at Dorchester-on-Thames, took control of the Oxford region and seized some of the local farms. Their descendants became peaceful farmers and the Saxon graves found in north Oxford may have been theirs

(Harden 1956). Archaeologists generally recognise that, although there was stability in social and economic patterns from the Eighth or Seventh Centuries B.C. until the late Fourth Century A.D., communications and the organization of villa estates broke down at the end of the Roman period. It was associated with a discontinuity in settlement patterns and a reduction in arable farming, particularly in rural areas (Hinchliffe & Thomas 1980: 107, 111; Hands & Walker 1981: 256; Robinson & Lambrick 1984). However, where continuity of land-use has been shown, as at Shakenoak, one can only say that it is likely that there may have been a reduction rather than a discontinuity in arable and grassland patterns. Postan (1972) points to the economic sense of continuing to cultivate land, which had been brought to a fine tilth by Iron Age people, during the Roman and Anglo-Saxon periods. Ford (1976: 294) cites several examples of medieval furlongs being aligned on Roman or earlier land divisions in the Warwickshire Avon valley. Archaeological evidence for continuity has been found in Northamptonshire where furlongs in medieval and later open-fields are bounded by earthworks, some of which appear to be of Roman date (Taylor & Fowler 1978; Taylor 1981: 37). If that is the case, then the adjacent pasture and hay meadows would have continued in use. Further research may show a similar situation in the upper Thames valley and so confirm that the Oxford grassland was part of the usual farming pattern at that time (See Hey 2004).

Evidence that the furlongs were divided into strips in the early Saxon period, if they existed then, has not yet come to light. It would be useful to take an opportunity to look at, and interpret, the contents of the Parish boundary ditch. In this area it has right-angled changes in direction, possibly associated with furlongs of arable or, more likely, hay strips.

During the Middle Saxon period many small, scattered settlements were abandoned and nucleated villages came into use. Taylor (1981: 37) puts forward the view that it was at this time that long furlongs were introduced. Their subsequent division, he suggests, was due to an increase in population, ecclesiastical and Royal taxes, and to a greater use of the heavy plough. Taylor suggests that one should look for the date of furlong division in villages where the long furlongs are in the centre and the more usual small furlongs appear to have been laid out beyond the original layout (see below).

5.2.G. THE POLITICAL BACKGROUND

During the Sixth and early Seventh centuries the Thames valley was the political centre of the Kingdom of Wessex (Myres 1954: 99). In the West Saxon campaign of A.D.

584, the Anglo-Saxon Chronicle records the death of Ceawlin's friend Cutha at the battle of Fethanleag in north Oxfordshire. When Ceawlin "returned in anger to his own" he may have buried Cutha under the "*hoga de Cudeslowe*" situated just east of Wolvercote, on the Banbury Road (which the Sheriff of Oxford was ordered to destroy in 1261 (Gelling 1953: 267)). The burial of princes in great barrows is known to have taken place in other parts of the Thames valley at, for example, Taplow and Asthall (between Witney and Burford) and at Cuckhamsley Knob on the Berkshire Downs.

In A.D. 634 St. Birinus became Bishop of the West Saxons at Dorchester-on-Thames, bringing Christianity to the area for the first time, but, by A.D. 670, Mercia had taken Essex, East Anglia and London and had forced the Bishop to move to Winchester, the new centre of Wessex. Mercian kings remained in control and styled themselves "King of All England" from A.D. 757 until Offa's successor, Cenwulf, died in A.D. 821. Thereafter Wessex fought back and regained supremacy after a series of campaigns. The Bishopric of Dorchester was, however, maintained until William I established Remegius at Lincoln before 1087 (Gelling 1953: 267; Myres 1954: 99; Wilson 1960: 31).

The presence of a Bishop at Dorchester-on-Thames led to the establishment of several monasteries in the area. A community predating the Benedictine Abbey of Abingdon was in existence by A.D. 700. In A.D. 727 St. Frideswide is said to have founded the house of nuns and cannons at Oxford on or near the site of the present cathedral (Hassall 1972), as well as a chapel at Binsey, and a large monastery was established at Eynsham in the Ninth Century. The land holding of these religious houses generally followed the pattern of the earlier conglomerate estates. (Documentary evidence shows that the St. Frideswide estate remained intact into the medieval period.) It was not until A.D. 850, however, that pressure from the Danes forced Wessex and Mercia to make peace. Laing (1979: 136) suggests that between A.D. 879 and 892 King Alfred established his line of *burhs* to protect Wessex against the Danes and Davis (1982) has taken back the dating of the Burghal Hidage, which includes Oxford, to *c.* 886.

The defences of these *burhs* consisted of a rampart of earth or turf with a pallisade on top, sharply scarped at the front and more gently sloping at the rear. A ditch generally lay in front of the main earth bank. The remains of such a bank and ditch have been found on the site of 31–34 Church Street, Oxford (Hassall 1972). Within the embankment was a town planned on a grid system with easy access to the walls for defence. By building Oxford at the south end of the Summertown-Radley Terrace the Sandford Gap was easily secured and movement up and down the Thames could be monitored. In addition, its situation on high ground surrounded by alluvial meadows, except on the north side, made it relatively easy to defend. The Burghal Hidage described a situation already well established and Port Meadow could have been given to the burghers when the town was founded, in the hope that they would support Alfred against the Danes.

5.2.H. A CONGLOMERATE ESTATE?

There is a little evidence at present which relates specifically to the Oxford grassland between the Romano-British period and the Eleventh Century, but the place-names of the surrounding villages and their field names show that there continued to be active farmers in the area. It is generally supposed that the mid Anglo-Saxons (7th-9th centuries) practised a well-organised farming system in which meadow and pasture played an essential part. The same may be the case in the Oxford grassland, where a double ditch divided the flood-plain into two parts. That by the river was used for haymaking and grazing, the part away from the river was pasture (Hey 2004). This boundary ditch can still be seen along the northern boundaries of West and Oxley Meads Yarnton and Wolvercote Lot Meadow.

Place-name evidence has been used to support the view that organised agriculture, based on a conglomerate estate with specialist settlements, was practised continuously from the Iron Age through the Anglo-Saxon period in this part of the Thames valley (McDonald 1983). The estate boundaries could have been the rivers Thames, Evenlode (known as Bladene in the earliest documents), Glyme and Cherwell. Belling (1953, 1974: 801) reminds us that these river names are derived from Celtic names and indicate contact between English settlers and the indigenous population. Anglo-Saxon charters mention that the river Evenlode (Bladene) was a boundary on the eastern side of an Eynsham estate to the west (Gelling 1979). The Headington Royal Estate was on both sides of the Cherwell, possibly stretching across to the Seacourt Stream. It may be significant that the southern boundary of the medieval Wootton Hundred (which, with two other Hundreds was administered from Wootton in 1087 (Morris 1978: 1.4)) lay along the southern boundary of the ecclesiastical parish of Wolvercote, while the franchise of Oxford in the early Fifteenth Century included the islands of "Wyke, Bunsey, Midley, Cropley et Portmanseyt" (Rogers 1891: 300) with the boundary itself following the Shiplake Ditch across Port Meadow.

Although elements of an estate are not necessarily contiguous, this estate, like that at Blewbury, Berkshire, could have been centred on a hillfort (Gelling 1974: 812; Ford 1976: 279–280). The hillfort on Bladon Heath, which

may have been deserted in the Iron Age in favour of a site beside the Evenlode at Cassington, is an obvious centre for an estate. It may have included, among others, the early settlements of Woodstock, Wootton, Shipton-on-Cherwell, Bladon, Kidlington, Thrupp, Begbroke, Gosford, Water Eaton, Cassington, Worton, Yarnton and Wolvercote. Their names suggest that they could provide the essential ingredients for a self-supporting conglomerate estate, namely, woodland, arable and grassland. The positions of the last four, with that of Stratfield Farm, lie along the edge of the first gravel terrace as outlined by the 61m contour (see Map 1) (which also outlines the maximum area of flooding). Each of these villages has an Old English name and is more or less equidistant from its neighbours. They may have comprised a network of villages, each specialising in such products as wood (of various sorts and uses), cress, vegetables, horses, sheep and cattle products (McDonald 1983).

The late Seventh or early Eighth Century laws of Ine, King of Wessex, describe a farming system which is considered to be similar to that existing in the Midlands in the same period (Fox 1981: 86; D. Hooke *pers. comm.*). It was, perhaps, also the farming system in the upper Thames valley which, as we have seen was under the influence of Wessex in the Sixth and early Seventh Centuries, but under Mercian rule between *c.* A.D. 670 and 821.

The recorded arable and meadow land of Ine's Celtic subjects may describe an established Celtic Iron Age practice which survived Saxon and Mercian rule as it had survived Roman. One of the laws contains the earliest known reference to "common meadow or other land divided in shares" (Whitlock 1955: 368–9). Although Gelling (1978) suggests that these may be equated with strips or doles, recent research suggests that the shares were blocks of land, rather than scattered strips surrounded by a ring hedge to exclude domestic and wild animals. The owner of each share was responsible for the repair of the part of the hedge adjacent to his land (Fox 1981: 86). These shares could, perhaps, be equated with the long furlongs described by Taylor from archaeological evidence in Northamptonshire (Taylor 1981, 34).

It is not unusual to find the fragmentation of large conglomerate estates, as a result of population pressure and partible inheritance during the middle or late Saxon period. Many settlements became the centres of independent estates which gradually evolved into modern parishes. Within a single pre-Conquest estate in Oxfordshire and Berkshire, for example, one might find four or more parishes which have continued relatively unchanged into the Twentieth Century (Aston 1958: 77; Sawyer 1974: 108; Jones 1976: 35; Gelling 1978: 206). Fox (1981: 100) argues that once arable and pastoral townships became independent they would be forced to find a way to make up the loss of the benefits formerly shared with other vills. Some arable would have to be put down to grass at the same time as pasture was being ploughed by one-time pastoralists in other villages. This is an intensification of farming practice during which the long furlongs may have been subdivided into lots or doles and grouped into furlongs of different sizes. It happened in Avon, Wiltshire, by A.D. 963 and in Himbledon, Worcestershire, by A.D. 975–8 (Hooke 1981: 58).

In Yarnton there were ten hides of common fields by A.D. 970 (or at his death in 982) when Earl Aethelmar left his estates to his son (Edwards 1866: 363). It must have been good land because its value was rated equivalent to 15 hides (10 in Chesterton and 5 in Studley) when Aethelmar obtained it from his kinsman Godwine (Gelling 1979: 138–9). These manors had changed hands again by 1005 when Eynsham Abbey was endowed by Earl Aethelmar; he had obtained them by exchange from his son-in-law, Aethelward (Salter 1907: vii). By this time field name evidence suggests that some land in Yarnton had already been enclosed, perhaps in the early Saxon period, for example the meadow or pasture, called Hayday, south-west of the village and Lincrofts to the south-east (Gelling *pers. comm.*, Hey 2004).

Problems, which the new form of land ownership produced, may have been solved by maintaining links between villages through the continuing common use of woods and pasture and by the eventual evolution of the Medieval three-field organisation which Grey (1915) first described as the Midland System and which Thirsk (1964, 1966) defined as a common-field system with four essential elements.

In the area of the Oxford grassland one might expect to find early settlement and arable fields on the gravel terraces and secondary settlement on brickearth. The clay lands would have been set aside as woodland and wood-pasture until pressure from an expanding population brought them under the plough. Evidence of this has not come to light in Yarnton, but a glance at Parsons' (1636) terrier and a pre-enclosure map of Wolvercote c. 1831 (St. John's College, Oxford, Muniment 58), together with a map of the surface geology, suggests the hypothesis that the church is a focal point in a nucleated settlement, with two crofts of similar size situated on the third gravel terrace to the east. The long furlongs grouped to the north and east are also on the third gravel terrace and include such names as Horslow and Hensler Furlongs. Just as the nearby village of Cutteslow is on the site of Cutha's barrow (see p.66) so these furlongs may be in the area of earlier settlement or funerary activity.

Radiating out from the long furlongs are short furlongs based on brickearth. It is possible that some of their names, for example King's Bush, Brier and Bourton Bush Furlongs reflect an area of scrub, possibly once a settlement, brought into cultivation or, conversely, arable fields left to "tumble down" to scrub, then brought back into the arable fields (Parsons 1636; St. John's College, Oxford, Muniment 58). If Taylor's hypothesis is correct and my tentative interpretation of furlong names is accepted (until a study of earlier versions of the furlong names has been conducted), we have a tantalising glimpse of early fields in Wolvercote. It confirms the hypothesis that there were people farming in Wolvercote in the "Dark Ages", perhaps earlier. They may have exercised rights of intergrazing over Wolvercote Moor and Hurst (as Wolvercote Common was called in the Sixteenth and Seventeenth Centuries) and over Port Meadow.

5.2.1. THE SUBDIVISION OF ESTATES

The campaigns fought by William the Conqueror had a great effect on the Oxford region. Oxford itself was devastated and the monks ran away from Eynsham Abbey presumably leaving the people of Yarnton in the hands of their Reeve (Salter 1907: vii; Morris 1978). The Domesday Book shows that William I did not grant blocks of conquered land to his Norman subjects but granted existing Saxon estates which were already sub-divided. For example, Roger d'Ivri held 9½ hides in Yarnton from the Bishop of Lincoln which belonged to Eynsham Abbey and half a hide (was it the glebe land?) from the Bishop of Bayeaux, who also held Bladon and Cassington (Morris 1978: 6.14, 7.22; Lennard 1959: 52). Earl William of Hereford held Worton and Begbroke, while Water Eaton had gone to Robert d'Oilly who also held Oxford. When Roger d'Ivri was distributing his manors of Holton, Horspath and Wolvercote, he gave Wolvercote and Holton to Godfrey rather than the neighbouring manors of Holton and Horspath (Morris 1978: 59.26, 59.11, 28.5, 29.8, 29.12, 29.23). Lennard (1959: 57) suggests that it would be unwise to give compacted land holdings to tenants who could then become too powerful but, in the light of the evidence of linked manors in Warwickshire (Ford 1976: 274–279) and in Wychwood Forest (Schumer 1984: 42) (which may be reflected in Eynsham's claim to common of pasture in Spelsbury, Oxon, renounced in 1306 (Salter 1907: 178)), the possession of Wolvercote with its 120 acres of meadow and 6x3½ furlongs of pasture would be complemented by the 2x1½ furlongs of woodland in Holton and would, therefore, make economic sense.

Income from the manors was received in the form of food-rents, military and public service, which were important elements in the feudal system carried over from the Saxon period. Oxford was no exception. The burgesses were expected, among other services, to send 20 of their number on a military expedition at the king's request, or pay £20 in lieu. "All burgesses of Oxford have a pasture outside the wall in common, which pays 6s 8d." (Morris 1978). Was this behind the grant of Port Meadow to the Portmen who would need adequate pasture for their war horses? Is it possible that the people of Binsey and Wolvercote already grazed their animals on the Meadow? The continuing fights between the Burgesses and these villages over their right to graze there (see below) suggests that this might be so.

5.2.J. SUMMARY OF ANGLO-SAXON LAND-USE

There is, therefore, evidence in favour of continuity of land-use of the Oxford grassland, beginning with the Bronze Age and Iron Age Celtic settlements on Port Meadow. During the Roman period, additional, and hitherto marginal, land in the Cotswolds was drained and brought into production, encouraging silt-laden floods in the valley bottom. Romano-British people abandoned their floodplain settlements and moved to drier ground on the first gravel terrace. The comparatively lush pasture of Wolvercote Common and Port Meadow continued to be grazed, however, by the flocks and herds of the people of Wolvercote and Wick (which Anthony Wood indicated was south west of Medley (Peshall 1773: 322). West and Oxford Meads, Yarnton, Wolvercote Lot Meadow and Picksey Mead, with their accumulating alluvium, were probably set aside for hay, perhaps from the spring solstice until about Midsummer Day, and then grazed by the herds and flocks of the people of Begbroke, Yarnton and Wolvercote until the following spring solstice or until the land was flooded. This practice may have undergone little change in Roman and Saxon times. Even when vills were moved from one part of an estate to another as the arable fields became infertile through overuse, the pasture and meadowland remained an important part of the economy. For administrative reasons, however, the conglomerate estate had been broken up into several manors of 5 or 10 hides each by Earl Aethelmar's death in the Tenth Century. There remains the impression, supported by archaeological, place-name and Anglo-Saxon Charter evidence, of the continued use of the Oxford grassland from the Iron Age to Domesday.

5.2.K. MEDIEVAL PERIOD – PORT MEADOW WITH WOLVERCOTE COMMON

The name Port Meadow is misleading. It. was first recorded in c.1285 (Gelling 1953) but there is no record of the land ever having been used for hay making, except during the Civil War (Clark 1891: 92; Ogle 1892). The name Port is likely to date back to the early years of Oxford. By that time most people were Christian and congregated for worship every day, often remaining near the church to buy and sell. The law frowned on transactions not conducted under the

eye of responsible officials who would see to it that tolls were paid, so regular markets, preferably in towns, were introduced. At a time when the military significance of the word *burh* was uppermost in the public mind, legislators applied another word, "port", borrowed from the administrative terminology of the Carolingians, to denote a market town, whether inland or on the coast (Applebaum 1972). King Edward the Elder (A.D. 899–924) prohibited all buying and selling, except in ports, and the English spoke of portmen where the Normans later on would speak of burgesses. The officer who collected the tolls and taxes for the king and whose presence authenticated commercial transactions, was called a "portreeve" (Harden 1956). The fact that the earliest record of Port Meadow in *c.* 1185 is to "Portmanneheit" i.e. the island of the Portmen (Gelling 1953) suggests that it had been given to the city before it was influenced by the Normans.

The size of the island given to the Portmen before Domesday is not known. It may have formed part of the Headington Royal estate, which may have extended westwards to the Seacourt Stream, before it was divided into the Headington and Northgate Hundreds. If this is so, then the Portmen's island was bounded by the Seacourt Stream on the west, Shiplake Ditch (a slow moving stream in the early Saxon period (Gelling 1953: 34)), and the stream which is now the Oxford canal to the east. In 1004 Ethelred confirmed Binsey island to the Monastery of St. Frideswide (see above) and this was again confirmed by the Empress Maud in 1142 when the island of Langney was added (Salter 1936). In 1138 the Burgesses gave "fenneit and Crepeleit" (Fidlers' Island and Cripley) *c.* 150 acres, to St. Frideswide and then rented it from them as grazing or hay for the Freemen's animals. After the dissolution of the monasteries they were enclosed in 1568 and 1532 respectively (Wigram 1894; Turner 1880).

In 1138 the Burgesses gave Midelheit (now Medley) to the town and then in 1147 to the Canons of Osney, on condition that they paid half a mark wherever bidden, in order to relieve themselves of the 6s 8d they owed to the king (Salter 1931). The ensuing dispute was not settled until 1191 when a Charter was signed giving Medley to Osney, and in a complicated agreement with the Monastery of St. Frideswide, the Burgesses agreed to pay them a yearly rent for Medley, and then granted the island to Osney at a slightly lower rent. This document is, incidentally, particularly interesting as it is the earliest known Oxford Charter in existence; is the first one which demonstrates that Oxford had an independent corporate body, and its seal is the earliest municipal seal in Great Britain (Davis 1968).

In 1148, when the buildings of Godstow Monastery were completed, the Burgesses endowed it with the "land in

Portmanneit which Sagrim held". This is probably Wycroft closes (in the northern part of Burgess Field Nature Park) amounting to *c.* 14 acres on the east side of Port Meadow, and "wyke, in portmanneit" which may be the island south of Port Meadow mentioned in an early Fourteenth Century charter of St. Frideswide (Clark 1906; Rogers 1891; Salter 1936).

Recent hypotheses relating the origin of common-field systems to a pre-Conquest period have been put forward and discussed by Taylor (1981) and those relating to their development and management, particularly after the Conquest, by, for example, Havinden (1961), Thirsk (1964, 1966), Titow (1965), and have been summarised by Dodgshon (1980). Their ideas were influenced by writers intent upon improving husbandry such as Walter of Henley (Oschinsky 1971) and Grosstete in the Thirteenth Century (Trans. Cripps-Day 1931) and by Fitzherbert (1523a; 1523b) in the Sixteenth Century. They gave advice on the advantages of enclosure, which nevertheless rendered many tenant farms unviable. Agricultural improvements in the common fields could not, however, be carried out in areas where the commoners could not agree on the new procedures.

The two- versus the three- or four-field crop rotation, which included the growing of clover, trefoil and sainfoin made into hay for winter fodder, may have reduced the value of hay meads, particularly those away from the village and situated near the parish boundary. The literature has to be read carefully because the binomial nomenclature of the plant and animal kingdoms was not invented by Linneaus (1707–1778) until the Eighteenth Century. For example, Ellis (1731: 80) and North (1759: 23–33) mentioned by Fussell (1950) refer to new or artificial grasses when they apparently mean sainfoin or other legumes and not new varieties of Gramineae such as ryegrass (*Lolium perenne*). An introduction to this literature is to be found in Fussell (1947, 1950). Fascinating as the agricultural and economic implications are, they relate to a general study of agricultural history and are not directly relevant to this specific study of the continuity of land-use of the Oxford grassland. It is, however, useful to allude to farming practices recorded in the Thames valley which may have been similar to those of the Oxford grassland.

5.2.L. IMPACT OF COMMON RIGHTS OF GRAZING

It is recorded that in 1279, the Abbess of Godstow's demesne yardlands in Wolvercote had common rights of pasture in Port Meadow attached to them (Crossley 1979). These are not the same as the "cottagers' rights" on which the rights of many of the Wolvercote Commoners are based today. This gift of land may have contributed to the

Nunnery's claim to Port Meadow which was contested by the Freemen in, for example, 1285, 1405 and 1518, until the matter was resolved in 1562 (Ogle 1892).

The Intercommoning Agreement (1562) (Turner 1880) indicates that intercommoning was still practised on Port Meadow and Wolvercote Common in the Sixteenth Century. This ancient method of farm management was described by Fitzherbert (1523b) as "common per cause of vicinage". It was a prescriptive right in which all the villages surrounding a piece of waste land (now called common land) had the right to graze their beasts on it. Commons "by cause of neighbourhood" were enjoyed only if the animals were in charge of a herdsman. Tethering animals on such common land was not allowed (Fitzherbert 1523b). Similarly in Clanfield, Oxfordshire, there were rights of intercommoning which predated the twofield system and were enjoyed by neighbouring settlements each with its own arable and fields (Pocock 1968). The origins of the rights over Port Meadow are probably of this nature. They may have survived the Royal Grant of Port Meadow to the Burgesses of Oxford at its founding *c.* 885. The Agreement between the Lord of the Manor of Wolvercote and the Freemen of Oxford, in 1562, mentioned that Wolvercote farmers could be stinted according to their yardland. These were "farmers' rights" or rights appendant. "Cottagers' rights" or rights appurtenant, as they are called, are acquired by prescription and were ignored. They must have been practised by a few tenants as they have continued to be exercised up to the present day. Prescriptive grazing rights to the Meadow did not receive official recognition, however, until 1972, when they were registered according to the Commons Registration Act 1965. As a result of the growth of Wolvercote and an increase in the number of suburban horse owners, they became the most important rights over the Meadow (Crossley 1979). The new status of the grazing rights means that they can now be let or sold, provided that the total number of animals registered is not increased.

There is no evidence of common rights to take turf, marl or gravel from Port Meadow, and any person caught removing such material was fined (Turner 1880). Nevertheless, large parts of both Port Meadow and Wolvercote Common have had gravel extracted (see Map 5) at some time in the past. Some of it will have been used by the Lord of the Manor of Wolvercote who had had the right to use it since 1562 at least, to mend the banks on Port Meadow and Wolvercote Common and for other necessities (Ogle 1892). However, in the course of the present survey a large bare patch was seen in the area of *Galium verum* (Type L) grassland, from which the turf had been illegally removed. Common grazing rights are based on customary law and, particularly on Port Meadow with Wolvercote Common, have been the subject of disagreements between the Freemen of Oxford and the owners of the Manors of Binsey and Wolvercote on many occasions (Hobson 1939, 1954, 1962; Hobson & Salter 1933; Turner 1880; Salter 1928; Bodleian Library G.A.Oxon.c.56; Christ Church Muniments relating to Binsey). Some of these are discussed below in relation to the very complex matter of managing the Meadow in the Twentieth Century.

5.2.M. REGULATING THE GRAZING

Stinting was at first very simple. Each Freeman was allowed to graze one beast (perhaps his war horse). In the Fourteenth Century when the population probably declined significantly, stinting may have lapsed. It would have been revived in the Fifteenth Century when the growth of the wool industry increased the value of even marginal pasture. By 1569 there were between 400 and 450 Freemen and the regulation of stints had become very sophisticated (see Table 22) there were 3 or 4 drives of the Meadow each year and a herdsman was employed to look after the Freemen's animals (Turner 1880).

FREEMEN	NO. OF BEASTS
The Mayor	8
Every Alderman	6
All Ex-Mayors	5
Every Bailiff	4
Every Chamberlain	3
All Common Councillors	2
Each of the Commonalty	1

TABLE 23. THE SIXTEENTH-CENTURY FREEMEN OF OXFORD REGULATED THE NUMBER OF ANIMALS GRAZING ON PORT MEADOW.

A Freeman's grazing rights in 1972 were registered as part of those of the Freemen body. They were rights in gross, personal to each Freeman not to his property, and could not in any way be loaned or assigned. (Register of Commons 1972; Campbell & Claden 1973). They would lapse when they died. The Freemen of Oxford remedied this anomaly by inserting a Clause in Section 27 of the Oxfordshire Act 1985. Their success was of great importance to holders of similar rights elsewhere in England and Wales.

The number of Freemen of Oxford at any one time may have a considerable bearing on the density of grazing on Port Meadow. Table 24 indicates the extent to which numbers of Freemen may have fluctuated during the last 450 years or so.

DATE	NO. OF FREEMEN
1520	300 – 350
1570	400 – 450
1630	c. 1,040
1650	c. 500
1835	2,500
1902	480
1923	300
1960	111
1973	178
1979	246

TABLE 24. FLUCTUATIONS IN THE NUMBER OF FREEMEN OF OXFORD MAY REFLECT THE GRAZING PRESSURES ON THE MEADOW

From the Fifteenth to the Nineteenth Centuries the Meadow was generally managed by Bailiffs acting for the Mayor and all the Freemen. Although a Freeman had the right to depasture an animal on Port Meadow, he was only allowed to exercise it on condition that he had somewhere to keep the cattle or horses during the winter. The Meadow was "hayned" i.e. left free from all manner of beasts from the 25th March until the 1st May each year (Turner 1880; Salter 1928). This allowed the grass to grow and the floods to go down. The Bailiffs appointed a herdsman to look after the animals. Any mangy cattle or horses infected with "the glaunders of the chyne" had to be killed (Turner 1880).

In 1920 there were 20 Freemen using their grazing rights (Oxford Freemen 1960-69). In 1969 the Freemen registered grazing rights for 350 cattle and 350 horses on both Port Meadow and Wolvercote Common. At the moment these are unstinted, because only one Freeman exercises his right. If more than a third of these rights were taken up, it would be in the interests of the Freemen to limit the number of grazing animals to the carrying capacity of the land. This would amount to not more than 400 cattle or 200 horses during the growing season. However, stinting can only be ordered at a meeting of Common Hall (the meeting of Freemen) with the Freemen's unanimous agreement and it is unlikely that the Freemen will want to put any controls on grazing until this pattern changes.

The Freemen have, in fact, increased the number of grazing animals by issuing 30 "permits" (valued at £25 p.a. in 1982) to allow Oxford people who are not Freemen to graze animals on the Meadow. This precedent was followed by the Wolvercote Commoners' Committee which issues 30 free permits to people living in Wolvercote who do not have registered grazing rights attached to their property. They did this in the belief that rights could not be sold or let, that many people living in Wolvercote did not register their rights and that, there should be a way in which village youngsters could enjoy owning and riding a pony without having to go outside the village for its pasture. However,

71

as a result of pressure from dealers and others wishing to put animals on the Meadow for commercial purposes, the fact that rights could be sold or let came to light after the Sheriff's Round-up in July 1984.

The Register of Commons shows the maximum number of animals allowed to graze on Port Meadow and Wolvercote Common. It is evident that in registering grazing rights no heed was paid to good pasture management. The number of animals allowed to graze the 400 acres is 1,365 horses, 1,890 cattle, 6 donkeys, together with 48 ducks and 1,192 geese. Of these, 451 horses and 832 cattle graze by right appendant. The others are rights appurtenant attached to suburban properties with no stables or even sheds in which to keep horses and cattle over the winter. Today, management of the Meadow is complex. It. is carried out by Oxford City Council through the Housing and Estates Committee which directs the City Officers, as owners of Port Meadow and Trustees of Wolvercote Common under the Commons Registration Act 1965. The Sheriff of Oxford, as Conservator of Port Meadow, has the responsibility to hold an annual drive (usually just before leaving office early in May). The date is usually "leaked" and illegal graziers remove their animals before they can be impounded. Owners with grazing rights or permits may retrieve their animals for a fine of 2p; those without rights pay a fine of £25 per head which, by today's values is very cheap grazing. The City Council looks after the boundaries, ditches, bridges and weed control. Apart from the money brought in by the drive they receive no income to balance the expenditure on this work.

The Lord of the Manor of Wolvercote had ceased to exercise his rights by the Second World War. The interests of Wolvercote Common are now looked after by the Wolvercote Commoners' Committee, which took over from Woodstock Rural District Council in 1928. It passes recommendations on to the Oxford City Housing and Estates Committee when it considers that the bridges, fences or ditches need repairing, but makes its own arrangements for cutting thistles and pulling ragwort. It obtains money for this by letting the Common for allotment gardens, fairs and other activities. It takes a keen interest in the quality of the grassland, but has no power to limit, or extend the grazing. When the floods are particularly high (Photograph 7) animals are taken off the Meadow at the request, of the Thames Valley Police and the Royal Society for the Prevention of Cruelty to Animals.

On paper the grassland and grazing on the Meadow is looked after by the Joint Management Committee of Freemen and Wolvercote Commoners (JMC) in association with Oxford City Estates Department and the Nature Conservancy Council. Methods of weed control

are discussed and agreed by the JMC and implemented, more or less, by them or the City Estates Department (see Chapter 6.3.B. Weed Control.). The need for regulating the grazing animals is also discussed. In practice this management, is ineffectual.

The JMC has proposed a plan to hold drives on other occasions but they cannot agree with the City Solicitor on the distribution of an income from a drive. The position is that the JMC and most members of the Wolvercote Commoners Committee understand that the grazing should be regulated but have no power at present. The graziers themselves have not yet seen the need to band together to call for a management plan under the Commons Registration Act.

5.2.N. ENCLOSURE/ENCROACHMENT

Problems arising from enclosure of manorial waste and encroachment have been the subject of disputes since at least the Thirteenth Century. Yates (1974), for example, cites several disputes arising in Staffordshire because pasture and wood pasture had been enclosed without the consent of fellow intercommoners or tenants. The Statutes of Merton (1235) and Westminster (1285) were brought in partly to alleviate these problems by attempting to control encroachment of the common pasture by the Lord of the Manor in particular. It was set down that sufficiency of pasture should be left for the grazing of all the tenants' or freeholders' animals for which there were rights over the area (Yates 1974). It was not, therefore, a unique situation when disputes between the Burgesses of Oxford and the Abbess of Godstow, who owned Wolvercote Common, continually arose about the ownership and management of the grazing animals over the Meadow (Turner 1880; Crossley 1979). In 1285 and 1405 the Abbess was accused of enclosing large parts of the Meadow; in 1494 when the Mayor and Bailiffs were charged with unlawful seizure of cattle at Wolvercote they claimed that all the Meadow lay in Oxford; in 1518 there was an affray on the Meadow between the Bailiffs and the Wolvercote husbandmen (Crossley 1979).

After the dissolution of Godstow Abbey, Wolvercote Manor was bought by Dr George Owen, Physician to Henry VIII, who considered that Wolvercote More and Hurst, Port Meadow and Cripley were all part of the estates of Godstow Nunnery and Rewley Abbey which he had received in 1541. The Burgesses had apparently been quick to take advantage of the lack of supervision of monastery land and were accused of enclosing Cripley in 1530. Dr Owen, encouraged by the University, sued the Mayor and Burgesses with the result that in 1552 the Privy Council forbade the renewal of leases of Cripley, told them to withdraw their sheep from Cripley and Port Meadow and to stop digging and raising the banks in the pastures until the matter of controversy between the City and Owen had been settled (Turner 1880). This was not very effective. On the 4th September, 1561, Mr Roger Tailler was given permission to fetch earth from Port Meadow to "mend his mounds of Cripley".

Both parties agreed to put mere stones on the boundary and not to enclose any land. Both parties, or their heirs, have tried to enclose and encroach on Port Meadow and Wolvercote Common but with varying success. In 1582 the Burgesses agreed to build a house for the herdsman above Port Meadow Gate. It fell down in 1629. In 1603, 1608 and 1625 temporary cabins were built beside it on Port Meadow for the use of plague victims (Turner 1880). In 1649 it was suggested that Port Meadow be enclosed and let, the money to go to the poor. Similar proposals were made in 1762, 1843, 1853 and 1923 to clear the City's debt (Hobson 1962; Salter 1928; Bodleian Library G.A.Oxon. c.56). In the Nineteenth Century Wolvercote people made "gardens" on the Common which were then built upon and became known as the Rookery.

In 1781 the owner of Wolvercote Common, the Duke of Marlborough, sold some of the Common to the Canal Company and effectively isolated what is now called Wolvercote Green and Goose Green from the rest of the pasture. In 1845 and 1850 more of Wolvercote Common was sold off, this time to the Railway Companies, while the Freemen and the City of Oxford sold part of Port Meadow to the same companies, and again, in 1941, a small part of Wolvercote Common was sold to the Great Western Railway Company (Oxford City Records PS.31, P26; Minn 1939).

Sometimes attempts to enclose part of the pasture for commercial purposes have been stopped by the Freemen. In 1896, for example, Mr Smith started a boat-building business on the Port Meadow bank of the Thames at Medley, he dug a slipway 5ft wide and 15ft into the Meadow which the Freemen asked him to fill in. He refused on the grounds that he had the Sheriff's permission (the Sheriff was the principal shareholder) and there the matter rested until another Sheriff was appointed and the Freemen were able to hold a public meeting after which the slipway was filled in and the bank made good in record time (Leach 1923).

Similarly, there was a problem at Medley Boat Station, on Port Meadow in the Twentieth Century. Despite the 1925 Law of Property Act and the 1965 Commons Registration Act, the proprietors of Medley Boat Station have expanded their business from the river onto the common land. An attempt by Oxford City Council to contain the business

was made in the High Court in 1979. In 1980, under Planning Law, Enforcement Notices were contested and the Appeal Inspector found in favour of Medley Boat Station. In January 1984 under Section 194 of the 1925 Law of Property Act, Oxford City Council, with Somerton Marine Ltd., (owners of Medley Boat Station) applied to the Secretary of State for permission to make part of Port Meadow into a boat yard. The application was made in the hope that the outcome would enable a "compromise agreement" to be reached to settle the High Court Case out of Court. Such an application is unusual because Local Authorities have a statutory obligation to protect common land from encroachment including encroachment by commercial companies. It can also be argued that there is some irregularity when the Local Authority is in a position to gain financially from such an application. Eventually, in 1989, Somerton Marine was bought out by Oxford City Council, the High Court case settled and the illegal houseboats given a licence to remain until the houseboat was let, sold or scrapped. Wolvercote Green also suffered from encroachment and plans to legalise parking on the common land foundered.

5.2.O. MEDIEVAL PERIOD – PICKSEY MEAD

Traditionally, hay meads as well as arable fields have been divided up into lots or doles. In Oxfordshire these are sometimes called "men's mowths" which is the amount of hay that can be cut by scythe in one day. Two methods of allocating these strips were practised to ensure that each farmer had an equal stake in the common fields and meadows. One method was to accord a particular farm every first or third strip (Dodgshon 1980: 33) or, as in some Welsh examples, account was taken of the position of the farmer's ox in the ploughteam (Seebohm 1914: 5). The second and possibly earlier method was to use a lottery. Examples of each have been found in the upper Thames valley. For example, in Begbroke, one farm was allocated every fifth strip in the common field in the 16th century, while in Cuxham in 1357 the hay was allocated by lot (Harvey 1965, 29).

A variant of this system which is called "intercommoning", was practised in Cuxham and Pyrton, Oxfordshire, until at least 1501 (Harvey 1965: 99, 100) and in North Aston, Oxfordshire, where the hay in Bestmoor was shared between two neighbouring parishes of North Aston and Duns Tew using tokens (or were they brand marks?) bearing the names Crown, Millrind, Snipe, plus some others, pictures of which may at one time have been scratched on tokens for allocating the hay by lot (Crossley 1990).

Similarly, some of the tokens which were used at Burford were called:

Double Cross	Pit and Dock
Single Cross	Pitt and Dockseed
Two Pitts	Pitt and Thorn
Three Pitts	Pitt and Stone

(Gretton 1920: 408)

It would be worth looking to see whether there is another set of tokens in Burford or a neighbouring village, with the names Pitt, Dock, Dockseed, Thorn and Stone (making a total of thirteen shares), which would be a logical start to the Burford series of names. There is no record of what the tokens actually looked like, but they seem to have been similar to the tokens used in Scotland to identify holdings or shares in the land. The Scottish tokens had the same character as those used in the act of seisin when property ownership passed from one person to another. They could take the form of earth, turf, stones, sticks or batons. Finberg was able to document their relevance to land holding as early as the Eleventh Century (Dodgshon 1980: 33).

The days recommended for cutting the hay, or for sowing seed are according to the pre-Gregorian calendar and so are 11 days earlier than what might otherwise be expected. Mowing should begin in the latter end of June in a good season when the hay is lush and green. To delay until July not only reduced the value of the hay crop but also interfered with the organization of the grain harvest. It took longer to make green hay, but the crop was more valuable because it had not shed its nutritious seeds and become dry and hard and, therefore, difficult to eat (Fitzherbert 1523b: 19).

Fitzherbert, a Circuit Judge (Fussell 1947: 6), whose work may well have taken him into the upper Thames valley, suggested that Quicke hay was the best for horses and beasts. It could be recognised by the presence of what he called Crofote:

"a plant growing flat, after the earth, with a yellow flower at least 18 inches high"

(Fitzherbert 1523b: 19)

This might be one of several plants, possibly a crowfoot in the Ranunculaceae, but bird's-foot trefoil (*Lotus corniculatus*) seems the most likely. It is a perennial plant with a yellow flower procumbent to ascending stems which grows up to 50cm tall (Stace 1997: 406). It is found in both pastures and meadows and, in view of Jones and Lyttleton's (1971) work on legumes that do not cause bloat, it is a particularly useful plant. Fitzherbert may have had in mind hay from alluvial meadows such as Picksey Mead.

From at least the Thirteenth Century people were aware of the different qualities of grassland and of the varying needs of their animals. That this is the case can be shown

by using the work of just two of several agricultural writers of the period. For example, Walter of Henley (Trans. Cripps-Day 1931: 84) could advocate the use of salt-marsh as prime pasture for dairy cattle when wood pasture, the aftermath in a meadow and the stubble after harvest were not so profitable in terms of the quantity of cheese and butter made in a season. (Each season ended on St. Michael's Day (29 September) in order to maintain the quality of the calves to be borne the following spring.) Both Walter of Henley and, later, Fitzherbert (1523b: 19), recommended that the hay should be cut by the Nativity of St. John (24th June) and that it should be properly dried and thatched before it could be spoilt by rain.

Anthony Fitzherbert (1523a) wrote the first English published text (Fussell 1947: 4) in which a thorough knowledge of both farming practice and customary farming management is displayed. Fitzherbert makes it clear that fields held in severalty were more valuable because the timing of tillage or pasture could be varied according to the weather and other factors, whereas the management of the common fields was regulated according to the Church calendar. He recommended that where there were common rights over a pasture, these rights should be stinted according to each man's yards, lands, or gages rents, a practice which was established over Port Meadow probably earlier than 1562 (Ogle 1892) and which reflected the number of animals each tenant farmer could keep under cover during the winter months.

How far the presence of pastures, in which cattle, horses, sheep or geese were grazed, implies an understanding on the part of farmer, of the feeding preferences of his stock, and the nutritional value of the different plants which make up a sward is difficult to determine. However, Fitzherbert appreciated the importance of grassland management in obtaining a high quality in pasture and meadow and particularly of controlling the amount of grazing in a pasture if its quality was to be maintained (Fitzherbert 1523b: 19). Port Meadow with Wolvercote Common would have benefited during periods such as those documented in the Sixteenth Century (Turner 1880) when the grazing was well controlled. Fitzherbert's criticisms of "rich men" who buy young cattle and put them out to graze in the early summer, and sell them in winter, might well be applied to legal and illegal users of the Meadow today.

The earliest record of Picksey Mead dates as far back as 1142, when Picksey Mead was given to Godstow Nunnery; the endowment included 5s for it to be mown on the Nativity of St. John's Day. This, incidentally, is a quarter day when payments are generally made and the day when a three-day fair began in Fair Close, south-west of Toll Bridge (Clark 1906: 651, 659). Such fairs frequently included an employment exchange, and extra mowers may have been readily available to cut hay which was normally harvested by that date (Walter of Henley in Cripps-Day 1931: 74; Fitzherbert 1523b).

Begbroke, Yarnton, Wolvercote and, possibly, Wytham all had rights of intercommoning in Picksey Mead but the limited evidence available suggests that since the Sixteenth Century at least, those of Yarnton and Begbroke were managed differently from the other two villages. Their rights to a customary acre in Picksey Mead were vested in the ownership of a token in the form of a small cherry-wood ball (see Photograph 10). At first the owner of a ball would receive one customary acre every time it was drawn so that each farmer had the chance of getting some good and some poor hay each year. The number of times the

balls, or set of tokens, were drawn differed according to the amount of meadowland available. In Burford there were four 'shots' or divisions of meadowland (Gretton 1920) while in Yarnton and Begbroke there were ten (two in Picksey Mead, five in West Mead, three in Oxhey Mead). The method of dividing the customary acres and allocating the lots is described in Appendix G.

Men's mowths were associated with a feudal villein's holding in the arable fields (Thomas, 1856; Gretton 1912: 55). Day (Crossley 1990) suggests that in Yarnton and Begbroke, neighbouring villages with hay and grazing rights in Picksey Mead, a customary acre was associated with a one-hide estate and with the ownership of a cherry-wood ball with which lots could be drawn (see Appendix H). Upon each of the balls one of the following names has been written:

William of Bladon, Parry, Geoffrey, Boat, White, Boulton or Bolton, Green, Rothe, Freeman, Harry, Watery Molly, Dunn and Gilbert.

These names can be equated with people recorded in the Hundred Rolls of Edward I as living in Yarnton and Begbroke in 1279. Some of the families represented by the balls are also recorded in the Yarnton Tax Assessments for 1317 and 1327 (Crossley 1990) but not in the Augmentation Office record for 1537, or a Churchwarden's notebook in 1615 (Exeter College Muniments; Stapleton 1893: 263). It is possible, therefore, that the balls were named sometime between 1279 (when the Hundred Rolls were made) and 1317 (when the tax assessment shows that the families in Yarnton were already changing). The names may indicate a re-allocation of the arable and meadowland in the late Thirteenth Century.

In Yarnton, at the end of the Thirteenth Century, there was a change in ownership of the Manor and, in 1294, settlement of a dispute over the hay tithes between Eynsham Abbey, as Rectors of Yarnton, and Rewley Abbey, the new owner. As a Cistercian foundation, Rewley was normally exempt from tithe (Thomas 1856). It is possible that the named families were living on the original homesteads in the village. Where there was expansion into the wastes and woodlands, the original holdings usually monopolised and maintained the rights of common (Feiling 1950).

Photograph 10. The late Mr E. Harris, First Meadsman, holding the cherry-wood balls used for allocating the hay on Picksey Mead by lot. 1983.

Photograph 11. The nineteenth-century merestone which separated the Begbroke Tydalls from those of Yarnton on Picksey Mead. It was rescued by Mr E. Harris after a contractor had cast the others into the Thames. Undoubtedly it had been placed on or near to previous stones. The Tydalls means land set aside in lieu of tythe.

Later evidence suggests that those responsible for managing Picksey Mead may have kept the traditional dates for closing the mead at Candlemas (2nd February), and cut the hay on or about the nativity of St. John the Baptist (24th June). The second crop may have been taken in late August, before opening the Mead for grazing again from Michaelmas (29th September) to Candlemas, floods permitting. It was, perhaps, at this time that the Tydalls or Tithalls were marked out with merestones (see Photograph 11). They were situated in the best part of the Mead (Stapleton 1893) in lieu of the Rectorial tithes due from the lot owners. The Rector of Yarnton (Exeter College) owned 2 acres and the Rector of Begbroke, 1 acre. When the population of Yarnton and Begbroke increased, the customary acres could be subdivided longitudinally into four divisions, or men's mowths, which were also known as a "yard" or "yerd", presumably meaning "belonging to a yardland".

Where land was enclosed in Yarnton in the Fifteenth and Sixteenth Centuries, the meadow lots survived, although the area on the ground may have been reduced (Leadham

1897: 386; Stapleton 1893). Similarly, in 1958, when six acres of Picksey Mead were taken in by the Oxford bypass, the remainder was divided up into 26 smaller lots (Map 10) and the ceremony of drawing the lots was recorded at a Public Inquiry in 1936 (Appendix H). It is, however, relevant to point out here that the Statutes of Merton (1235) and Westminster (1285) were brought in to control enclosure/encroachment of the common pasture by the Lord of the Manor in particular. It was set down that sufficient waste should be left for the grazing of all the tenants' animals (Richardson 1974). These Statutes must also have applied to the encroachment of lot meads, which were an equally important part of a tenant's yardland.

5.2.P. WATER MEADOWS

Stamp (1948: 78–82) and Kerridge (1953: 105–18) refer to the practice of "floating" specially constructed water meadows in order to provide an early bite for ewes in spring and an extra bite when pasture becomes short later in the year. Tucker (1978/9) points out that they were also used to increase hay production and that near Edinburgh a water meadow was said to have produced six hay crops in one year. It was a practice most used in calcareous areas of chalk and limestone in the North and South Downs and the Southern Cotswolds. Ridges or "beds" were formed along which channels containing streams directed water which overflowed down the ridge into the adjacent furrow and then into other channels where it was directed back into the river. Young (1813: 265) stated that there was "No watered meadow in the county" of Oxfordshire. This was true until 1843–5 when the Duke of Marlborough had 69 acres of alluvial meadow near Bladon converted into water meadow (Sutton 1962–3).

In 1608 the rent for 4 acres (the 4th, 5th, 6th, and 7th closes) in Picksey Mead was £3 2s. per annum (15s. 6d. per acre), on condition that not more than half an acre was ploughed up for water furrows without the consent of the Lord of the Manor of Wolvercote (St. John's College, Oxford, Muniment 89). Could this have been a reference to water meadow (as opposed to flood meadow) management which was being promoted in Wiltshire, Gloucestershire, Dorset and Berkshire at that time (Fussell 1950: 121; Sheail 1971a)? Before the river dredgings raised the banks of Picksey Mead (in the Twentieth and, perhaps, the Seventeenth Centuries) it would have been feasible to abstract water from between King's Weir and Wolvercote Mill Weir for irrigating at least part of Picksey Mead. The water would have drained away through the ditch system which emptied into the river near Godstow Bridge. No structural evidence has been found to prove that this occurred on Picksey Mead.

The Duke of Marlborough's Piece

317

318

319

The Yarnton Farmers' Piece

316

320

Wytham Piece

321

322

323 324

325

326

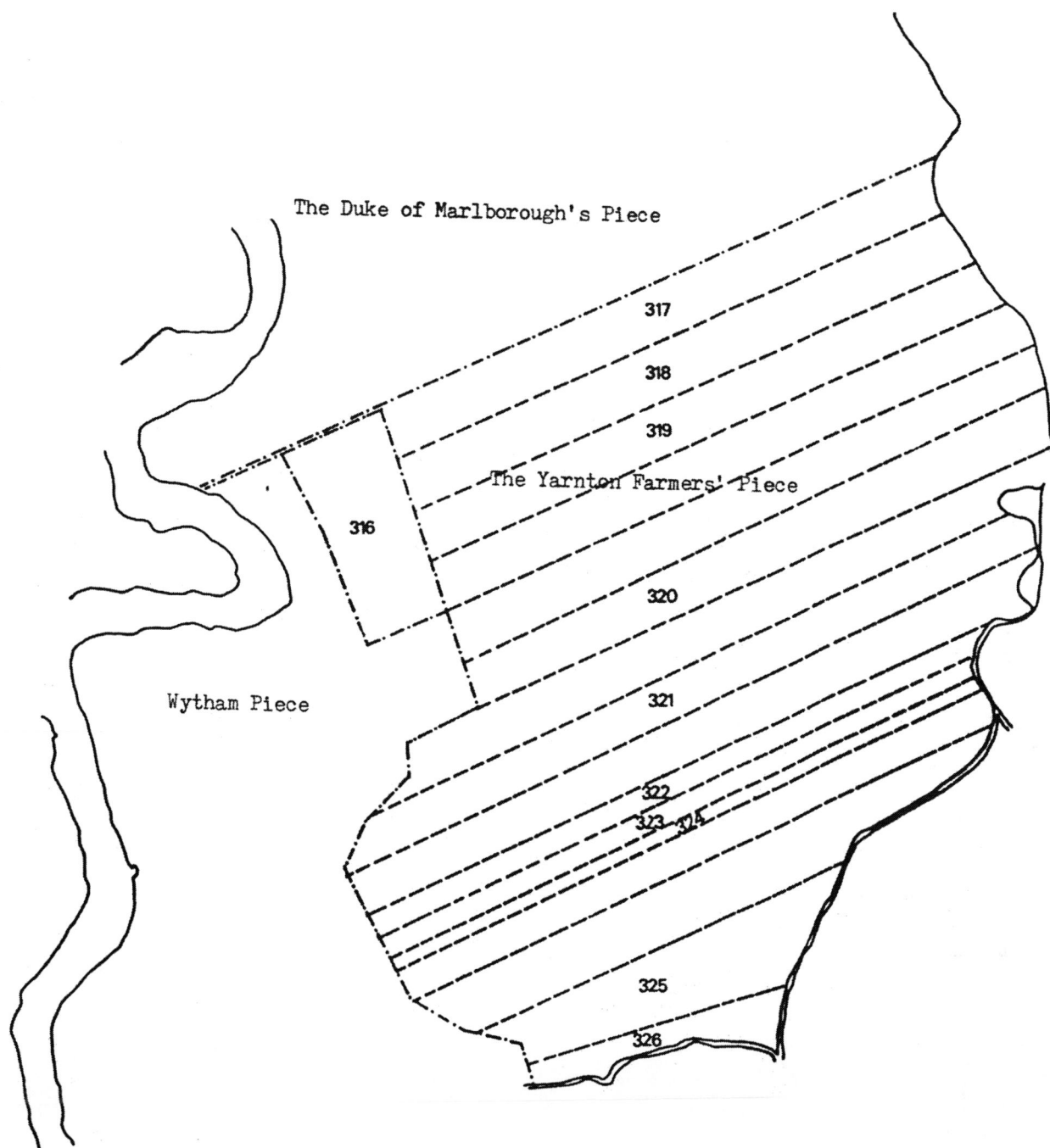

Map 10a. Redistribution of the hay lots on Picksey Mead 1845

5.2.Q. SIXTEENTH CENTURY LAMMAS LAND

The earliest existing survey of the Manor of Wolvercote was made at the dissolution of Godstow Nunnery in 1535. The demesne lands in Picksey Mead included 52a 2r 30p valued at £4. (*c.* 18d. per acre) plus 40 acres which were common "*post prima vestur*" (after the first cut) also valued at 18d. each. The latter are the customary acres commmon to Begbroke and Yarnton. It is not known whether or not Picksey Mead was

Lammas land, (i.e. open to grazing on the 1st August with the implication that only one crop of hay was taken, before the Sixteenth Century or) like South Mead (25 acres) in the same survey, it may have been open to grazing after St. Michael's Day (29th September). This would have allowed two hay crops to be taken each year (Valor Ecclesiasticus (Rec. Com.) 1535: 191). The site of South Mead has not been established. It might have been the south west part of Picksey Mead now referred to as the Wytham Piece.

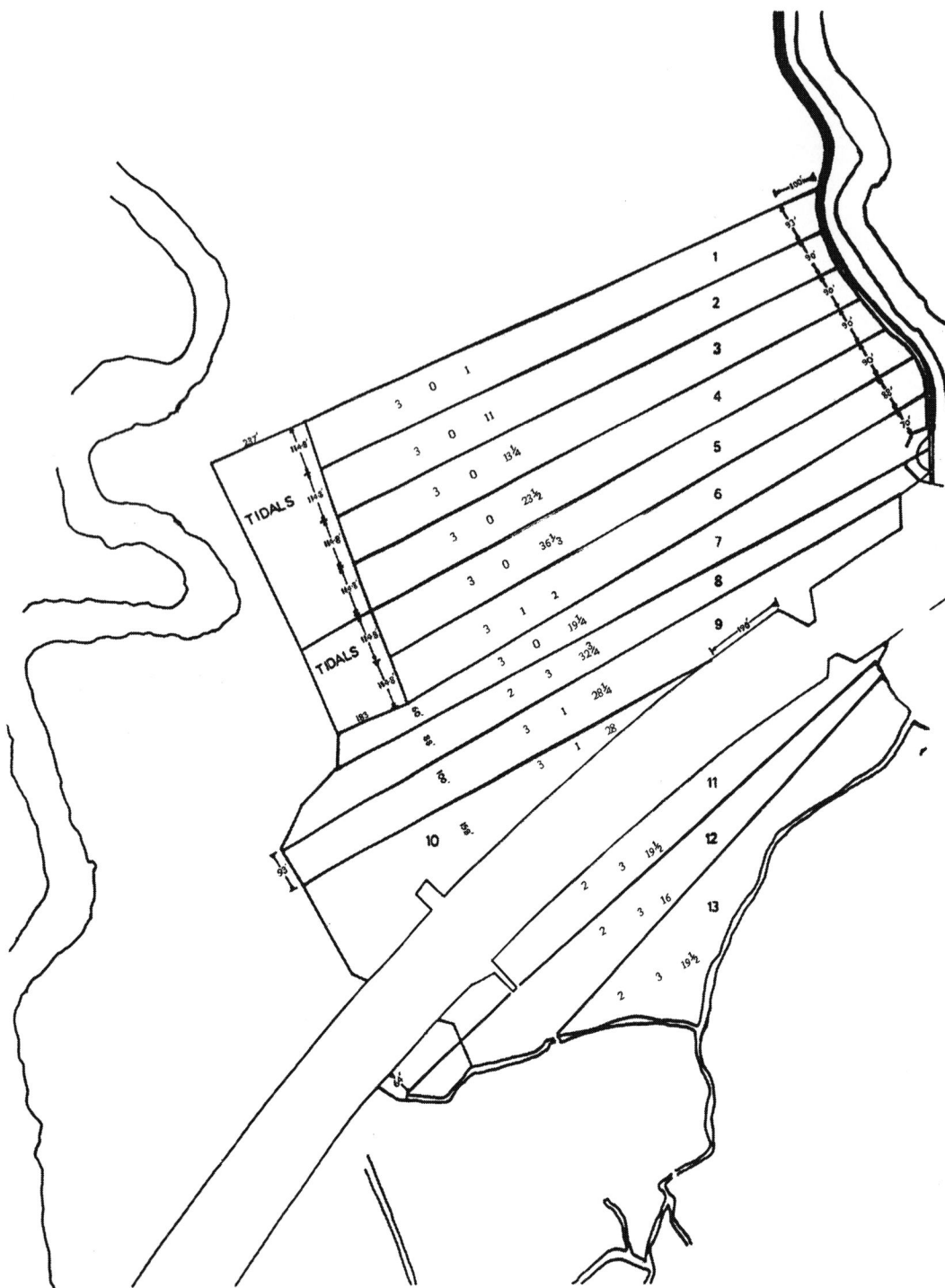

Map 10b. Redistribution of the hay lots on Picksey Mead 1958

5.2.R. SEVENTEENTH CENTURY MANAGEMENT

The management of the grazing of the aftermath on Picksey Mead was similar to that at Eynsham and Shifford where the landlord took all the hay in alternate years (Gretton 1912: 56–7). On Picksey Mead the right to graze the aftermath went alternately to Yarnton and Begbroke one year, when the cattle were regulated at 10 per hay-lot, and, possibly, to the Manor of Wolvercote the next. If this is the case then the Wolvercote demesne right to pasture in the aftermath "*sans nombre*" has now passed via the Duke of Marlborough and the Earl of Abingdon to Mrs. Wise of Wytham and the number of animals she may graze has now been registered under the Registration of Common Land Act 1965. Animals belonging to Yarnton farmers were branded, in hot tar, with the letter "E" (see Photograph 12) deriving from Eardington, the earlier name for Yarnton. The Lord of the Manor, or his agent, would have ensured

Photograph 12. A branding iron and hot tar were used to mark Yarnton animals put into Picksey Mead to graze the aftermath. The letter "E" stands for Eardington, the old name for Yarnton.

that the number of animals grazing the aftermath was not above the carrying capacity of the land.

A survey dated 1636 shows that in Picksey Mead 52a. 2r. 30p. of demesne meadow was in unenclosed strips allocated by number, rather than by names, as in the Yarnton and Begbroke part of Picksey Mead. It is not clear whether the position of the demesne meadow in 1636 is the same as that owned by the present Duke of Marlborough who inherited the Manor of Wolvercote. (Bodleian Library MSS.Top Oxon.c.334; d.502, f.86). Two hams amounted to 1a. 2r. 25p. and may have been enclosed and valued at 25–30s. per acre. Except for two Wytham acres, which were worth only 20s. per annum, the rest were valued at 26s. 8d. per acre. The Ordnance Survey (1877) shows the position of all these areas and names the 23 acres in the south west as belonging to Godstow "formerly ex-parochial".

In 1694 Picksey Mead was again recorded as having been mown twice a year. Each acre was let at £5 per annum (Oxfordshire Record Office Dashwood XV/i/24). Such intensive management suggests that floods spread rich alluvium over the Mead each winter, which nourished the next crop of hay. The land must have been relatively dry during the growing season.

Picksey Mead continued to be allocated by lot long after the arable lands had been enclosed: Yarnton and

Begbroke by *c.* 1635 and Wolvercote by 1834 (Wolvercote Enclosure Award 1834; Yarnton and Begbroke Tithe Award 1845; Crossley 1990). This may have reflected its considerable value in a dairy farming area (Thomas Bodleian Library MS Top Oxon b.19, f.93; Young 1813), or the likelihood that at no time were ALL the farmers with rights in Picksey Mead prepared to give up their hay or grazing rights, in order that one of them could enclose the whole or even part of the mead. A different course was followed in Wolvercote where, in 1698, the Lord of the Manor permitted the enclosure of Wolvercote Lot Meadow situated to the east of Oxhey Mead and divided from it by Honeybourne (*alias* Honeycut or King's Bridge) stream. Each of the tenants received compensation in the form of money or a piece of the meadow, according to the number of strips he owned in the meadow. The tenant could fence his part of the meadow, provided that it remained open for common grazing as usual from the 21st September until the 24th February each year. A special clause was added to the effect that no sheep were to be grazed on the land until All Saints Day (1st November) (Oxfordshire Record Office Dashwood XVI/i/a/24).

5.2.S. EIGHTEENTH CENTURY MANAGEMENT

The Eighteenth Century was a period during which there was considerable experiment in and publication of improved farming methods (Fussell 1947: 1). In 1731 William Ellis, in particular, discussed the advantages of what he called natural and artificial grass, sainfoin, clover and lucerne. Many farmers put these ideas into practice in their enclosed fields but the common lands and meads remained, to a large extent, under their traditional management. Many of the open-field meadows in Oxfordshire were still divided into narrow strips allocated by lot annually (Young 1969: 205). Davis (Young 1969), in the 1790s, recounted how they were generally situated at the edge of a parish, some distance away from the village, and were somewhat neglected because there was seldom any dung left over from the wheat crop to manure them in spring. Where the aftermath was the property of all the occupiers in the village, and there was no fixed time for admitting the cattle, the grass could deteriorate as a result of over-grazing or the hay crop might be ruined by allowing it to stand too long (Young 1969: 205). A 1796 set of rules for Eynsham tenants shows very clearly the importance placed upon the upkeep of mounds and ditches and the regular movement of sheep and cattle to and from the Lammas grounds and the open fields (Minn Bodleian Library MS.Top Oxon. e.384)). The management of Picksey Mead was, therefore, by no means unique.

By the Eighteenth Century much of the common land in England had been enclosed, but hay meadows continued to represent the best use of the floodplain of river valleys (Scruby 1979; Allen 1978), where floodwater would have ruined crops and eroded ploughed soils in winter time. The value of the meadow land in Yarnton and Wolvercote decreased as a result of the Act of 1751 For The Better Carrying On And Regulating The Navigation Of The River Thames. The new locks and weirs built under the terms of this Act at the end of the Eighteenth Century ruined the drainage of the land upstream. The raising of the water at King's Weir by 4 or 5 feet, and the consequent rise in the water-table:

> "changed some of the best pasturage in Yarnton
> into coarse, worthless grass"
> (Thomas, Bodleian Library MS.top Oxon.b.19).

At the same time access to Picksey Mead from Yarnton was prohibited by the drowning of the ford between Picksey and Oxhey Meads (Thomas Bodleian Library MS.Top Oxon. b.19).

Between about 1770 and 1813 the value of meadowland in England was depressed as a result of an increase in the production of sainfoin (*Onobrychis viciifolia* Scop.) and other trefoils (Thirsk 1957: 276). In 1770 good meadowland was let at 40s. per acre, while in 1813 it had only doubled in price (other land values had more than doubled). Cassington meadows realised from 30s

to 45s per acre. Not enclosed until 1800, the Cassington meads' value may have reflected the difference between lot-meadow management and that of enclosed land. In this part of Oxfordshire a ready market (and transport via the nearby railway and canal) for veal and dairy products meant that enclosed lot meadows often became pasture for dairying and veal production, rather than continuing as hay meadows (Young 1969: 205).

5.2.T. NINETEENTH CENTURY CHANGES

The custom in 1817 was to cut the hay in each mead in one day. Haymaking began in Yarnton in Oxhey on the first Monday after old St. Peter's Day, West Mead on the following Monday and Picksey Mead on the Monday after that. This was a possibility when, as in 1745, the mowths were held by men working their own small farms (Thomas, Bodleian Library MS Top Oxon b.19, f.94). But as the lots came into the hands of fewer and fewer farmers, 100 mowers had to be imported from Oxford and the neighbouring villages. Inevitably, with so many extra people in Yarnton, there was a good deal of competition, which led to noise and fighting between the incomers and the villagers. Sometimes it went on all night to the dismay of the Vicar and no doubt to many of his parishioners. The death of a parishioner in a fight finally provided the Vicar, the Rev. Vaughan Thomas, with the motivation to get each of the lot meads cut in three days instead of one.

In order to make the change in the hay cutting the Rev. Thomas had to get the agreement of everyone who owned the lot balls (Appendix H) and he went to considerable trouble to get it. He believed that the new arrangement was for the benefit of the village in general and in particular to Mr R. Osborne who had wanted the change for at least 7 years. Osborne had 10 men's mowths which could be cut by 3 men in 2 days and so save him the cost of 4 meals. This was only partly true, because the size of the lots varied between 3 and 5 statute acres (Map 10a & b). The largest lots were on Picksey Mead and were allocated in pairs, one on either side of a central path. Osborne had also acquired 84 of the 146 grazing rights.

The Rev. Thomas found that he had the support of most of the farmers and wrote to Sir Henry Dashwood, Lord of the Manor of Yarnton and Begbroke, asking him to authorise any farmer with mowths in the meads to cut them in 3 days, instead of in one. The following effects were expected:

> "1. The farmer having three days to cut his lot
> in instead of one, need not hire out-of-town men
> to cut it, his own labourers being fully adequate
> to the purpose.

2. By employing his own labourers to cut it, the farmer would get rid of a most expensive practice, that of entertaining his out-of-town mowers with breakfast, and eating and drinking all day long.

3. By employing his own labourers he would be putting money into their pockets instead of the pockets of strangers.

4. And above all the village would be saved from the regular return of Uproar, Drunkenness, Fighting.

5. And the rising generation to whose education Sir Henry has lately contributed so liberally would be saved from the sights of this most pernicious practice."
(Thomas, Bodleian Library MS.Top Oxon.b.19)

Mr Treadwell Strange, the tenant of the Manor House was against the Vicar's plan. He did not use the Manor's rights, yet he strongly opposed the new arrangement, on behalf of the absent Lord of the Manor, fearing that delay in cutting the meads would injure the lattermath or grazing. The Rev. Thomas records that Mr Strange enjoyed and helped to organize the "entertainments" provided for the haymakers. He was, however, finally persuaded that whether the hay was cut on the Monday, Tuesday or Wednesday would make little difference to the strength of the lattermath because the meads would not be opened to stock until six weeks later on the Monday after St. Bartholomew's Feast Sunday (c. 24th August). The Rev. Thomas was happy to remind Mr Strange that there had been no complaint when Mr North of Cassington had left his hay standing for a fortnight after the other lots were cut (Thomas, Bodleian Library MS.Top Oxon.b.19, f.143).

These problems arose because the lots were owned by fewer people, some of whom lived outside Yarnton and Begbroke. Mr Morris of Woodstock, for example, let his lot to Mr North of Cassington (MS Top Oxon. b.19, f.143). The owners of the farms to which the lots belonged no longer considered the meads to be the asset they had been in the 13th century. The flooding in summer caused by the navigation aids on the Thames (Chapter 4) had reduced the quality of the hay and in some years rendered it valueless. The small farmers who used to rely on it for winter fodder could do so no longer. Fortunately for the Rev. Thomas' peace of mind, Sir Henry Dashwood readily gave his consent and his instructions to cut the hay in 3 days instead of one, were passed to the Meadsmen.

The apparent change in management, from two crops to one crop of hay in the Eighteenth Century, may have been due to one or a combination of causes. A change

in stocking practices may be indicated by the fact that when Sir William Spencer died in 1608, the demesne lands of Yarnton Manor were recorded as supporting horses and sheep (Woodstock Museum Archives). At the end of the Eighteenth Century, records suggest that the area was used only for veal and dairy farming (Bodleian Library MS.Top Oxon.b.68; Young 1813: 205). Alternatively, change may have been prompted by the summer flooding associated with the raising of the level of King's Weir at the end of the Eighteenth Century which could have reduced the value of the hay because the higher water-table may have provided conditions in which the unpalatable Meadowsweet (*Fililpendula ulmaria*) Meadow Rue (*Thalictrum flavum*) and Willow Herb (*Epibolium hirsutum*), for example, could flourish at the expense of more nutritive herbs and grasses (Young 1813: 213–25; Appendix I). This vegetation can be seen in Picksey Fen (*Phragmites australis* (Type O) grassland which is gradually developing, perhaps as a result of water ponding up beside the Oxford Western Bypass which is interfering with the drainage in that part of the mead. In Water Eaton, for example, the loss of the season's hay crop due to floods could amount to £500 (Young 1813: 205). At a time when the benefits of sainfoin, clover and other trefoils were being discussed, as, for example in Lincolnshire (Thirsk 1957: 276) it is possible that they were being grown to make up for the poor quality hay, as well as to improve the fertility of the arable land.

5.2.U. TWENTIETH CENTURY MANAGEMENT

By the Twentieth Century the divisions had become complicated and, with a contraction in the number of farmers wanting the hay, the lots for the year could be sold by auction to people from outside the village. In 1921, for example, the lots were advertised as:

Harry in the first mead (Oxey)
¼ Bolton in the second mead (West Mead)

In the same way grazing rights were auctioned in lots of 10. Forty commons were auctioned in 1918, and 70 in 1921 (Sale advertisements, Oxford City Library).

Photograph 13 shows the lots being allocated in 1911 (Taunt c. 1911). The tools required included a scythe for cutting the first swathe on the lot allocated, and a knife with which to cut into the turf the initials of the new owner. Two men, usually owners of lots, were needed to "run the treads" through the standing hay to delineate the lot (see Appendix H). The First Meadsman is holding a bag containing the 13 named balls which are drawn out of the bag one at a time, usually by the senior lady present (Mr E. Harris, First Meadsman, *pers. comm.*).

Photograph 13. The Meadsman and his team allocating hay on Yarnton Mead (Taunt 1911).

The traditional management of Picksey Mead ceased in 1958 when the Oxford Bypass was constructed over some of the lots. A map was drafted to show how the remaining land could be divided up should the tradition ever be restored (see Map 10). During the past few years the quality of management of Picksey Mead has been poor. The grazing is let each year to a contractor who depastures intermittently either sheep or cattle between August and February. The decline in the amount of dung thus put on the Mead, the cessation of flooding, and with it the annual addition of nutrients, means that there is little replenishment of nutrients taken off the Mead in the form of hay and stock. In the early 1980s the vegetation was sparse in places.

PART III – COMPARISONS

CHAPTER 6

THE OXFORD GRASSLAND IN THE LIGHT OF MANAGEMENT

6.1 FLUXES IN GRASSLAND SYSTEMS

6.1.A. INTRODUCTION

It is generally accepted that grassland is an ecosystem dominated by grasses. These, with herbs and bryophytes, make up a turf which varies in composition and density according to the underlying edaphic factors of soil chemistry, water-status and climate. Mammalian and invertebrate predators and management by man are also reflected in the turf. The growth pattern of grass is well suited to the oceanic climate of the British Isles with its normally cool summers, well-distributed rainfall and almost constant supply of cool air (Davidson & Lloyd 1977: 13). The presence of leaf-base meristems (growth points) enables grass to withstand cropping by grazing animals, scythe or machine. Grazing and trampling by stock prevent the establishment of taller, broad-leaved plants, and arrest the natural succession through scrub to woodland.

In judging whether or not pasture and meadows are of high quality, one must first establish the criteria. Agriculturalists favour a dense, fast growing, sward dominated by easily digested ryegrass (*Lolium perenne*). Nature conservationists look for species-richness and the presence of rare plants. Old grassland can be "direct drilled" with commercial seed mixtures to maximise the grass crop at the expense of more delicate grasses and herbs. Sown swards may be left without chemical fertilizers or other disturbances and, with time, will appear to be comparable with old grassland because the sown species die out and the grassland will increasingly reflect and be determined by the prevailing edaphic and climatic conditions, as well as by management. The nature of the soil may be "improved" by inorganic fertilisers to increase nutrient availability. Equally important are the natural heterogeneities in the composition of the soil and its depth for the provision of a species-rich sward. Alterations in the grazing regime or stocking density, time of grazing or kind of animal, can also cause dramatic changes in the presence and abundance of the species in grassland (Fenton 1937; Stapledon 1937, 1939; Jones 1933; Milton 1940, 1947; Davies 1952; Brenchley 1958; Voisin 1960, 1961; Watt

1938, 1947; Hunter 1962; Arnold 1964; Nicholson 1971; Nicholson *et al.* 1970; Rawes & Welch 1969; Norman 1957; Kydd 1964; Wells 1971; Fitter 1982).

6.1.B. EFFECT OF DEFOLIATION

Grassland would not exist in lowland Britain without constant defoliation of woody species by cutting or by grazing. Mowing can affect the composition of the sward, which can be changed by the varying the intervals between cuts and the height of the cutter (Wells 1971). Cutting the hay in late June means that only the plants which flower and set seed before that time or reproduce vegetatively, and are not restricted by low light levels in May and June, can flourish. These include the following species which occur in Picksey Mead:

Alopecurus pratensis	Meadow foxtail
Arrhenatherum elatius	Oat grass
Bromus commutatus	Meadow brome
Filipendula ulmaria	Meadowsweet
Lathyrus pratensis	Meadow vetchling
Lychnis flos-cuculi	Ragged robin
Primula veris	Cowslip
Sanguisorba officinalis	Great burnet
Succisa pratensis	Devil's-bit scabious
Thalictrum flavum	Meadow rue
Vicia cracca	Tufted vetch

The number of times the word "Meadow" is included in these common names must be significant.

Grazing also defoliates the vegetation but, unlike hay making, nutrients mainly derived from the stems and leaves are removed from the sward and may be later returned in the form of dung and urine. There are three types of plants which are adapted to grow on pasture, such as Port Meadow with Wolvercote Common; each has different needs and mechanisms to survive grazing:

1. herbs requiring plenty of light which may not flower and set seed in the dense shade of a hay field in early summer include:

Plantago media	Hoary plantain
Trifolium repens	White clover

2. adventive plants which prefer disturbed areas:

Plantago major	Great plantain
Potentilla anserina	Silverweed

3. plants adapted to grazing by their low growth-habit or vegetative reproductions:

Agrostis stolonifera	Creeping bent
Bellis perennis	Daisy

The following species are included in good quality meadow and pasture:

Dactylis glomerata	Cocksfoot
Festuca pratensis	Meadow fescue
F. rubra	Red fescue
Lolium perenne	Ryegrass
Lotus corniculatus	Bird's-foot trefoil
Plantago lanceolata	Ribwort
Taraxacum officinale	Dandelion
Trifolium pratense	Red clover
Trifolium repens	White clover

Some pasture plants are prevented from seeding by grazing animals; seeds of other species do not survive even in an anaerobic situation. Even the quantity of seeds in the soil can vary significantly. For example, Chippindale & Milton (1934) found that out of a sample of 6,494 viable seeds in a lightly grazed pasture 2,315 were *Ranunculus repens* while Champness & Morris (1948) and Champness (1949) found between 4,940 and 18,000 per square metre in new sown leys. Nevertheless, archaeologists have distinguished between broad categories of vegetation such as woodland, grassland or heathland.

Perennial grasses are likely to be dominant in permanent grassland, their seed production may be low, compared with many annual species, and unpredictable, because of the dependence on season and grazing activities (Rabotnov 1956; Leith 1960). Ecologists have so far mostly investigated the viable seed bank which could be a small proportion of the total number of seeds shed and accumulated in successive years. This could be a problem for environmental archaeologists when interpreting assemblages of a generally non-viable seed bank in which seeds of some species, such as *Trifolium repens*, are thought to be unrepresented due to the shortness of the time they survive in the soil as a result of germination and attack by fungal, bacterial and other decomposers.

6.1.C. IMPACT OF FERTILIZER

A long term experiment in an old hay field was set up at Rothamsted Experimental Station, Hertfordshire, in 1884,

to test the effect of fertilizer applications. Named the Park Grass Plots, they were mown once a year to simulate light grazing (Lawes *et al.* 1888; Brenchley 1958). After about 50 years the plots could be described as having reached an equilibrium. A few new species had appeared and some others dropped out. This experiment highlights the kind of changes that may occur in two circumstances. Firstly, when plants are regularly removed and insufficient nutrients are returned to the soil, and secondly, when fertilizers, and particularly nitrogen, are applied. Because a few species like ryegrass (*Lolium perenne*) can respond quickly to a high nitrogen status, these plants soon shade out the less vigorous species and low species numbers can be correlated with high productivity (Brenchley 1958; Page 1980; Silvertown 1980). Plot 19 of the Park Grass experiment received no chemical fertilizers but manure was applied every four years in order to reproduce hay meadow conditions in which the aftermath only was grazed. If the data collected from this plot were compared on an annual basis one might be able to show changes with time in species composition of the sward of a dry-hay meadow. One would need information from several sites, however, (which is not available) in order to show a pattern of species composition and, therefore, a pattern which might be related to quality control of hay meadows.

6.1.D. EFFECT OF GRAZING ANIMALS

6.1.D.i. Impact of dung on grassland

What might be called a side effect of grazing is the pattern of dunging and urination in a pasture which recycles the nutrients within the grassland ecosystem. Most nitrogen and potassium returns to the pasture in urine and all the phosphorus and calcium in the dung; these affect the plant species in the pasture. For example, dung only applied to a pasture results in a clover-dominant sward while the urine-only sward is dominated by grasses (Herriott & Wells 1963). Jones (1933) showed how the composition of the sward can be changed by adding dung or by resting a pasture in early or late autumn. Areas that receive urine in winter are generally avoided by cattle for six to seven months, but spring applications when leaves and tillers are more nutritious only deter the stock for up to four weeks. Dung application sites are, however, avoided by stock for thirteen to eighteen months but this may be reduced to four months if the availability of other herbage is limited. Dung deposited in a normally damp summer is broken down more quickly than that dropped in winter so heavy grazing in December and January may necessitate the use of a rake to spread the manure in latrine areas to lessen the effect of dunging on the site (Wells 1974).

Rakes are not used on the Meadow, but horse dung is collected by gardeners for use on the allotments. In the dry summer of 1921, when no rain fell between February and September, all dung dried on the Meadow and there was practically no decay. Port Meadow was distinctly blackened and there was more dung than grass (Church 1922). This forced the cattle to invade the river where they ate all the marginal and aquatic vegetation (Baker 1937).

The depositing of dung and urine on a meadow produces mosaic effects within a grazed system that add to the heterogeneities caused by selective grazing. For example, a 350kg cow voids c. 34kg of dung (5–6kg dry weight) and covers c. 0.75 sq.m. of ground each day (Maclusky 1960). The cowpat smothers the plants beneath, which also suffer from the exclusion of light. Few grasses can grow through a solid cowpat, but a few dicotyledons, such as thistles (e.g. *Cirsium arvense*), can emerge through a cowpat or even raise it. The growth habits of some species, for example the stoloniferous creeping buttercup (*Ranunculus repens*), allow the plant to spread quickly over a dung patch without rooting in it (Harper 1977: 449).

Both dung and urine are nutrient rich, representing mineral elements collected over a large area and deposited on a small one. This causes a local disturbance of the nutrient relations within the pasture which may extend beyond the patch itself. The grazing animal is, therefore, a diversifier of the fertility regimes in its environment. In the immediate circle around a dung patch there is often a zone of increased plant growth. This may be due to local stimulation of the plants by phosphate released from the dung and to the unwillingness of animals to graze close to their own dung or that deposited by other individuals of the same species (Marten & Donker 1966). Animals also generally avoid plants that have grown rank through being ignored. As the dung disintegrates through invertebrate and bacterial action, so it leaves a bare patch of earth available for colonisation by new plant species in the neighbourhood (Harper 1977: 450). In areas, such as Port Meadow, which are grazed throughout the winter, the grasses are slower to colonise new areas in spring than are dicotyledons, such as thistles (*Cirsium spp.*) and ragwort (*Senecio jacobaea*), which germinate in winter and early spring (Sheldon 1974).

6.1.D.ii. Feeding preferences

The selective grazing habit of individual animal species has been studied for many years. Linnaeus in 1748 carried out tests to see which plants are eaten, which are ignored and which are avoided by, amongst other animals, sheep, cattle, and horses (Duffey *et al*. 1974: 175). The results suggested that sheep showed the least discrimination, but subsequent research, using faecal analysis, has shown that

sheep are much more selective feeders than previously suggested (Martin 1964). Selection or avoidance can be attributed to many factors, including the presence of toxins, prickles, hairiness, taste or palatability, amount of fibre, and the stage of growth of the plants. The example may be cited of hill sheep in Argyllshire which showed seasonal grazing preferences. It was apparent that the maximum intake of a plant species occurred at the time of the year when that plant was most palatable and nutritious, with secondary grazing occurring when the sheep were able to exercise little or no choice (Hunter 1962; Martin 1964; Duffey *et al*. 1974: 176–8).

Material selected by grazing animals is usually higher in nitrogen, phosphorus and gross energy than unselected food. Not surprisingly, at high stocking-densities, the most abundant species in the grassland are likely to make the highest contribution to the diet (Duffey *et al*. 1974: 179).

Sheep tend to move in a horizontal plane as they graze and select in a vertical plane. Because they eat the top part of the growing leaves first, it may take 2 or 3 grazings to reduce a leaf from 15cm to 2cm. Cattle, on the other hand, curl their tongue round a tuft of vegetation and tear away the plant tissue, leaving the grassland as a mosaic of tufts set within a sea of shorter vegetation. Their eating method is probably less selective than that of sheep. Horses are the most selective of domestic animals, they bite the vegetation close to the ground, always choosing the most nutritive and palatable species. They tend to overgraze areas where these species occur; other areas untouched become coarse and rank. It has, however, been shown at Willington, Bedfordshire, that, if the stocking rate is very high and herbage availability low, the turf will become uniformly short, with no coarse vegetation present. Horses have even been seen to eat stinging nettles (*Urtica diotica*) but this is generally in the autumn when the plants are dying down. Like other animals, horses will, therefore, become less selective as preferred food becomes scarce (Arnold 1960; Duffey *et al*. 1974: 180) .

The most nutritious, and therefore the preferred species in grassland, tend to be ryegrass (*Lolium perenne*), cocksfoot, (*Dactylis glomerata*), meadow fescue (*Festuca pratensis*), Timothy (*Phleum pratense*) and tall fescue (*Festuca arundinacea*) (see Appendices I and J). As a native species, ryegrass (*Lolium perenne*) is a perennial, rich in nutrients, and well adapted to withstanding the trampling and grazing of animals. It responds quickly to applications of nitrogenous fertilizers and tends to grow better when associated with a legume such as white clover (*Trifolium repens*) which can incorporate atmospheric nitrogen into the soil where it then becomes available to other plants. Ryegrass is a major constituent of fattening

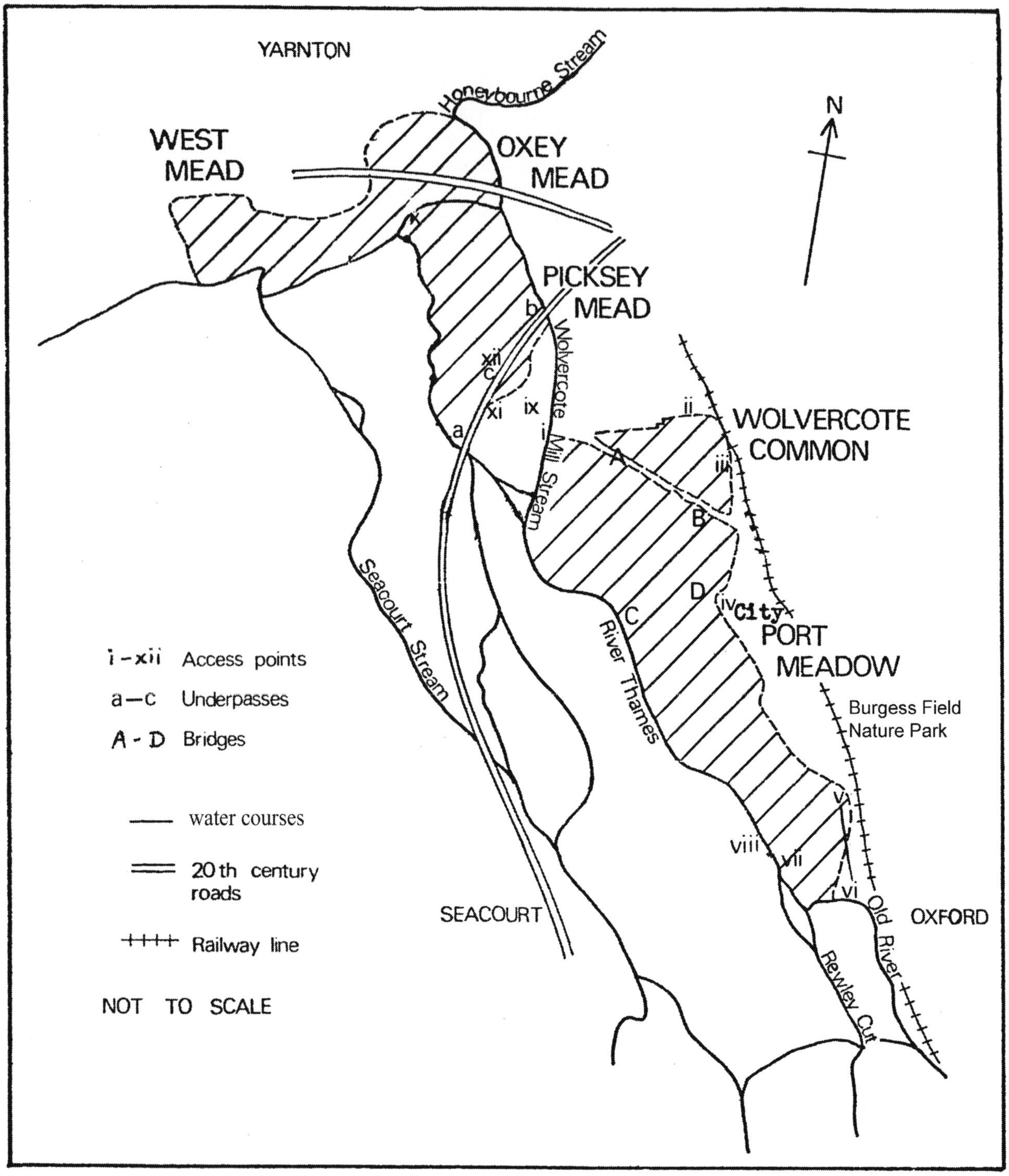

YARNTON

WEST MEAD

OXEY MEAD

Honeybourne Stream

PICKSEY MEAD

WOLVERCOTE COMMON

Wolvercote Mill Stream

Seacourt Stream

River Thames

City
PORT MEAD

PORT MEADOW

Burgess Field
Nature Park

SEACOURT

Rewley Cut

Old River

OXFORD

i – xii Access points

a – c Underpasses

A - D Bridges

——— water courses

═══ 20th century roads

+++++ Railway line

NOT TO SCALE

LEGEND

i	Wolvercote bathing place	vii	Medley Bridge
ii	Jubilee gate	viii	Binsey or Peel Yate Ford
iii	Railway crossing	ix	Picksey Lane
iv	Wycroft Lane	x	King's Weir or Mead Lane Ford
v	Aristotle Lane	xi	Cowleys gate
vi	Walton Well Road gate	xii	Bypass gate

Map 11. Water courses and potential areas of disturbance in the Oxford grassland.

pastures where it is often associated on alluvial soils with 8 or 10 other grasses and a few herbs. This ryegrass is sometimes called darnel and must not be confused with white darnel (*Lolium temulentum*) which is an introduced annual weed of cereal crops and threshed grain (Green 1972; Beddows 1967).

6.1.D.iii. Impact of treading and poaching

"Grazing animals frequently sit, lie, scratch and paw on the pasture in addition to walking, running and jumping on it"

(Spedding 1971, 114)

Both the growth and botanical composition of grassland can be affected by these activities. The extent of any change will, however, depend upon the nature of the soil and its moisture-content as expressed in terms of a reduction of water penetration, aeration and plant regrowth. On wet alluvial marshes the open structure of the soil can be rapidly destroyed by excessive treading, which leads to "poaching". Poaching is a term used to describe treading which breaks up the vegetation cover and disturbs the ground surface. The literature shows that the effect of human trampling can be as great as that of animals (Burden & Anderson 1972; Wells 1974; Canaway 1975; Liddle 1975a, 1975b; Crawford & Liddle 1977; Warwick 1980).

Poaching is most noticeable beside water troughs and gateways, where the vegetation is often eroded leaving bare ground to be colonised by resistant plants such as swine cress (*Coronopus squamatus*), knotgrass (*Polygonum aviculare*) and pineapple weed (*Matricaria matricarioides*) (Wells 1974). The sharp hooves of cattle sink into the soft ground crushing and tearing the plants, and churning-up the soil. Plants show different degrees of tolerance to such activity, which tends to reduce plant growth and helps to extend areas available for plant colonisation (Canaway 1975). The pressure of the hooves can be very great. For example, a South Devon cow with hoof area of 350 sq. cm., and live weight *c.* 500–560kg will exert a pressure of 1,430-1600g/sq.cm. when walking (Spedding 1971: 115). Poached areas are prominant on the Oxford grassland at the access points (see Map 11 and Appendix K), particularly in winter when owners feed their horses near the gates into the Meadow and sheep or cattle are moved on or off Picksey Mead. Poaching occurs on the edge of the Long Pond on Wolvercote Common and in Port Meadow Marsh. It also occurs where cattle, horses and people gather near the gates and tread paths fanning out from the entrances, in feeding areas near these gates, and at the edge of the ponds where the animals drink.

Trampling during winter grazing helps to break up the layer of litter and may reduce the competitive ability of coarse grasses during a period when many dicotyledons are dormant, with little growth above ground. In this way poaching helps to preserve species diversity, but must be controlled, particularly in periods of low growth, in order to avoid the entry of unpalatable and winter germinating species such as ragwort and thistles.

Variations in grazing intensity have had a great effect on Port Meadow with Wolvercote Common. The reduction in the grazing area as a result of winter flooding (see Fig. 6) is easily underestimated and leads to concentrations of grazing animals in small areas of relatively high ground. The effect of an increase in the number of horses grazing the pasture, even in winter, compared with the decrease in the number of cattle (see Fig. 7) should not be discounted. Even more damage can be caused by shod horses, as they accelerate to gallop across the Meadow in groups of up to 12 or so, or paw the ground beside posts and the merestones along Shiplake Ditch which mark the Oxford City boundary lying between Port Meadow and Wolvercote Common.

6.1.D.iv. Overgrazing

The effects of overgrazing pasture, especially during the winter months, are discussed in Chapter 6.3.B. Weed Control.

6.1.D.v. Undergrazing

Undergrazing can be equally damaging to a species-diverse sward. It allows the coarse unpalatable herbs and grasses, and the litter of dead herbage, to increase. This causes areas to be overshadowed and the death of more delicate species. Woody species are able to invade leading eventually to some form of the natural climax vegetation which is deciduous forest. *Bromus commutatus* (Type P) grassland (p.50) shows evidence of this where it grows in the shade of shrubs and trees on Picksey Mead. On Port Meadow seedling hawthorn (*Crataegus monogyna*) was recorded in 1968 (Woodell 1969) but no hawthorn bushes can survive the heavy grazing. Even the hedge, which was planted in 1966 at the north end of Port Meadow to act as a windbreak, never became established (Oxford Times 1st July 1966). The wire and posts erected to afford protection have been removed because they were a danger to grazing animals.

6.2 DISTURBANCE TO THE OXFORD GRASSLAND

Grassland disturbance takes many forms. The most important in terms of the Oxford grassland are described below.

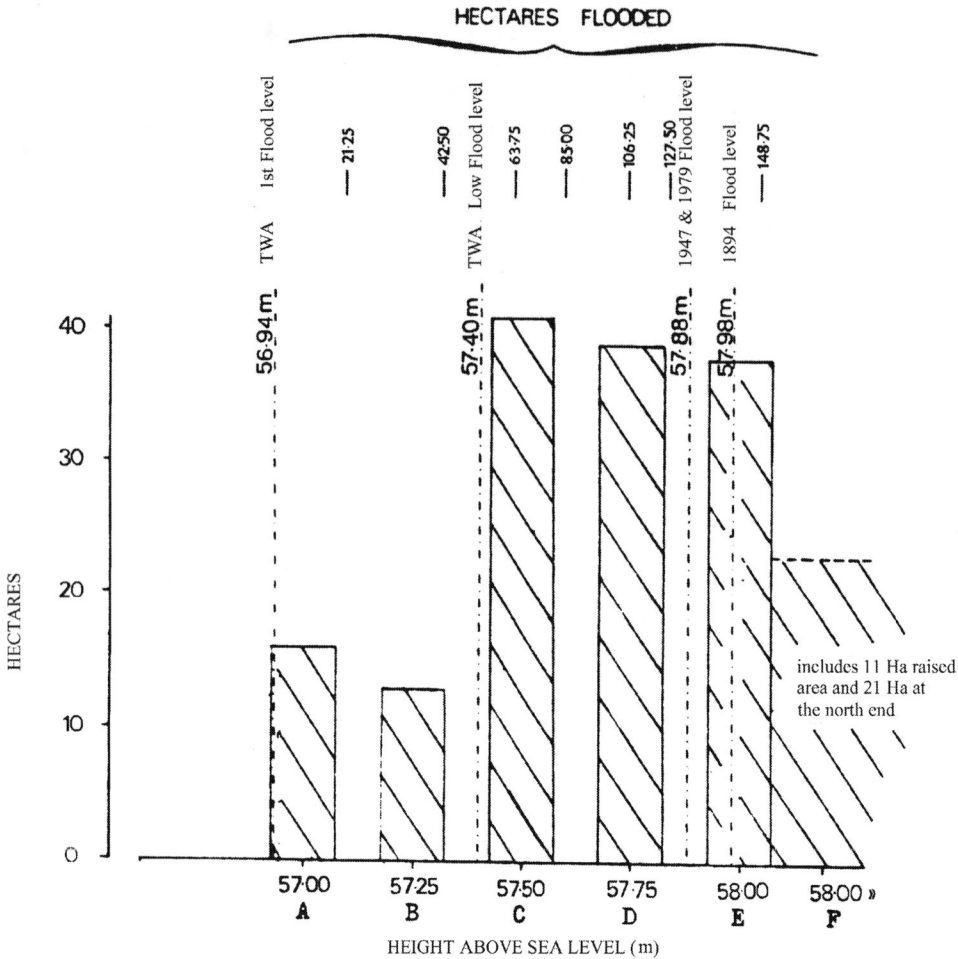

Left:
Fig. 6. The reduction in pasture as a result of the river flooding. The letters A to F correspond with the Inundation Zones on Map 4.

Below:
Fig. 7. Fluctuations in the number of animals counted at the animal drive. (Oxford City Solicitor pers. comm.)

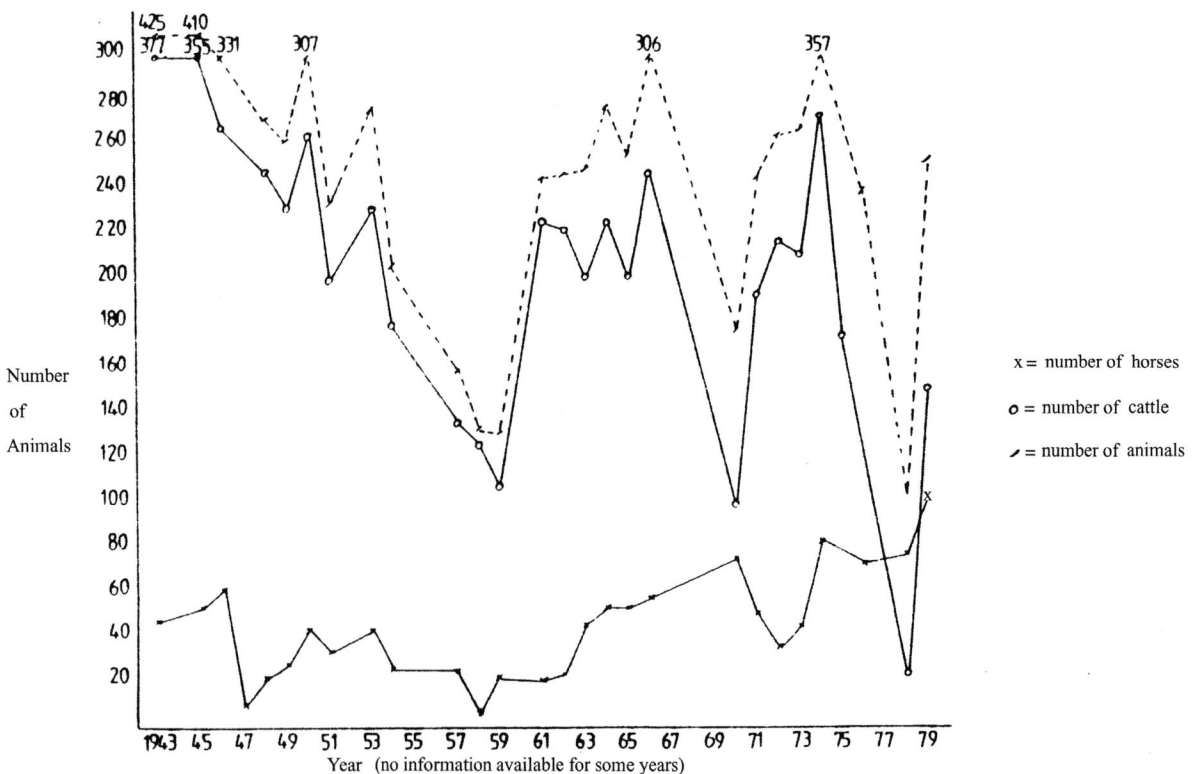

x = number of horses

o = number of cattle

╱ = number of animals

6.2.A. ACCESS POINTS

Treading and poaching of animals' hooves produces an unpalatable, disturbed pasture vegetation. It is a particular problem where paths converge in gateways and other points of access to grassland and at focal points such as bridges and merestones. Shown on Map 11, and explained in more detail in Appendix K, are situations where this vegetation grows on the Meadow and Picksey Mead. The major areas of disturbance in 1983 are at Medley Boat Station, Walton Well Road Gate, Jubilee Gate, Wolvercote Bathing Place and, to a lesser extent, the Bypass Gate. The total area of lost grassland, excluding the railway and the land beyond it, could be as much as a hectare.

6.2.B. ANIMAL REFUGE/RUBBISH TIP

Rubbish was first tipped on the south-eastern edge of Port. Meadow in 1883 at the instigation of the local Board (Crossley 1979) and with the acquiescence of the Freemen of the City of Oxford who wanted a refuge for their animals in times of flood (see Photograph 14). The turf was first lifted to make a place for rubbish to be tipped and then relaid on the top of it. Naturally enough, the marsh species were unable to tolerate the dry conditions and it took a long time for a new sward to be formed. (Minn Bodleian Library MS.Top Oxon.d.502). Domestic and builders' rubbish and the street sweepings of Oxford continued to be dumped at the south end of Port Meadow in the area of the present humps and hollows until the 1920s.

6.2.C. DUMP ROAD

In 1935 part of Port Meadow was leased from the Freemen at £5 p.a. on which to build a road from Walton Well Gate to a new City Dump to the north of the Trap Grounds Allotment Gardens and east of Port Meadow (Map 11). The Agreement between the then City Council and the Freemen's Committee provides that:

> "upon completion of the work, the Council is required at its own cost to remove the track and to restore the Meadow to the same condition as before."
> (Wolvercote Commoners' Committee January 1982)

Informal discussions between the City Council, the Freemen and the Wolvercote Commoners' Committee suggested that the Council found it expedient to keep the Dump Road as access to the reconstituted City Dump, Burgess Field Nature Park, once it had time to settle. Local residents were concerned that the retention of the road not only reduced the pasture but also encouraged people to drive motorcycles and cars over the common land.

6.2.D. ALLOTMENT GARDENS

6.2.D.i. Port Meadow

The tip covered about 15 acres by 1916 and had consolidated sufficiently for the Land Cultivation Committee to propose

Photograph 14. Horses making use of the "refuge" during the floods of January 1982.

Photograph 15. Plantago major *(Type F) grassland has developed on the levelled allotment gardens on Port Meadow since 1968*

that it be divided into 240 x 10 pole plots and let at 5s. per plot as allotment gardens. The Committee apparently felt justified in making this suggestion because of the poverty of the turf. In spite of the Freemen's protests at the possible loss of grazing and of a refuge for their animals, the plan went ahead and the allotments remained in use until 1963. At that time they were levelled, and sown with an unknown seed mixture, and now support *Plantago major* (Type F) grassland (see Photograph 15).

6.2.D.ii. Wolvercote Common

15 acres of Wolvercote Common were taken over by the Ministry of Agriculture, Fisheries and Food in 1940 to help the Second World War "Dig for Victory" campaign. Approximately 4 acres were returned to the Common, but not seeded, in 1968 and another acre in 1984 (Wolvercote Commoners Committee Minutes). A further acre at the north end of the Allotments was returned to pasture in 2000.

6.2.E. OXFORD MODEL AIRCRAFT CLUB

Photograph 16 shows the effect of mowing an area *c.* 20m x 20m each summer for the benefit of, and by the members of the Model Aircraft Club. It has reduced the thistles (*Cirsium arvense*) to rosette forms and has produced a sward in which daisies (*Bellis perennis*) are abundant.

6.2.F. PORT MEADOW AIRFIELD (1917–1922)

The airfield had a considerable impact upon the flora of Port Meadow, both from the point of view of disturbance, and that of the transportation of alien plant species on the wheels of aircraft (see Appendix F). Stand 8 was sampled in an area under which were concrete foundations of one of the Airfield buildings. These are shown in the background of Photograph 17 which shows a short turf in which there is a shooting target (?Junkers) in the foreground. Photograph 18 shows a circular bombing target and rifle butts on Port Meadow at the end of the First World War. Godstow Weir can be seen in the background on the right. The buildings were sold and removed in 1922 (Bodleian Library MS.Top Oxon.d.502).

6.3 MANAGEMENT PROBLEMS ON THE OXFORD GRASSLAND

6.3.A. INTRODUCTION

Port Meadow with Wolvercote Common shows signs of neglect since the Second World War. This is manifested in large areas which have been colonised by the plants avoided by cattle and horses on account of their prickles or toxicity. These plants include thistles (*Cirsium arvense,*

90

Photograph 16. The Oxford Model Aircraft Club mow their "flying area" and so provide a short turf in which daisies (Bellis perennis) *are abundant.*

Photograph 17. Shooting target on Port Meadow Airfield in 1918 (H. Minn).

Photograph 18. Bombing target and rifle butts on Port Meadow Airfield in 1918. Godstow Weir is in the background (H. Minn).

Photograph 19. Rotting hay and wheel ruts indicate poor management on Picksey Mead, January 1983.

C. vulgare, C. acaule, C. eriophorum and *Onopordum acanthium*) and ragwort (*Senecio jacobaea*), which have arrived since Baker carried out his survey in 1923. Buttercups (*Ranunculus acris, R. bulbosus, R. repens*) were already present, but the abundance of meadow buttercup (*Ranunculus acris*) has increased. Although unpalatable in a pasture, they are not a problem in hay fields because their toxicity is lost once the hay has been made.

On Picksey Mead, where mole hills have not been spread in the traditional manner, the annual hemiparasite, yellow rattle (*Rhinanthus minor*) invades at the expense of more palatable plants. When the hay, belonging to the Yarnton and Begbroke farmers, was cut in the wet month of September 1982, instead of in early July, much of it lay in rows or bales all winter. Photograph 19 shows some of the damage that was done to the sward by the wheels of heavy farm machinery.

6.3.B. WEED CONTROL

Weeds such as thistles (*Cirsium sp.*) and ragwort (*Senecio jacobaea*) may occur in any grassland. They become a problem when grazing pressure is not regulated to the carrying capacity of the land. On the Meadow, weed problems are related to overgrazing.

Ragwort (*Senecio jacobaea*) and creeping thistle (*Cirsium arvense*) are abundant on Port Meadow with Wolvercote Common (see Map 13). They are classified as noxious weeds under the schedule to the Corn Production (Repeal) Act (1921) amended in the Agriculture Act 1947. As owners of Port Meadow and Trustees of Wolvercote Common, Oxford City Council has the responsibility for weed control. The Injurious Weeds (Delegation to County Borough Councils) Order 1948, gave the Council the necessary powers.

Ragwort is a sand-dune species but has become a common weed of low-grade grassland where the soils are not waterlogged (Harper 1958). It is dangerous to cattle and horses because it contains toxic alkaloids (Barger and Blackie 1937). Not only do these remain active, but the ragwort becomes more palatable after it has been cut. Between September 1947 and October 1948, 51 animals which had died of ragwort-poisoning were received at a knackery (Willmott 1949). Attempts to reduce the robustness of ragwort by cutting have to be accompanied by taking the cut plants out of the pasture.

Normal control of ragwort is achieved by maintaining an actively-growing closed sward which is ungrazed in winter. The first year rosettes must be shaded out by tall herbage such as a hay crop. The land can, alternatively be ploughed and planted with shading crops such as potatoes (Hexter 1950; Harper 1956). Although the first of these options could be adopted on the Meadow, it is impossible to achieve without strict control of grazing animals. *Senecio jacobaea* germinates in open ground between December and March where its light-demanding rosettes can become established before lateral-growing species, such as grasses and clovers, become active in spring (Sheldon 1974). Ragwort is known to have a cyclical habit, but the reasons for its sudden disappearance are far from clear (Holly *et al.* 1952; Gillham 1955).

The first record of ragwort on Port Meadow was made by Professor A.D. Bradshaw (*pers. comm.*) in the autumn of 1948 (or the spring of 1949). The rosettes had become frequent by 1954 when Chief Inspector Waite, R.S.P.C.A., advised closing the Meadow for three winter months in order to improve the grazing (Wolvercote Commoners' Committee (W.C.C.) Minutes 28.9.54). As early as 1952/3 Harper and Sagar (1953: 262) considered Port Meadow to be heavily overgrazed. In 1955 a dense growth of ragwort covered about 40 hectares of Port Meadow, and discussions took place between the Oxford City Council's Estates Department, Oxford University and the Nature Conservancy (N.C.C.). An agreement was reached whereby the City Council would cut and burn the ragwort and thistles on Port Meadow (Harper & Wood 1957; N.C.C. Southern Region). This operation apparently took longer than expected. The Wolvercote Commoners' Committee found it necessary to request the City to open the Meadow gates as soon as possible (W.C.C. Minute 19.8.55).

The following year no consultation took place, and 62 hectares at the north end of Port Meadow were sprayed with 2,4-D amine solution. Co-operation between Oxford City Council and Oxford University would have been very helpful at this point. Ecologists could have informed the Estates Committee that the ragwort had almost disappeared. Only 3 flowering shoots were seen growing on Port Meadow (Harper & Wood 1957). The action, however, forced a closer liaison between Oxford City Council, Oxford University and the Berkshire, Buckinghamshire and Oxfordshire Naturalists Trust (B.B.O.N.T.). It was agreed after some discussion, that 5 hectares at the south end of Port Meadow should be sprayed with herbicide. This is now *Achillea millefolium* (Type E) grassland (see Map 12) (N.C.C. Southern Region).

Despite the application of herbicide in 1956 the ragwort problem became worse. The 2,4-D amine solution killed all broadleaved species and some grasses. The bare ground which was exposed, together with the disturbance caused by winter grazing (see Photograph 20), provided ideal

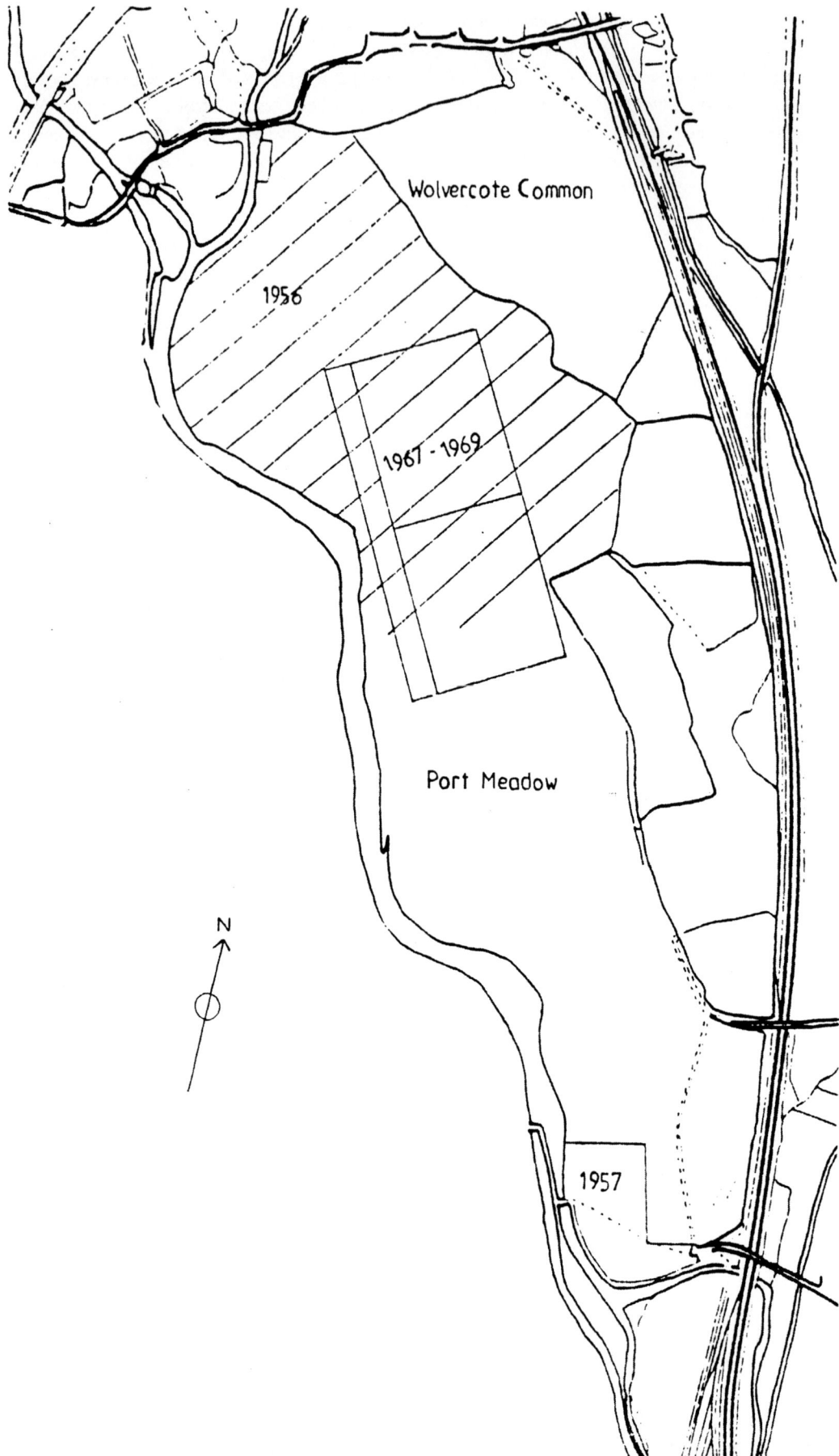

Map 12. 2,4-D amine solution was sprayed over Port Meadow on several occasions.

Photograph 20. Inundation Zones E and F on Port Meadow are overgrazed in winter by ponies belonging to the Wolvercote commoners.

germinating conditions for seeds already in the ground and those derived from, for example, the tow path at Binsey or the railway embankment and blown onto the Meadow. *Senecio jacobaea* seeds remain viable for at least 8 years (Sheldon 1974).

By 1963 the Wolvercote Commoners' Committee was reporting the spread of ragwort into Port Meadow from the river bank and in 1965 were not optimistic about a plan to use cinnabar moth caterpillars to control it (W.C.C. Minutes 7.8.63; 24.2.65). Nevertheless, an attempt was made by Dr Roger Clarke of B.B.O.N.T. in order to allay increasing pressure to use a selective herbicide (N.C.C. Southern Region). Lack of success was attributed to the impossibility of introducing a sufficient number of the larvae of *Tyria jacobaea* L. Other factors were also involved. The moth pupates in October on, or just below, the soil surface, where it is subject to predation by rooks and crows (Cameron 1935). On Port Meadow gulls and plover seen searching for invertebrates may also take the pupae. Although the winter conditions at the north end of the Meadow may be within the tolerance of *Senecio jacobaea*, they are too wet for cinnabar moth pupae. During 1981, 1982 and 1983, cinnabar moth caterpillars were found on ragwort growing on the road embankment

at the north end of Wolvercote Common and on the Aristotle Lane embankment, but were not seen on the Meadow itself.

In 1967 Ragwort had invaded the area of dense thistle outlined on Map 13. The thistles had been a problem for many years and regular cutting of them on Wolvercote Common had been carried out since at least 1931. By 1953 the Commoners were feeling that this was a waste of time, since the thistles on Port Meadow were allowed to seed (W.C.C. Minutes 27.8.31; 5.8.53). Unfortunately it is not recorded whether the thistles were creeping thistle (*Cirsium arvense*), which are a problem today, or spear thistle (*Cirsium vulgare*), which was frequent on the north end of Port Meadow in the 1920s and 30s (Baker 1937). Minn (Bodleian Library MS Top Oxon.d.502) also comments on the thistles and other "coarse weeds of cultivation at the north end of the Meadow", but does not specify which. However, thistle seed, especially *Cirsium arvense*, rarely germinates (Harper undated). Cutting the thistles is intended not so much to stop them seeding, but rather to weaken their growth and prevent their spreading vegetatively. But in view of the increasing density of the thistles, one wonders whether success can be achieved by this method.

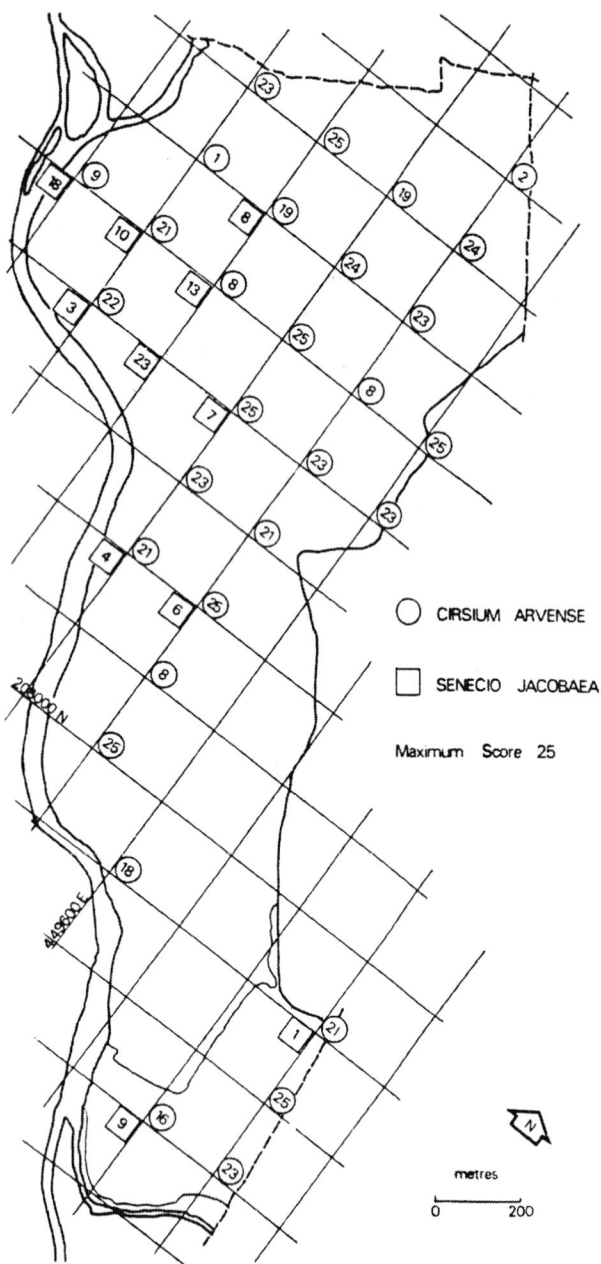

Map 13. Distribution of weed species on Port Meadow with Wolvercote Common, 1981.

After considerable discussion between Oxford City Council, Oxford University and B.B.O.N.T. it was agreed that 1967–69 should be an experimental period during which the efficiency of three methods of ragwort control would be tested:

1. Hand pulling (1.25 ha)
2. Spraying with 2,4-B amine solution (15 ha)
3. Cutting with a forage harvester (15 ha)
4. Control (no treatment)

The results showed that the effect of spraying was cumulative and that both herb and grass species were killed by the herbicide while forage harvesting and hand pulling reduced the ragwort and thistle but retained species diversity (see Table 25 and Appendix L).

	1967		1968		1969	
	Grass	Herbs	Grass	Herbs	Grass	Herbs
Control	14	20	12	22	16	19
Hand pulled	11	22	10	23	8	22
Forage harvested	11	18	14	19	13	20
Sprayed	15	22	10	15	9	6

TABLE 25. RAGWORT CONTROL EXPERIMENT SHOWED THAT NEITHER FORAGE HARVESTING, NOR HAND PULLING, REDUCE SPECIES-RICHNESS, AND HERBICIDE PRODUCED A SPECIES-POOR SWARD. FROM: WOODELL 1969.

Contrary to Woodell's recommendations, the Council arranged for *c.* 50 ha in the northern part of Port Meadow to be sprayed in 1970 (map unavailable). Between 1971 and 1977 ragwort was handpulled by members of B.B.O.N.T. and the British Trust for Conservation Volunteers. There was too much ragwort in 1978 for the Volunteers to cope with. After consultation with the N.C.C., the City Estates Department arranged for the flat areas to be forage harvested and for the rest to be cleared by hand. This form of management continued through 1983, and the extent of the area cut by forage harvester is shown by the distribution of creeping thistle (*Cirsium arvense*) shown on Map 13.

Forage harvesting removes the ragwort and thistles as well as the tops of other species. It encourages the growth of grasses, particularly ryegrass (*Lolium perenne*) which may then shade out more light demanding species. Its long term effect may be to reduce even further the species richness and nutrient status of the infrequently flooded parts of Port Meadow. Its effect, as can be seen in Photograph 21, is similar to taking a crop of hay.

The Park Grass Experiment at Rothamstead has shown very clearly that such management will produce sparse and poor vegetation, if unaccompanied by the addition of some form of fertiliser (Brenchley 1958). On the Meadow the results may not appear as quickly as at Rothamsted because some manure is derived from the grazing animals.

On Wolvercote Common the same condition could occur as the result of the grassland being cut for the Sheriff of Oxford's Races (200 bales of hay were harvested in 1983 (the late Mr R. Bateman, Chairman, W.C.C. *pers. comm.*)). The W.C.C. was pleased to have the herbage cut and carried at the expense of the Sheriff's Races Committee because it saved them the cost of cutting the thistles. It also had the effect of encouraging grass growth and left

Photograph 21. Port Meadow after the Thistles had been cut. The height of the vegetation in the background suggests that the Meadow is not overgrazed in summer. August 1983.

the Common looking fresh and green. The graziers (some of whom were on the Sheriff's Races Committee) did not object to the cutting of the hay because they considered that the Meadow was undergrazed in summer.

6.4. CHANGING COMMUNITY PATTERNS IN THE TWENTIETH CENTURY

6.4.A. INTRODUCTION

It can be argued that, since PCA showed a continuum of species composition (see Chapter 1.3.D.), the four communities described in Chapter 3 are simply an artefact of the program Twinspan. This is not entirely the case. Four types of grassland can be distinguished which differ in relation to the height of the water-table and flooding, and the amount of grazing pressure including poaching. On Port Meadow the distinction between the communities formed by *Dechampsia cespitosa* (Type H) grassland and *Agrostis capillaries* (Type I) grassland perhaps caused by the effects of disturbance, is no doubt a flaw in the classification attributable to Twinspan. This community is being subjected to an increase in the dominance of species with a wide ecological amplitude and resistance to grazing and trampling, such as *Cirsium arvense*, *Senecio jacobaea*, *Plantago major* and *Poa*

annua. It would have been interesting, therefore, had time allowed, to run the Twinspan program again taking these species out of the list, in turn, and in combinations. Despite this problem, the present classification of the Oxford grassland allows comparisons with the flora recorded on earlier occasions.

The characteristic community of Port Meadow Marsh is *Myosotis scorpioides* (Type B) grassland. *Poa trivialis* (Type A) and *Galium palustre* (Type C) grasslands are both ecotones with dry and wet facies respectively. All may be distinguished by the scent of mint (*Mentha aquatica*) crushed underfoot. Port Meadow Moist Pasture is a miscellaneous collection of disturbed grassland Types, the least disturbed of which is *Deschamsia cespitosa* (Type H) grassland. This is similar to *Agrostis capillaris* (Type I) grassland, classified with Port Meadow Dry Pasture. Together they make up a community mentioned above and distinguishable by a springy turf which is quite different from the hard short sward of *Galium verum* (Type M) grassland – the most characteristic community of Port Meadow Dry Pasture. *Cirsium vulgare* (Type L) and *Carex panicea* (Type N) grasslands are again ecotones which, together with *Galium verum* (Type M) grassland, comprise the calcareous loam community in the north-west part of the Meadow. The presence of the calcicole

Cirsium eriophorum in *Cirsium arvense* (Type K) grassland suggests that this, too, formed part of the same community before the spread and eventual dominance of creeping thistle after the Second World War.

There is no doubt that the fourth community indicated by Twinspan, the *Rhinanthus minor* and *Lathyrus pratensis* Community on Picksey Mead, is not an artefact of Twinspan nor, indeed, of PCA. All the grassland Types within it are subject to the same management of hay-making followed by grazing, in contrast to the pasture on Port Meadow with Wolvercote Common. The Types themselves are also distinguishable on the ground, even though there is a continuum apparently based on soil-moisture tolerance. In the southern, lowest portion of Picksey Mead is the wettest *Phragmites australis* (Type O) grassland which modulates through *Cardamine pratense* (Type R) and *Arrhenatherum elatius* (Type S) grasslands to the drier *Succisa pratensis* (Type D) grassland on the higher ground to the north. *Bromus commutatus* (Type P) grassland has also been isolated and is exceptional in that it occurs on river dredgings which form a levée along the river bank.

In natural conditions where grassland is not cut or grazed it can progress through the seral stages from scrub to woodland. In other conditions, such as managing the grassland as pasture or mead, while constant edaphic factors are maintained, progression can be arrested and the plant communities reach an equilibrium. Such an equilibrium has been demonstrated at the Rothamsted Park Grass experiment, monitored since its establishment in 1856 (Lawes *et al.* 1888; Brenchley 1958). Because of the long history of continuity in land-use, outlined in Chapter 5, one might expect that the plant communities in the Oxford grassland have also reached an equilibrium. This Chapter will suggest that this is not the case. Chapter 2 shows that the edaphic factors have not remained constant in the past. There is too little detail of the management practices described in Chapter 5, particularly that relating to stocking densities, for relationships such as cause and effect to be shown. It is apparent, however, that the vegetation over the Oxford grassland has been controlled by the management, or not, of the Freemen of Oxford, the Wolvercote Commoners Committee and Oxford City Council over Port Meadow with Wolvercote Common, and the Duke of Marlborough's Agent and the Yarnton farmers over Picksey Mead. The control of the River Thames, and therefore of the water-table, by Thames Water and its predecessors, has also played an important part.

Although both Baker (1937) and Tansley (1939: 568) describe Port Meadow as alluvial grassland, Chapter 2 shows that this is not entirely the case. Zones E and F on Map 4 at the north end of the Meadow are islands of first gravel terrace which rise above the alluvium and upon which a calcareous loam grassland has developed. A more accurate description of the Meadow vegetation would be mesotrophic or neutral grassland since Tansley (1939: 559) includes communities based on both alluvium and loam over gravel within this group.

6.4.B. CHANGE IN WATER-TABLE AND FLOODING LEVELS

Chapter 4.2. shows that since Baker (1937) collected his data in 1922–4, Medley Weir has been removed (1931) and Osney Weir and Hagley Weirs enlarged (1958) to allow water to flow out of the Oxford area more quickly, particularly in times of flood. The number of days that flood water lies on the Meadow was dramatically reduced in 1931 and the graph presented in Figure 4 shows that between 1931 and 1958 the number of flood days oscillated between one and thirty (excluding the exceptional >50 days in 1951) and that after 1958 the oscillations were reduced by approximately one third, but that in most years the water was above low flood level (57.43m above O.D. described by the Thames Water Authority as "banks brimming") for at least one week. Figure 7 shows that because of the topography of Port Meadow this actually means that 42½ ha (Zones A and B) are under water and a further 42½ ha (Zone C) are very wet, when the river reaches 57.4m (low flood level). This change in water-regime may have had little affect on the vegetation at the north end of the Meadow (Zones E and F on Map 4; Baker's Area C on Map 14) which is well above low flood level. It could, however, have affected the plant communities at the south end, particularly Zones A, B and C on Map 4.

The dumping of rubbish including builders' rubble, in the late Nineteenth and early Twentieth Centuries (see Chapter 6.2.B.) (under Stands 38, 41, 42 and 43) may impede the surface drainage in what is now called Port Meadow Marsh. Under this raised area was a

"large deep drain running some distance up the
Meadow and draining into the old river"
(Minn, Appendix L).

It is shown on the First Edition of the Ordnance Survey (see Map 8) and the silted up remains may be under Stands 33 and 34. When the City Council constructed a road in 1935, to the new City dump on the Trap Grounds adjacent to Port Meadow, they built a culvert to take water from Port Meadow to the Line Ditch running along the eastern boundary of the Meadow, and thence into the

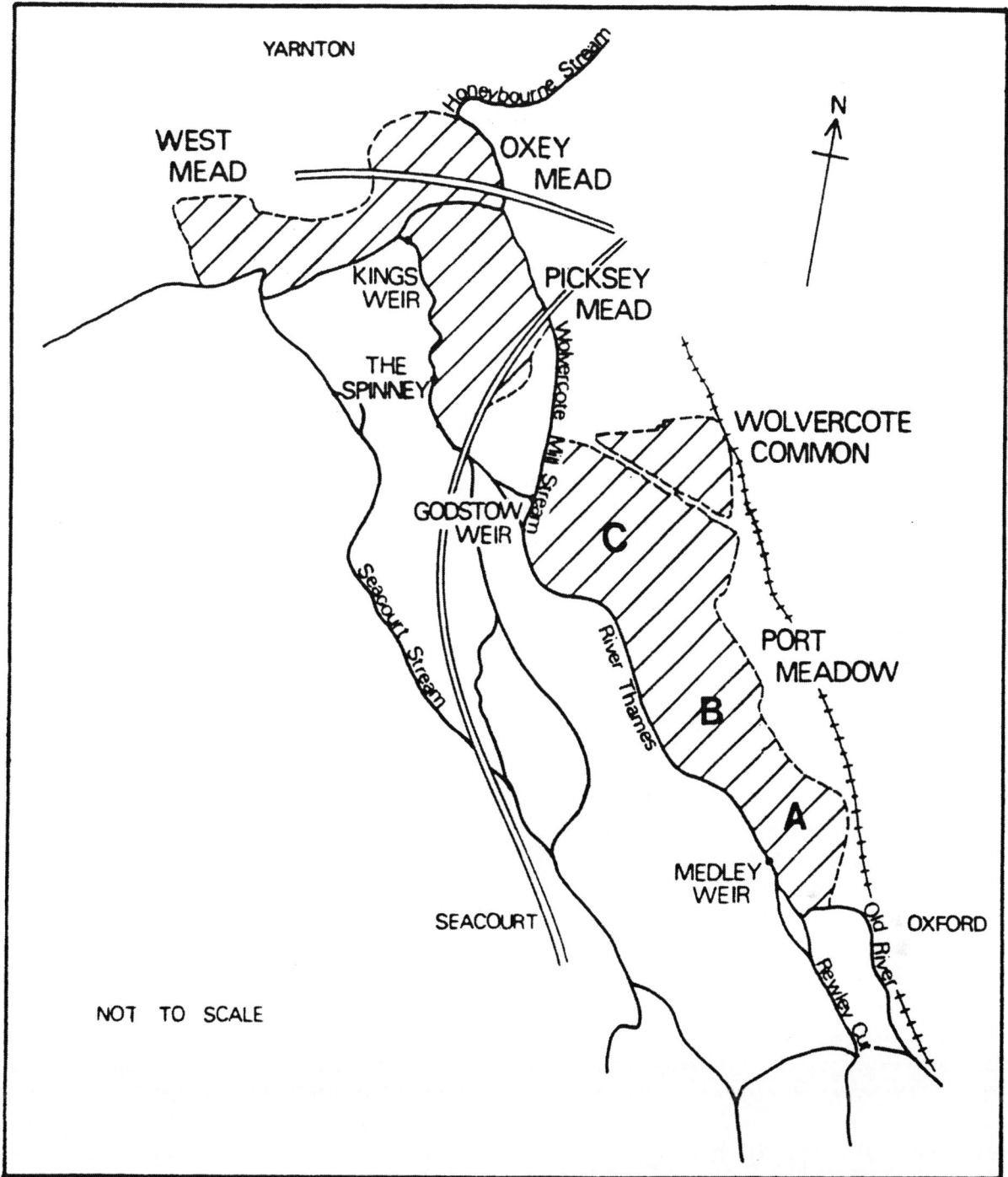

Map 14. The position of Areas A, B and C on Port Meadow according to Baker (1937).

Old River at a point where it passes under the railway bridge. The fact that there is no longer any outflow at this point suggests that the Old River is now higher than in the past. Since 1923 nutritious meadow species in Zones A and B have been replaced by mint (*Mentha aquatica*) which is avoided by cattle and horses. The quality of the grazing in this part of the Meadow has therefore declined as a result of changes in soil moisture and selective grazing.

The pattern of ground-water movement, with its seasonal change in direction to and from the river (see Chapter 3) is different from that of surface drainage. The very wet conditions in the south-central part of the Meadow (Zones A and B) may, therefore, be the result of water "ponding" up behind the rubbish dumped onto the south end. The situation is probably made worse because the culvert built in 1935 has now silted up. Oxford City Council and the Thames Water Officers are at present investigating this matter.

99

6.4.C. THE OXFORD GRASSLAND IN THE 1920s

H. Baker (1937) of the Botany School, Oxford, compared the floristic composition of Port Meadow with that of Yarnton and Picksey Meads between 1923 and 1937 (Appendix L). He not only recorded a significant difference in the vegetation between Port Meadow and the two other sites, but he suggested that this reflected the fact that Port Meadow had been pasture since the time of the Domesday Book (1087) whereas the Meads had been cut for hay and grazed. This section of my study will show how the grassland in Baker's areas A, B and C (see Map 14) has changed and suggests why this might have occurred. In making the comparison one must take into account the differences in techniques practised in the 1920s and the 1980s. For example, the methods set out in Chapter 1 of this study must be set against the impression that Baker compiled his species list by walking over areas which he had already decided were different from each other and he almost certainly measured pH by colorimetric methods. Nevertheless, certain trends in vegetation change can be seen.

6.4.C.i. Area A – Now Port Meadow Marsh

Area A, on Map 14, is situated in the lowest part of Port Meadow. Although in the 1920s almost the whole Meadow was generally inundated from November until March, its drainage was excellent. As soon as the river level fell the pasture began to dry out (Minn in Appendix F). The western part of Area A (to the north and south of Stand 39) was, at that time, a mud bank on which a colourful semi-aquatic community grew which was well documented. The most notable species, marsh marigold (*Caltha palustris*), forget-me-not (*Myosotis laxa*), mint (*Mentha aquatica*), flowering rush (*Butomus umbellatus*), purple loosestrife (*Lythrum salicaria*) and yellow loosestrife (*Lythrum vulgaris*) were remembered by Henry Minn writing in 1939 (Bodleian Library MS. Top Oxon. d.502; Appendix F). Photograph 22 shows a mud bank community including marestail (*Hippuris vulgaris*), fringed water lily, (*Nymphoides peltatum*), yellow water lily (*Nuphar lutea*), mint (*Mentha aquatica*), and bulrushes (*Schoenoplectus lacustris*) photographed by A.M. Church (1922), also of the Botany School, Oxford. In addition Baker (1937) found marestail (*Hippuris vulgaris*), watercress (*Nasturtium officinale*), thread-leaved water crowfoot (*Ranunculus trichophyllus*), and water parsnip (*Berula erecta*).

This community disappeared from the river bank after the removal of Medley Weir in 1931 and the dredging of the river bed that followed. Several acres were thus added to the pasture as the mud flats dried out and were colonised by *Poa trivialis* (Type A) grassland. Remnants of the mud bank community remain in the form of floating sweet-grass (*Glyceria fluitans*), mint (*Mentha aquatica*) and spike rush (*Eleocharis palustris*) which are constituents of *Myosotis scorpioides* (Type B) and *Galium palustris* (Type C) grasslands. The evidence here points to a change from a marsh to a wet grassland community which is illustrated in Photograph 23.

The reverse trend appears in the rest of Area A (Stands 30, 31, 33, 34, 36, 37, and 40), where Baker noted a short meadow fescue (*Festuca pratensis*), white clover (*Trifolium repens*) sward. The wetland community, including the annual or biennial, forget-me-not (*Myosotis laxa*), rough stalked meadow grass (*Poa trivialis*), creeping bent (*Agrostis stolonifera*), creeping buttercup (*Ranunculus repens*) and brooklime (*Veronica beccabunga*), were abundant. They were, however, unusual for their miniature forms each about one inch high or prostrate. This habit allowed them to flower despite the closeness of the grazing. If the grazing pressure were removed, Baker predicted that a marsh community would develop in seral succession to the reed sweet-grass (*Glyceria maxima*) community growing near the river at Medley. Photograph 24 taken in 1911 (Bodleian Library Minn Collection Negative 5/23) and Photograph 25 in June 1917 (Taunt National Monument Records CC54/367) show sheep grazing on the Meadow. The presence of sheep as well as geese, would account for the closeness of the turf. Since 1923, and particularly during the last 20 years, the grazing pressure has only been relaxed to the extent that sheep have been excluded. Nevertheless, the turf in Area A no longer contains miniature plant forms. There is now a loose springy sward about 15 to 30cm tall.

Chapter 6.4.B. shows that the water regime has also changed. This has not, however, led to any increase in the number of pasture (as opposed to marsh) species, growing in Area A today. On the contrary, the community growing there now is dominated by floating sweet-grass (*Glyceria fluitans*), of which there was very little in 1923, and mint (*Mentha aquatica*), which Baker did not mention. Meadow fescue (*Festuca pratensis*) was dominant in 1923, but is now found only in Area. B. White clover (*Trifolium repens*) was co-dominant in Area. A in 1923, and now occurs only on the drier parts. The comparison seems to highlight the importance of changes in the minimum height of the river and, therefore, of the water-table as well as changes in pasture management.

6.4.C.ii. Area B – Now Moist Pasture

Area B was described by Baker (1937) as "intermediate" in relation to flooding and aeration. This now supports

Photograph 22. A mud bank community growing on Port Meadow opposite Binsey before Medley Weir was removed in 1931 (A.H. Church 1922).

Photograph 23. Poa trivialis *(Type A) grassland has developed in the mud bank area since the river was confined to a deeper channel. August 1983.*

Photograph 24. Sheep were grazing on Port Meadow in 1911 and the willows along the Line Ditch were pollarded (H. Minn).

Photograph 25. Contrary to all reports, sheep were also grazing on the Meadow in 1917. The view is the same as in Photograph 3. The trees in the hedge between Hook Meadow and Wolvercote Common have gone and the Long Ditch has a rich aquatic community (H. Taunt).

Deschampsia cespitosa (Type H) and *Agrostis capillaris* (Type I) with some *Poa annua* (Type J) grasslands. Only two species, field woodrush (*Luzula campestris*) and silverweed (*Potentilla anserina*) were confined to Area B in 1922/3. Field woodrush is now rare in Area B. It was sampled only at Stand 25, but is more common in Port Meadow Dry Pasture in the drier northwestern part of the Meadow. It is a rare component of *Cirsium arvense* (Type K), *Cirsium vulgare* (Type L), *Galium verum* (Type M) and *Carex panicea* (Type N) grasslands. Creeping cinquefoil (*Potentilla reptans*) is, however, still common in Area B.

The abundance of both *Poa trivialis* and *Phleum pratense* appears to have increased in Area B since 1922/3. Although this is still an intermediate zone between the wet and dry parts of the Meadow, it is probably wetter now than in the 1920s. The most significant change is shown by the invasion and dominance in the central part of the Meadow (Map 13) of creeping thistle (*Cirsium arvense*).

6.4.C.iii. Area C – Now Dry Pasture

Area C appears to be drier now than in 1922/3 and supports a more diverse flora. Additional species include yellow oat grass (*Trisetum flavescens*), lady's bedstraw (*Galium verum*), creeping thistle (*Cirsium arvense*), woolly thistle (*C. eriophorum*) and ragwort (*Senecio jacobaea*) which Baker did not mention. Baker only found yarrow (*Achillea millefolium*) in Area B; it is now abundant in Area C. The increasing number of horses overwintering on the Meadow (pers. obs.) keep the turf short and may be giving a competitive advantage to other species, such as the light-demanding yarrow, as well as the weed species described in Chapter 6.3.B. which germinate between December and March, before the grasses begin to grow.

6.4.C.iv. Summary of change on Port Meadow

In general the changes in the grassland noted on Port Meadow reflect changes in management and the movement of the water-table. Changes in the management of the grazing animals are reflected in the absence of the miniature community in Area A, due to the exclusion of sheep and a reduction in the number of domestic geese, with an increase in ragwort and thistles in Areas B and C, corresponding to an increase in winter grazing of horses.

The presence of Port Meadow Marsh reflects an increase in soil moisture, despite the decrease in flooding, due to the removal of Medley Weir, and perhaps selective grazing of the more nutritious species and avoidance of water mint (*Mentha aquatica*).

6.4.C.v. Picksey Mead

Floristically, Picksey Mead remains species-rich but Baker (1937) does not distinguish the wet and dry areas on his map showing Picksey Mead. He does, however, give their pH at 3in. soil depth as 7.3 and 7.6 respectively. Table 2 shows that there is a general trend towards an increase in the acidity of the soil between 1922/3 and 1981. This may reflect a decrease in flooding due to the raising of the river bank, with material dredged from the river and an associated increase in leaching of the soil. The reasons for the wide range in pH values (5.2 – 7.6) today are not clear, but may include poor drainage (Stand 47), leaching and the filtering effect of the gravel banks and alluvium on the groundwater. A more detailed study would be needed to elucidate this.

Although the construction of the bypass makes it difficult to relate the grassland Types recorded in 1982 to Baker's "drier" and "wetter" areas, it is possible to discern significant changes in the abundance of particular species. Baker's omission of cowslips (*Primula veris*) and *Orchidaceae* may have reflected the time of year when he carried out his survey, or that winter flooding at that time precluded their growth. A closer comparison of the two species lists suggests that by 1981 a new fen community, *Phragmites australis* (Type O) (see Map 3) and a variant of the "wetter" community, *Succisa pratensis* (Type Q), had developed. These are situated on either side of the bypass and may have evolved as the result of disturbance to the surface-water drainage. In 1923 the "wetter" community is likely to have been associated with water ponding up above Godstow Weir at the south end of Picksey Mead, and above King's Weir at the north.

Bulbous buttercup (*Ranunculus bulbosus*) is abundant in *Bromus commutatus* (Type P) and *Cardamine pratense* (Type R) grasslands and on Stands 59 and 61 in *Arrhenatherum elatius* (Type S) grassland. It is, significantly, absent from *Phragmites australis* (Type O) grassland and Stands 63, 64, 65, 66 and 67 in *Arrhenatherum elatius* (Type S) grassland near the river, where the water level has been raised by King's Weir. In September 1978 (Thames Water Map) the water level was 58.5m above King's Weir and 58.4m at the point where it flowed into Duke's Cut. This compares with 58.6m, 59.1m, 58.8m and 59.1m for the Stands, respectively. The moisture tolerant creeping buttercup (*R. repens*) was not found on Stand 59 but was otherwise frequent in the *Phragmites australis* (Type O) and *Arrhenatherum elatius* (Type S) grasslands. Meadow buttercup (*R. acris*) was abundant all over Picksey Mead, including the *Phragmites australis* (Type O) grassland, in 1982. The "Buttercup Test" (see Chapter 6.3.D and Harper & Sagar 1953) applied to Picksey Mead in 1982, shows that most of the Mead is drier now than it was in 1923.

6.4.D. PORT MEADOW IN THE 1950s

There were at least three people recording plants on the Oxford grassland in this decade including graduate students J.L. Harper and G.R. Sagar and the excellend amateur botanist H.J.M. Bowen (Appendix L).

6.4.D.i. Moisture tolerances of some *Ranunculus* species.

Harper and Sagar (1953), working from the Department of Agriculture, Oxford University, studied the ecology of meadow buttercup (*Ranunculus acris*), bulbous buttercup (*R. bulbosus*) and creeping buttercup (*R. repens*) on Port Meadow. These species are closely related, yet they co-exist successfully in the same community. Harper & Sagar (1953) found that their distribution was non-random, not only as a result of the clumping of seedlings round the parent plants, but also because each species has different moisture tolerances. This showed up clearly in 1952 on the ridge and furrow grassland at Binsey, just across the river from Port Meadow (Harper & Sagar 1953).

Today the three species may be picked out most easily in May on a Bronze Age barrow on Port Meadow. By the time the flowering of the bulbous buttercup is ending on the high relatively dry central part within the ring ditch, meadow buttercup is flowering on the side of the ditch and in the surrounding Meadow. The creeping buttercup, which tolerates the high soil-moisture in the bottom of the ditch, has not yet come into flower (see Photograph 26).

A comparison of the abundance of these buttercups between 1923/4, 1952 and 1981 provides ecological evidence for changing patterns in the height of the water-table on Port Meadow. Their distribution in 1923/4 is shown on Table 25 (Baker 1937).

Species	Area A	Area B	Area C
	wet	medium	dry
R. repens	a	a	o
R. acris	o	f	f
R. bulbosus	–	–	f
R. flammula	f	–	–
a = abundant	f = frequent	o = occasional	

TABLE 26. COMPARISON OF *RANUNCULUS* SPECIES GROWING ON PORT MEADOW IN 1923/4 (BAKER 1937)

The relative abundance of the species growing in each area in 1923/4 confirms Harper and Sagar's work on the buttercups' soil-moisture preferences. In 1923/4 creeping buttercup (*R. repens*) was the most abundant on Port Meadow, but in 1952 Harper and Sagar (1953) report that bulbous buttercup (*R. bulbosus*) is the most frequent *Ranunculus* species on the Meadow. This may indicate that they took their samples from Zones E or F, or an increased dryness of the Meadow. The latter could be attributed to the removal of Medley Weir in 1931 and the dredging of the river bed, which forced the water into a deeper, narrower channel. Figure 4 shows that flooding did, indeed decrease sharply after 1931 but that from

Photograph 26. The different moisture tolerances of Meadow, Bulbous and Creeping Buttercups are illustrated on a Bronze Age barrow.

1956 there may have been a slight increase in the number of days the Meadow was flooded, but not to pre-1931 levels.

The distribution of these *Ranunculus* species on Port Meadow and *Ranunculus flammula* which is confined to Port Meadow Marsh, in 1981 (see Map 15), broadly corresponds with their distribution in 1923/4. It suggests that, after a period in which the Meadow dried out, increased moisture has favoured the growth of meadow buttercup (*Ranunculus acris*) but not the other two species.

After the removal of Medley Weir in 1931, the land dried

out and bulbous buttercup (*Ranunculous bulbosus*) replaced creeping buttercup (*R. repens*) as the dominant. Meadow buttercup (*R. acris*) is now the most abundant *Ranunculus* species. It indicates an increase in soil-moisture since 1953 (Chapter 6.4.B). The only exception is Inundation Zone F (Map 4) which has only flooded once (1981) since Harper and Sagar (1953) did their work on buttercups.

6.4.D.ii. *Agrostis* hybrids

Bradshaw (1958) studied the natural hybridisation of common bent (*Agrostis capillaris*) with fiorin or creeping bent (*A. stolonifera*) on Port Meadow. He found that they produce vigorous but generally sterile plants which were abundant in the regions of *Agrostis capillaris* (Type I) and *Cirsium arvense* (Type K) grasslands; almost to the exclusion of the parent species. The dominance of the hybrid in that area reflects, not only the vegetative spread of one hybrid plant, but also the repeated formation of different hybrids which were F1, F2 or even back-cross generations.

Bradshaw suggested that the high frequency of these hybrids on Port Meadow was remarkable on such an ancient and, therefore, closed community as Port Meadow. The present study has shown that this ancient grassland is an open community. For example, the distubance caused by horses grazing and kicking up the turf in winter could have given ragwort (*Senecio jacobaea*) a competitive advantage at the time of his survey. It may well have played a similar part in the establishment of the *Agrostis* hybrids.

It is extremely difficult to distinguish, in the field, between these two *Agrostis* species and their hybrids. In the 1981–3 survey, the distinction was based, in the absence of panicles, mainly upon the character of the ligule. Plants with a ligule that was relatively long and pointed were accepted as creeping bent (*Agrostis stolonifera*), while those with a relatively short and blunt ligule were recorded as common bent (*A. capillaris*). The distribution of the hybrids was not recorded.

In view of the changes noted in the vegetation on the Meadow in this Chapter, the possibility that the distribution of the hybrids has changed since 1958 should also be considered. More research is needed, however, before such a change can be described.

6.4.D.iii. *Festulolium loliacium*

This hybrid grass is adapted to moderately grazed pastures in contrast to its parents, meadow fescue (*Festuca pratensis*) which grows where grazing is very light and

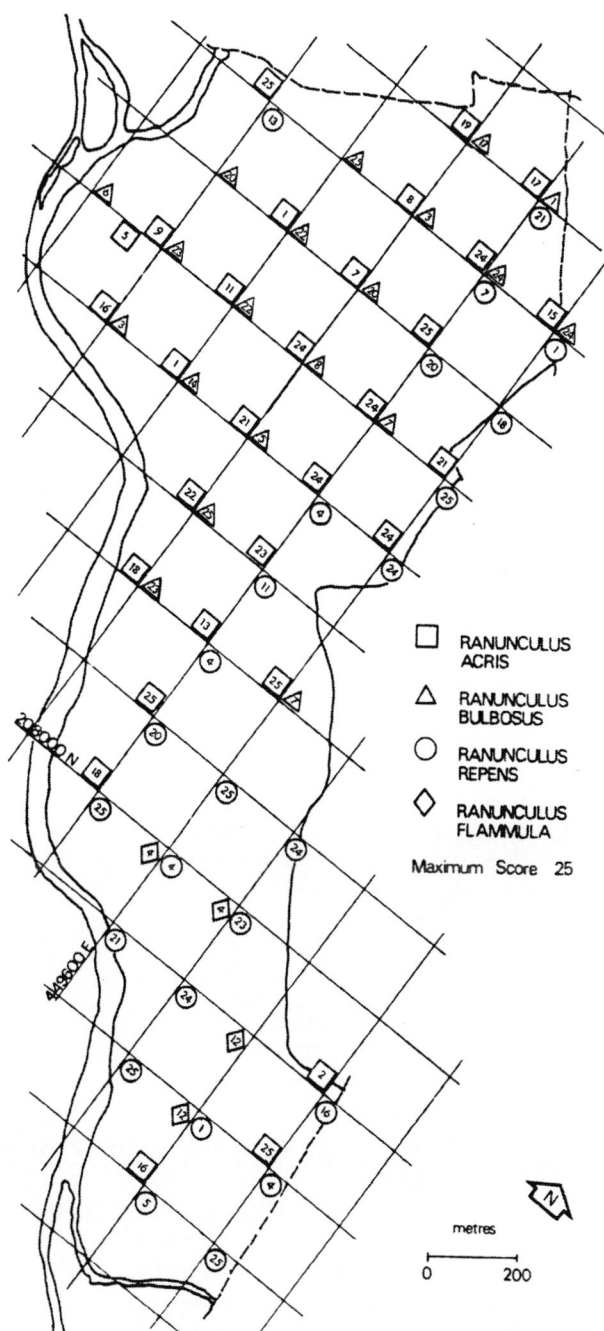

□ RANUNCULUS ACRIS

△ RANUNCULUS BULBOSUS

○ RANUNCULUS REPENS

◇ RANUNCULUS FLAMMULA

Maximum Score 25

metres

0   200

Map 15. Distribution of Ranunculus species on Port Meadow 1981.

ryegrass (*Lolium perenne*), which can tolerate very heavy grazing. It was found in quantity on Port Meadow in the mid-1950s (Bradshaw 1958) but only in small amounts on Stands 13, 9, 14, 15, 4, 19 and 27 in 1981. It was clearly a minor constituent of the grasslands Type I, K, L, M and N, which are the relatively dry, undisturbed areas of the Meadow. The apparent reduction in the quantity of the fescue-ryegrass hybrid may also be attributed to increased grazing pressure.

6.4.E. THE OXFORD GRASSLAND IN THE 1970s

6.4.E.i. Introduction

The Nature Conservancy Council scheduled Port Meadow and Picksey Mead as part of a Grade I Site of Special Scientific Interest (SSSI) in 1952 (N.C.C.Southern Region). The Conservation Management Plan of Port Meadow with Wolvercote Common, drawn up the following year, did not include Picksey Mead (Nature Conservancy Council 1973). It summarised the published ecological history of the area and included vegetation maps based on botanical surveys carried out in 1971 and earlier years, which are no longer available for study. Map 16 is taken from the map representing the vegetation as it was in 1973. Species lists of 1969 (at location F on Map 17) and 1973 (at locations A to E) are presented in Appendix K. The surveys distinguished three types of grassland, namely, Lower, Mid and Higher Level Grassland, and an area of dense creeping thistle (*Cirsium arvense*). Various ditches and part of the river bank were described separately, as being of special botanical interest (see Map 16) but had no species lists with which to compare the 1981–3 survey.

A comparison of these data suggests that the vegetation of Port Meadow with Wolvercote Common has changed between 1973 and 1983 in the following ways:

6.4.E.ii. Lower-level grassland.

Apart from the record of meadow buttercup (*Ranunculus acris*) which was not found in any part of Port Meadow Marsh in 1973 or 1981, this grassland (N.C.C. Site A) is similar to *Galium palustre* grassland (Type C), which now extends northwards into that which was Mid-Level Grassland (Photograph 27). (It is more likely that the reference is SP499075). Stand 36 and the N.C.C. Site B

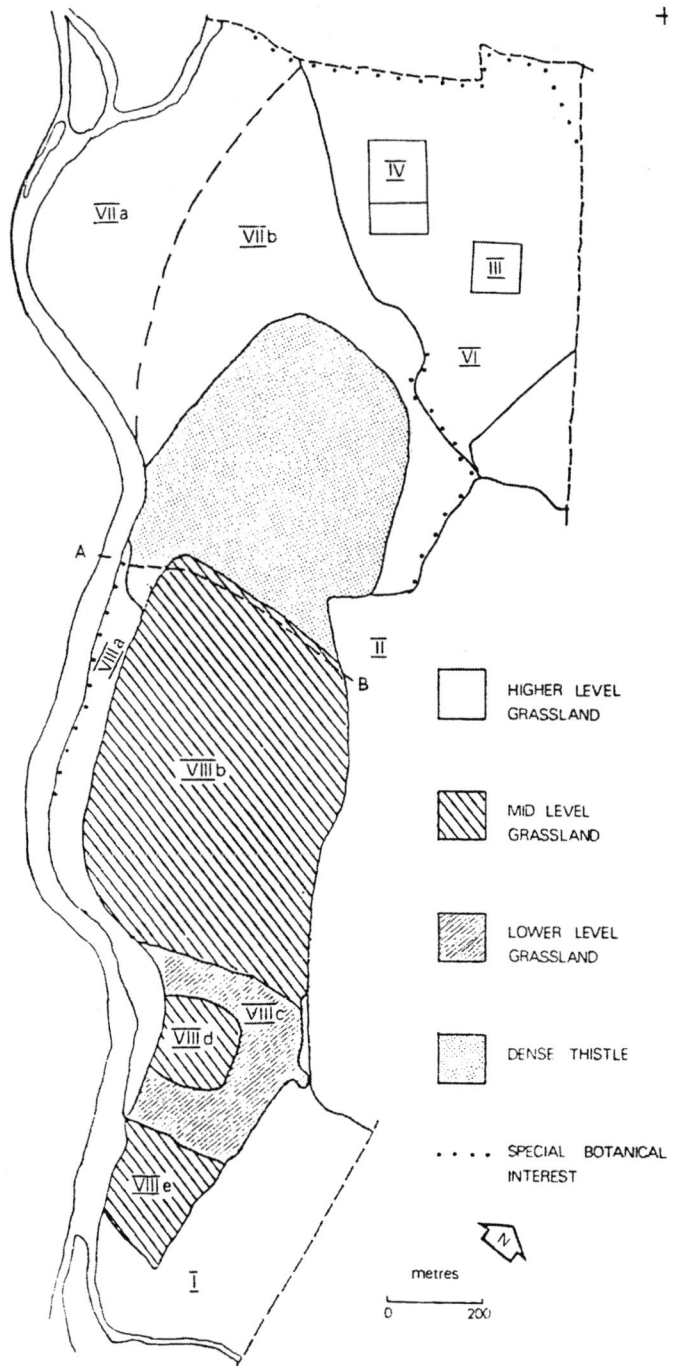

LEGEND:

I to IV	Exclude from S.S.S.I.
VI	Little interest except for parts of ditches
VIIa	Interesting calcicole flora to be protected
VIIb	Area sprayed with herbicides
VIIIa	Thistle infested area with botanically interesting river bank
VIIIb, d, e	Very important mid level grassland: Not to be drained
VIIIc	Marshy area
A– – –B	Southern limit of ragwort except for on the raised area

Map 16. Nature Conservancy Council's Vegetation Map of Port Meadow with Wolvercote Common.

6.4.E.iii. Mid-level grassland

The two southern areas of this species-rich grassland type have now been replaced by *Poa trivialis* (Type A) grassland. The area of dense thistle along the riverbank has extended eastwards and is now described as Wet Pasture, *Alopecurus geniculatus* (Type G) and *Deschampsia cespitosa* (Type H) grasslands. The Mid-Level Grassland itself (N.C.C. Site C) has thus been reduced in area and corresponds with *Agrostis capillaris* (Type I) grassland.

6.4.E.iv. Higher-level grassland

Stand 20 and the N.C.C. Site D are samples from the same area, SP490088, described in Chapter 3 as *Carex panicea* (Type N) grassland. The characteristic species of Higher-Level Grassland, *Lotus corniculatus, Briza media, Galium verum, Anthoxanthum odoratum, Festuca/Agrostis* and *Cirsium acaule*, are also characteristic of the Dry Pasture, *Cirsium vulgare* (Type L), *Galium verum* (Type M) and *Carex panicea* (Type N) grasslands which occur on the highest part of Port Meadow (Photograph 28). Fig. 8 shows that the grassland is still species-rich (31 species recorded in 1973 and 30 in 1981) but for reasons which are unclear, only 18 of those species were recorded on both dates. This leaves a large area of Disturbed Pasture, *Agrostis capillaris* (Type I) and *Poa annua* (Type J) grasslands with *Cirsium arvense* (Type K) grassland providing a link between the two areas. This evidence suggests that the area of Higher-Level Grassland has been considerably reduced in size or that the damper areas were ignored for the survey in favour of the more interesting calcicolous community.

6.4.E.v. Area of dense thistles

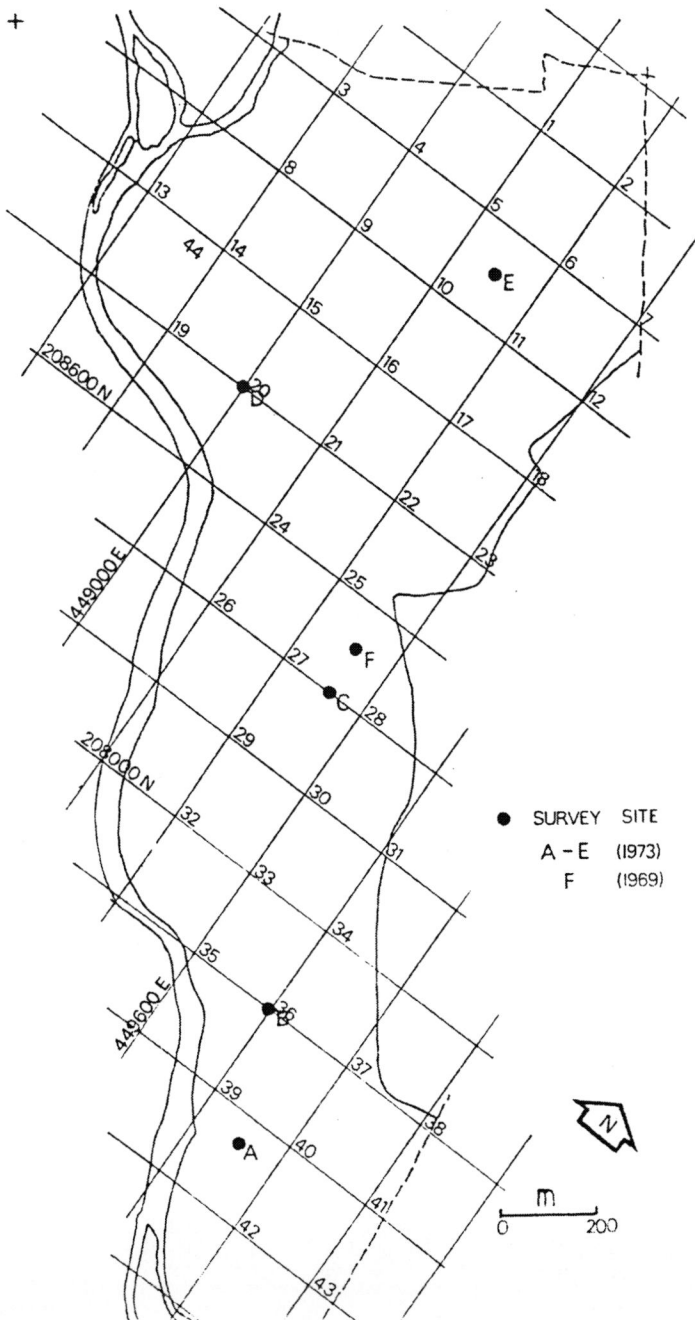

Map 17. The Nature Conservancy Council's recording sites on Port Meadow with Wolvercote Common in 1969 and 1972.

Cirsium arvense is still dense in the area marked on Map 16 but it has spread into the surrounding grassland and can now be found all over Port Meadow with Wolvercote Common, except in Port Meadow Marsh. Map 10 shows that its density is variable but that the problem has increased since 1973 (see Chapter 6.3.B.).

6.4.E.vi. Consequences of changing community patterns.

As a result, of the 1973 Survey, the Nature Conservancy Council redefined the boundaries of the botanical communities and these are shown on map 16. Because of the historic interest of Port Meadow communities in 1983 SSSI was re-notified and extended to the whole of Port

have the same Ordnance Survey grid reference but the only 6 species in common are those adapted to wet soil conditions. (*Deschampsia cespitosa* was seen in the area in 1981 but was not sampled.) The *Ranunculus* species are very interesting in this respect because those recorded in 1973 were the relatively dry land species, *R. acris* and *R. bulbosus*, while those recorded in 1981 were *R repens* and *R. flammula* which have a competitive advantage in damp ground. Their present distribution on Port Meadow is shown on Map 15 and suggests an increase in soil moisture in Port Meadow Marsh between 1973 and 1981.

Photograph 27. The horses mark the edge of Port Meadow Marsh which has spread into the Mid-Level Grassland (N.C.C.) since 1972.

Photograph 28. Most of the grass in the High-Level Grassland (N.C.C.) dies down in summer and can be seen as a light-coloured line behind the animals.

Species occurring in Stand 20 in 1981 (25 sq. m.) SP490088	Species occurring in both samples	Species occurring in Site D in 1973 (3 sq. m.) SP490098
Anthoxanthum odoratum	Achillea millefolium	Alopecurus pratensis
Bellis perennis	Agrostis stolonifera	Carex caryophyllea
Carex panicea	Briza media	Carex flacca
Cerastium fontanum	Cirsium acaule	Centaurea nigra
Cirsium eryopherum	Cirsium vulgare	Cirsium arvense
Festuca pratensis	Cynosurus cristatus	Dactylis glomerata
Galium verum	Lolium perenne	Helictotrichon pubescens
Phleum pratense	Lotus corniculatus	Hieracium pilosella
Plantago major	Luzula campestris	Hypochoeris radicata
Ranunculus acris	Plantago lanceolata	Medicago lupulina
Trifolium dubium	Plantago media	Poa trivialis
Trisetum flavescens	Poa pratensis	Prunella vulgaris
	Potentilla reptans	Danthonia decumbens
	Ranunculus bulbosus	
	Senecio jacobaea	
	Taraxacum officinale	
	Trifolium pratense	
	Trifolium repens	

Fig. 8. A comparison of the species recorded in 1981 (this study) and 1973 (N.C.C.) typifies the problems faced in the interpretation of species lists. Are the differences due to misidentification, to changed environmental factors or simply to the dynamic state of grassland communities?

Meadow with Wolvercote Common, with the exception of the Wolvercote Allotment Gardens. The closure of the Allotments on Port Meadow and the reduction of those on Wolvercote Common are well documented. Future surveys will, therefore, have a base line from which to monitor succession and colonization in these areas. The rest of Port Meadow with Wolvercote Common are important as a gene bank of species particularly well adapted to heavy grazing which may become important in the development of agricultural leys. Despite the area adjacent to Medley Boat Station being within the Site of Special Scientific Interest since 1954, its vegetation and, therefore its scientific interest, was destroyed during the 1970s and early 1980s by oil spillage and the spreading of gravel by the owner of Medley-Boat Station. The illegal use of this part of Port Meadow as a boat yard was contested by the General Public. Despite two Public Inquiries finding in favour of the boat yard the City Council bought it in 1989 and confined all activity to the river.

6.4.F. OTHER RECENT CHANGES ON THE OXFORD GRASSLAND

It is generally true to say that changes in management of the Oxford grassland, or changes in soil-moisture conditions, which took place even thirty years ago, have a direct bearing on the present vegetation where their effect has not been nullified by later adjustments. This principle is illustrated in several areas. Certain trends are apparent at the south end of Port Meadow, where, for example, there is the possibility that *Poa trivialis* (Type A) grassland (now growing on the river bank above Medley Boat Station) could not survive if the conditions reverted to the bi-weekly inundations which took place prior to the removal of Medley Weir in 1931.

Changes in the effect and timing of grazing (which have never been recorded in detail on the Oxford grassland) could be seen on Port Meadow Marsh in 1984 where water mint (*Mentha aquatica*) is spreading, partly as a result of its unpalatability and partly as a result of its tolerance of soils with a high moisture content. In Port Meadow Dry Pasture, the *Galium verum* (Type M) grassland is augmented by creeping bent (*Agrostis stolonifera*) which appears to take advantage of the moist conditions in ditches dug in the First World War and as long ago as the Iron Age; and in the advance of ragwort (*Senecio jacobaea*) and creeping thistle (*Cirsium arvense*) since winter grazing increased on Port Meadow with Wolvercote Common after the Second World War.

It is known that *Plantago major* (Type F) grassland has developed over the old allotment gardens since 1968. It has been invaded by weed species such as curled dock (*Rumex crispus*) creeping thistle (*Cirsium arvense*) and ragwort (*Senecio jacobaea*) and by ruderals such as great plantain (*Plantago major*). It has not yet been colonised by normal constituents of old neutral grassland such as meadow fescue (*Festuca pratensis*), meadow foxtail (*Alopecurus pratense*) or Yorkshire fog (*Holcus lanatus*) all of which occur on Stand 18 which was also classified as *Plantago major* (Type F) grassland.

Changes in management are shown to have influenced the Spinney on Picksey Mead which has probably acquired species since it was managed as an osier bed before the 1920s. In the Twentyfirst Century meads have high diversity value for their flora and invertebrate fauna. This has evolved under traditional management of hay-cutting in late June and aftermath grazing by cattle from 1st August to 1st November and by sheep from 2nd November to 1st February. Cattle grazing in the autumn promotes greater bio-diversity in mead grassland than either sheep grazing or hay-cutting with no grazing (McDonald 2001, Woodcock *et al* 2005, Woodcock *et al* 2006). Despite all this evidence it is, nevertheless, impossible to say how long it takes for such changes to be accomplished in particular areas without taking annual measurements.

6.5 COMPARISONS WITH OTHER GRASSLANDS

6.5.A. INTRODUCTION

In Britain grassland has evolved in close relationship with the grazing pressures of both domestic and wild animals. Chapters 3 and 5 show that the total area has fluctuated considerably over the centuries. The outline of Celtic fields can be seen on the Berkshire Downs (Bradley & Richards 1978), which were tilled during the Iron Age when an expanding population brought marginal pasture land under cultivation. In the Medieval period when a reduction in grazing occurred, grassland reverted to a form of deciduous forest as in, for example, Wychwood Forest, Oxfordshire (Schumer 1984).

The number and type of sheep on the Downs has closely reflected the high price of wool in relation to the use of the land for crops or other livestock. During the Napoleonic wars wheat prices were relatively high and extensive areas of chalk grassland were brought under the plough. Again in the mid-Nineteenth Century, Lavergne, a French topographer, noticed that half of Salisbury Plain had been converted to arable. This was also a time of high corn prices (Wells *et al.* 1976). Ridge and furrow shows up in the floodplain of the upper Thames valley indicating a period of arable farming on what is now pasture (see Photograph 2, Sutton 1964). In other words, there have been several periods in British history when it was more profitable to cultivate the land rather than to put sheep, or other animals, on it. In this respect, Port Meadow with Wolvercote Common and Picksey Mead are outstanding for having remained unploughed for more than two thousand years.

Grasslands in the upper Thames valley, in line with other British river systems such as the Trent and the Severn,

have been subjected to intensive agricultural improvement, which has escalated since the end of the Second World War. The Ministry of Agriculture, Fisheries and Food and the European Economic Community administer grant aid to farmers, including sums for drainage and hedge clearance and easy terms for hiring or buying agricultural machinery. Direct drilling ancient grassland, as well as leys, with grasses suitable for intensive grazing or silage production has increased since the first equipment was tested at the A.R.C. Weed Research Organisation, Begbroke Hill, Oxford, in the 1960s. Trials testing the effect of nitrogen on ancient alluvial hay mead continued on the Oxford University Farm, Wytham, (Harper unpublished) for a similar period, despite the fact that the area had been designated a Site of Special Scientific Interest in 1952. This is unfortunate but, looking to an oilless future, it might provide a base from which a comparison of highly productive grassland, in which a few species provide stock with easily digested bulk, could be compared with unimproved grassland such as Picksey Mead (on the opposite bank of the Thames). Picksey Mead lacks bulk, but contains a wide variety of trace elements within the species-rich community.

6.5.B. LOWLAND ENGLAND

Interest in the description and ecology of grassland has gradually increased during the Twentieth Century. At first the work closely reflected the interests of agriculturalists: now it is the nature conservation interest that tends to be foremost in studies of ancient grassland.

Stapledon (1925) classified pastures into five groups. The best were fatting pastures based on loam or silt where ryegrass (*Lolium perenne*) and white clover (*Trifolium repens*) were prominent and there were generally no more than 20–25 species of flowering plants most of which were grasses. Yarrow (*Achillea millefolium*) was a common herb which Stapledon picked out. The next group were dairy pastures which were found on a greater variety of soils. Those on chalk or limestone had, as might be expected, a greater number of species (up to 30). Bent grass (*Agrostis spp.*), crested dog's tail (*Cynosurus cristatus*), red clover (*Trifolium pratense*), bird's-foot trefoil (*Lotus corniculatus*) and meadow vetchling (*Lathyrus pratensis*) were more dominant than ryegrass (*Lolium perenne*). The description in Chapter 3.3.D. (p.38) suggests that these pastures may be comparable with Port Meadow Dry Pasture.

Tansley (1939: 571–2) compared the Hampshire Water Meadows (Fream 1888) with the Rothamsted Park Grass plots (Lawes *et al.* 1882) and suggested that the following "core" species were present because of their tolerance of poor soil and their inability to compete successfully when neutral grassland has been manured.

Anthoxanthum odoratum	*Lolium perenne*
Cardamine pratensis	*Lotus corniculatus*
Cerastium fontanum	*Plantago lanceolata*
Cynosurus cristatus	*Poa pratensis*
Deschampsia cespitosa	*Poa trivialis*
Festuca pratensis	*Ranunculus acris*
Holcus lanatus	*Trifolium pratense*
Leontodon autumnalis	*Trifolium repens*

These species grow on the Oxford grassland where the limiting factor for the distribution of *Cardamine pratensis*, for example, appears to be not so much eutrophic soil conditions or grazing, but a dependence upon soil moisture. It is rather surprising that ryegrass (*Lolium perenne*) occurs on this list because it is now well known to be the species *par excellence* for taking advantage of high nitrogen status.

Ratcliffe (1977:1, 185–6) was able to divide the neutral grasslands, as defined by Tansley, into nine groups. Some of these Groups *viz*. 1(a) Base rich marshes, 4(a) Tall grass washlands, 7(a) Alluvial meadows and 9(a) Calcareous loam pastures have affinities with parts of both Picksey Mead and Port Meadow with Wolvercote Common. Rodwell (1992) went further in his National Vegetation Classification by defining 13 types of "mesotrophic grassland", of which six – MG4, 5, 6, 8, 11 and 13 – are similar to parts of the Oxford grassland.

In some places the management of common land which has continued to be managed as pasture can be used as an example which the Freemen of Oxford and the Wolvercote Commoners' Committee might follow. The Parish of Cookham, Berkshire, may be cited as an example having two commons, Cockmarsh (132 acres) and Widbrook (65 acres) (Whittingdon 1964). They are both enclosed manorial waste over which grazing is stinted (rationed), not in the traditional way, according to the number of animals a grazier could maintain on his farm over the winter, but by dividing the total number of animals which the pasture can support, equally between the interested parties. Such a regime could remove the overgrazing problem encountered in the management of Port Meadow with Wolvercote Common, but attention must be drawn to the fact that once graziers have been brought together to agree a stint they may also agree to other management practices such as an application of inorganic fertiliser. This may already have happened in Cookham where the common pasture is not included as a Site of Special Scientific Interest in A Nature Conservation Review (Ratcliffe 1977).

The Oxford grassland is also outstanding in that it has retained its early management despite the pressures exerted by an expanding Oxford. Other areas of common land have not been so fortunate. In Leatherhead, for example, the Common Meadow over which "the lords and tenants of the local manors exercised 'entercommon'" is now preserved under the Commons Registration Act 1965 as a public open space beside the river (Benger 1968). Cookham Dean Common, Berkshire, as well as grasslands in Suffolk, were requisitioned during the Second World War and were still under arable crops in 1964 (Whittingdon 1964; Trist 1981). Snelsmore Common, Newbury, is no longer a pasture but has been designated a Site of Special Scientific Interest for its wood and heathland (Ratcliffe 1977) and Greenham Common was notorious as a base for nuclear weapons, but encouragingly is now a nature reserve.

Portholme, a Grade 2 Site of Special Scientific Interest, on the banks of the river Ouse in the Parish of Bampton, Huntingdon (Ratcliffe 1977), has affinities with both Picksey Mead and Port Meadow with Wolvercote Common. Its traditional management is similar to Picksey Mead and has resulted in a similar Alopecurus-Sanguisorbetum Association (Nature Conservancy Council 1968). Its history reminds one of Port Meadow. In Edward the Confessor's reign Portholme was part of Bampton Royal Estate (Port Meadow might have been part of the Headington Royal Estate). Portholme was probably the "large meadow" mentioned under Bampton in the Domesday Book (1086) and in 1205 (like Picksey Mead) its common grazing rights appendant and hay rights are recorded (Sheail 1971b). There was an eighteenth-century racecourse (compared with a seventeenth-century course shown on Benjamin Cole's (1696) map of Port Meadow (Bodleian Library Shop)), large crowds assembled for cock fights (the Rev. Vaughan Thomas complained of those on Port Meadow in the Nineteenth Century (Bodleian Library MS.Top Oxon. b.19)). Both Portholme and Port Meadow supported an Air Field in the First World War and had devices to prevent enemy gliders landing in the Second World War (Sheail 1971b; the late Mr Ron Bateman *pers. comm.*).

A second example of Alopecurus Sanguisorbetum, a species-rich hay meadow community including the snake's head fritillary (*Fritillaria meleagris*) occurs at Mottey Meadows National Nature Reserve, Staffordshire. The Nature Conservancy Council report (1982) shows that it is a series of enclosed meadows on clay loam through silt alluvium to peaty gleyed soils, which have been mown for many years by a variety of owners. Like Picksey Mead the 26 small fields tend to be flooded in winter and have dried out by June. However, their past history is different. Two of the meadows show remnants of "ridge and furrow" agriculture of unknown date; others have been subjected to overgrazing and inorganic fertilizers. Their future management by the Nature Conservancy Council should allow the latter meadows to return to a species-rich state and, if funds were available, would make an excellent study of such a transition.

North Meadow National Nature Reserve, Cricklade, is also a flood meadow noted for *Fritillaria meleagris* and an Alopecurus-Sanguisorbetum Association conditioned by the height of the water-table (Ratcliffe 1977). North Meadow is Lammas land with a history possibly dating from the foundation of the town by King Alfred (Whitehead 1982). By the early Nineteenth Century North Meadow, unlike Picksey Mead, included two hedged enclosures bordering the Thames, described as "water mead" and assessed at 1s. per acre more than the rest of the Meadow which Whitehead (1982) relates to mapped channels distinguishable on the ground. Fream (1888) in describing Hampshire water meadows, points out the importance of water channels in increasing the number of plant species growing in a meadow by providing conditions suited to marsh plants in what would otherwise be a hay meadow community.

6.5.C. THE UPPER THAMES VALLEY

Alluvial grasslands on the calcareous gravels of the upper Thames valley generally have a pH *c*. 7.0. In the first "ecological" description of "neutral grasslands", made by Tansley (1911), there is the following statement:

"To include semi-natural grasslands whose soil is not markedly alkaline nor very acid mostly developed on the clays and loams ... as well as on many of the tracts of alluvium in the valleys of the north and west ... with pH between 6 and 7."

Church (1922–3) described the vegetation and its annual succession round Oxford, illustrating it with a selection from his fine collection of photographs now in the Library of the Department of Plant Sciences, Oxford. The wealth of detailed observations made of plants and their communities on and beside the river Thames included the changes imposed on them by agricultural practices.

Baker (1937) made a more detailed comparison of pasture and hay mead communities based on a survey of Port Meadow and Yarnton and Picksey Meads. He drew attention to the similarity of the pH in the two areas over which contrasting communities grew, and concluded that management was the controlling factor.

In his later edition of "The British Islands and their Vegetation" (1939: 559) Tansley included Baker's (1937) comparison of Thames-side alluvial meadows on which the pH was between 6.6 and 8.0. In a revised definition, the emphasis was placed on the plants growing on an area, rather than on the pH of the soil. In Tansley's words, "Neutral grasslands" now include grasslands characterized:

"Neither by markedly 'calcifuge' nor markedly 'calcicole' species rather than (by the) neutrality of the soil solution."

(Tansley 1939: 559)

It is tempting to think that the interest shown in Port Meadow and Picksey Mead, among other places, by Church and Baker was instrumental in Tansley's *volte face*.

Allen (1979) surveyed all the land which had never been ploughed, drained or spread with inorganic fertilizers or herbicides in an area which covers the Thames valley from Lechlade to Abingdon, including the Windrush valley as far as Witney. She recorded 144 sites of unimproved grassland amounting to 960.17 ha. They remain unimproved largely because of the annual flooding of the river Thames. In this area the Thames water has passed through the oolitic limestone of the Cotswolds and the limestone gravel river terraces. Some of its calcium carbonate has been absorbed and has given the water a pH of 7.9. By the time floodwater has been leached through the meadow soils by rainwater (pH *c*. 5.6) the grassland tends to have a pH between 6 and 7 and therefore comes into the above categories. Allen (1979) showed that, of the 144 species-rich sites recorded (including 8 on the Coralline Rag limestone over clay), most were fragmented into fields less than 10 ha. Of the 23 remaining sites only 4 were over 20 ha. The fact that the latter included Port Meadow with Wolvercote Common (155 ha) and Picksey Mead (41 ha) gives added significance to the Oxford grassland and to its present and future management. This becomes increasingly important as farmers continue to "improve" their wet grassland. Two years after Allen's survey Welsh (1981) showed that 5.5% of the unimproved grassland Allen had recorded had been drained or otherwise destroyed.

In their different ways, all these studies show that it is the human element that is the controlling factor on the neutral grassland in the upper Thames valley; other elements are secondary.

6.6 CONCLUSIONS

The following conclusions are based on observation of the present day situation, on historical evidence and, in some places, on inference drawn from what is known about the features of grasslands elsewhere. All evidence is discussed in detail in the relevant place in the text.

A. About 6,000 years ago the upper Thames valley was probably occupied by various types of woodland, including alder carr in the wetter places. Clearance probably began in the Neolithic period (4,000–2,400 B.C.) and was probably substantially completed by about 1,500 B.C. The vegetation is now a mosaic of different types of neutral grassland on alluvium and calcareous gravel maintained by indigenous and particularly domestic animals.

B. The changes up to the present in river control, the intensity of settlement, and nature of land-use, have each affected the grassland communities. Although the changes recorded must have resulted in changing patterns of grassland, there may also have been a few local instances of reversion to scrub or woodland before the recent period.

C. It is not possible to describe in any detail the results of human activities on the distribution of grassland types in the past. One could argue by analogy, however, that a study of the effects of recent changes, which are more fully documented, may show how previous changes under similar conditions could have taken place.

D. The present management practices have, in general, been carried out for a long time and the major differences in the grassland can be accounted for in broad terms by differences in land-use, whereas more local differences are related to the intensity of flooding.

E. Within the grassland the greatest contrast is between the mead which has been managed for hay, and the pasture which has been grazed for millennia. This was suspected by Baker (1937). The main contrast is in the species-richness of the mead, up to 63 species per Stand, compared with a maximum of 36 species per Stand in the pasture, and in the large number of species with features such as tall growth and seed set by early summer confined to the mead contrasted with species with rosette forms and vegetative reproduction which are confined to the pasture and are thus suited to particular management practices. These floristic differences have been known for some time (Tansley 1939: 568) but the present study allows some inferences about their possible origin.

F. The change in emphasis from the stinted grazing of the Freemen's and Wolvercote farmers' animals in the Nineteenth Century, to the unstinted grazing of the Commoners' and illegal graziers' animals in the Twentieth Century, is reflected in the increasing dominance of weed species, such as thistles and ragwort, in all but the wettest part of the Meadow.

G. Some of the features described for Port Meadow with Wolvercote Common, such as the area raised by the dumping of rubbish, and the allotment gardens, are certainly of recent origin and may be related to management practices which would not have occurred in the traditional past. Similarly on Picksey Mead, the few arable weeds present can be associated with the use of modern machinery. A certain lack of management can be seen in the degradation of the sward of Port Meadow with Wolvercote Common and its invasion by ragwort and thistles as a result of overgrazing in

winter. It is shown that neither spraying the grassland with the weed-killer 2,4-D amine solution, nor forage harvesting, were successful methods of controlling the weeds. A rigorous policy of regulating the grazing, according to the season and the carrying capacity of the land, should therefore be put in hand. This could be followed by the manual eradication of ragwort and thistle rosettes in spring when the grass is growing fast enough to colonise the gaps left in the sward. The weed problem is now sufficiently great for such a labour intensive solution to be fully justified.

H. The destruction of the sward near Medley Boat Station by a commercial enterprise showed that the scheduling of the Oxford grassland as a Grade 1 Site of Special Scientific Interest in 1952 and the Wildlife and Countryside Act, 1981, were no guarantee of the survival of unimproved grassland. It was unfortunate that The Nature Conservancy Council did not, for whatever reason, ensure that a site of national importance was managed in a way that would enhance its scientific interest.

I. Although Picksey Mead continues to be mown for hay, there have been appreciable changes in recent years which are having or could have considerable influence on the grassland and which could affect its conservation status. For example, the effect of letting the hay lots and grazing to a single contractor should be watched with care. The problems related to not cutting the hay in July 1982 have been discussed but the changes to the flora inherent in changing from cattle to sheep grazing in August have not been looked into. Natural England is now, however, aware that it might affect the composition of the sward. Indeed Woodcock *et al* (2005) showed that the biodiversity of both flora in most years and invertibrate fauna was greater under cattle grazing the aftermath, than sheep.

6.7 CONSIDERATIONS FOR FUTURE MANAGEMENT

The traditional management of the Meadow and Picksey Mead is reflected in their present vegetation and is of considerable historic interest. For this reason such management should be continued and the modern agricultural methods of herbicidal weed control or draining, for example, should be excluded.

6.7.A. PORT MEADOW WITH WOLVERCOTE COMMON

6.7.A.i. Overgrazing in winter

Year-round grazing, particularly in Inundation Zones D, E and F (Map 4) allows colonization of the Meadow by thistles (*Cirsium spp.*) and ragwort (*Seneceo jacobaea*). These species are avoided by grazing animals and so spread over the Meadow until they are stopped by adverse environmental conditions such as a high water-table. Control by forage harvester has been tried but has not so far been effective. This method is unacceptable because it is equivalent to taking a crop of hay. The last time this occurred was during the Civil War. To kill the weeds by further applications of herbicide is also unacceptable on a Site of Special Scientific Interest where other species are of possible interest to agricultural and conservation plant-breeding programmes.

An acceptable method of controlling these particular weeds would be to exclude stock from the Meadow from the 1st December until the 31st March so that the number of germination sites is reduced. This could be done with the co-operation of those with registered grazing rights. At the same time an increase in the number of cattle grazing in early summer, before the thistle and ragwort has grown too tall, would reduce the amount of vegetation removed by a forage harvester clearing ragwort and topping thistles. The animals' dung would return nutrients to the soil.

6.7.A.ii. Port Meadow Marsh

The grazing in this part of the Meadow would be improved if the ditches and culverts on its eastern border were cleared out. This would allow surface water from Port Meadow to flow into the Line Ditch and then into the Old River. There is at present no flow at the junction of the Line Ditch and the Old River which is also silted up. If the headwater of the next weir downstream was lowered by as little as 20cm, it could set up a sufficient water-movement to drain the Meadow in summer time. The substrate would become less suitable for mint (*Mentha aquatica*) and more suitable for the nutritious species such as smooth-stalked meadow-grass (*Poa pratensis*), ryegrass (*Lolium perenne*) and other nutrient-rich grasses (Appendix J).

6.7.B. PICKSEY MEAD

In considering the future management of the Mead, two aspects should be borne in mind, namely, its historic interest as a hay mead and its scientific interest as an unimproved grassland site. With careful management these should not be conflicting interests. The *Phragmites australis* (Type O) grassland is slowly becoming a Reed swamp, similar to that on the west side of Picksey Lane. In order to preserve the mead species, the ditches to the south of Picksey Mead should be cleared out to provide a flow of surface water into the river. It is normal farming practice to clear ditches every 30 years or so. Because the river is generally high in winter and early spring, there is a high water-table at

that time of year, which would allow the early flowering fen species to continue and yet the quality of the hay and grazing would be improved.

To improve the sparse vegetation in the centre of Picksey Mead to the north of the bypass, the autumn and early winter grazing of stock should be increased and controlled to provide a light dressing of dung and the removal of dead grass. A controlled experiment should be conducted which would include the breaking down of the raised bank at strategic points along the northern border of the Mead, so that river water could reach the surface of the central part. This could be beneficial, provided that the ditch along the northern side of the Bypass embankment is cleared out to provide a means for the water to flow off the Mead, back into the river below King's Weir. This would increase the quality of the hay and grazing but would not affect the species-rich fen community south of the Spinney.

6.8 FUTURE RESEARCH AND DEVELOPMENT

6.8.A. AVAILABILITY OF MINERAL SALTS IN THE SOIL AND SOIL WATER

i. Movement of minerals from the dumped material to the east of Port Meadow, onto the Meadow itself, is suggested by the high conductivity readings in the Port Meadow Marsh. These minerals, which may include heavy metals, should be identified and, if toxic, measures should be taken to stop their movement onto the Meadow where they could become dangerous to stock.

ii. Movement of nutrients from the river into both Port Meadow with Wolvercote Common, and Picksey Mead should be traced to measure the amount of filtering, if any, that takes place as the ground water passes through the gravel and alluvium. Such analyses should be accompanied by an ecological survey to trace the way the mineral composition of the soil and soil water may be reflected in the floristic composition of the sward.

6.8.B. VARIATION OF pH IN THE OXFORD GRASSLAND

The wide range of pH in the Oxford grassland should be investigated in relation to species diversity and the importance and cause of seasonal fluctuations in pH values of the soil.

6.8.C. COMPARISON BETWEEN PASTURE AND MEADOW SEED BANKS

On many occasions when crossing the Meadow during the preparation of this volume, small plants of, for example, great burnet (*Sanguisorba officinalis*) and moon daisy (*Leucanthemum vulgare*) were seen. An investigation of the seed bank may show the proportion of these so-called hay meadow species, seen growing on the Meadow, to those lying dormant in the soil.

Similarly, on Picksey Mead, the damage caused by tractor wheels in 1982 might have provided an opportunity to monitor the seed bank and to record the regeneration of these areas. Are the species which occur only on Port Meadow excluded entry into Picksey Mead simply by competition, or by another factor?

6.8.D. SERAL MOVEMENT

If stock could be excluded from the Meadow, what community would replace the present one? There is said to be a correlation between cutting the hay in July and species-richness. If two crops of hay are taken off Picksey Mead, as in the Seventeenth Century, how would this affect the flora? What would happen if a return to the management recommended by Fitzherbert (1523a, 1523b) was made? How would it compare with the regime carried out at the Butser Ancient Farm Research Project?

6.8.E. POLLINATION AND SEED SET

Picksey Mead has many invertebrates active in early summer. How many of them are pollinators of the mead flowers? Should some of them be encouraged? Are the seeds of grasses or other species in a hay crop more nutritious for stock? If so, which?

6.8.F. ARE THERE SIGNIFICANT ASSOCIATIONS BETWEEN PAST MANAGEMENT OF UNIMPROVED GRASSLAND AND INDIVIDUAL PLANT SPECIES?

Port Meadow with Wolvercote Common, and Picksey Mead, are only part of a Grade I Site of Special Scientific Interest (SSSI) which is adjacent to a second grassland SSSI. Several of the fields have received different management in the past yet they are all species-rich. Similarly, Wendlebury Meads Site of Special Scientific Interest is a suite of meadows in the Ray valley in which hay meads may be distinguished from pasture despite similar soil and water conditions (Nature Conservancy Council 1979). If it could be established that certain species are excluded or included in a sward, because of its management, the knowledge would be useful in the maintenance of grassland SSSI's generally, in the future.

6.8.G. AUTECOLOGY

Warwick & Briggs (1979) have identified prostrate forms of *Achillea millefolium* and *Plantago major* on Port Meadow and erect early flowering variants of *Prunella vulgaris* and *Plantago lanceolata* on Picksey Mead. Are there other species showing such phenotypic differences? Observations made during the summers of 1981–84 suggest that other species such as *Leucanthemum vulgare*, *Succisa pratensis* and *Trifolium pratense* on Picksey Mead are different from phenotypes of the same species found, for example, on roadside verges. Is there a genetic difference too?

GLOSSARY

Customary acre   The amount of land which could be scythed by one man in one day

Ecotones   A transitional zone between two ecological communities, as between a forest and grassland or a river and its estuary. An ecotone has its own characteristics in addition to sharing certain characteristics of the two communities.

Edaphic   describes the effect of soil characteristics, especially chemical or physical properties, on plants and animals

Fishing bucks   fish trap attached to the upper side of a bridge over a river or stream

Genecological   study of the genetics and ecology of plants

Gleying   water-logging in the soil causing anoxic (airless) conditions in which plant and insect remains are fossilized

Hide   measure of land: in Old English law, a measure of land equal to 120 acres

Holocene   approximately the last 10,000 years

Merestone   boundary stone

Meristem   growing plant tissue: embryonic plant tissue that is actively dividing, as found at the tip of stems and roots

Monothetic   a divisive statistical method made on the basis of one attribute, character or species, eg. Association Analysis.

Partible   divisible: able to be divided – a partible inheritance

Polythetic   a divisive statistical method made on the basis of partitioning the first axis of an ordination of Stands and/or species, eg. TWINSPAN

Pound lock   gated section of canal or river: a short section of a waterway in which the water level can be altered to enable boats to pass to a higher or lower part of the waterway. The lock has gates at each end with a mechanism for letting water in or out.

Seral   successive changes in flora and fauna: the series of different communities of plants and animals that occupy a specific site and create a stable system during the process of ecological succession

Stint   ration

Terrier   a book or roll in which the lands of private persons or corporations are described by site, boundaries, acreage etc.

Vill   a small town or village, a hamlet; a parish or part of a parish

Appendix A

GRID REFERENCES TO STANDS AND DATE OF SAMPLING PORT MEADOW WITH WOLVERCOTE
COMMON AND PICKSEY MEAD

1.	(49200960)	23.06.81		35.	(49600780)	30.07.81
2.	(49400960)	24.06.81		36.	(49800780)	30.07.81
3.	(48800940)	25.06.81		37.	(50000780)	28.07.81
4.	(49000940)	15.06.81		38.	(50200780)	28.07.81
5.	(49200940)	05.08.81		39.	(49800760)	31.07.81
6.	(49400940)	28.05.81		40.	(50000760)	31.07.81
7.	(49600940)	03.06.81		41.	(50200760)	03.08.81
8.	(48800920)	19.06.81		42.	(50000740)	04.08.81
9.	(49000920)	17.06.81		43.	(50200740)	04.08.81
10.	(49200920)	25.06.81		44.	(48660889)	10.08.81
11.	(49400920)	11.06.81		45.	(48450965)	05.05.82
12.	(49600920)	08.06.81		46.	(48480963)	16.05.82
13.	(48600900)	29.06.81		47.	(48470984)	18.05.82
14.	(48800900)	22.06.81		48.	(48050945)	20.05.82
15.	(49000900)	26.06.81		49.	(48200960)	23.05.82
16.	(49200900)	02.07.81		50.	(48200960)	24.05.82
17.	(49400900)	02.07.81		51.	(48200980)	01.06.82
18.	(49600900)	06.07.81		52.	(48250985)	07.06.82
19.	(48800880)	08.07.81		53.	(48402100)	08.06.82
20.	(49000880)	08.07.81		54.	(48452105)	09.06.82
21.	(49200880)	07.07.81		55.	(48202100)	16.06.82
22.	(49400880)	07.07.81		56.	(48252105)	15.06.82
23.	(49600880)	06.07.81		57.	(48402120)	10.06.82
24.	(49200860)	10.07.81		58.	(48052105)	17.06.82
25.	(49400860)	10.07.81		59.	(48202120)	18.06.82
26.	(49200840)	13.07.81		60.	(48252125)	28.06.82
27.	(49400840)	14.06.81		61.	(48402140)	28.06.82
28.	(49600840)	15.07.81		62.	(48052125)	30.06.82
29.	(49400820)	21.07.81		63.	(48202140)	01.07.82
30.	(49600820)	19.07.81		64.	(48252145)	02.07.82
31.	(49800820)	16.07.81		65.	(48402140)	08.07.82
32.	(49400800)	24.07.81		66.	(48452145)	06.07.82
33.	(49600960)	27.07.81		67.	(48252145)	05.07.82
34.	(49800800)	27.07.81				

APPENDIX B

ALL SPECIES RECORDED IN THIS MONOGRAPH

Achillea millefolium	Yarrow	Climacium dendroides	
Achillea ptarmica	Sneezewort	Crataegus monogyna (seedling)	Common hawthorn
Agrostis capillaris	Common bent	Cratoneuron filicinum	
Agrostis stolonifera	Creeping bent	Crepis biennis	Rough hawk's-beard
Ajuga reptans	Bugle	Crepis capillaris	Smooth hawk's-beard
Alisma lanceolatum	Narrow-leaved water-plantain	Cynosurus cristatus	Crested dog's-tail
Alisma plantago-aquatica	Water plantain	Dactylis glomerata	Cock's-foot
Allium vineale	Wild onion	Dactylorhiza fuchsii	Common spotted-orchid
Alopecurus geniculatus	Marsh foxtail	Dactylorhiza incarnata	Early marsh-orchid
Alopecurus pratensis	Meadow foxtail	Dactylorhiza praetermissa	Southern marsh-orchid
Amblystegium humile		Danthonia (Sieglingia) decumbens	Heath-grass
Amblystegium riparium		Deschampsia cespitosa	Tufted hair-grass
Angelica sylvestris	Wild angelica	Eleocharis palustris	Common spike-rush
Anisantha sterilis	Sterile brome	Eleocharis uniglumis	Slender spike-rush
Anthoxanthum odoratum	Sweet vernal-grass	Elytrigia repens	Common couch
Anthriscus sylvestris	Cow parsley	Epilobium hirsutum	Great willow-herb
Apium inundatum	Lesser Marshwort	Equisetum arvense	Field horsetail
Apium nodiflorum	Fool's water-cress	Equisetum palustre	Marsh horsetail
Apium repens	Creeping marshwort	Eurhynchium praelongum	
Arrhenatherum elatius	False oat-grass	Eurhynchium speciosum	
Atriplex prostata (hastata)	Spear-leaved orache	Eurhynchium swartzii	
Baldellia ranunculoides	Lesser water-plantain	Festuca arundinacea	Tall fescue
Bellis perennis	Daisy	Festuca pratensis	Meadow fescue
Brachythecium mildeanum		Festuca rubra	Red fescue
Brachythecium rutabulum		Festulolium loliaceum	Hybrid fescue
Briza media	Quaking-grass	Filipendula ulmaria	Meadowsweet
Bromus commutatus	Meadow brome	Fraxinus excelsior	Ash
Bromus hordeaceus hordeaceus	Soft brome	Galium aparine	Cleavers
Bromus lepidus	Slender soft-brome	Galium mollugo	Hedge bedstraw
Butomus umbellatus	Flowering rush	Galium palustre	Common marsh-bedstraw
Calliergon cuspidatum		Galium uliginosum	Fen bedstraw
Callitriche obtusangula	Blunt-fruited water-starwort	Galium verum	Lady's bedstraw
Callitriche stagnalis	Common water-starwort	Geranium dissectum	Cut-leaved crane's-bill
Callitriche seedling/sp	Water starwort	Geranium molle	Dove's-foot crane's-bill
Caltha palustris	Marsh marigold	Glechoma hederacea	Ground-ivy
Calystegia sepium	Hedge bindweed	Glyceria fluitans	Floating sweet-grass
Campylium stellatum		Glyceria maxima	Reed sweet-grass
Cardamine flexuosa	Wavy bitter-cress	Glyceria notata	Plicate sweet-grass
Cardamine pratensis	Cuckoo flower	Helictotrichon pratense	Meadow oat-grass
Carduus crispus multiflorus	Welted thistle	Heracleum sphondylium	Hogweed
Carex acuta	Slender tufted sedge	Holcus lanatus	Yorkshire fog
Carex caryophyllea	Spring sedge	Hottonia palustris	Water violet
Carex acutiformis	Lesser pond-sedge	Hordeum secalinum	Meadow barley

Carex disticha	Brown sedge	Hypericum tetrapterum	Square-stalked St. John's-wort
Carex flacca	Glaucous sedge	Hypochoeris glabra	Smooth cat's-ear
Carex hirta	Hairy sedge	Hypochoeris radicata	Cat's-ear
Carex lepidocarpa	Long-stalked yellow-sedge	Iris pseudacorus	Yellow flag
Carex nigra	Common sedge	Juncus articulatus	Jointed rush
Carex panicea	Carnation sedge	Juncus bufonius	Toad rush
Carex riparia	Greater pond-sedge	Juncus compressus	Round-fruited rush
Centaurea nigra	Common knapweed	Juncus conglomeratus	Compact rush
Cerastium arvense	Field mouse-ear	Juncus inflexus	Hard rush
Cerastium fontanum	Common mouse-ear	Koeleria macrantha (gracilis)	Crested hair-grass
Chaerophyllum temulentum	Rough chervil	Lathyrus palustris	Marsh pea
Chenopodium vulvaria	Stinking goosefoot	Lathyrus pratensis	Meadow vetchling
Cirsium acaule	Dwarf thistle	Leontodon autumnalis	Autumn hawkbit
Cirsium arvense	Creeping thistle	Leontodon hispidus	Rough hawkbit
Cirsium eriophorum	Woolly thistle	Leontodon taraxacoides	Lesser hawkbit
Cirsium palustre	Marsh thistle	Leucanthemum vulgare	Oxeye daisy
Cirsium vulgare	Spear thistle	Limosella aquatica	Mudwort
Linum catharticum	Fairy flax	Ranunculus repens	Creeping buttercup
Listera ovata	Common twayblade	Rhinanthus minor	Yellow rattle
Lolium perenne	Perennial ryegrass	Ribes rubrum	Red current
Lotus corniculatus	Common bird's-foot trefoil	Ribes uva-crispa	Gooseberry
Luzula campestris	Field woodrush	Rorippa palustris	Marsh yellow-cress
Lychnis flos-cuculi	Ragged Robin	Rorippa sylvestris	Creeping yellow-cress
Lysimachia nummularia	Creeping Jenny	Rosa canina	Dog-rose
Lythrum salicaria	Purple-loosestrife	Rubus idaeus	Raspberry
Medicago lupulina	Black medick	Rumex acetosa	Common sorrel
Mentha aquatica	Water mint	Rumex conglomeratus	Clustered dock
Myosotis discolor	Changing forget-me-not	Rumex crispus	Curled dock
Myosotis laxa caespitosa	Tufted forget-me-not	Rumex obtusifolius	Broad-leaved dock
Myosotis scorpioides	Water forget-me-not	Sagittaria sagittifolia	Arrowhead
Myosotis secunda	Creeping forget-me-not	Salix cinerea	Grey willow
Nasturtium officinale	Water-cress	Salix fragilis	Crack willow
Nuphar lutea	Yellow water-lily	Salix viminalis	Osier
Nymphoides peltata	Fringed water-lily	Sambucus nigra	Elder
Oenanthe fistulosa	Tubular water-dropwort	Sanguisorba officinalis	Great burnet
Oenanthe silaifolia	Narrow-leaved water-dropwort	Schoenoplectus lacustris	Common clubrush
Ophioglossum vulgatum	Adder's-tongue fern	Senecio aquaticus	Marsh ragwort
Pedicularis palustris	Marsh lousewort	Senecio jacobaea	Common ragwort
Persicaria hydropiper	Water-pepper	Silaum silaus	Pepper-saxifrage
Persicaria lapathifolia	Pale persicaria	Sonchus arvensis	Perennial sow-thistle
Persicaria laxiflora	Tasteless water-pepper	Sonchus palustris	Marsh sow-thistle
Persicaria maculosa	Redshank	Sparganum erectum	Branched bur-reed
Persicaria minor	Small water-pepper	Stellaria alsine	Bog stitchwort
Phalaris arundinacea	Reed canary-grass	Stellaria graminea	Lesser stitchwort
Phleum pratense	Timothy	Stellaria media	Common chickweed
Phragmites australis	Common reed	Stellaria palustris	Marsh stitchwort
Pilosella officinarum agg	Mouse-ear hawkweed	Stratiotes aloides	Water-soldier
Plagiomnium affine		Subularia aquatica	Awlwort
Plagiomnium undulatum		Succisa pratensis	Devil's-bit scabious

Plantago lanceolata	Ribwort plantain	Symphytum officinale	Common comfrey
Plantago major	Greater plantain	Taraxacum officinale agg.	Dandelion
Plantago media	Hoary plantain	Thalictrum flavum	Common meadow-rue
Poa annua	Annual meadow-grass	Thuidium tamariscinum	
Poa compressa	Flattened meadow-grass	Tragopogon pratensis	Goat's-beard
Poa pratensis	Smooth-stalked meadow-grass	Trifolium campestre	Hop trefoil
Poa trivialis	Rough-stalked meadow-grass	Trifolium dubium	Lesser trefoil
Polygonum arenastrum	Equal-leaved knotgrass	Trifolium fragiferum	Strawberry clover
Polygonum aviculare	Knotgrass	Trifolium pratense	Red clover
Potamogeton perfoliatus	Perfoliate pondweed	Trifolium repens	White clover
Potentilla anserina	Silverweed	Triglochin palustre	Marsh arrowgrass
Potentilla erecta	Tormentil	Trisetum flavescens	Yellow oat-grass
Potentilla reptans	Creeping cinquefoil	Urtica dioica	Stinging nettle
Primula veris	Cowslip	Utricularia australis (neglecta)	Bladderwort
Prunella vulgaris	Selfheal	Valeriana dioica	Marsh valerian
Prunus spinosa (seedling)	Blackthorn	Veronica anagallis-aquatica	Blue water-speedwell
Quercus robur (seedling)	Pedunculate oak	Veronica beccabunga	Brooklime
Ranunculus acris	Meadow buttercup	Veronica scutellata	Marsh speedwell
Ranunculus aquatilis	Common water-crowfoot	Veronica serpyllifolia serpyllifolia	Thyme-leaved speedwell
Ranunculus bulbosus	Bulbous buttercup	Viburnum opulus	Guelder rose
Ranunculus ficaria	Celandine	Vicia cracca	Tufted vetch
Ranunculus flammula	Lesser spearwort	Vicia sativa	Common vetch

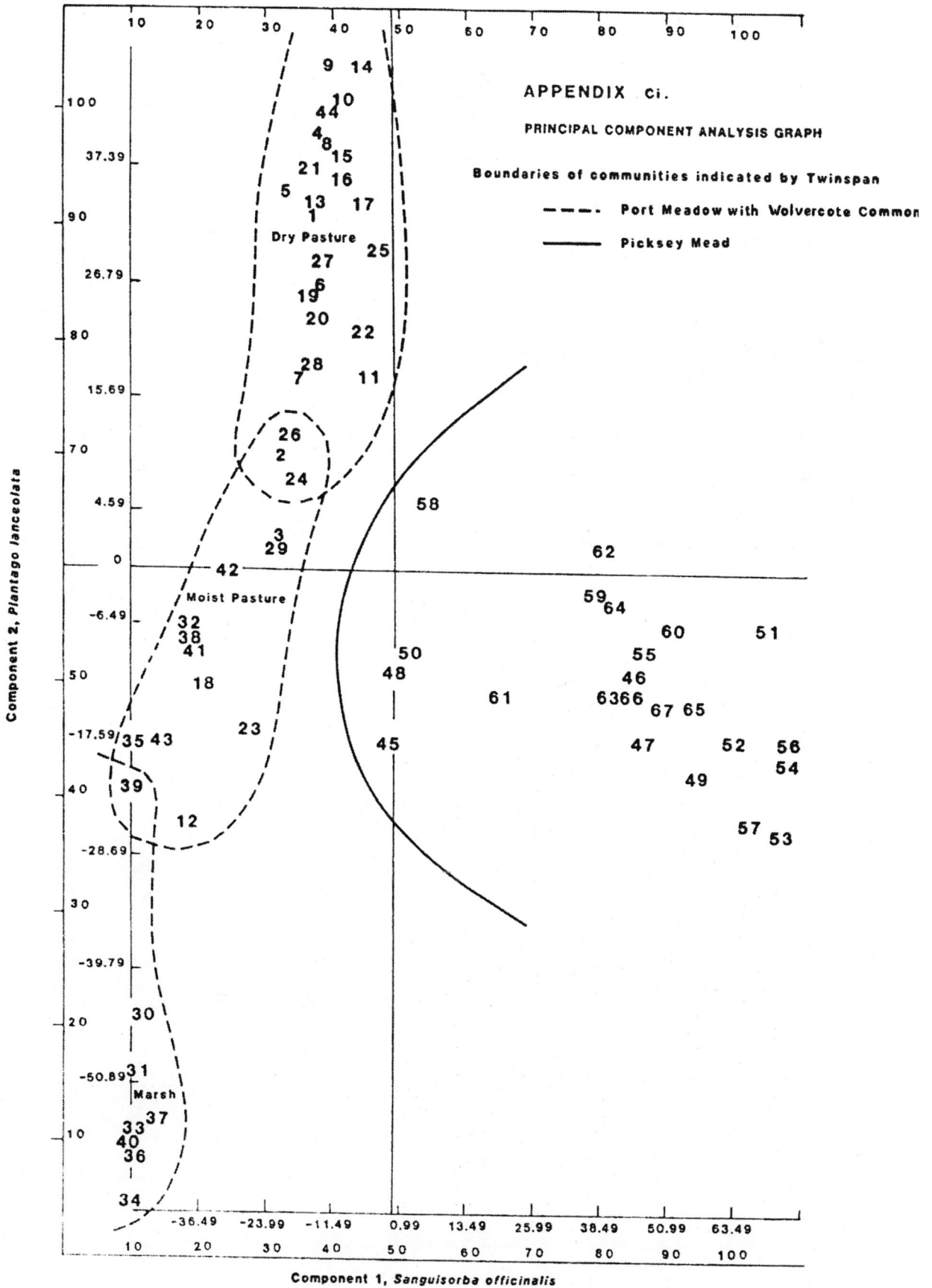

Component 2, *Plantago lanceolata*

10   20   30   40   50   60   70   80   90   100

9 14

100

10

37.39   44

4

8 15

21

16

90   5

13   17

1

Dry Pasture

26.79   27   25

6

19

80   20

22

15.69   28

7   11

26

70   2

24

4.59   58

3   62

0   29

42

Moist Pasture   59 64

-6.49   32   60   51

38

41   55

50   46

18   50   61   6366   67 65

48

-17.59 35 43   47   52   56

23   54

40   39   45   49

12   57 53

-28.69

30

-39.79

20   30

-50.89 31

Marsh

33 37

10   40

36

34

-36.49 -23.99 -11.49   0.99   13.49   25.99   38.49   50.99   63.49

10   20   30   40   50   60   70   80   90   100

Component 1, *Sanguisorba officinalis*

APPENDIX Ci.

PRINCIPAL COMPONENT ANALYSIS GRAPH

Boundaries of communities indicated by Twinspan

— — — — Port Meadow with Wolvercote Common

———— Picksey Mead

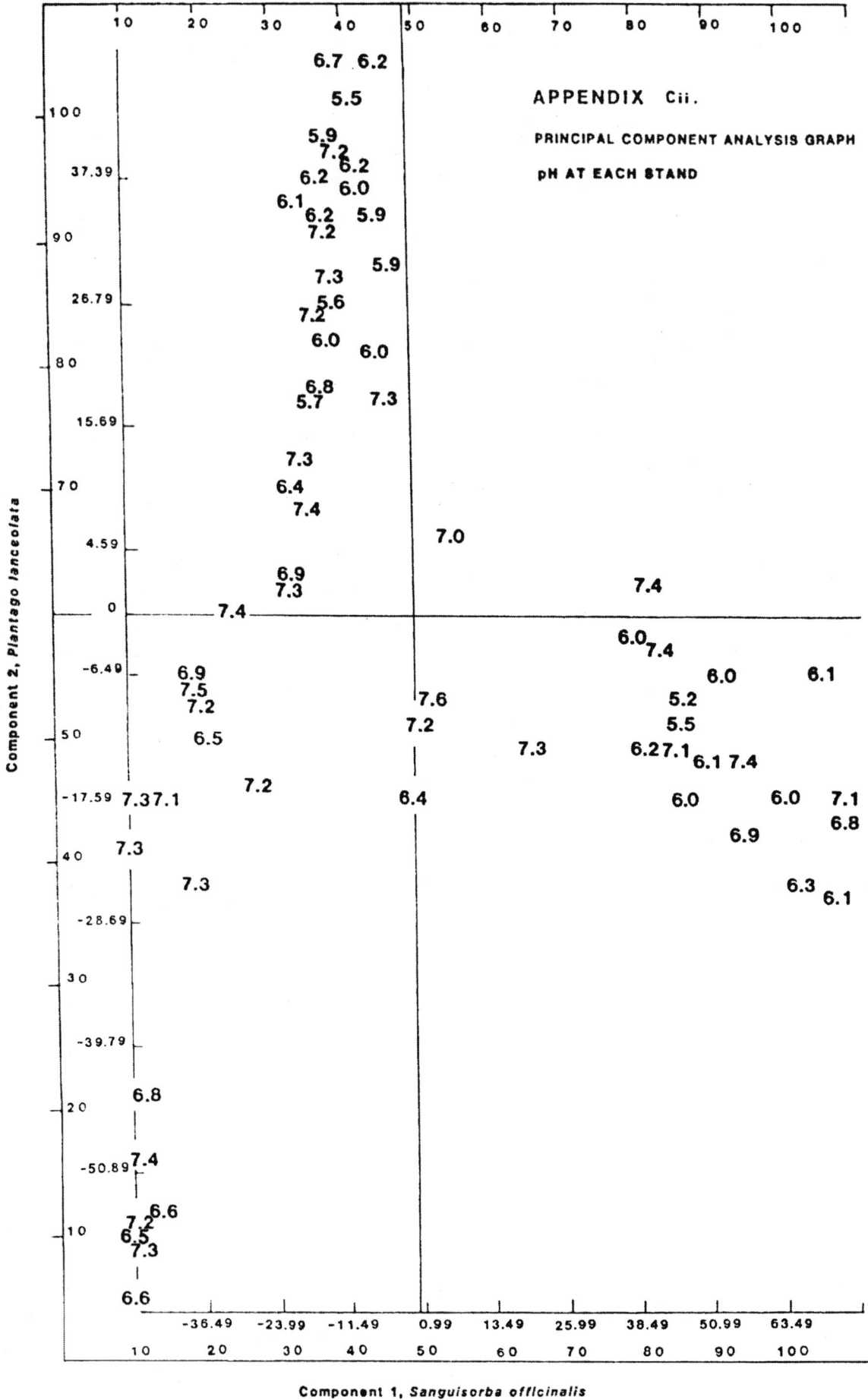

APPENDIX Cii.

PRINCIPAL COMPONENT ANALYSIS GRAPH

pH AT EACH STAND

Component 2, *Plantago lanceolata*

Component 1, *Sanguisorba officinalis*

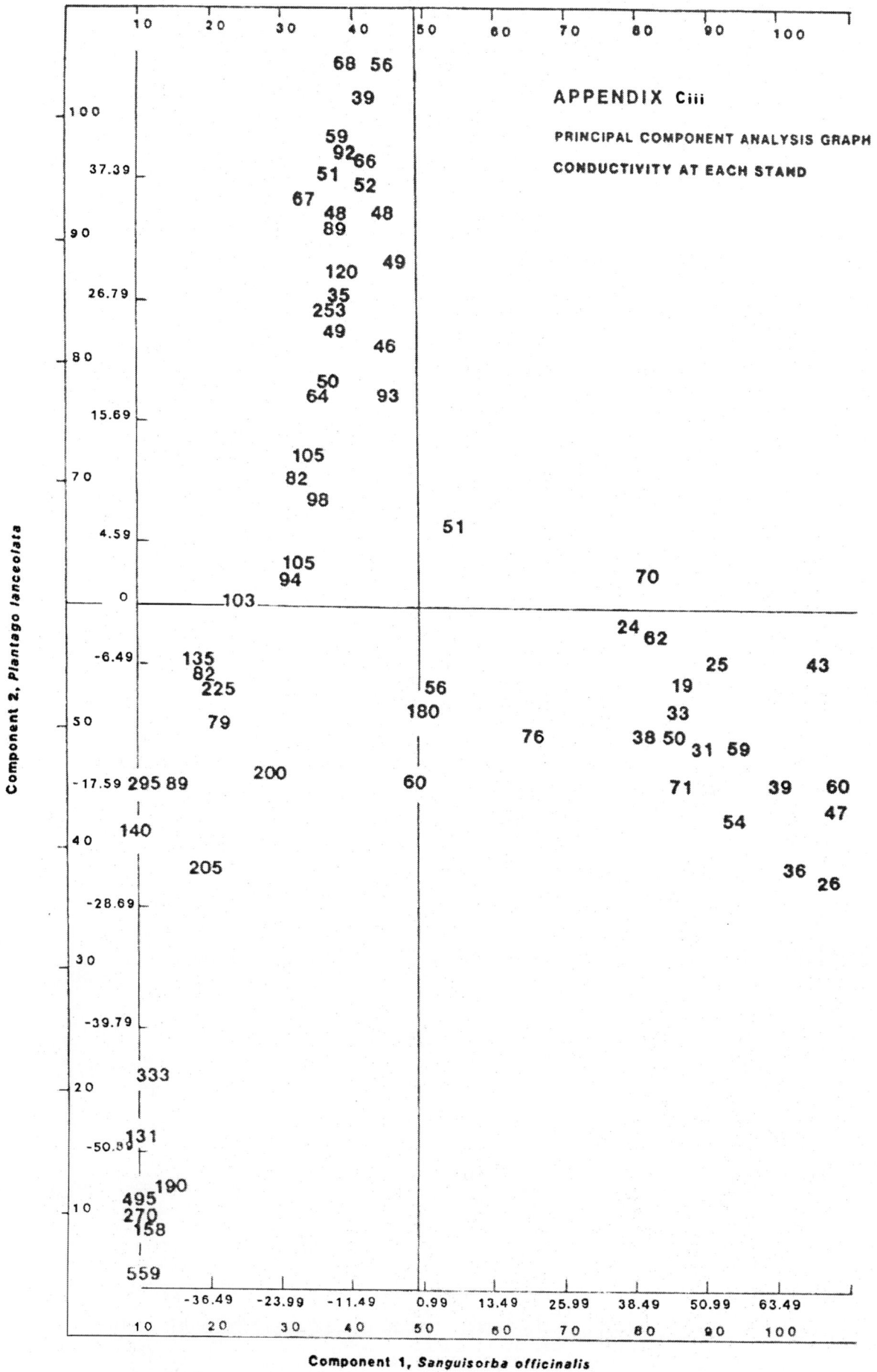

Component 2, *Plantago lanceolata*

Component 1, *Sanguisorba officinalis*

APPENDIX Ciii

PRINCIPAL COMPONENT ANALYSIS GRAPH

CONDUCTIVITY AT EACH STAND

68 56
39
59
92 66
51 52
67
48 48
89
49
120
35
253
49 46
50 93
64
105
82
98
51
105 70
94
103
24 62
135 25 43
82
225 19
180 33
56
79 38 50 31 59
76
200 71 39 60
295 89 60 54 47
140
205 36 26
333
131
495 190
270
158
559

Top axis: 10 20 30 40 50 60 70 80 90 100

Left axis: 100 37.39 90 26.79 80 15.69 70 4.59 0 -6.49 50 -17.59 40 -28.69 30 -39.79 20 -50.89 10

Bottom axis: -36.49 -23.99 -11.49 0.99 13.49 25.99 38.49 50.99 63.49

Bottom axis (lower): 10 20 30 40 50 60 70 80 90 100

125

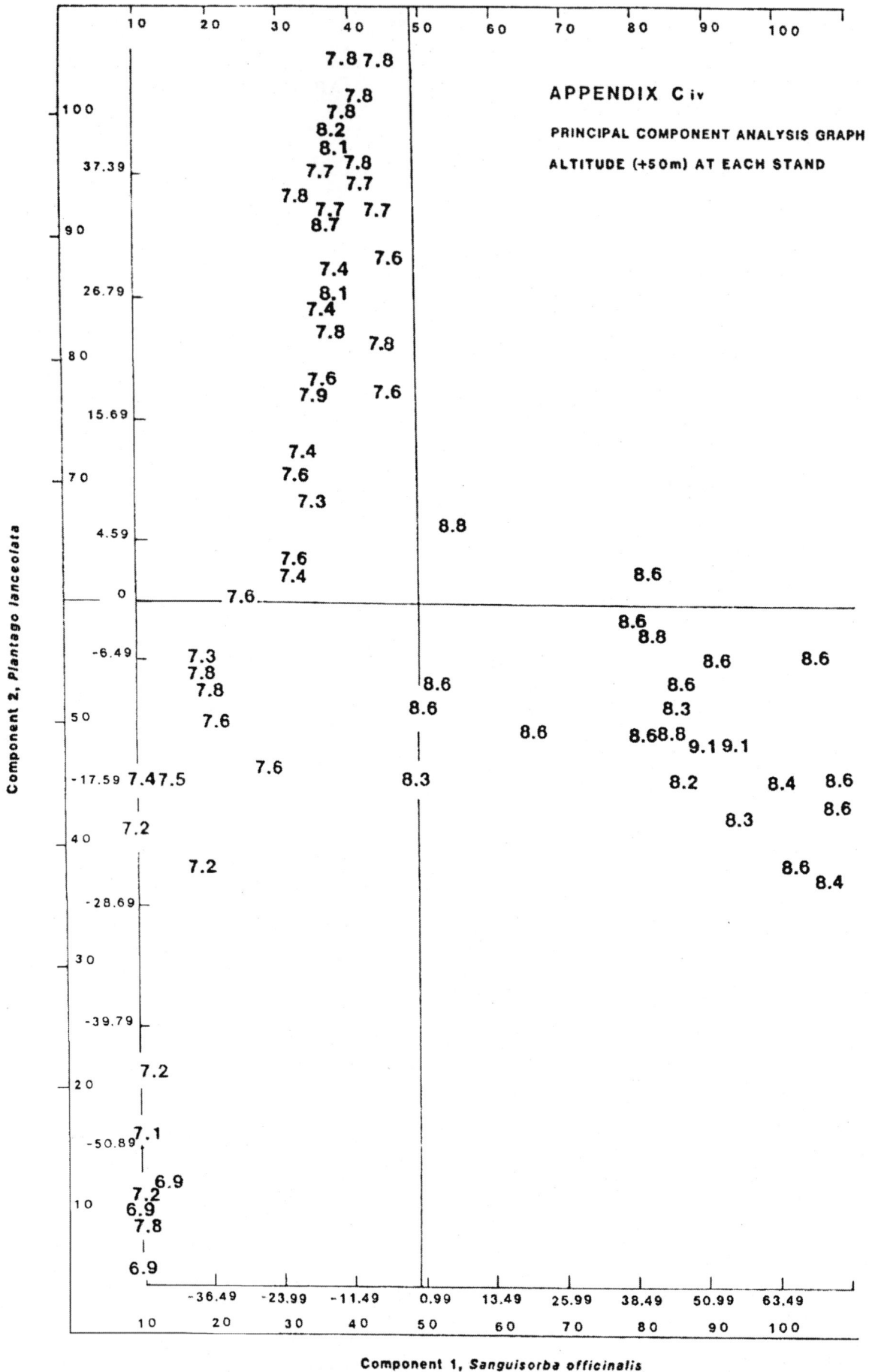

APPENDIX C iv

PRINCIPAL COMPONENT ANALYSIS GRAPH

ALTITUDE (+50m) AT EACH STAND

Component 2, *Plantago lanceolata*

Component 1, *Sanguisorba officinalis*

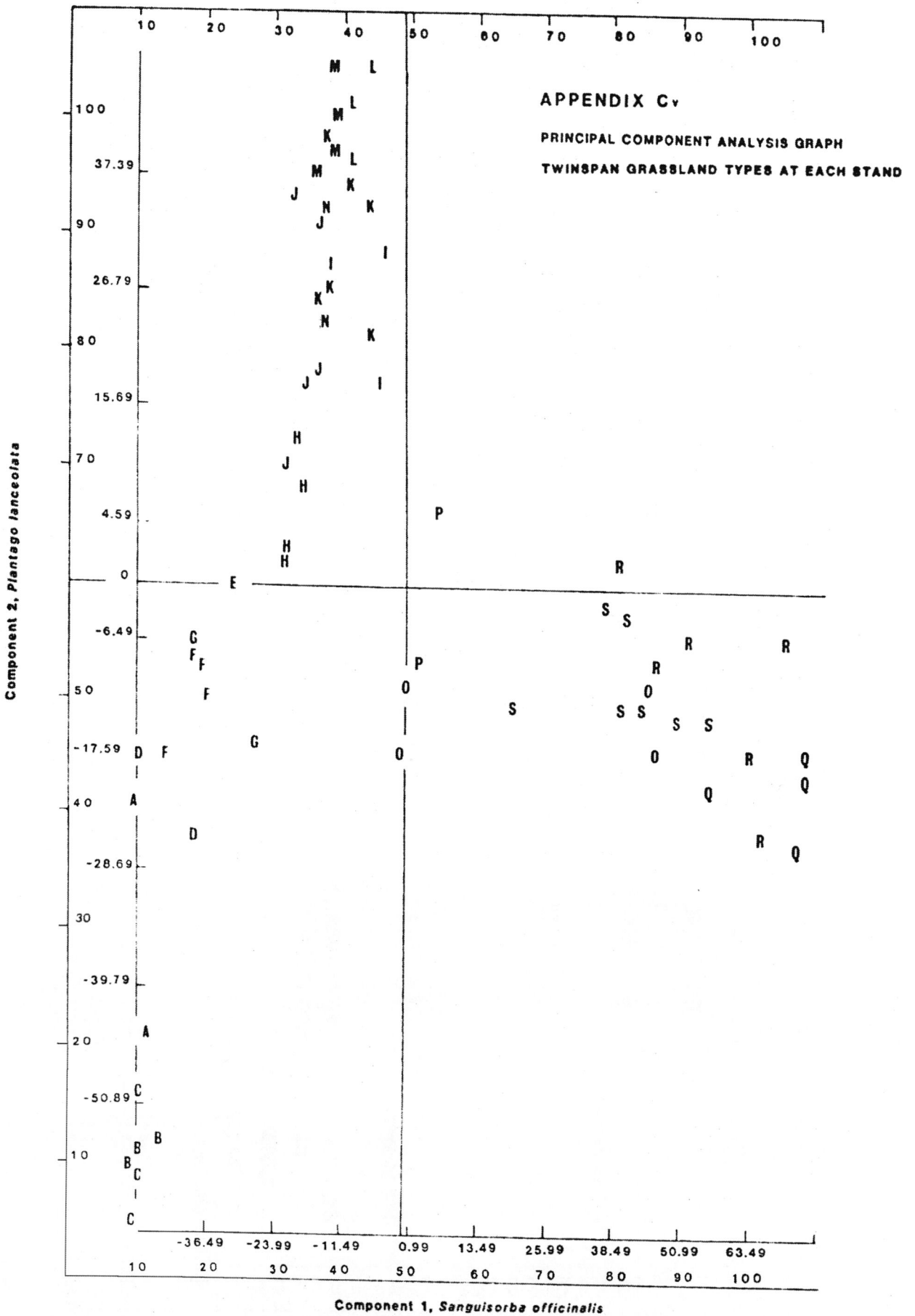

APPENDIX Cᵥ

PRINCIPAL COMPONENT ANALYSIS GRAPH

TWINSPAN GRASSLAND TYPES AT EACH STAND

Component 2, *Plantago lanceolata*

Component 1, *Sanguisorba officinalis*

APPENDIX D

MAKE-UP OF RIVER GRAVELS ON THE OXFORD GRASSLAND

Diagram to show the descriptive categories used in the classification of sand and gravel

APPENDIX E

MINERALS IN PORT MEADOW SOIL WATER (INSTITUTE OF HYDROLOGY) (SEE MAP 5)

WELL N°:   PTM 1

DEPTH: 6.00m (5.20m to bedrock)

GEOLOGY: Terrace 1/Oxford Clay

DATE: 1st/2nd October 1979

Sample depth	0.9 - 1.4m		1.4 - 2.1m		2.1 - 3.1m		3.1 - 3.7m		3.7 - 6.0m	
Sample N°	00021		00022		00023		00024		00025	
	mg/1	meq/1								
Ca	213	10.63	249	12.43	185	9.23	219	10.93	209	10.43
Mg	42	3.45	70	5.76	70	5.76	74	6.09	62	5.10
Na	94	4.09	120	5.22	124	5.39	127	5.52	133	5.79
K	31	0.79	55	1.41	62	1.59	57	1.46	49	1.25
Total	18.96		24.81		21.97		24.00		22.57	
HCO_3	460	7.54	700	11.47	626	10.26	700	11.47	656	10.75
SO_4	420	8.74	490	10.20	480	9.99	460	9.58	460	9.58
Cl	103	2.91	123	3.47	125	3.53	125	3.53	132	3.72
NO_3	<2		<2		<2		<2		<2	
Total		19.19		25.15		23.78		24.58		24.05
Si	4.7		6.5		5.0		5.2		4.9	
Sr										
E.C.	1700		2100		2100		2200		2100	
pH	7.4		7.4		7.4		7.4		7.2	
Balance error	− 0.60%		− 0.61%		− 3.96%		− 1.19%		− 3.17%	

WELL N°:   PTM 2

DEPTH: 5.00m (4.40m to bedrock)

GEOLOGY: Alluvium/Terrace 1/Oxford Clay

DATE: 3rd/4th October 1979

Sample depth	1.1 - 2.1m		2.1 - 3.1m		3.1 - 4.1m					
Sample N°	00026		00027		00028					
	mg / l	meq/l								
Ca	343	17.12	809	40.37	431	21.51				
Mg	40	3.29	64	5.26	76	6.25				
Na	110	4.79	164	7.13	201	8.74				
K	10.4	0.27	10.6	0.27	10.2	0.26				
Total		25.47		53.04		36.76				
HCO_3	479	7.85	479	7.85	497	8.15				
SO_4	670	13.95	910	18.95	152	3.16				
Cl	140	3.95	188	5.30	236	6.66				
NO_3	<2		<2		<2					
Total		25.75		32.10		17.97				
Si	5.2		5.8		7.0					
Sr										
E.C.	2100		2600		3000					
pH	7.4		7.4		7.2					
Balance error	− 0.54%		24.59%		34.34%					

WELL N°:   PTM 3

DEPTH: 4.90 m (4.70 m to bedrock)

GEOLOGY: Alluvium/Terrace 1/Oxford Clay

DATE :   22nd/23rd October 1979

Sample depth	1.0 - 2.0 m		2.0 - 3.0 m		3.0 - 4.0 m		4.0 - 4.7 m		
Sample N°	00051		00052		00053		00054		
	mg/l	meq/l							
Ca	151	7.53	152	7.58	163	8.13	151	7.53	
Mg	5.1	0.42	5.9	0.49	5.6	0.46	4.7	0.39	
Na	21	0.91	23	1.00	25	1.09	26	1.13	
K	3.7	0.09	5.0	0.13	7.3	0.19	7.4	0.19	
Total		8.96		9.20		9.87		9.24	
HCO_3	326	5.34	288	4.72	357	5.85	349	5.72	
SO_4	27	0.56	133	2.77	139	2.89	91	1.89	
Cl	38	1.07	66	1.86	47	1.33	41	1.16	
NO_3	2	0.03	3	0.05	<2		<2		
Total		7.01		9.40		10.07		8.77	
Si	3.2		3.3		4.0		2.7		
Sr									
E.C.	620		900		920		840		
pH	7.6		7.3		7.6		7.5		
Balance error	12.23%		−1.08%		−1.02%		2.61%		

WELL N°:   PTM 5

DEPTH: 6.00m (5.70 m to bedrock)

GEOLOGY: Terrace 1/Oxford Clay

DATE: 24 October 1979

Sample depth	1.8 - 2.8 m		2.8 - 4.1 m		4.1 - 5.2 m		5.2 - 5.7 m		
Sample N°-	00055		00056		00057		00058		
	mg/l	meq/l							
Ca	89	4.44	126	6.29	132	6.59	126	6.29	
Mg	2.8	0.23	3.2	0.26	4.2	0.35	4.2	0.35	
Na	11	0.48	16	0.70	20	0.87	20	0.87	
K	4.4	0.11	8.4	0.21	9.4	0.24	9.6	0.25	
Total		5.26		7.46		8.05		7.76	
HCO_3	253	4.15	293	4.80	326	5.34	303	4.97	
SO_4	54	1.12	74	1.54	86	1.79	84	1.75	
Cl	28	1.52	48	1.35	43	1.21	46	1.30	
NO_3	13	0.21	3	0.05	<2		3	0.05	
Total		6.27		7.74		8.34		8.07	
Si	2.9		2.7		3.3		2.7		
Sr									
E.C.	600		730		720		770		
pH	7.7		7.4		7.6		7.5		
Balance error	−10.24%		−1.86%		−1.77%		−1.96%		

MEMORIES OF PORT MEADOW (H. MINN, 1947)

The condition of Port Meadow has greatly changed from the time of my early recollection in the 1880. Before the raising of the south portion of the Meadow with the City refuse the lower end was very wet and before the extensive dredging of the river and the enlarging of the weirs at Osney the whole Meadow was usually flooded from November to March to a depth sufficient for sailing boats and during frosts good skating, the latter often giving employment to the workless with chairs putting on skates which at that period were all of the wooden type with screw and straps. But the drainage was very much better than it is now (1939) there being one large and deep drain running some distance up the Meadow and draining into the old river and all the ditches round the Meadow were then quick running streams and swarming with crayfish.

Once the river having fallen the Meadow drained and dried up very quickly and formed fairly good cricket pitches, the Clarendon Press Club played there and a roller was kept on the Meadow, earlier still in 1760 the Rev. Jas. Woodforde while an undergraduate at New College records playing in a cricket match on Port Meadow between "the Winchester against the Eaton arid we Wintons beat them". With the great improvements effected in the Thames under the Thames Drainage Act only the lower part of the Meadow now floods and that usually only for a few days. This reduction in the extent and period of the floods has caused a great change in the Flora of the Meadow and the marshy plants have given way especially at the top end of the Meadow to coarse weeds of cultivation, thistles, nettles, hawkweeds and some few additions were made to the flora by seeds brought on the wheels of the aeroplanes in 1916–18 but these have mostly vanished. The ditches round the Meadow are now all silted up and many flowers have now disappeared, notably the water violet *Hottonia palustris* which at one time existed in large patches.

The river has also greatly changed between Medley and Godstow. Up to the early nineties (1890) it was shallow quick running water with a fine gravel bottom, forming one of the best short punting courses in the Thames. It was only navigable for heavy boats on "flash" days, Tuesdays and Fridays, on the flush of water. In summer the water was rather choked with water plants. The yellow water lily *Nuphar luteum* being very abundant and in the late summer the surface along the Meadow side gloriously golden with masses of *Lymnantheum nymphaeoides*. The banks were clothed in their seasons with Kaltha (Marsh Marigold), Forget-me-not, masses of the Mints, *Butomus* (Flowering Rush) Purple and Yellow Loosestrife, and many other waterside plants. Between Binsey and Black Jack's Hole the river was very much wider than it is now, for the lowering of the bed of the river by dredging has added several acres to Port Meadow.

The shallow water swift running over a gravel bottom swarmed with fish and I have seen old Jack Bossom with one throw of a cart net (now prohibited) catch more fish than would now be caught in a month's fishing, for the last deep dredging during the late 1920s and 1930 has left the river only a deep muddy canal leaving the fish no shelter and no shallow water in which to spawn and clean after spawning. Up to about 1880 crayfish existed in great abundance and the local boatmen would take up a punt load of creels in the evening drop them and lift the following morning after taking many hundreds during the night, but during the 1880s the whole of the crayfish in both the Thames and its tributaries and in the Oxford canal perished of some unknown disease, and all efforts to re-establish them have been without success, but I think the dredging is responsible for this as crayfish cannot exist in deep water.

The Towing Path was formerly one of the most pleasant walks near Oxford. It ran between the river and a ditch and was a glory with wild flowers during the summer and autumn. It is now a dreary arid waste formed by the gravel dredged from the river.

The Meadow and the river made a perfect paradise for birds especially the waders, and marsh birds. I have seen Redshank, Greenshank, Ruff and Reeves, Snipe, Dunlin, Godwit, etc., once a stork, heron are common, swan I have counted as many as 42 at one time. Moorhen and dabchick were common but are now decreasing owing to lack of cover, the great crested grebe was occasionally seen, and once a Red-throated diver. Gulls and terns are fairly common, in the winter of 1938–9 gulls appeared in larger numbers than I had ever seen, in a flock of 7 or 8 hundred. When the Meadow is flooded large flocks of coot and many of the duck species and an occasional wild goose may be seen. In the spring lapwing and golden plover are common on the Meadow.

Perhaps the greatest change in the appearance of the river is in the boating. From about 1880 up to 1900 the Bossoms and Beesley of Medley owned between them several hundred boats and the river up to Godstow was crowded with them on a summer evening, but now one can often walk to Godstow in the summer evening without seeing a boat, the advent of motors has put an end to this form of pleasure. I very much doubt if the lock-keeper at Godstow now lets through in 12 months boats equalling the number passing through in a single week as the above date.

As late as 1814 salmon were sometimes found as visitors in the upper reaches of the Thames. Lampreys were locally known under the name of "Pride". The only time I have seen these fish in the Thames was about the year 1885 when I saw 30 or 40 small ones 6 or 7 inches long on a large stone at the overflow to "Swift's ditch" near Godstow. (H.M.)

In this summer (1940) the upper part of the Meadow is covered with tents forming a large army camp and posts have been put up all over the Meadow to prevent enemy aeroplanes landing in case of an invasion.

In the summer of 1901 I gathered several specimens of *Aristolochia clematitis* on the bank of the Sanctuary ditch in the west side of the Nunnery enclosure at Godstow. It was recorded on the same spot by Sibthorpe in 1794 and again by Walker in 1832. In 1907 and for some years after there was a small patch of *Gentiana amarella* in the north-west corner of the Port Meadow.

Some additions to the flora of the Meadow were made by seeds and plants adhering to the landing wheels of the aeroplanes stationed on the Meadow 1914–18.

Now, 1947, the upper part of the Meadow has been allowed to become covered with thistles and other weeds of cultivation.

APPENDIX G

IRON AGE SPECIES LIST (DR M.A. ROBINSON)

	1.	*Cruciferae indet.*
P	2.	*Cerastium cf. holosteoides*
A	3.	*Stellaria media gp.*
A–B	4.	*Arenaria sp.*
A	5.	*Chenopodium rubrum or botryodes*
A	6.	*Atriplex sp.*
P	7.	*Potentilla anserina*
	8.	*Anthriscus caucalis*
	9.	*Polygonum aviculare agg.*
A	10.	*P. persicaria*
A	11.	*P. lapathifolium or nodosum*
A	12.	*P. convolvulus*
A–B	13.	*Rumex maritimus*
	14.	Another *Rumex sp.*
	15.	*Gramineae indet.*
A	16.	*Urtica urens*
P	17.	*U. dioica*
	18.	*Myosotis sp.*
A–B	19.	*Hyoscyamus niger*
P	20.	*Mentha sp.*
P	21.	*Ballota nigra*
A–B	22.	*Carduus sp.*
P	23.	*Achillea sp.*
B	24.	*Onopordum acanthium*
P	25.	*Leontodon sp.*
A	26.	*Galium aparine*
P	27.	*Juncus sp.*
	28.	*Lemna sp.*
P	29.	*Carex sp.*
	30.	*Eleocharis s. palustris sp.*

Of these species, the following are common on Iron Age settlement sites in the upper Thames valley: *Atriplex sp., Hyoscyamus niger, Ballota nigera, Onopordum acanthium, Galium aparine, Anthriscus caucalis.*

Was *Onopordum acanthium* cultivated for its blanched leaves or oil from its seeds?

Of the ten Coleoptera identified by the end of January, 1983, four were dung beetles and one (*Ananthius*) prefers umbelliferous flowers and so may indicate tall grassland, possibly, meadow.

KEY
A = annual   P = perennial
A–B = annual or biennial

APPENDIX H

OWNERSHIP OF YARNTON AND BEGBROKE LOT BALLS

The names of the balls with alternative spellings cited.

LOT BALLS ASSOCIATED WITH BEGBROKE FARMS
(R.H. = Rotuli Hundredorum II)

WILLIAM OF BLADON
Associated with Begbroke Rectory in 1912 (Gretton 1912: 59). Possibly named for a member of Agnes and Richard de Bladene's family who lived in Begbroke in 1279 (R.H.: 857).

PARRY
(Parry: Charlett 1936; Perry: Bretton 1912: 58)
Possibly named after Richard de Pyrie who was a tenant of John Giffard in 1279 (R.H.: 857).

GEOFFREY
(Geoffrey: Charlett 1936; Walter Jefferey: Thomas (1858 MB Top Oxon B.19, f.174; Water Geoffrey: Gretton 1910: 53; Water Jeoffrey, Gretton 1912: 42)
This ball belonged to Begbroke Hill Farm in 1860 and its ownership can be traced through the Fitzherbert family to the Gifford family (Blenheim Mun, Box 21). John Gifford had a servus called Walter Godefrey in 1279 (R.H.: 857).

BOAT
It is often the case that errors creep in when script writing is deciphered. It is possible, therefore, that Richard de Cote, who lived in Yarnton in 1279, was the original owner of this ball (Gretton 1912: 58). Another possibility is the family of William Hoat who was assessed in Yarnton at 2d in 1317 (P.R.O. E.179/161/8). However, this ball belonged to Begbroke Hall in 1908 and the Hall's ownership can be traced back to the Thirteenth Century. It may have belonged to the Prioress of Studley"s three yardlands in 1279 (Christopher Day pers. comm.)

LOT BALLS ASSOCIATED WITH YARNTON FARMS

HARRY
This may be a familiar form of William Henr's name. He lived in Yarnton in 1279 (R.H.: 855). The ball belonged to Exeter College, as Rectors of Yarnton, in the 20th century.

WHITE
Simon le Wyte lived in Yarnton in 1279 (R.H.: 855) and the ball now belongs to Paternoster Farm, Yarnton (Mr E. Harris, First Meadsman, *pers. comm.*)

BOULTON
(Booton, Thomas MS. Top Qxon. b. 19, f . 174; Gretton 1912: 58) This may be a corruption of Bovetone, a family living in Yarnton and Begbroke in 1279, since it would not be difficult to confuse a script "ve" for "ul" (Gretton 1912: 58). The Bovetone family continued to live in Yarnton in 1327 (P.R.O. E.179/161/9) and in 1817 the ball belonged to Mr Robert Osborne's Farm. He lived in the Manor House and owned 84 commons and ten men's mowths. Boulton now belongs to Stonehouse Farm, which at one time acted as the home farm to the Manor. This may be added evidence that this ball belonged to a Yarnton farmstead rather than to one in Begbroke.

GREEN
This name may be a corruption of Agnes de Juvene's name (Gretton 1912: 58) but Will at Green is probably a more likely candidate. Both are recorded as living in Yarnton in 1279 (R.H.: 855) and Miles at Green was there in 1327 (P.R.O.).

ROTHE

This name is a problem. Richard de Cote could be a corruption of either Boat (q.v.) or Rothe (Gretton 1912, 58). But, a deed dated 1632 and related to a property which belonged to John Weston and which, in 1749, belonged to Exeter College, mentions "a lot called 'Roffe' lying and being in a meadow called Pixey Mead" (Exeter Col. Mun.). Bearing in mind thedifficulties encountered when deciphering script, Roffe may come from Rosse, which, in turn, may have been derived from Basse. John Basse lived in Yarnton in 1279 (R.H. 855) and the family was still there in 1327 (P.R.O. E.179/161/8 and 9).

FREEMAN

Contrary to Gretton's opinion (1912: 58) there was a freeman living in Yarnton in Domesday (Morris 1976: 6.14). He is re-ferred to as a "maino" "he could go where he will". However, the freeman in question is more likely to have been Thos le Frankleyn who lived in Yarnton in 1279 (R.H.: 855) or Thos le Freeman in 1327 or Ric and Mic Freeman who lived in Yarnton in 1317 and 1327 respectively (P.R.O.). The ball belonged to Jackson's Farm in the twentieth century (Merton Col. Mun.).

WATERY MOLLY

Watery Molly: Charlett 1936; Water Molley: Gretton 1912: 59; Walter Molly: Stapleton 1893: 309; Walter de Molly: Thomas 1858, MS Top Oxon b.19, f.174.
This name could be an abbreviation of Molendinarius and the ball could be named after a relative of John of the Mill (Gretton 1912: 59). It may have belonged to Springhill Farm (Christopher Day *pers. comm*). Gretton (1912: 58) associates it with Windmill Hill Farm but this farm appears to be a relatively new property which had no allotment in the Thames meadows in the early Nineteenth Century (Thomas M.S. Top Oxon. b.19.f. 192). An alternative is that the ball was associated with the land of a water mill, possibly at Cassington, Summerton or Thrupp (R.H. 855).

DUNN

Will Dun lived in Yarnton in 1294 (R.H. 855) and Wm and Wal Don in 1317 and 1327 respectively (P.R.O. E.179/161/8 and 9).

GILBERT

Thomas Gileberd lived in Yarnton in 1279 (R.H. 855). This could be a variant of the spelling of Gilbert. Certainly the Gilbert family lived in Yarnton in 1317 and 1327 (P.R.O. E. 179/161/8 and 9). The ball belonged to Yarnton Manor in 1952 (Kohlhorst, Oxford City Library).

THE TYDALLS

"The Tydalls are pens of the best land stoned out in each meadow for the tithe owner, to discharge the rest from tithe" (Stapleton 1893)

In Picksey there are three statute acres (Charlett 1936). The Tydalls belonged to Merton College as Rectors of Begbroke and Exeter College as Rectors of Yarnton. The Tydalls were laid down before 1774, when Henry Smith notes on his survey (MS Top Oxon b.19.f.97) that the lands in Oxhey, West Meadow and Picksey Meadow are valued as tithe free lands to the tenants. They may have been laid down at any time between the earliest known record in 1754 (MS Top Oxon b.19.f.216) and, perhaps, 1294 when, contrary to their normal practice, Rewley Abbey agreed to pay tithes to Eynsham Abbey (M.S. Top Oxon.B.9.f.12.).

MOWING THE MEADS

The ceremony of drawing the lots seems to have been unchanged for generations and was arranged in the following manner:

"On the day for the drawing of Oxhey the party including the two Meadsmen one of them carrying the 13 balls in the bag start from the end of the metalled road opposite the entrance to "Mead Farm" pass through the farmyard and thence down the grass lane (in winter often a complete bog) till they reach the gate at the point marked A on Plan 2 at the northwest corner of Oxhey Mead. They then walk across the first Division of Oxhey till they reach the grass track shown on Plan 2 as separating the first from the second Division. Then they walk down that grass track east to the point C. Arrived at point C the Meadsman with the bag holds out the bag with the balls in it holding the mouth closed so that a person cannot see the balls or the names thereon and someone is invited (if a lady visitor as is usually the case is present she is invited) to draw first. He or she puts in a hand draws one ball looks at it and calls out the name written thereon for instance "William of Bladon" and this is verified by the Meadsmen. The person claiming to own the ball "William of Bladon" in Oxhey or generally or some one acting for him says "I am William of Bladon" and thereupon at the point C with a scythe cuts a few feet then with a knife he cuts his own initials or his master's on the grass left by that scythe cutting. Several persons then following each other in single file walk down the whole of the western and eastern boundaries as shown in the plan of Strip No. 1 of first Division. This is done to stamp the grass down and thus trace accurately the exact boundaries of the drawer's strip and to prevent his trespassing on his neighbours. There is no physical boundary between each of the thirteen strips that make up each of the first second and third divisions. But there are posts on the grasstrack which runs west to east between the first and second Divisions shewing the exact starting points of each strip in these divisions and similarly at the proper places there are posts showing the starting point of each of the thirteen strips in the third Division and farther along posts in line so as to enable the true line in each case to be kept. Strip No. 1 of the first Division having thus been drawn and the line each side trod down as above the ball "William of Bladon" is of course not returned to the bag but kept in the Meadsman's pocket. The same course is followed successively as regards each of the strips 2 to 13 of the first Division till the western hedge is reached. At this point of course no ball is left in the bag. When all thirteen balls are put back into the bag and the thirteen strips of the second Division shown on the plan are similarly drawn in succession till the party this time walking eastwards arrive at the point D. They then walk eastwards down the rest of the grass track and up the eastern boundary of strip 1 of the first Division till they arrive at the point E and the thirteen balls being again replaced in the bag they draw similarly the 13 strips of the third Division this time walking southwards till they reach the river. The same process of drawing scything cutting and treading boundaries that I have described in regard to Strip 1 of the first Division is repeated in the case of each strip in each Division. It results that in drawing Oxhey each ball is drawn three times but as I said before Tydalls is never drawn for."

(Frederick Charlett First Meadsman, 1936)

Appendix I

HORSE AND COW FEEDING PREFERENCES

Grazing preferences of horses and cattle (Archer 1973; Ivins 1952).
1 = least favourite species.
26 = most favourite species.

Horses' preferences

1.	*Agrostis tenuis*	Browntop
2.	*Trifolium pratense*	Red Clover
3.	*Achillea millefolium*	Yarrow
4.	*Festuca rubra*	Red fescue S.59
5.	*Cichorium intybus*	Chicory
6.	*Plantago lanceolata*	Ribgrass
7.	*Poa pratensis*	Smooth-stalked meadow-grass
8.	*Taraxacum officinale*	Dandelion
9.	*Poa trivialis*	Rough stalked meadow-grass
10.	*Alopecurus pratensis*	Meadow foxtail
11.	*Cynosurus cristatus*	Crested dogstail
12.	*Lolium perenne*	Perennial ryegrass S.24
13.	*Dactylis glomerata* and *Poa trivialis*	Cocksfoot/rough-stalked meadow-grass
14.	*Festuca rubra*	Canadian creeping red fescue
15.	*Trifolium repens*	Wild white clover – Kentish
16.	*Lolium perenne*	Perennial ryegrass S.23
17.	*Lolium perenne*	Perennial ryegrass – midas
18.	*Festuca arundinacea*	Tall fescue – alta
19.	*Lolium perenne*	Perennial ryegrass S.321
20.	*Phleum pratense*	Timothy S.48
21.	*Phleum pratense*	Timothy S.50
22.	*Dactylis glomerata*	Cocksfoot S.143
23.	*Lolium perenne*	Perennial ryegrass – petra
24.	*Lolium perenne*	Perennial ryegrass – melle
25.	*Lolium perenne*	Perennial ryegrass – sceempter
26.	*Lolium perenne* *Festuca pratensis* *Dactylis glomerata* *Phleum pratense* *Trifolium repens*	Dryland mixture

Cows' preferences

1.	Trefoil	10.	Timothy S.48
2.	S.143 Cocksfoot	11.	Meadow fescue S.215
3.	Cockle Park Type Mixture	12.	Ribgrass
4.	Irish perennial ryegrass		
5.	Danish cocksfoot		
6.	Montgomery L.F.R.C.		
7.	American timothy		
8.	Perennial ryegrass S.23		
9.	White clover S.100		

APPENDIX J

POACEAE SPECIES OF GRASSLAND INTEREST

Elymus repens	A troublesome weed on most arable land.	Perennial
Agrostis capillaris	Nutritive value and palatability low. Not sown in seed mixtures except for the formation of lawns and greens.	Perennial
Alopecurus pratensis	Nutritive value and palatability extremely high. Productivity of some indigenous strains high throughout growing season. Very leafy in early spring and very winter green. Seed difficult to establish, not normally recommended for seed mixtures.	Perennial
Anthoxanthum odoratum	Nutritive value low and not recommended for including in seed mixtures. Originally an inhabitant of woodland.	Perennial
Arrhenatherum elatius	Proportion of leaf:stem low. Cannot stand up to grazing, but produces heavy hay crop on light land.	Perennial
Helictotrichon pratensis	Nutritive value low, used for rough grazing on dry chalky soils.	Perennial
Brachypodium pinnatum	Nutritive value low.	Perennial
Brachypodium sylvaticum	Nutritive value low.	Perennial
Bromus mollis	Nutritive value and palatability low, not very persistent.	Biennial
Cynosurus cristatus	Nutritive value and palatability high. Productivity highest during late summer. Rapidly develops wiry flowering stems unattractive to stock. Very winter green and valuable as a bottom grass on upland pastures and poor dry soils. Originated in dry grassland.	Perennial
Dactylis glomerata	Nutritive value high and very palatable in young stage. Productivity high. Starts growth early in spring and recovers quickly in the absence of grazing. Agricultural strains developed for grazing and hay.	Perennial
Deschampsia cespitosa	Nutritive value low, a weed in wet shady places.	Perennial
Festuca ovina	Nutritive value and palatability moderately high. Productivity low. Hardy and drought resistant.	Perennial
Festuca pratensis	Nutritive value high. Palatability decreased with age. High proportion of leaf to stem. Recommended for permanent leys.	Perennial
Festuca rubra	Nutritive value and palatability high. When young indigenous strains are productive and often remain green in winter. On good soils it tends to suppress white clover.	Perennial
Holcus lanatus	Palatability low, indigenous strains sometimes recommended for improving upland pastures.	Perennial

Lolium perenne	Nutritive value and palatability high. Productivity high throughout growing season and persists over a number of years. Agricultural strains developed for grazing and hay.	Perennial
Phleum pratense	Nutritive value and palatability high. Susceptible to grazing but produces heavy hay crops on good soils. Originated in dry grassland.	Perennial
Poa annua	Nutritive value low.	Annual
Poa pratensis	Nutritive value and productivity high. Sometimes recommended for sowing in seed mixtures as a bottom grass in open, rich soils, and for hard wearing lawns.	Perennial
Poa trivialis	Nutritive value and palatability high. Productivity high during early summer. Persistent on account of its creeping habit.	Perennial
Trisetum flavescens	Nutritive value and palatability high. Productivity low. High proportion of stem to leaf.	Perennial

(Baker 1937; Percival 1910; Stapledon 1933; Thomas & Davies 1949).

APPENDIX K

ACCESS POINTS TO THE MEADOW AND PICKSEY MEAD

This Appendix is designed to expand some historical aspects of Chapters 5.2.N Encroachment/Enclosure and 6.1.D.iii. Impact of treading and poaching.

i. WOLVERCOTE BATHING PLACE
At the north end of Port Meadow next to the Toll Bridge (named as a reminder of the place where people paid a toll at the entrance to a fair held in Fair Close in the time of King Stephen and Queen Matilda) an area of pasture is lost due to the building of a car park and the exclusion of cattle and horses from the grass in the Bathing Place. The pound, built in 1982, simplified arrangements for driving animals, but did not exclude them from the grassland because the two gates were normally kept open. Gateways are badly poached and parts of the grassland within the pound are worn by children repeatedly schooling their ponies.

ii. JUBILEE GATE
From Godstow Road to the west of the railway bridge, onto Wolvercote Common. The name Jubilee Gate was given to this access in celebration of the Jubilee of Queen Elizabeth II. This gate leads to a path which Mr Coomb of Wolvercote Mill built up in 1863, in order to take his carts of paper to Wolvercote Halt (Bodleian Library G.A.Oxon.c.56). It suffers considerably from the feet of people taking exercise as well as from dogs, horses and cattle moving on and off the Common. It is used by heavy vehicles on Fair Days, such as the Sheriff's Races and Wolvercote Horticultural Show, and the damage extends over at least 100 sq. m.

iii . RAILWAY CROSSING
From First Turn, Wolvercote, the lane passed over the canal bridge and railway level crossing. The latter was closed for safety reasons by British Rail in 1962 and replaced by a foot bridge next to Godstow Road bridge (W.C.C. Minute 6.11.61). There is little damage here.

iv. WYCROFT LANE
This lane was also called Our Lady's Way. It formed part of the boundary of Oxford from at least the Fifteenth Century. The land between it and Port Meadow had once been part of the Freemen's pasture but was given to Godstow Nunnery circa. 1143, when it was referred to as "the land that Sagrim held" (Clark 1905). The Abbess of Godstow and, later, the Lords of the Manor of Wolvercote, was responsible for the upkeep of Wycroft Lane until, in 1563, an agreement was reached with the City of Oxford that Richard Owen would repair and widen it and, in return, the City's Freemen would have free use of it and keep it in repair in perpetuity (Ogle 1892: 255). Two thirds of this land and of Wycroft Lane is now covered by the grassed over Oxford City Dump now called Burgess Field Nature Park. The disturbance at this entrance is caused by animals sheltering from the east wind, particularly in winter.

v. ARISTOTLE LANE
This lane, previously called Broman's Well Lane, was originally the main entrance to Port Meadow from Oxford. It is on the route of an ancient trackway which is thought to have forded the Cherwell at Magdalen Bridge (first built before 1004 (Crossley 1979)), followed the Green Ditch (now under St. Margaret's Road), crossed Port Meadow and forded the river at Binsey or Peel Yate ford (Map 1). The track then wound round Wytham Hill towards Eynsham and the west (Biddle 1961/2). This is the entrance beside or over which the herdsman's house was built in 1582 (Turner 1880) which had become a poor house by 1596 and was then used by plague victims until it fell down in 1629 (Hobson & Salter 1933). The entrance known as Old Man's Gate was a little to the east of the present gate which was reset when the railway lines and High Bridge were built (Minn Bodleian Library MS.Top Oxon. d.502).

People and animals using this entrance tend to keep to the raised path which is bordered on both sides by ditches containing *Potentilla anserina* (Type D) grassland. This was not so in the past when it suffered so much from damage by cattle that it was closed, for example, from July 1652 to October 1653 when 20s. were paid for a causeway to be built within the gate. Although the City Council ordered that the gate be locked and chained, this was not effective and on August 17th they ordered Thomas Pavyer to stand near Bromans Well (near the Anchor Inn on the corner of Hayfield Road and Polstead Road) to ensure that "only horses, mares, geldings or nags, laden or unladen" were driven down Aristotle Lane to Port Meadow. Cows, heifers, bullocks and calves had to be directed along Wycroft Lane (further north along Hayfield Road and turning north-west almost opposite Frenchay Road) (Hobson 1939).

vi. WALTON WELL ROAD GATE

Walton Well Road entrance, like Jubilee Gate suffers from considerable disturbance by people, animals and cars. It is not shown on Cole's Map, but Walton Ford was often used as a short cut to Medley, Binsey and Wytham. The way was closed in 1701 to prevent carting over the Meadow (Hobson 1954). During the Eighteenth Century the Freemen of Oxford had was a long dispute with Christ Church and Alderman Swete on behalf of their tenants in Binsey and Medley. They wanted to take their carts and carriages over Port Meadow, but did not prove their right to do so until 1797 (Hobson 1954). This was a Pyrric victory, as Medley flash weir had just been built. This raised the level of the river at Peel Yate Ford except after a "flash" of water had gone by on Tuesdays and Fridays. Walton Well Road Gate became the main entrance to Port Meadow after 1841 when Sheriff James Hunt opened the bridge over the railway lines to give easy access to the Meadow as well as to Medley, Binsey and the towpath (Bodleian Library G.A. Oxon c.201(8), c.56)

Pasture was lost when the railway was built in 1856 (Oxford City Council Archives P.S.31). Two remnants survive to the east of the bridge on either side of Walton Well Road. On the north it is a Victorian rubbish dump on which grass cuttings containing ragwort and thistles, forage harvested from Port Meadow, were dumped in the early 1980s (Chapter 6.3.B.). In 1990 this remnant of common land was converted into an informal garden for the benefit of the residents of the new estate nearby. On the south are allotment gardens. West of the railway more pasture has been lost to provide a car park and access road to Medley Boat Station and to the City Dump. Land for the latter was let by the Freemen in 1935 on condition that the grassland was reinstated as soon as the Dump was closed (Oxford City Council Archives). The Dump was closed in August 1982 but the road has not been removed.

vii. MEDLEY BRIDGE

In the Eighteenth and Nineteenth Centuries there was a ferry here (see map 11; Minn in Appendix F) until the Rainbow Bridge was built in 1866 between the Binsey bank and the central island and a wooden bridge over the weir from the island to Port Meadow. The present Bailey Bridge was built in 1947 by the Royal Engineers to replace an earlier one swept away by floods (Minn unpub.). In this area the disturbance to the vegetation is increased by the activities generated at Medley Boat Station which has expanded onto Port Meadow (Chapter 6).

viii. PEEL YATE OR BINSEY FORD

This was known as Peel Yate Ford by Jessup in 1789 (Thacker 1911: 105). Clark (1889: 46) notes:

> "Some years ago it was customary to turn horses out to grass on Port Meadow; there they became so wild that it was generally impossible to catch them on that extensive space and they were therefore driven by beaters across the ford onto Binsey Green, in whose confined corners they were more easily captured. Recent dredgings have, however, so deepened the channel, that it is now dangerous to attempt this ford."

ix. PICKSEY LANE

Until the end of the eighteenth century there were three ways into Picksey Mead, two of which carried Picksey Lane, part of the road out of Oxford leading to Yarnton and the north-west.

The existence of this lane in 1165 is assumed from the fact that there was a ferry on it to take people to the Godstow Abbey Fair (Clark 1906; 659). Later the ferry was replaced by a bridge (now called Toll Bridge). To get to Cassington and the West from Oxford one crossed the Toll Bridge and turned right into Picksey Lane passing between Great Baynhams and the Cowleys and so into Picksey Mead (Blenheim Estate Map 1765). It passed down the middle of the Mead where the hay lots belonging to the Yarnton and Begbroke farmers were identified by merestones laid out on either side. It probably left the Mead along the causeway at the north-west corner, outlined by the 58.75m and 59m contours, to cross the river by King's Weir ford and so on into Mead Lane, Yarnton. There is no disturbance here now, but could this land be associated with the *Arrhenatherum elatius* (Type S) grassland growing at the north end of Picksey Mead today? This is the way King Charles is supposed to have taken when he escaped from Oxford during the Civil War (Bodleian Library MS. Top Oxon. b.19; Stapledon 1893).

x. KING'S WEIR FORD

After crossing the Mead the road went over a ford (which was drowned in the 1790s (see Chapter 4.3)) across the centre of Oxey Mead and so along Mead Lane and Froggledown Way to Cassington. After the ford was drowned the Begbroke and Yarnton farmers, who owned hay rights and rights of common in Picksey Mead, had to take their hay off by the southern Picksey Lane entrance (see Map 11).

xi. COWLEYS GATE

The south-west corner of Picksey Mead is bounded on the north-east by a silted up ditch which turns this part of the Mead into a 20 acre island. Wytham farmers, who were possibly the tenants of Godstow Abbey and the Lords of the Manor of Wolvercote, used a gate in East Cowleys (Map 11) to reach what is now the Wytham piece of Picksey Mead.

xii. BYPASS GATE

A Public Inquiry was held on the 19th November 1958, (Nature Conservancy Council 1958) into objections to the proposed route of the A34, Oxford Western Bypass. Bearing in mind Section 4 of the Restriction of Ribbon Development Act, 1935, and the Common Law rights, the pros and cons of using a crossing or underpasses to take hay and animals on and off the mead were examined. Evidence was given that the road was designed to take traffic moving at speeds of up to 50 miles per hour and that this would give farmers with hay waggons a safety factor of 4 if they used a gate straight onto the bypass. It was therefore felt that it would be unnecessary to build an underpass with minimum dimensions 15ft wide and 14ft high, for Picksey Lane (Nature Conservancy Council 1958). In retrospect this decision seems to have been foolhardy. By 1983 holiday and other traffic were using the bypass at speeds which may exceed the 70 mile per hour speed limit, at the same time as the farmers, or their contractor, are taking the hay off the Mead.

xiii. UNDERPASSES

Access for animals to move between the main part of Picksey Mead and the eight acre remnant in the south was made by underpasses, one near the river, 14ft 6in. high with a lane south of the road embankment into the remnant and a second 11ft 6in. high between the remnant and the rest of the Mead near the Mill Stream. The soil suffers from disturbance by sheltering sheep or cattle on the southern side. A third and much lower underpass, known as a cattle creep, to the west of the Picksey Lane crossing, was built over a natural depression in the Mead. All three underpasses were designed to take flood water off the Mead whenever necessary (Nature Conservancy Council 1958). A fence stops animals getting onto the bypass and from using these underpasses, except for the one by the Mill Stream which can be used for shelter.

xiv. BRIDGES

During the Eighteenth Century the ditches on Port Meadow were wet enough to require bridges. These were repaired at the City's expense in, for example, 1773–4, 1785, 1790 and 1799. The four lower ones were made of wood with timber supports to the arches (Hobson 1962). In 1796 the Duke of Marlborough built stone bridges on the eastern edge of Port Meadow so that he could take carriages to the Races. The two other bridges are now also made of stone and, like the others, have been repaired with concrete and are again in need of repair. The bridges seem to be in appropriate places to take the race track shown on Cole's (c. 1696) map.

Appendix L

Plant Species Found on Port Meadow between 1923 and 1973

	A			B			C						1968 Ragwort Control in C			
	1973	1973	1923	1973	1973	1923	1973	1973	1923	1954	1970	1970				
	NCC SP499074A	NCC SP498078B	H. Baker	NCC SP495085F	NCC SP495084C	H. Baker	NCC SP490088D	NCC SP493092E	H. Baker	H.J.M. Bowen	H.J.M. Bowen	Dr. Richards	Hand-pulled	2,4–D amine 1967	Forage harvested	Control
SPECIES	1	2	3	4	5	6	7	8	9	10	11	12	13	14	15	16
Achillea millefolium				1			1	1	1				1	1	1	1
Achillea ptarmica							1									
Alisma lanceolatum										1						
A. plantago-aquatica										1						
Agrostis stolonifera	1	1	1	1	1	1	1	1	1				1	1	1	1
Alopecurus geniculatus	1	1	1	1												
A. pratensis		1		1	1		1	1							1	
Anthoxanthum odoratum				1					1						1	
Apium nodiflorum			1	1												
A. repens										1						
Baldellia ranunculoides												1				
Bellis perennis		1			1	1	1		1				1		1	1
Berula erecta		1														
Briza media					1		1						1		1	1
Bromus mollis													1		1	1
Butomus umbellatus										1						
Callitriche obtusangula												1				
C. stagnalis				1												
Cardamine flexuosa				1												
C. pratensis		1	1	1	1	1										
Carduus acanthoides													1		1	
Carex acuta												1				
C. caryophyllea							1		1							
C. disticha	1															
C. flacca			1	1	1		1									
C. hirta	1			1												
C. lepidocarpa												1				
C. panicea																1
Centaurea nigra					1		1		1						1	1
Cerastium arvense							1									
C. fontanum				1	1				1			1	1	1	1	1
Chaerophyllum temulentum							1									
Cirsium acaule							1		1							
C. arvense	1				1			1					1	1	1	1
C. eriophorum								1				1	1			
C. vulgare					1		1	1	1						1	1

SPECIES	1	2	3	4	5	6	7	8	9	10	11	12	13	14	15	16
Crataegus monogyna																1
Cynosurus cristatus				1	1		1	1	1				1	1	1	1
Dactylis glomerata			1		1		1	1					1	1	1	1
Dactylorchis incarnata												1				
D. praetermissa												1				
Deschampsia cespitosa		1	1	1	1	1		1	1					1		
Eleocharis palustris				1												
Elymus repens									1							
Festuca pratensis		1	1		1	1							1			
F. rubra	1	1		1	1		1	1	1				1	1	1	1
Filipendula ulmaria				1												
Galium palustre	1		1	1												
G. veris (verum)				1				1					1	1	1	1
Glyceria fluitans	1	1	1	1												
G. maxima											1					
Helictotrichon pratense													1			
H. pubescens							1									
Hippuris vulgaris			1								1					
Holcus lanatus			1	1	1	1		1	1					1	1	1
Hordeum secalinum				1												
Hottonia palustris												1				
Hypochoeris radicata					1	1	1									
Juncus articulatus	1		1	1		1										
J. compressus				1							1					
J. inflexus				1												
Koeleria macrantha									1							
Lathyrus pratensis				1												
Leontodon autumnalis			1		1	1			1							
L. hispidus				1												
Leontodon taraxacoides									1							1
Limosella aquatica											1					
Lolium perenne			1	1	1	1	1	1	1				1	1	1	1
Lotus corniculatus				1	1	1	1	1	1				1	1	1	1
Luzula campestris						1	1	1						1	1	1
Medicago lupulina							1						1	1	1	
Mentha aquatica	1															
M. scorpioides	1		1	1												
M. secunda											1					
Nasturtium officinale			1													
Nuphar lutea											1					
Nymphoides peltata											1					
Oenanthe fistulosa	1		1								1					
O. silaifolia												1				
Persicaria lapathifoliua											1					
P. maculosa				1												
Phleum pratense			1	1		1			1				1			
Pilosella officinarum							1									
Plantago lanceolata				1	1	1	1		1				1	1	1	1
P. major				1	1											
P. media							1		1				1		1	1
Poa annua			1			1			1					1	1	1
P. compressa														1		

SPECIES	1	2	3	4	5	6	7	8	9	10	11	12	13	14	15	16
P. pratensis		1			1	1	1	1					1	1	1	1
P. trivialis		1	1	1	1		1	1					1	1	1	1
Potamogeton perfoliatus											1					
Potentilla anserina		1	1	1	1				1					1		
P. erecta				1												
P. reptans		1		1	1	1	1	1					1	1	1	1
Prunella vulgaris			1		1		1		1							
Ranunculus acris	1	1	1	1	1	1		1	1				1	1	1	1
R. aquatilis											1					
R. bulbosus		1			1	1	1	1	1				1	1	1	1
R. droueti			1													
R. flammula			1								1					
R. repens			1		1	1			1				1	1	1	1
Rumex acetosa					1	1		1					1	1	1	1
R. obtusifolius				1												
Sagittaria sagittifolia												1				
Schoenoplectus lacustris											1					
Senecio jacobaea					1		1						1	1	1	1
Sieglingia decumbens							1									
S. latifolium												1				
Sparganum erectum												1				
Stellaria alsine	1															
S. graminea					1											
S. palustris											1					
Stratiotes aloides												1				
Subularia aquatica												1				
Taraxacum officinale				1	1	1	1	1	1						1	1
Trifolium dubium									1							
T. fragiferum												1				
T. pratense		1			1	1	1	1	1				1	1	1	1
T. repens	1	1	1	1	1	1	1	1	1				1	1	1	1
Trisetum flavescens				1												
Urtica dioica				1												
Utricularia neglecta												1				
Veronica anagallis-aquatica			1													
V. beccabunga			1		1											
V. scutellata			1								1					

This table is compiled from data collected by Baker (1937) and Doctors Bowen, Richards, Wells and Woodell (Nature Conservancy Council Southern Region) and adapted from Appendix K in McDonald (1980).

APPENDIX M

SURVEY OF THE HEDGE SPECIES ON THE EASTERN BOUNDARY OF PORT MEADOW. (McDONALD 1980)

During the survey thirteen species of shrub or tree were identified. The hedge was divided into 30yd blocks (30 paces) and the number of different species in each block counted in order to ascertain the approximate age of the hedge (Hooper 1970).

HEDGE SPECIES IDENTIFIED

Acer pseudoplatanus
Acer campestre
Crataegus monogyna
Fraxinus excelsior
Malus sylvestris
Prunus spinosa
Rhamnus catharticus
Rosa canina
Salix caprea
Salix alba
Salix fragilis
Sambucus nigra
Ulmus procera

THE NUMBER OF SPECIES IN EACH BLOCK WITH LANDMARKS WHERE APPROPRIATE

There is no hedge on the Wolvercote Common/Railwayline boundary. From there to the Aristotle Lane footbridge species were recorded in successive 30yd blocks.
Corner of Hook Meadow and the Railway line.
1, 1, 1, 3, 3, 2, Drinking trough, 2, 2, 1, 3, 4, 2, 2, Merestone 1886 (R. Buckell Mayor, F. Twining Sheriff), 2, 1, Hook Meadow/Trapp Ground boundary corner, 3, 3, 3, 3, 3, 3, 3, 2, 3, 4, 4, 4, 5, 5, Merestone 1840 (Mallam Mayor, Wyatt Sheriff) 4, 2, Trapp Ground/City Dump boundary and public footpath, 4, 3, 3, 4, 3, 4, 3, 5, 2, 3, 3, 3, 5, 4, 3, 4, 3, 4, 1, 3, 5, 1, 4, 3, 4, 4, 5, 3, 4, 3, 4, 4, 6, 5, 3, 2, 2, Gate to City Dump, 2, 3, City Dump/Trapp Ground Allotments boundary, 2, 2, 2, 3, 2, Gate to Trapp Ground Allotments, 3, 3, 4, 5, 1, Footbridge to Aristotle Lane.

CONCLUSIONS

The hedge bounding Hook Meadow is at present sparse with many gaps in it. The dominance of *Crataegus monogyna* suggests that this was the only species planted. The average number of species in the Hook Meadow hedge is 2, giving a date for planting of 1780, but we know that this hedge was in good condition when Benjamin Cole made his drawing of Port Meadow *c.* 1696. So this is not a good indication of the age of the hedge. When we get to the Trapp Ground the average number of species is 3, increasing to 4 or 5 as the public footpath which used to be known as Our Lady's Way is approached. This suggests a planting date of about 1480 but one would expect that this hedge, and that now surrounding the City Dump, would have been planted soon after 1139 when the Abbey of Godstow was given this land by the Freemen of Oxford (Salter 1936), or possibly before then when the land was held by Sagrim in 1086.

One reaches the conclusion, therefore, that although this method of dating hedges may be very effective in some cases it must also be treated with caution. Neglect, disease (e.g. Dutch Elm disease) and trampling by animals can all cause a hedge to lose species over the centuries and in this case the composition of the hedge may also have been affected by flooding which was particularly bad around the turn of the 20th century.

Historical Sources Not Included Under Author's Name

BLENHEIM PALACE, WOODSTOCK, OXFORD
Box 31. Deeds of Begbroke Hill Farm, Yarnton, Oxford.
Estate map of Wolvercote, Oxford. 1765.

BODLEIAN LIBRARY, OXFORD UNIVERSITY
Oxford City Notices: Works done in Port Meadow 1841-1862, showing how they were respectively paid for and receipts. G.A. Oxon.c.201.
Miscellaneous notes on Port Meadow. G.A. Oxon.c.56.
MS. Top Oxon.b.19.f.12

MERTON COLLEGE, OXFORD
Deeds of Jackson's Farm, Yarnton, Oxford.

OXFORD CITY LIBRARY, WESTGATE CENTRE, OXFORD
Oxford City Records P.S.31. Proposed Cheltenham and Oxford railway 1946.
Disposal of refuse 1888-1889.
Exeter Farm, Yarnton, Sale Advertisements.
Advertisements for auction of Yarnton mead hay lots and grazing.

OXFORDSHIRE COUNTY COUNCIL
Register of Common Land.

OXFORDSHIRE COUNTY MUSEUM, WOODSTOCK
Index of field names and small finds.

OXFORDSHIRE COUNTY RECORD OFFICE
Survey of Yarnton, Begbroke and Medley estate 1694. DASHWOOD XV/i/24.
Copy/release 1719, includes common rights in Picksey Mead. DASHWOOD XV/ii/3
Railway plans and sections Ref:62, 1853, Plan and reference includes Picksey Mead.
Wolvercote Enclosure Award 1834.
Wytham Enclosure Award 1814.
Yarnton and Begbroke Tithe Award.

PUBLIC RECORD OFFICE
Tax Assessments, Yarnton. 1317 and 1327. E/179/161/89.

ST. JOHN'S COLLEGE, OXFORD
Wolvercote Enclosure Award 1834 with pre-enclosure field boundaries shown. Muniments 29 and 58.
Grant from Owen to Bell, 26 Sept. 1611, includes commons in Port Meadow. Muniment 40.9.
Wolvercote Rental. Muniment 89.

THAMES WATER, READING
New locks and river improvements above Oxford 1928.
Photogrammetric map of the upper Thames valley 1978.
Daily water level records at Godstow lock tail water.

WOODSTOCK ARCHIVES, TOWNHALL, WOODSTOCK
SPENCER, Sir Thomas, Inventory of effects 1622. B.35(1)/4.

Sources cited under Author's Name

SOURCES CITED UNDER AUTHOR'S NAME

ADAM P. (1976) *Plant sociology and habitat factors in British salt-marshes*. Thesis (Ph.D) University of Cambridge. Unpublished.

ADAMS S.N. (1975) Sheep and cattle grazing in forests: a review. *Journal of Applied Ecology* 12, 143-152.

ALLEN J.A. (1979) *Survey to find unimproved pasture in Oxfordshire: Thames valley*. Nature Conservancy Council Southern Region, Newbury. Unpublished.

ALLEN Stewart E. (ed.) (1974) *Chemical analysis of ecological material*. Blackwell Scientific Publications. Oxford.

APPLEBAUM S. (1972) Roman Britain. In: H.P.R. Finberg (ed.) *The Agrarian History of England and Wales A.D. 43–1042* Cambridge University Press.

ARCHER M. (1973) The species preferences of grazing horses. *Journal of the British Grassland Society* 28, 123–138.

ARNOLD G.W. (1960) Selective grazing by sheep of two forage species at different stages of growth. *Australian Journal of Agricultural Research* 11, 1026–1033.

ARNOLD G.W. (1964) Factors within plant associations affecting the behaviour and performance of grazing animals. *Symposium of the British Ecological Society* 4, 133–154.

ASTON T.H. (1958) The origins of the manor in England. *Transactions of the Royal Historical Society*, 5th Series 8, 59–83.

ATKINSON R.J.C. (1942) Archaeological sites on Port Meadow, Oxford. *Oxoniensia* 7, 22–35.

ATKINSON R.J.C. (1946) New archaeological sites at Binsey and Port Meadow. *Oxoniensia* 11, 81–84.

BAKER H. (1937) Alluvial meadows: a comparative study of grazed and mown meadows. *Journal of Ecology* 25, 408–420.

BARCLAY A.M. & CRAWFORD R.M.M. (1982) Plant growth and survival under strict anaerobiosis. *Journal of Experimental Botany* 33, 541–549.

BARGER G. & BLACKIE J.J. (1937) Alkaloids of *Senecio* III. Jacobine, jacodine and jaconine. *Journal of the Chemical Society* 584–586.

BATES G.H. (1935) The vegetation of footpaths, sidewalks, cart tracks and gateways. *Journal of Ecology* 23, 470–487.

BEARDMORE & LEACH (1869) *Thames Conservancy Report*. Unpublished.

BEDDOWS A.R. (1967) Biological flora of the British Isles No. 107. *Lolium perenne* L. *Journal of Ecology* 55, 567–587.

BENGER F.B. (1968) Leatherhead Common Meadow. *Proceedings of the Leatherhead and District Local Historical Society* 3, 51–55.

BERSU G. (1940) Excavations at Little Woodbury. *Proceedings of the Prehistoric Society* 6, 61–62.

BIDDLE M. (1961/2) Medieval village of Seacourt. *Oxoniensia* 27, 68–201.

BLASHFIELD R.K. & ALDENDERFER M.S. (1978) The literature on cluster analysis. *Multivariate Research* 13, 271–295.

BOWLER D. & ROBINSON M. (1980) Three round barrows at King's Weir. *Oxoniensia* 45, 1–8.

BRADLEY R. & RICHARDS J. (1978) Prehistoric fields and boundaries on the Berkshire Downs. In: H.C. Bowen & P.J. Fowler (eds) *Early land allotment in the British Isles*, British Archaeological Reports 48, 53–60.

BRADSHAW A.D. (1958) Natural hybridization of *Agrostis tenuis* Sibthorpe and *Agrostis stolonifera* L. *New Phytologist* 57, 66.

BRADSHAW A.D. (1959a) Population differentiation in *Agrostis tenuis* Sibth. I. Morphological differentiation. *New Phytologist* 58, 208.

BRADSHAW A.D. (1959b) Studies of variation in bent-grass species. II. Variation within *Agrostis tenuis* Sibth. *Journal of the Sports Turf Research Institute* 35, 6.

BRADSHAW A.D. (1960) Population differentiation in *Agrostis tenuis* Sibth. III. Populations in varied environments. *New Phytologist* 59, 92.

BRAUN-BLANQUET J. (1932) Plant sociology. In: G.D. Fuller & H.S. Conrad (trans. and eds) *The Study of Plant Communities*. McGraw Hill, New York and London.

BRAUN-BLANQUET J. & TÜXEN R. (1952) Irische Pflanzengesellschaften. *Die Pflanzenwelt Irlands*. Veroff Geobot. Inst. Rubel., 25, 224–421.

BRENCHLEY W.E. (1958) *The Park Grass plots at Rothamsted 1856–1949*. (Revised by Katherine Warington). Rothamsted Experimental Station, Harpenden.

BRIGGS D.J. & GILBERTSON D.D. (1980) Quarternary processes and environments in the upper Thames valley. *Transactions of the Institute of Geography*. New Series 5, 55–65.

BRILLOUIN L. (1956) *Science and information theory*. 2nd edition 1962. Academic Press. New York.

BRODRIBB A.C.C., HANDS A.R., & WALKER D.R. (1972) *Excavations at Shakenoak Farm, near Wilcote, Oxfordshire. III, Site F*. Privately printed.

BRUMMER G. (1974) Redoxpotentiale und Redoxprozesse von Mangan-Eisen und schwefelverbindungen in hydromorphen Boden und Sedimenten. *Geoderma* 12, 207–222.

BURDEN R.F. & ANDERSON P.F. (1972) Quantitive studies of the effects of human trampling on vegetation as an aid to the management of semi-natural areas. *Journal of Applied Ecology* 9, 439.

BURDON J.J. (1983) Biological flora of the British Isles. *Trifolium repens* L. *Journal of Ecology* 71, 307–330.

CAIN S.A. & CASTRO G.M. de O. (1959) *Manual of vegetation analysis*. Harper, New York.

CAMERON E. (1935) A study of the natural control of ragwort (*Senecio jacobaea* L.). *Journal of Ecology* 23, 265–322.

CAMPBELL I. & CLAYDEN P. (1973) *The law of commons and village greens*. Commons Open Spaces and Footpaths Preservation Society, Henley-on-Thames.

CANAWAY P.M. (1975) Turf wear, a literature review. *Journal of Sports Turf Research Institute* 51, 92.

CARTER H. (1957) *Wolvercote Mill*. Oxford University Press. 2nd edition 1974, pp. 4, 62.

CASE H.J. (1954) The prehistoric period. In: A.F. Martin & R.W. Steel (eds) *The Oxford Region*. Oxford University Press. pp. 76–84.

CHAMPNESS S.S. (1949) Notes on the buried seed populations beneath different types of ley in their seedling year. *Journal of Ecology* 37, 51–56.

CHAMPNESS S.S. & MORRIS K. (1948) The population of buried viable weed seeds in relation to contrasting pasture and soil types. *Journal of Ecology* 36, 149–173.

CHARLETT F. (1936) *Account of the lot ceremony at Yarnton*. Woodstock Museum, Oxfordshire. Unpublished.

CHIPPINDALE H.G. & MILTON W.E.J. (1934) On viable seeds present in the soil beneath pastures. *Journal of Ecology* 22, 508–531.

CHURCH A.H. (1922) Introduction to the plant life of the Oxford District. *Botanical Memoirs 13*. Oxford University Press, 102.

CLAPHAM A.R., TUTIN T.E. & WARBURG E.F. (1962) *Flora of the British Isles*. Cambridge University Press.

CLAPHAM A.R., TUTIN T.G. & WARBURG E.F. (1981) *Excursion flora of the British Isles*. 3rd edition. Cambridge University Press.

CLARK A. (ed.) (1889) *Wood's City of Oxford*. Clarendon Press, Oxford. p. 46.

CLARK A. (ed.) (1891) *The life and times of Anthony Wood 1632–1695 I*. Oxford Historical Society. p. 92.

CLARK A. (ed.) (1905) *The English register of Godstow Nunnery near Oxford*. Kegan Paul, London. pp. 651, 659.

CLARKE G.R. (1954) 'Soils' in A.F. Martin & R.W. Steel (eds), *The Oxford Region*. Oxford University Press.

CLYMO R.S. (1980) Preliminary survey of the peat bog Hummell Knowe Moss using various numerical methods. *Vegetatio* 42, 129–148.

COETZEE B.J. & WERGER M.J.A. (1975) On association analysis and the classification of plant communities. *Vegetatio* 30, 201–206.

COLE B. (*c*. 1696) *Map of Port Meadow*. Bodleian Library, G.A. Oxon.a.64.f.58.

COLES J.M. & ORME B.J. (1980) Prehistory of the Somerset Levels. *Somerset Levels Project* 36. Cambridge University Press.

COLLINSHAW S.J. & ALDER F.E. (1960) The grazing preferences of cattle and sheep. *Journal of the Agricultural Science Club* 54, 257–265.

CONWAY V.M. (1940) Aeration and plant growth in wet soils. *Botanical Review* 6 (4), 149–163.

COULT D.A. & VALLANCE K.B. (1958) Observations on the gaseous exchanges which take place between *Menyanthes trifoliata* L. and its environment II. *Journal of Experimental Botany* 9, 384.

COUNTRY LIFE (1939) *Old Thames weirs*. 17 June 1939, 653.

CRAWFORD A.K. & LIDDLE M.J. (1977) The effect of trampling on neutral grassland. *Biological Conservation* 12, 135.

CRAWFORD R.M.M. (1966) Alcohol dehydrogenase activity in relation to flooding tolerance in roots. *Journal of Experimental Botany* 18 (56), 458–464.

CRAWFORD R.M.M. (1969) The physiological basis of flooding tolerance. *Bericht der Deutschen botanischen Gesellschaft* 82 (1/2),111–114.

CRAWFORD R.M.M. & MCMANNON M. (1968) Inductive responses of alcohol and malic acid dehydrogenases in relation to flooding tolerance in roots. *Journal of Experimental Botany* 19 (60), 435–441.

CRAWFORD R.M.M. & TYLER P.D. (1969) Organic acid metabolism in relation to flooding tolerance in roots. *Journal of Ecology* 57, 235–244.

CRIPPS-DAY F.H. (1931) *The Manor Farm*. Bernard Quaritch Ltd., London.

CROSSLEY A. (ed.) (1979) *Victoria County History of the Counties of England 4, The City of Oxford*. Oxford University Press.

CROSSLEY A. (ed.) (1990) *Victoria County History of the Counties of England. Wootton Hundred*. Oxford University Press.

CROVELLO T.J. (1970) Analysis of character variation in ecology and systematics. *Annual Review of Ecology and Systematics* 1, 55–98.

CUNLIFFE B.W. (1974) *Iron Age communities in Britain*. Routledge & Kegan Paul. London.

DALE M.B. & ANDERSON D.J. (1973) Inosculate analysis of vegetation data. *Australian Journal of Botany* 21, 253–276.

DAVIDSON J. & LLOYD R. (eds) (1977) *Conservation and agriculture*. John Wiley & Sons, London.

DAVIES W. (1952) *The grass crop*. Spon, London.

DAVIS R. (1794) A general view of the agriculture of the county of Oxfordshire (Board of Agriculture Report) London. In A. Young (1813) *General View of Agriculture of the Oxfordshire Board of Agriculture*, 2nd edition 1968, David S. Charles, Newton Abbot.

DAVIS R.H.C. (1968) An Oxford charter of 1191 and the beginnings of municipal freedom. *Oxoniensia* 33, 53–65.

DAVIS R.H.C. (1973) The ford, the river and the city. *Oxoniensia* 38, 260.

DAVIS R.H.C. (1982) Notes and documents: Alfred and Guthrum's frontier. *English Historical Review* 97, 803–810.

DAVY A.J. (1980) Biological flora of the British Isles: *Deschampsia cespitosa* L. Beauv. No. 149. *Journal of Ecology* 68, 1075–1096.

DAWKINS B.W. (1968a) *Association analysis program*. Department of Forestry, Oxford University. Unpublished.

DAWKINS B.W. (1968b) *Principal component analysis*. Department of Forestry, Oxford University. Unpublished.

DAWKINS H.C. & FIELD D.R.B. (1978) *A long term surveillance system for British woodland vegetation*. Department of Forestry, Oxford. Commonwealth Forestry Institute Occasional Papers 1.

DODGSHON R.A. (1980) *The origin of British field systems: an interpretation*. Academic Press.

DUFFEY E. & WATTS A.S. (eds) (1971) *The scientific management of animal and plant communities for conservation*. 11th symposium of the British Ecological Society. University of East Anglia, Norwich. 7-9 July 1970.

DUFFEY E., MORRIS M.G., SHEAIL J., WARD L.K., WELLS D.A. & WELLS T.C.E. (1974) *Grassland ecology and wildlife management*. Chapam & Hall. London.

EDWARDS E. (ed.) (1866) *Liber Monasterii de Hyda*. Longmans Green, Renders & Dyer, London. Roll Series 45. pp. 254, 363 n.2.

ELLENBERG H. (1978) *Vegetation Mitteleuropas mit den Alpen*. 2nd edition. Eugen Ulmer, Stuttgart.

ELLIS W. (1731) The modern husbandman, or practice of farming. Cited by G.E. Fussell (1950) *More old English farming books*. Crosby Lockwood & Son Ltd., London.

ENGLAND RECORD COMMISSION (1810–34) *Valor Ecclesiasticus tempus Henry VIII*. Auctoritate Regia Institutus.

ETHERINGTON J.R. (1981) Limestone heaths in south-west Britain. *Journal of Ecology* 69, 277–294.

FEILING K. (1950) *A history of England: from the coming of the English to 1918*. 2nd edition 1972. Book Club Associates.

FENTON E.W. (1927) The composition of Devon pastures. *Agricultural Progress* 4.

FENTON E.W. (1931a) The influence of sectional grazing and manuring on the flora of grassland. *Journal of Ecology* 19, 75–97.

FENTON E.W. (1931b) A botanical survey of grasslands in the south and east of Scotland. Journal of Ecology 19, 392–409.

FENTON E.W. (1937) The influence of sheep on the hill grazings in Scotland. *Journal of Ecology* 25, 424–430.

FITTER A.H. (1982) Influence of soil heterogeneity on the co-existence of grassland species. *Journal of Ecology* 70, 139–148.

FITZGERALD Lady R. (1984) The Gearagh – a rare habitat in Co. Cork. *Botanical Society of the British Isles News* No. 36, 8–9.

FITZHERBERT A. (1523a) Boke of surveying: a statute ordained for Edward I. In: F.H. Cripps-Day (ed.) *The Manor Farm*. Bernard Quaritch Ltd., London.

FITZHERBERT A. (1523b) A boke of husbandry. In: F.H. Cripps-Day (ed.) *The Manor Farm*. Bernard Quaritch Ltd., London.

FOIN T.C. & JAIN S.K. (1977) Ecosystems analysis and population biology: lessons for the development of community ecology. *Biological Science* 27, 532–538.

FORD W.J. (1976) Some settlement patterns in the central region of the Warickshire Avon. In: P.H. Sawyer (ed.) *Medieval Settlement: Continuity and Change*. Arnold, London.

FOX H.S.A. (1976) Approaches to the adoption of the midland system. In: P.H. Sawyer (ed.) *Medieval Settlement: Continuity and Change*. Arnold, London.

FOX H.S.A. (1981) Origins of the two and three field system. In: T. Rowley (ed.) *The Origins of Open-Field Agriculture*. Croom Helm, London .

FREAM W. (1888) On the flora of water-meadows, with notes on the species. *Journal of the Linnean Society (Botany)* 24, 454–464.

FUSSELL G.E. (1947) *The old English farming books from Fitzherbert to Tull 1523 to 1730*. Crosby Lockwood & Son Ltd, London.

FUSSELL G.E. (1950) *More old English farming books from Tull to the Board of Agriculture 1731 to 1793*. Crosby Lockwood & Son Ltd. London.

GAUCH H.G. (1982) *Multivariate analysis in community ecology*. Cambridge university press.

GAUCH H.G. & WHITTAKER R.H. (1981) Hierarchical classification of community data. *Journal of Ecology* 69, 537–557.

GELLING M. (1953/4) *The place-names of Oxfordshire.* Vols I & II. Cambridge University Press.

GELLING M. (1974) *The place-names of Berkshire.* Vol. II. English Place Names Society.

GELLING M. (1978) *Signposts to the past.* J.M. Dent & Sons Ltd, London.

GELLING M. (1979) *The early charters of the Thames valley.* Leicester University Press.

GILBERT E.W. (1954) The growth of the city of Oxford. In: A.F. Martin & R.W. Steel (eds) *The Oxford Region* Oxford University Press.

GILLHAM M.E. (1955) Ecology of the Pembrokeshire islands. III. The effect of grazing on the vegetation. *Journal of Ecology* 43, 172–206.

GODWIN H. (1943) Coastal peat beds of the British Isles and North Sea. *Journal of Ecology* 31, 199.

GODWIN H. (1956) *History of the British flora.* 2nd edition 1975, Cambridge University Press. p. 465.

GOODALL D.W. (1953) Objective methods for the classification of vegetation. I. The use of positive interspecific correlation. *Australian Journal of Botany* 1, 39–63.

GOODALL D.W. (1954) Objective methods for the classification of vegetation. III. An essay in the use of factor analysis. *Australian Journal of Botany* 2, 304–324.

GRAY H.L. (1915) *English field systems.* Cambridge Massachusetts. Reprinted London, 1959.

GREEN J.O. (1972) *A sample survey of grassland in England and Wales, 1970–72.* Grassland Research Institute, Hurley, Maidenhead, Berkshire.

GRETTON R.H. (1912) Historical notes on the lot meadow customs at Yarnton, Oxon. *Economic Journal.* March pp. 55, 58, 60.

GRETTON R.H. (1920) *Burford records: a study in minor town government.* Oxford University Press. p. 408.

GRIFFITHS G.J. (1926) The upper Thames and its works. *Journal of Cambridge University Engineering and Aeronautical Society.*

GRIME J.P. (1963) Calcifuge species on calcareous substrata. *Journal of Ecology* 51, 375–390.

GRUBB P.J., GREEN H. E & MERRIFIELD R.C.J. (1969) Calcicole-calcifuge and acidification. *Journal of Ecology* 57, 175–210.

HANDS A.R. & WALKER D.R. (1981) *The environment of man.* British Archaeological Report 87.

HARDEN D.B. (ed.) (1956) *Dark Age Britain.* Clarendon Press, Oxford.

HARPER J.L. (undated) *Report of ragwort problem on Port Meadow* Nature Conservancy Council Southern Region. Newbury (unpublished).

HARPER J.L. (1956) The evolution of weeds in relation to the resistance to herbicides. *Proceedings of the 3rd British Weed Control Conference* (Blackpool) 1, 179–188.

HARPER J.L. (1958) The ecology of ragwort (*Senecio jacobaea* L.) with especial reference to control. *Herbage Abstracts* 28, 152–157.

HARPER J.L. (1977) *Population biology of plants.* Academic Press.

HARPER J.L. & CLATWORTHY J.N. (1963) Analysis of the growth of *Trifolium repens* and *T. fragiferum* in pure and mixed populations. *Journal of Experimental Botany* 14, 172–190.

HARPER J.L. & SAGAR G.R. (1953) Some aspects of the ecology of buttercups in permanent grassland. *Proceedings of the National Weed Control Conference,* 256–265.

HARPER J.L. & SAGAR G.R. (1964) Biological flora of the British Isles. *Plantago major, P. media* and *P. lanceolata. Journal of Ecology* 52, 189–221.

HARPER J.L. & WOOD W.A. (1957) Biological flora of the British Isles. *Senecio jacobaea* L. *Journal of Ecology* 45, 617–37.

HARVEY P.D.A. (1965) *A medieval Oxfordshire village, Cuxham: 1240–1400.* Oxford University Press.

HASSALL T.G. (1972) *Oxford: The city beneath your feet.* Oxford Archaeological Excavation Committee, Oxford.

HAVINDEN M.A. (1961) Agricultural progress in open-field Oxfordshire. *Agricultural History Review* 9, 73–83.

HENSHAW G.G., COULT D.A. & BOULTER D. (1962) Organic acids of the rhizome of *Iris pseudacorus* L. *Nature* 4828, 579–580.

HERRIOT J.E.D. & WELLS D.A. (1963) The grazing animal and sward productivity. *Journal of Agricultural Science Cambridge* 61, 88–99.

HEXTER G.W. (1950) Ragwort: control by pasture improvement. *Journal of the Department of Agriculture, Victoria,* 48, 217–218.

HEY G. (2004) *Yarnton: Saxon and medieval settlement and landscape.* Published for Oxford Archaeology by Oxford University School of Archaeology as part of the Thames Valley Landscapes Monograph Series.

HILL M.O. (1977) Use of simple discriminant functions to classify quantitive phytosociological data. In: E. Diday, L. Lebart, J.P. Pages & R. Thomassone (eds) *First International Symposium on Data Analysis and Informatics.* Le Chesnay Institut de Recherche d'Informatique et d'Automatique, France, 181–199.

HILL M.O. (1978) *TWINSPAN computer program.* Cornell University, Ithaca, New York.

HILL M.O. (1979) *TWINSPAN – A FORTRAN Program for arranging multivariate data in an ordered two-way table by classification of the individuals and attributes.* Cornell University, Ithaca, New York.

HILL M.O., BUNCE R.G.H. & SHAW M.W. (1975) Indicator species analysis, a divisive polythetic method of classification, and its application to a survey of native pinewoods in Scotland. *Journal of Ecology* 63, 579–613.

HINCHLIFFE J. & THOMAS R. (1980) Archaeological investigations at Appleford. *Oxoniensia* 45, 108.

HOBSON M.G. (1939) *Oxford council acts 1666–1701.* Oxford Historical Society, Clarendon Press, Oxford.

HOBSON M.G. (1954) *Oxford council acts 1701–1751.* Oxford Historical Society, Clarendon Press, Oxford.

HOBSON M.G. (1962) *Oxford council acts 1752–1801.* Oxford Historical Society, Clarendon Press, Oxford.

HOBSON M.G. & SALTER H.E. (1933) *Oxford council acts 1626–1665.* Oxford Historical Society, Clarendon Press, Oxford.

HOLLY K., WOODFORD E.K. & BLACKMAN G.E. (1952) The control of some perennial weeds in permanent grassland by selective herbicides. *Agriculture* 59, 19–32.

HOOK D. (1981) Open-field agriculture – the evidence from pre-Conquest charters of the West Midlands. In: T. Rowley (ed.) *The origins of open-field agriculture.* Croom Helm, London.

HOOPER M.D. (1970) Dating hedges. *Area* 4, 63–65.

HOTELLING H. (1933) Analysis of a complex of statistical variables into principal components. *Journal of Educational Psychology* 24, 417–441, 498–520.

HUBBARD C.E. (1968) *Grasses.* 2nd edition. Penguin Books, Harmondsworth.

HUNTER R.F. (1962) Hill sheep and their pasture: a study of sheep grazing in south-east Scotland. *Journal of Ecology* 59, 651–680.

INSTITUTE OF HYDROLOGY (1979) *Report of the hydrology of the Thames flood-plain near Oxford.* Wallingford. Unpublished.

IVEMEY-COOK R.B. & PROCTOR M.C.F. (1966) The application of association-analysis to phytosociology. *Journal of Ecology* 54, 179–192.

IVINS J.D. (1952) The relative palatability of herbage plants. *Journal of the British Grassland Society* 7, 43–54.

JERMY A.C. & TUTIN T.G. (1982) *British sedges. A handbook of the species of Carex found growing in the British Isles.* 2nd Edition. Botanical Society of the British Isles, London.

JONES G.R.J. (1973) Field systems of North Wales. In: A.R.H. Baker and R.A. Butlin (eds) *Studies of Field Systems in the British Isles.* Cambridge University Press, pp. 430, 436, 439.

JONES G.R.J. (1976) Multiple estates and early settlement. In: P.H. Sawyer (ed.) *Medieval Settlement: Continuity and Change.* Arnold, London.

JONES M. (1981) The development of crop husbandry. In: M. Jones and G.W. Dimbleby (eds) *The Environment of Man: the Iron Age to Anglo-Saxon Period.* British Archaeological Reports 87, 95-127.

JONES M. (1984) Regional patterns in crop production. In: B.W. Cunliffe and D. Miles (eds) *Aspects of the Iron Age in Southern Britain.* Committee for Archaeology, University of Oxford: Monograph No. 2.

JONES M.G. (1933) Grassland management and its influence on the sward. *Journal of the Royal Agricultural Society of England* 94, 21–41.

JONES R. (1972) Comparative studies of plant growth and distribution in relation to waterlogging. V. The uptake of iron and manganese by dune and dune slack plants. *Journal of Ecology* 60, 141–145.

JONES R. & ETHERINGTON J.R. (1971) Comparative studies of plant growth and distribution in relation to waterlogging. IV. The growth of dune and dune slack plants. *Journal of Ecology* 59, 793–801.

JONES W.T. & LYTTLETON J.W. (1971) Bloat in cattle. 34. A survey of legume forages that do and do not cause bloat. *New Zealand Journal of Agricultural Research* 14, 101–107.

KERRIDGE E. (1953) The floating of the Wiltshire Watermeadows. *Wiltshire Archaeological Magazine* 55, 105–118.

KERRIDGE E. (1973) *The farmers of old England.* George Allen & Unwin Ltd., London.

KERSHAW K.A. (1964) *Quantitative and dynamic ecology.* Edward Arnold, London.

KOLKHORST G.H. (1952) *Notes on Yarnton Manor.* City Library, Westgate Centre, Oxford. Unpublished.

KREBS C.J. (1978) *Ecology. The experimental analysis of distribution and abundance.* 2nd edition. Harper & Row, New York. pp. 273, 456.

KYDD D.D. (1964) The effect of different systes of cattle grazing on the botanical composition of permanent downland pasture. *Journal of Ecology* 52, 139–149.

LADD P.G. (1979) Past and present on the Delegate river in the highlands of eastern Victoria. I. Present vegetation. *Australian Journal of Botany* 27, 167–184.

LAING L. (1979) *Celtic Britain.* Book Club Associates, London.

LAMBERT J.M. (1972) Theoretical models for large-scale vegetation survey. In: J.N.R. Jeffers (ed.) *Mathematical Models in Ecology.* Blackwell Scientific Publications, Oxford. pp. 87–109.

LAMBERT J.M. & WILLIAMS W.T. (1962) Multivariate methods in plant ecology. IV. Nodal analysis. *Journal of Ecology* 50, 775–802.

LAMBERT J.M. & WILLIAMS W.T. (1966) Multivariate methods in plant ecology. VI. Comparison of information-analysis and association analysis. *Journal of Ecology* 54, 635–664.

LAMBRICK G. (1984) Pitfalls and possibilities in Iron Age pottery studies – experiences in the upper Thames valley. In: B.W. Cunliffe and D. Miles (eds) *Aspects of the Iron Age in Southern Britain*. Committee for Archaeology, University of Oxford: Monograph No. 2.

LAMBRICK G. & McDONALD A.W. (1985) The archaeology and ecology of Port Meadow with Wolvercote Comon. In: G. Lambrick (ed.) *Archaeology and nature conservation*. Oxford University Department for External Studies.

LAMBRICK G. & ROBINSON M. (1979) *The Iron Age and Roman riverside settlements at Farmoor, Oxon*. Oxfordshire Archaeological Unit Report 2, Council for British Archaeology Research Report 32.

LANE C. (1980) The development of pastures and meadows during the sixteenth and seventeenth centuries. *Agricultural History Review* 28, part 1.

LAWES J.B., GILBERT J.H. & MASTERS M.T. (1882) *Results of experiments on the mixed herbage of permanent meadow. II. Botanical results*. Philosophical Transactions of the Royal Society. London.

LEACH H. (1923) *Memoirs of an Oxford freeman, 1894–1923*. Local History Section, Oxford City Library. Unpublished notes.

LEADAM I.S. (1897) The domesday of enclosures 1517–1518. Longmans Green & Company, London. p. 386.

LEGENDRE L. & LEGENDRE P. (1983) *Developments in environmental modelling: numerical ecology*. Elsevier Scientific Publishing Company, Amsterdam, Oxford, New York.

LEITH H. (1960) Patterns of change within grassland communities. In: J.L. Harper (ed.) *The Biology of Weeds*. Blackwell, Oxford. pp. 27–39.

LENNARD R. (1959) *Rural England 1086–1135: a social study of agrarian conditions*. Clarendon Press, Oxford.

LIDDLE M.J. (1975a) A selective review of the ecological effects of human trampling on natural ecosystems. *Biological Conservation* 7, 251.

LIDDLE M.J. (1975b) A theoretical relationship between the primary productivity of vegetation and its ability to tolerate trampling. *Biological Conservation* 8, 251.

LIMBREY S. (1978) Changes in quality and distribution of the soils of lowland Britain. In: S. Limbrey & J.B. Evans (eds) *The Effect of Man on the Landscape: the Lowland Zone* Council for British Archaeology Research Report 21, 21–27.

LIMBREY S. (1978) Changes in quality and distribution of the soils of Lowland Britain. In: S. Limbrey & J.B. Evans (eds) *The Effect of Man on the Landscape: The Lowland Zone*. Council for British Archaeology Research Report No. 21.

LLOYD P.S. & PIGOTT C.D. (1967) The influence of soil conditions on the course of succession on the chalk of southern England. *Journal of Ecology* 55, 137–146.

MACLUSKY D.S. (1960) Some estimates of the areas of pasture fouled by the excreta of dairy cows. *Journal of British Grassland Society* 15, 181–188.

MARGALEF D.R. (1958) Information theory in ecology. General Systems 3, 36–71.

MARTEN G.C. & DONKER J.D. (eds) (1966) Proceedings of the 10th International Grassland Conference, Helsinki. pp. 359–363.

MARTIN D.J. (1964) Analysis of sheep diet utilising plant epidermal fragments in faeces samples. *Symposium of the British Ecological Society* 4, 173–188.

McDONALD A.W. (1980) *The historical ecology of Port Meadow with Wolvercote Common*. B.Sc. Project. Oxford Polytechnic. Unpublished.

McDONALD A.W. (1983) Continuity of land-use in the upper Thames valley near Oxford. *Oxfordshire Local History* 1 (6).

McDONALD A.W. (2000) Meadow dandelions near Oxford. *Fritillary* 2, 19–23.

McDONALD A.W. (2001) Succession during the re-creation of a flood-meadow 1985-1999. *Applied Vegetation Science* 4, 167–176

McDONALD A.W. and LAMBRICK C.R. (2006) *Apium repens* creeping marshwort. Species recovery programme 1995-2005. English Nature Research Reports, No. 706.

McMANNON M. & CRAWFORD R.M.M. (1971) A metabolic theory of flooding tolerance: the significance of enzyme distribution and behaviour. *New Phytologist* 70, 299–306.

MILES D. (1979) Claydon Pike, Lechlade/Fairford. *Council for British Archaeology Group 9, Newsletter* 10, 160–164.

MILES D. & PALMER S. (1983) Claydon Pike. *Current Archaeology* 86, 88–93.

MILTON W.E.J. (1940) The effect of manuring, grazing and liming on yield, botanical and chemical composition of natural hill pastures. *Journal of Ecology* 28, 326–356.

MILTON W.E.J. (1947) The yield, botanical and chemical composition of natural hill herbage under manuring, controlled grazing and hay conditions. I. Yield and botanical section. *Journal of Ecology* 35, 56–89.

MINN H. (1939) *Notes on Port Meadow and Oxford city*. Bodleian Library. MS. Top. Oxon.d.502. Unpublished.

MINN H. (undated) *Notes on Yarnton and Eynsham manors*. Bodleian Library, MS. Top Oxon. e.384. Unpublished.

MINN H. (undated) *Photographic collection*. Bodleian Library. Negative Numbers: 5323, 6318B, 6318C. Unpublished.

MOORE J.J. (1962) The Braun-Blanquet system: a reassessment. *Journal of Ecology* 50, 761-769.

MOORE J.J., FITZSIMONS S.P., LAMBE C. & WHITE J. (1970) A comparison and evaluation of some phytosociological techniques. *Vegetatio* 20, 1–20.

MOORE P.D. (1982) Survival mechanisms in wetland plants. *Nature* 299, 581–582.

MORRIS J. (ed.) (1978) *Domesday Book: Oxfordshire.* Phillimore, Chichester.

MUELLER-DOMBOIS D. & ELLENBERG H. (1974) *Aims and methods of vegetation ecology.* John Wiley & Sons. pp. 50–51.

MYERS J.N.L. (1954) The Anglo-Saxon period. In: A.F. Martin & R.W. Steel (eds) *The Oxford Region.* Oxford University Press. pp.96–102.

NATURE CONSERVANCY COUNCIL SOUTHERN REGION Unpublished records. Foxhold House, Newbury, Berkshire.

NATURE CONSERVANCY COUNCIL (1958) *Report of Public Inquiry into objections to the proposed A34 (Oxford Western Bypass) across Picksey Mead.* Unpublished.

NATURE CONSERVANCY COUNCIL (1968) *A list of flowers which grow on Port Holme, Huntingdon.* Unpublished.

NATURE CONSERVANCY COUNCIL (1973) *Conservation management plan of Port Meadow Site of Special Scientific Interest.* Unpublished.

NATURE CONSERVANCY COUNCIL (1982) *Mottey Meadows, Staffordshire.* Unpublished.

NICHOLSON I.A. (1971) Some effects of animal grazing and browsing on vegetation. *Transactions Proceedings of the Botanical Society of Edinburgh* 41, 85–91.

NICHOLSON I.A., PATTERSON I.S. & CURRIE A. (1970) A study of vegetational dynamics: selection by sheep and cattle in *Nardus* pasture. *Symposium of the British Ecological Society* 10, 129–143.

NORMAN M.J.T. (1957) The influence of various grazing treatments upon the botanical composition of a downland permanent pasture. *Journal of British Grassland Society* 12, 246–256.

NORTH R. (1759) Account of the different kinds of grasses propagated in England. Cited by Fussell G.E. (1950) *More old English farming books from Tull to the Board of Agriculture 1731 to 1793.* Crosby Lockwood & Son Ltd., London. pp. 40–41.

ODUM E.P., FINN J.T. & ELDON H.F. (1979) Pertubation theory and the subsidy-stress gradient. *Bioscience* 29 (6), 349–352.

OGLE O. (1892) *Royal letters addressed to Oxford.* James Parker & Co., Oxford.

ORDNANCE SURVEY (1877) *Map including Port Meadow.* Her Majesty's Stationery Office, London.

OSCHINSKY D. (ed.) (1971) *Walter of Henley.* Oxford University Press.

O'SULLIVAN A.M. (1965) A phytosociological survey of Irish lowland pastures. Cited in: M.L. Page (1980) *A phytosociological classification of neutral grasslands in the British Isles.* Ph.D Thesis. Exeter University. Unpublished.

O'SULLIVAN A.M. (1968a) A phytosociological survey of Irish grasslands. In: R. Tüxen (ed.) *Pflanzensoziologie und Landschaftsokologie.* The Hague.

O'SULLIVAN A.M. (1968b) The lowland grasslands of County Limerick. An Foras Taluntais. *Irish Vegetation Studies* 2.

O'SULLIVAN A.M. (1968c) Irish Molinietalia communities in relation to those of the Atlantic region of Europe. In: R. Tüxen (ed.) *Pflanzensoziologishe Systematik.* The Hague.

OXFORD FREEMEN (1960–1969) *Extracts from the Journal of the Freemen of Oxford.* Oxford City Library, Local History Section, Westgate Centre, Oxford. Unpublished.

OXFORD TIMES 1st July 1966. *Report of damage to hedge on Port Meadow.*

PAGE M.L. (1980) *A phytosociological classification of neutral grasslands in the British Isles.* Unpublished Ph.D. Thesis. Exeter University.

PANNET D.J. (1981) Fish weirs of the river Severn. In: T. Rowley (ed.) *The Evolution of Marshland Landscapes.* Oxford University Department of External Studies, Oxford.

PARSONS S. (1636) *Survey of Wolvercote and Godstow.* Bodleian Library. MS Top Oxon.c.334. Unpublished.

PASSARGE H. (1964) Pflanzengesellschaften des nordostdentschenflachlands. I. *Pflanzensoz* 13.

PEARSON K. (1901) On lines and planes of closest fit to systems of points in space. *Philosophical Magazine Sixth Series* 2, 559–572.

PEET R.K. (1974) The measurement of species diversity. *Annual Review of Ecological Systematics* 5, 285–307.

PERCIVAL J. (1910) *Agricultural botany.* Fourth edition, Duckworth & Co., London.

PESHALL J. (1773) *Anthony Wood and additions by the Rev. Sir J. Peshall Bart: the ancient and present state of the county of Oxford.* Printed for J. & F. Rivington in St. Paul's Churchyard.

PETERKEN G. (1981) *Woodland conservation and Management.* Chapman & Hall, London & New York.

PIELOU E.C. (1966) The measurement of diversity in different types of biological collections. 5. *Theoretical. Biology* 13, 131–144.

PIGOTT C.D. & TAYLOR K. (1964) The distribution of some woodland herbs in relation to the supply of nitrogen and phosphorus in the soil. *Journal of Ecology* 52, (Supplement) 175–185.

POCOCK E.A. (1968) First fields in an Oxfordshire parish. *Agricultural History Review* 16, 85–100.

POORE M.E.D. (1955) The use of phytosociological methods in ecological investigations. I. The Braun-Blanquet System. *Journal of Ecology* 43, 226–244.

POORE M.E.D. (1962) The method of successive approximation in description ecology. *Advancement of Ecological Research* 1, 35-68.

POSTAN M.M. (1972) *The medieval economy and society: an economic history of Britain in the Middie Ages*. Weidenfeld and Nicolson, London.

POSTAN M.M. (1973) *Essays on medieval agriculture and general problems of the medieval economy*. Cambridge University Press.

PRIOR M. (1982) *Fisher Row: Fishermen, bargemen and canal boatmen in Oxford 1500–1900*. Clarendon Press, Oxford.

RABOTNOV T.A. (1956) [Some data on the content of living seeds in soils of meadow communities.] In: *Akademica V.N. Sukacheva K.75 – letiyo so duia rozhdeniia*, Akademica Nauk. S.S.S.R. Moskva-Leningrad, (In Russian). pp. 481–499.

RACKHAM O. (1974) *Hayley Wood: its history and ecology*. Cambridge and Isle of Ely Naturalists' Trust.

RACKHAM O. (1980) *Ancient woodland: its history, vegetation and uses in England*. Arnold, London.

RAHMAN M.S. (1976) A comparison of the ecology of *Deschampsia caespitosa* (L.) Beauv. and *Dactylis glomerata* L. in relation to the water factor. 1. Studies in field conditions. *Journal of Ecology* 64, 449–462.

RATCLIFFE D.A. (1977) *A conservation review*. Vols 1 and 2. Cambridge University Press. pp.129,185-187.

RAWES M. & WELCH D. (1969) Upland productivity of vegetation and sheep at Moor House National Nature Reserve Westmorland, England. *Oikos*. Supplement No. 11, 7–72.

REGISTER OF COMMON RIGHTS (1972) Port Meadow and Wolvercote Common. Yarnton and Pixey Meads. County Solicitor, Oxfordshire County Council. Unpublished.

RHODES P.P. (1949) New archaeological sites at Binsey and Port Meadow, Oxford. *Oxoniensia* 14, 81–84.

RICHARDS A.J. (1972) The *Taraxacum* flora of the British Isles. *Watsonia* 9, Supplement.

RICHARDSON J. (1978) *The Local Historian's Encyclopaedia*. 2nd edition. Historical Publications. London. p.25.

ROBINSON M.A. (1981) *Investigations of paleoenvironments in the upper Thames valley, Oxfordshire*. PhD Thesis, London. pp. 82, 124, 180.

ROBINSON M.A.(1982) Water-logged plants and invertebrates. *Council for British Archaeology Group 9. Newsletter* 12, 178–181.

ROBINSON M.A. & ALLEN T.G. (1978) Hardwick with Yelford, Mingies' Ditch. *Council for British Archaeology Group 9. Newsletter* 8, 17–19.

ROBINSON M.A. & LAMBRICK G.H. (1984) Holocene alluviation and hydrology in the upper Thames basin. *Nature* 308, 809–814.

ROBSON P. (1976) The sand and gravel resources of the Thames valley, the country between Lechlade and Standlake. *Institute of Geological Science. Mineral Assessment Report* 81, 6–10.

RODWELL J.S. (ed.) (1991a) *British Plant Communities. Vol. 1. Woodlands and Scrub*. Cambridge University Press.

RODWELL J.S. (ed.) (1991b) *British Plant Communities. Vol. 2. Mires and heaths*. Cambridge University Press.

RODWELL J.S. (ed.) (1992) *British Plant Communities. Vol. 3. Grasslands and montain communities*. Cambridge University Press.

RODWELL J.S. (ed.) (2000) *British Plant Communities. Vol. 5. Maritime communities and vegetation of open habitats*. Cambridge University Press.

ROGERS J.E.T. (1891) *Oxford city documents 1268–1665*. Clarendon Press, Oxford.

RORISON I.H. (1971) The use of nutrients in the control of the floristic composition of grassland. In: E. Duffey & A.S. Watt (eds) *The Scientific Management of Animal and Plant Communities for Conservation*. Oxford University Press. pp.65–77.

ROTULI HUNDREDORUM II (1535) Record Commission. pp. 185–191.

ROWLEY T. (ed.) (1981) *The origins of open-field agriculture*. Croom Helm. London Record Commission.

SALISBURY C. (1980) The Trent, the story of a river. *Current Archaeology* 74, 88-91.

SALTER H.E. (1907) Eynsham cartulary. *Oxford Historical Society Publication* 49 & 50. Clarendon Press. Oxford.

SALTER H.E. (1928) *Oxford city records 1583–1626*. Oxford Historical Society. Clarendon Press, Oxford.

SALTER H.E. (1931) *Cartulary of Oseney Abbey*. 3,343. Oxford Historical Society, Clarendon Press, Oxford.

SALTER H.E. (1936) *Medieval Oxford*. Oxford Historical Society, Clarendon Press, Oxford.

SANDFORD K.S. (1954) River development and superficial deposits. In: A.F. Martin and R.W. Steel (eds) *The Oxford Region*. Oxford University Press. pp. 21–23

SCHUMER B. (1984) *The evolution of Wychwood to 1400: pioneers, frontiers and forests.* Leicester University Press.

SCRUBY M.A. (1979) *Survey of Wendlebury Meads, Oxon.* Nature Conservancy Council, Southern Region. Unpublished.

SEEBOHM F. (1914) *Customary acres and their historical importance.* Longmans Green & Co., London.

SELLWOOD L. (1984) Tribal boundaries viewed from the perspective of numismatic evidence. In: B.W. Cunliffe and D. Miles (eds) *Aspects of the Iron Age in Southern Britain.* Committee for Archaeology, University of Oxford: Monograph No. 2.

SHEAIL J. (1971a) The formation and maintenance of water meadows in Hampshire, England. *Biological Conservation* 3 (2). pp. 101–106.

SHEAIL J. (1971b) *Notes on the history of Portholme, Huntingdon.* Nature Conservancy Council. Unpublished.

SHEAIL J. & WELLS T.C.E. (eds) (1969) *Old grassland: its archaeological and ecological importance.* Symposium proceedings by Lowland Grasslands Research Section Monkswood. Unpublished.

SHELDON J.C. (1974) The behaviour of seeds in soil. III. The influence of seed morphology and the behaviour of seedlings on the establishment of plants from surface lying seed. *Journal of Ecology* 62, 47–66.

SHIMWELL D.W. (1968) *The phytosociology of calcareous grasslands in the British Isles.* PhD thesis. University of Durham. Unpublished.

SHIMWELL D.W. (1971) *The description and classification of vegetation.* Sidgwick & Jackson. pp. 12, 14, 257.

SILVERTOWN J. (1980) The dynamics of a grassland ecosystem: botanical equilibrium in the Park Grass experiment. *Journal of Applied Ecology* 17, 494–504.

SIMON H.A. (1962) The architecture of complexity. *Proceedings of the American Philosophical Society* 106, 467–682.

SMARTT P.F.M. (1978) Sampling for vegetation survey: a flexible systematic model for sample location. *Journal of Biogeography* 5, 43–56.

SMITH A.G. (1970) The influence of Mesolithic and Neolithic man on British vegetation: a discussion. In: D. Walker & R.G. West (eds) *Studies in the Vegetational History of the British Isles.* Cambridge University Press. pp. 81–96.

SMITH A.J.E. (1980) *The moss flora of Britain and Ireland.* Cambridge University Press.

SPEDDING C.R.W. (1971) *Grassland ecology.* Clarendon Press, Oxford.

STACE C. (1997) New flora of the British Isles. 2nd edition. Reprinted 2001. Cambridge University Press.

STAMP L.D. (1948) *The land of Britain: its use and misuse.* Longmans, Green & Co. in conjunction with Geographical Publications Ltd., London.

STAPLEDON R.G. (1925) Permanent grass. *Farm Crops* 3, 74–136.

STAPLEDON R.G. (1933) *4 addresses on the improvement of grassland.* University College of Wales, Aberystwyth.

STAPLEDON R.G. (1936) *The hill-lands of Britain.* Faber & Faber, London.

STAPLEDON R.G. (1939) *The plough-up policy and ley farming.* Faber & Faber, London.

STAPLETON Mrs. B. (1893) *Three Oxfordshire parishes: Begbroke, Yarnton and Kidlington.* Oxford Historical Society, Clarendon Press, Oxford. pp. 310, 315.

STOCK R.V.W. (1951) *Thames Conservancy report of operations and proceedings under the Land Drainage Act 1930 and 1937–51.* H.M.S.B.

SUTTON J.E.G. (1963) Water meadows at Bladon. *Oxoniensia* 28.

SUTTON J.E.G. (1964) Ridge and furrow in Berkshire and Oxfordshire. *Oxoniensia* 29–31, 95-115,

SÝKORA K.V. (1982) Syntaxonomy and synecology of the Lolio-Potentillion Tüxen 1947 in the Netherlands. *Acta botanica neerlandica* 31, 65–95.

TANSLEY A.G. (ed.) (1911) *Types of British vegetation.* Cambridge University Press.

TANSLEY A.G. (1953) *The British Islands and their Vegetation.* 2nd edition. Cambridge University Press. p. 213.

TAUNT H.(*c.*1911) *From Oxford westward, includes photographs of Port Meadow and Yarnton lot meadows.* Unpublished.

TAYLOR C.C. (1981) Archaeology and the origins of open-field agriculture. In: T. Rowley (ed.) *Origins of Open-Field Agriculture.* Croom Helm, London. pp. 13–21.

TAYLOR C.C. & FOWLER P.J. (1978) Roman fields into medieval furlongs. In: H.C. Bowen & P. (eds) Fowler *Early Land Allotment in the British Isles.* British Archaeological Reports 48.

THACKER F.S. (1911) *The Thames highway.* Reprinted 1968. David & Charles, Newton Abbot.

THAMES CONSERVANCY (1928) *New locks and river improvements above Oxford.* Unpublished.

THAMES WATER (THAMES CONSERVANCY DIVISION) (1978) Photogrammetric map of the upper Thames valley. Unpublished.

THAMES WATER (THAMES CONSERVANCY DIVISION) *Daily water levels at Godstow lock tail-water, 1894–1979.* Unpublished.

THIRSK J. (1957) *English peasant farming.* Routledge & Kegan Paul, London.

THIRSK J. (1964) The common fields. *Past and Present* 29, 3–29.

THIRSK J. (1966) The Origin of Common Fields. *Past and Present* 33, 142–147.

THOMAS J.D. & DAVIES L.J. (1969) *Common British grasses and legumes*. Green & Longmans, London.

THOMAS V. (1817) *Yarnton parish church*. Bodleian Library. G.A. Oxon.8.147(19). (Unpublished).

THOMAS V. (1856) *Notes on Yarnton tithes and lot meadows*. Bodleian Library. MS Top Oxon. b.19. Unpublished.

TINSLEY H.M. (1981) The Bronze Age. In: I. Simmons and M. Tooley (eds) *The Environment in British Prehistory*. Duckworth, London.

TITOW J.Z. (1965) Medieval England and the open-field system. *Past and Present* 32, 86–102.

TRIST P.J.O. (1981) *Fritillaria meleagris* L. Its survival and habitats in Suffolk, England. *Biological Conservation* 20, 5–14.

TUCKER D.E. (1978/9) Water meadows. *Water Space* No. 15, Winter.

TURNER W.H. (1880) Oxford City records 1509–1583. Oxford Historical Society. Clarendon Press, Oxford.

TÜXEN R. (1937) *Die Pflanzengesellschaft en Nordwestdeutschlands Mitteilungen der Florislisch-soziologischen Arbeitsgemeinschaft in Niedersachsen*. Engelhard, Hanover.

TÜXEN R. (1947) Der Pflanzensoziologische Garten in Hanover und seine bisherige Entwicklung. *Jahresbericht der Naturhistorischen Gesellschaft zu Hannover*, 113–288.

VALOR ECCLESIASTICUS (1535) Record Commission.

VERNON-HARCOURT L.F. (1883) *The Floods around Oxford: their causes; their effects; and the means of mitigating them*. Clarendon Press, Oxford.

VICTORIA COUNTY HISTORY See Crossley, A. (ed.)

VINOGRADOFF P. (1882) *Villainage in England*. Swan, Sonnenschein.

VOISIN A. (1960) *Better grassland sward*. Crosby Lockwood, London.

VOISIN A. (1961) *Grass productivity*. Crosby Lockwood, London.

WALTERS S.M. (1949) Biological flora of the British Isles: *Eleocharis palustris* and *E. uniglumis*. *Journal of Ecology* 37, 192–202, 203–206.

WARWICK S.I. (1980) The genecology of lawn weeds. VII. The response of different growth forms of *Plantago major* L. and *Poa annua* L. to simulated trampling. *New Phytologist* 85, 461–469.

WARWICK S.I. & BRIGGS D. (1978a) The genecology of lawn weeds. I. Population differentiation in *Poa annua* L. in a mosaic environment of bowling green lawns and flower beds. *New Phytologist* 81, 711–723.

WARWICK S.I. & BRIGGS D. (1978b) The genecology of lawn weeds. II. Evidence for disruptive selection in *Poa annua* L. in a mosaic environment of bowling green lawns and flower beds. *New Phytologist* 81, 725–737.

WARWICK S.I. & BRIGGS D. (1979) Genecology of lawn weeds. III. Cultivation experiments with *Achillea millefolium* L., *Bellis perennis* L., *Plantago lanceolata* L., *Plantago major* L. and *Prunella vulgaris* L. collected from lawns and contrasting grassland habitats. *New Phytologist* 83, 509–536.

WARWICK S.I. & BRIGGS D. (1980a) Genecology of lawn weeds. IV. Adaptive significance of variation in *Bellis perennis* L. as revealed in a transplant experiment. *New Phytologist* 85, 275–288.

WARWICK S.I. & BRIGGS D. (1980b) The genecology of lawn weeds. V. The adaptive significance of different growth habit in lawn and roadside populations of *Plantago major* L. *New Phytologist* 85, 289–300.

WATT A.S. (1938) Studies on the ecology of Breckland III. The origin and development of the Festuco-Agrostidetum on eroded sand. *Journal of Ecology* 26, (1), 1–37.

WATT A.S. (1947) Pattern and process in the plant community. *Journal of Ecology* 35, (1/2), 1–22.

WATT A.S. (1971) Factors controlling the floristic composition of some plant communities in Breckland. In: E. Duffey & A.S. Watt (eds) *The Scientific Management of Animal and Plant Communities for Conservation*. Oxford University Press.

WELLS D. (1974) In E. Duffey *et al. Grassland Ecology Wildlife Management*. Chapman & Hall, London. pp. 59–60.

WELLS D. (1981) Meadow recording card. Nature Conservancy Council. Unpublished.

WELLS T.C.E. (1971) A comparison of the effects of sheep grazing and mechanical cutting on the structure and botanical composition of chalk grassland. *Symposium British Ecological Society* No. 11, 497–515.

WELLS T.C.E., SHEAIL J., BALL D.F. & WARD L.K. (1976) Ecological studies on the Porton Ranges: relationships between vegetation, soils and land-use history. *Journal of Ecology* 67, 589–626.

WELSH P. (1981) *A botanical survey of selected alluvial grassland sites in the Ray and Upper Thames basins, Oxfordshire*. Nature Conservancy Council. Unpublished.

WESTHOFF V. & MAAREL E. van der (1973) The Braun-Blanquet approach. In: R.H. Whittaker (ed.) *Handbook of Vegetation Science*. Part V. Ordination and Classification of Communities. Junk, The Hague. pp. 617–726.

WHEELER B.D. (1980) Plant communities of fen-rich systems in England and Wales III. Fen meadow, fen grassland and fen woodland communities, and contact communities. *Journal of Ecology* 68, 761–789.

WHITEHEAD B.J. (1982) The topographical history of North Meadow, Cricklade. *Wiltshire Archaeological and Natural History Magazine* 76, 129–139.

WHITELOCK D. (1979) *English Historical Documents c. 500–1042.* 2nd edition.

WHITTINGDON G. (1964) The common lands of Berkshire. *Transaction and Papers of the Institute of British Geographers* 35, 129–148.

WIGRAM S.R. (1884) *Cartulary of the Monastery of St. Frideswide.* Clarendon Press, Oxford.

WILLIAMS C.B. (1964) *Patterns in the Balance of Nature and Related Problems in Quantitative Ecology.* Academic Press, New York.

WILLIAMS J.T. (1968) The nitrogen relations and ecological investigations on wet fertilised meadows. *Veroff. geobotanische Institut Zurich* 41, 70–193.

WILLIAMS T.E. & DAVIS A.G. (1946) A grasslands survey of the Monmouthshire "moors". *Journal of British Grassland Society* 1.

WILLIAMS W.T.& GILLARD P. (1971) Pattern analysis of a grazing experiment. *Australian Journal of Agricultural Research* 22, 245–260.

WILLIAMS W.T. & LAMBERT J.M. (1959) Multivariate methods in plant ecology. I. Association-analysis in plant communities. *Journal of Ecology* 47, 83–101.

WILLIAMS W.T. & LAMBERT J.M. (1960) Multivariate methods in plant ecology. II. The use of an electronic digital computer for association analysis. *Journal of Ecology* 48, 689–710.

WILLIAMS W.T. & LAMBERT J.M. (1961) Multivariate methods in plant ecology. III. Inverse association analysis. *Journal of Ecology* 49, 717–729.

WILLMOTT F.C. (1949) Stock poisoning by ragwort. *Journal of the Department of Agriculture, Dublin* 46, 22.

WILSON D. (1981) *The Anglo-Saxons.* 3rd edition. Penguin Books, London.

WOLVERCOTE COMMONERS' COMMITTEE, OXFORD *Minutes 1929–1983. Including Oxford City Council Report December 1981.* Unpublished.

WOODCOCK, B.A., LAWSON C., MANN D.J. AND McDONALD, A.W. (2005) Re-creation of a lowland flood-plain meadow: management implications for invertebrate communities. *Journal of Insect Conservation* 3: 207–215.

WOODCOCK, B.A., LAWSON C., MANN D.J. AND McDONALD, A.W. (2006) Effects of grazing management on beetle and plant assemblages during the re-creation of a flood-plain meadow. *Agriculture, Ecosystems and Environment* 116: 225–234.

WOODELL S.R.J. (1969) *Report of weed control experiment on Port Meadow 1967–69.* Nature Conservancy Council, Southern Region. Unpublished.

YATES E.M. (1974) Enclosure and the rise of grassland farming in Staffordshire. *North Staffordshire Journal of Field Studies* 14, 46–60.

YOUNG A. (1968) *General view of agriculture of the Oxfordshire Board of Agriculture,* [1813]. 2nd edition. David Charles, Newton Abbot. pp. 205–215.